Use R!

Advisors:
Robert Gentleman
Kurt Hornik
Giovanni Parmigiani

For other titles published in this series, go to
http://www.springer.com/series/6991

Richard M. Heiberger · Erich Neuwirth

R Through Excel

A Spreadsheet Interface for Statistics, Data Analysis, and Graphics

Richard M. Heiberger
Department of Statistics
Temple University
Philadelphia PA 19122
USA
rmh@temple.edu

Erich Neuwirth
University of Vienna
Fakultät für Informatik
Dr.-Karl-Lueger-Ring 1
A - 1010 Vienna
Austria
erich.neuwirth@univie.ac.at

Series Editors

Robert Gentleman
Program in Computational Biology
Division of Public Health Sciences
Fred Hutchinson Cancer Research Center
1100 Fairview Avenue
N. M2-B876
Seattle, Washington 98109
USA

Kurt Hornik
Wirtschaftsuniversität Wien, Vienna
Austria

Giovanni Parmigiani
Johns Hopkins University
Baltimore, MD
USA

ISBN 978-1-4419-0051-7 e-ISBN 978-1-4419-0052-4
DOI 10.1007/978-1-4419-0052-4
Springer Dordrecht Heidelberg London New York

Library of Congress Control Number: 2009929743

Printed on acid-free paper

Springer is part of Springer Science+Business Media (www.springer.com)

Let's not kid ourselves: The most widely used piece of software for statistics is Excel.

Brian D. Ripley
"Statistical Methods Need Software: A View of Statistical Computing." Opening lecture Royal Statistical Society 2002, Plymouth (September 2002).

Preface

Abstract MS Excel, the most widely available spreadsheet on MS Windows machines, is often used for data collection, manipulation, and storage. Elementary and medium-complexity mathematical and statistical functions are included with Excel. More advanced and highly reliable statistical analysis in Excel requires an add-in package. R is one of the best statistics programs available. It is an extensible system of software facilities for data manipulation, statistical analysis, and graphical display. With RExcel, the entire R environment (including more than a thousand contributed packages) can be treated as an extension of Excel.

This book is a supplementary text to any introductory course in statistics. The book supports the instructor by giving students step-by-step screenshots showing access to state-of-the-art statistical computations in R directly from the menu bar in Excel.

The book can also be used as a computational introduction by data analysts who already have basic statistical skills.

R is a program for statistical analysis and graphical display of data.

R is one of the best programs for statistical analysis and graphical display of data. It is maintained and distributed by an international team of statisticians and computer scientists working in universities and industry. R is one of the major tools used in statistical research and in applications of statistics in science, social science, economics, and business. R used in both academia and industry.

Among other things, R has

- data handling and storage facilities.
- a suite of operators for calculations on arrays, in particular matrices.
- a large, coherent, integrated collection of intermediate tools for data analysis.

- graphical facilities for data analysis and display either directly at the computer or on hardcopy.
- a well-developed, powerful, and effective programming language (called S) that includes conditionals, loops, user-defined functions (including recursive functions), functions for creating complex data structures, and input and output facilities. (Indeed, most of the system-supplied functions are themselves written in the S language.)
- A large selection of demonstration datasets used in the illustration of many statistical methods.

Excel is the most widely used spreadsheet program.

Microsoft Excel® [Microsoft, 2008a] is the most widely available spreadsheet. Entering data, cleaning data, and simple data processing (including simple statistics) are very easily done on spreadsheets. As a consequence, much statistical data is available as, or even created in, Excel worksheets.

Spreadsheets have a different paradigm for representing mathematical formulas than statistical (and mathematical) programming languages. The spreadsheet paradigm is much more visual and action-oriented than the functional or procedural paradigm of statistical programming languages. This problem of different paradigms can be overcome. In this book, we illustrate some of the ways the two paradigms can be made to work with each other. [Neuwirth and Arganbright, 2004] discuss in detail how to represent the development and structure of spreadsheets in printed form and how spreadsheets can be used to do serious mathematical work.

Excel is easy to use, but statisticians have found it has some deficiencies in the area of numerical precision. Statistical software is usually perceived as difficult to learn. This can be a major obstacle for potential users of advanced statistical methods. As this book shows, using R within Excel allows access to both the easy-to-use tools for data entry and manipulation available in Excel and the power and precision of the advanced statistical methods available via R.

RExcel is an interface program that uses R as an add-in to Excel.

RExcel is an add-in to Excel on MS Windows [Microsoft, 2008b] machines that allows the use of R as a "helper application" for Excel. Data can be transferred between Excel and R (in both directions), and Excel can call R functions to perform calculations and then transfer the results to Excel.

RExcel offers the following features:

- allows the use of R functions in Excel cell formulas, effectively controlling R calculations from Excel's automatic recalculation mechanism.
- connects R dataframes and Excel data lists.

- handles missing data.
- allows the creation of a standalone RExcel application that hides R almost completely from the user and uses Excel as the main interface to R. (Instructions are given in RExcel's help file.)
- if R Commander [Fox et al., 2007] is available, RExcel optionally places the Rcmdr menus on an Excel menu bar. Any menu item integrated into the Rcmdr menu using an Rcmdr plugin will also be available on the RExcel Rcmdr menu.
- works with the statconn (D)COM server (previously called R(D)COM server) server, turning R into an (invisible) background server for Excel.
- works with the rcom package, turning R into a (visible) foreground server for Excel. Using this configuration, the user can access the same instance of R either from Excel or from the command line in an R GUI Console window.
- supports R processes running under the control of RServerManager. R server is attached to Excel from a server pool. Different instances of Excel (running on different machines) may access the same R process with the same data. We do not use this capability in this book.

The RExcel interface is described in [Baier and Neuwirth, 2007]. RExcel is built on the the rcom and statconn (D)COM (previously called R(D)COM) packages, which we use for communication between R and the Microsoft Office software [Baier, 2007]. Basic information on the installation of R, RExcel, and Rcmdr is in Appendix A. Full information on RExcel is available at http://rcom.univie.ac.at/.

Rcmdr is an R package that provides GUI menu access to R.

Rcmdr (R Commander) is a platform-independent menu interface to R. The menu items implemented by Rcmdr are primarily designed for introductory courses. They can be extended by the Rcmdr plugin facility to provide a clickable graphical user interface (GUI) to any statistical procedure coded in R.

Audience

There are two audiences for this book:

1. students learning statistics.
2. people analyzing data.

Students

Introductory courses in statistics, and introductory statistics components of courses in all other subjects, require access to a software system for the collection and analysis of data.

This book is a supplementary text for an introductory course in statistics. We include examples of all the standard data analysis techniques that are introduced in such courses. We also include some of the elementary probability examples from those courses.

Many examples are structured parallel to similar presentations for other software that appears in such texts. The outline for such examples is as follows:

1. Read data into Excel from a textbook CD.
2. Put data into R from the RExcel menu.
3. Construct standard analysis tables and graphs from the Rcmdr menu installed in the Excel menu bar.
4. Cut and paste the tables and graphs into a document describing the results of the analysis.

We have two worksheets, using Excel and R only, that are used to illustrate the fundamental concepts of hypothesis testing, the construction and interpretation of confidence intervals, and the ideas behind least-squares fitting. We have several other worksheets that are used to illustrate data transfer between R and Excel and to illustrate additional statistical techniques.

Data Analysts

See the Students section above for an introduction to the use of RExcel and Rcmdr to access many of the analysis and graphical capabilities of R. It is possible to write additional menu items to access specialized functions written in R directly from the Rcmdr menu installed in the Excel menu bar. See the RExcel and Rcmdr documentation for details.

Updates and Additional Information

RExcel has a Wiki at http://rcom.univie.ac.at/.

Update material for this book will be available from the book's website at Springer http://www.springer.com/978-1-4419-0051-7.

A video on RExcel, including both the material in this book and additional material, is available at http://rcom.univie.ac.at/RExcelDemo/.

Acknowledgments

First and foremost, we have to thank Thomas Baier, without whose work [the rcom package and the statconn (D)COM server (previously called R(D)COM server)] RExcel and the book built on it would not have been possible. It should be noted that his design, now more than 10 years old, has not needed any change—a very uncommon event in the software world.

Christian Ritter has been the premier user of RExcel, and he has contributed many ideas to the design of the system.

We wish to acknowledge our students at Temple University and the University of Vienna who have used preliminary versions of this book and the RExcel software in class and made many helpful suggestions that have been incorporated into this version. We wish to thank Burt Holland at Temple University for teaching with an earlier version of the book and software. Our early experiences using RExcel in teaching are described in [Baier et al., 2006].

We wish to acknowledge John Fox of McMaster University both for the Rcmdr menu system [Fox et al., 2007] and especially for his willingness to incorporate changes into his system that were needed to make Rcmdr and RExcel cooperate. Rcmdr was designed as a platform-independent menu system. We have moved the Rcmdr menu to the Excel toolbar as part of our integration of Excel and R.

We wish to thank R Core for the R program [R Development Core Team, 2008].

Philadelphia and Vienna
July 2009

Richard M. Heiberger
Erich Neuwirth

Notes to Readers

Notation

Much of this book is focused on the the use of a clickable menu to access the statistical functions in R. We use several typographical conventions to describe the menus and the formulas.

Description	Sample font
Menu items	sans serif font
Cascading menus	Menu item ► Submenu name
File name	`typewriter font`
Pathname in Excel	`c:\path\with\backslash\filename.xls`
Pathname in R	`c:/path/with/forwardslash/filename.R`
Excel formula	sans serif font
R formula	`typewriter font`
Mathematical notation	Standard math notation (using math italic font) $t = \frac{\bar{x} - \mu_0}{\frac{s}{\sqrt{n}}}$

We use the following terminology to describe clicking in Excel.

click	Press the Left mouse button.
right-click	Press the Right mouse button.
menu bar	Clickable horizontal list at the top of the Excel window. In Excel 2003, each item expands to a menu. In Excel 2007, each item expands to a toolbar in the Ribbon.
toolbar	Specialized menu.
RExcel–Rcmdr toolbar	In Excel 2007, the RExcel–Rcmdr toolbar appears on the Ribbon when we click Add-ins ► RExcel ► RCommander ► with Excel menus In Excel 2003, the RExcel–Rcmdr toolbar appears below the standard toolbars when we click RExcel ► RCommander ► with Excel menus
Ribbon	Excel 2007 only. A set of clickable icons and menus that appears below the menu bar and depends on which menu bar item has been clicked.
menu	List of clickable actions that appears on a taskbar or menu bar or when you hover the mouse on an active item.
context menu	Menu that appears when you right-click on any Excel object, for example, a spreadsheet cell. Its appearance and list of items depend on the current context. RExcel adds several items to the standard Excel context menu for spreadsheet cells when R and Rcmdr are running.

Presentation

Classroom Usage

The default font size for the Rcmdr window works well for a single user on a computer screen. The Rcmdr default font size is too small for classroom projection. We therefore wrote the Tools ► Large Font for Projectors (HH) menu item to increase the font size in the Rcmdr window and to change the default plotting character to solid dots (denoted by the number 16).

The R and Rcmdr default for presentation of hypothesis test results includes stars to indicate the level of significance. The stars can be turned on or off with the Tools ► R Options (HH) menu item.

The Tools ► Options... menu item opens a dialog box for control of font sizes and other Rcmdr options and for a few R options.

Any other R options can be controlled by typing R commands in the Rcmdr Script Window.

R Version

Most of the screenshots in this book were taken with R 2.8.1. Some of our screenshots show earlier version numbers, the version of R current at the time the screenshot was taken. R has scheduled releases of new versions about four times a year. Version 2.9.1 was the current version as we went to press.

Writing Reports

Reports designed to be read on paper have different conventions than output designed to be read on a computer screen. Screen images are normally inappropriate in reports. The tables and graphs themselves, not emulated screen images of the tables and graphs, are required for paper reports.

This book is a user manual for a set of computer programs. The graphs here are screen images to show exactly what you type or click and exactly what you will see in response on the screen.

A written report on your job is not a computer manual. A written report needs to show graphs, not screenshots of windows showing graphs. See Figs. 4.21 and 4.22 for illustrations of the two different formats.

Computer Notation and Mathematics Notation

Computer arithmetic, both Excel and R, uses notation that is similar to standard math notation. The notations are not identical, and you are required to know both and to use them correctly. They don't mix in the same formula. Computer notation in the R language is always in the Courier font because spacing, especially the alignment of tables on the decimal point, makes that assumption. Computer tables designed for Courier that are printed in Times Roman usually do not align and are therefore very difficult to read.

Concept Font	Math notation *Math Italic*	Computer `Courier`	Number written out and aligned at decimal point Times Roman
Multiplication	$\times$	`*`	
Power	a^b	`a^b`	
Small numbers	1.23×10^{-12}	`1.23e-12`	0.00000000000123
Big numbers	4.56×10^8	`4.56e+08`	456000000.000

The computer notation with the letter "e" is standard in almost all computer programs (in particular, both R and Excel). It means, as illustrated in the table above, "times 10 to the power". It is written in ordinary-size type on the line. It is not a subscript, nor is it a superscript. It has nothing to do with the base of the natural logarithms. It is a historical artifact left over from the time when computer input and output devices were teletypes with only one font and no special characters. It is absolutely necessary to understand how to read it.

Statements written in the R language and in math notation distinguish between lowercase and uppercase letters. There are frequent examples of both "X" and "x" appearing in the same formula with different meanings [for example, $E(X) = \sum_{i=1}^{n} x_i f(x_i)$ is the mean of a discrete probability distribution]. Names of functions in Excel formulas are case-insensitive, and in many cases Excel changes between uppercase and lowercase when formulas are entered.

Alignment of Decimal Points in Tables

Good: Same precision in each column		Correct: Decimal points aligned		Wrong: Decimal points unaligned	
12.34	567.890000	12.34	567.89	12.34	567.89
43.20	98.760000	43.2	98.76	43.2	98.76
443.00	8.765432	443.	8.765432	443.	8.765432

Rounding

Intermediate numbers in a calculation should not be rounded. Only the final answer may be rounded. For example, the full-precision numbers lead to rejection of the null hypothesis at the $\alpha = .025$ one-sided level and the rounded values lead to non-rejection.

```
> 4.2222 * .46444
[1] 1.960959
> 4.22 * .464
[1] 1.95808
```

Data values and simple summaries should not be displayed with more precision than is justified. For example, if the data values are recorded with one decimal position, then it makes sense to report two decimal positions for the mean and the standard deviation, but not three. Computing programs (including R and Excel) do not always determine and display the appropriate number of digits.

Output Appearance—Width

Tables from computer output (and, actually, most tables) are designed to be read as well-defined rows and columns. For legibility, they must be presented as designed. Many word processing systems interfere with legibility by changing the font or spacing of a table pasted into the word processor. This illustration shows the effects of folding lines that the word processor thinks are too long. The single line of interpretation of the significance stars, which is easily read in the correctly aligned table, becomes difficult to read in the incorrectly folded table when the symbols and *p*-values no longer alternate.

Correct width—columns are aligned.

```
Coefficients:
             Estimate Std. Error t value Pr(>|t|)
(Intercept)   576.799    514.020   1.122 0.264576
Space          90.605      6.477  13.990  < 2e-16 ***
Water           9.657      2.412   4.004 0.000122 ***
---
Signif. codes:  0 '***' 0.001 '**' 0.01 '*' 0.05 '.' 0.1 ' ' 1
```

Width too narrow for this table—each row is folded. The visual first column includes items from the last column of the intended alignment. Thus, in this example, it looks like `Pr(>|t|)`, `(Intercept)`, `0.264576`, ... are in the same column. The usual repair is to decrease the margins or decrease the font size.

```
Coefficients:
             Estimate Std. Error t value
Pr(>|t|)
(Intercept)   576.799    514.020   1.122
0.264576
Space          90.605      6.477  13.990
 < 2e-16 ***
Water           9.657      2.412   4.004
0.000122 ***
---
Signif. codes:  0 '***' 0.001 '**' 0.01
'*' 0.05 '.' 0.1 ' ' 1
```

Output Appearance—Font and Spacing

Tables from R computer output are designed to look right in a monowidth font such as Courier. They are often illegible in a proportional font such as Times Roman. For legibility, they must be presented as designed. In MS Word, programs and transcripts must be highlighted and then explicitly placed into Courier.

Here is an example of the issue. The Courier rendition is consistent with the design of the output by the program designer. The Times Roman is exactly the same text dropped into an environment that is incorrectly attempting to space it in accordance with English-language typesetting rules.

`Courier` (correct spacing)	Times Roman (incorrect spacing)
`> summary(Long)`	> summary(Long)
`          y             group`	y group
`  Min.    :-2.000   A:12`	Min. :-2.000 A:12
`  1st Qu.: 3.217   B:12`	1st Qu.: 3.217 B:12
`  Median : 5.150   C:12`	Median : 5.150 C:12
`  Mean   : 5.815`	Mean : 5.815
`  3rd Qu.: 8.700`	3rd Qu.: 8.700
`  Max.   :13.090`	Max. :13.090

Input Notation—Case

R is a case-sensitive system. Uppercase (ABC) and lowercase (abc) letters are not the same. Variable names and function names in R must be written with the correct case if they are to be understood by the program.

Excel is not case-sensitive. Cell formulas written in lowercase (a1:c12) letters will be converted to uppercase (A1:C12) when they are displayed.

Nonsense Notation

As instructors, we often see nonsensical statements on student papers. This is one of the most flagrant:

Nonsense:	$\alpha/2 = .025 = 1.96$
Correct:	$z_{\alpha/2} = z_{.025} = 1.96$

The nonsense statement claims that .025 and 1.96 have the same value. The correct statement shows the relationship, through the normal table, of the two values.

Basic Writing

1. Organization. Introduction, sections, summary, placement of tables and figures in text, automatic numbering and referencing of tables and figures.
2. Mechanics. Appropriate ways to cut tables and graphs from R and to paste them into documents.
3. Style. Styles for writing simple homework analyses, case reports, and technical reports.
4. Distribution media. We emphasize that reports designed to be read on paper have different conventions than output designed to be read on a computer screen. Screen images are normally inappropriate in reports. The tables and graphs themselves, not emulated screen images of the tables and graphs, are required for paper reports.

Internationalization

All examples in this book have been developed on Windows systems running in an English language locale. When both R and Excel use the same locale, they will behave consistently in their use of decimal notation and/or time conventions. For example, English locales use the period "." for the decimal indicator and many European locales use the ",".

When R and Excel are using different locales, there may be strange interpretations of input values.

R (and therefore Rcmdr) uses the operating system's information. See the R help file `?locales` and `?localeconv` for further information.

Excel uses information on the Windows Start ► Control Panel ► Regional and Language Options ► Regional Options ► Customize... dialog boxes and on the Excel Tools ► International tab.

RExcel has a worksheet function RNumber which, when dealing with numbers as strings, always does the right thing in conversion.

Contents

Chapter 1
Getting Started

Abstract Once RExcel has been installed on your computer (see Appendix A for details), it can be started by clicking the RExcel with RCommander or RExcel2007 with RCommander icon. The icon is initially placed on your Desktop by the RExcelInstaller. It may have been copied or moved by your lab manager to your Start menu, or to a menu reached from the Start menu. It is possible to start Excel first and then start R and Rcmdr from the RExcel menu. Most of our illustrations show screenshots from Excel 2007 on Windows. Everything works with Excel 2003 or Excel 2002 on Windows, with only minor differences in the appearance of the menus.

In this chapter, we present several alternate starting scenarios. Most users will need only one of them. RExcel can be started from the RExcel icon or from a running Excel window. Rcmdr can be started from Excel or from an R window.

1.1 Starting RExcel with the RExcel Icon

The easiest way to start is to use the RExcel icon in Fig. 1.1. On a personal machine, the icon is normally on the Desktop. On a university laboratory machine, the icon may have been moved by the lab manager to the Quick Launch toolbar, or to a menu accessible from the Start menu.

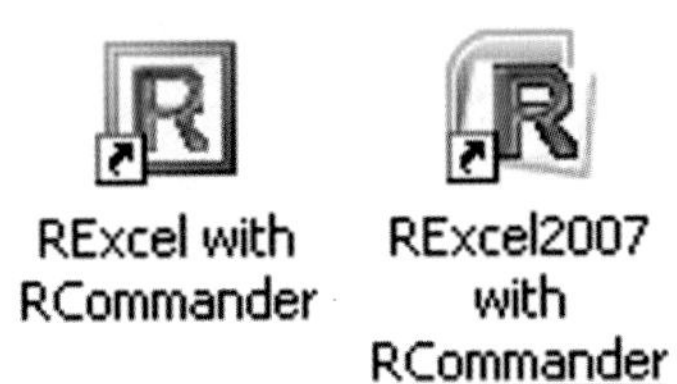

Fig. 1.1 Double-click the RExcel with RCommander (Excel 2003 or 2002) or the RExcel2007 with RCommander icon on the Desktop to get Fig. 1.2.

R.M. Heiberger, E. Neuwirth, *R Through Excel*, Use R,
DOI 10.1007/978-1-4419-0052-4_1,

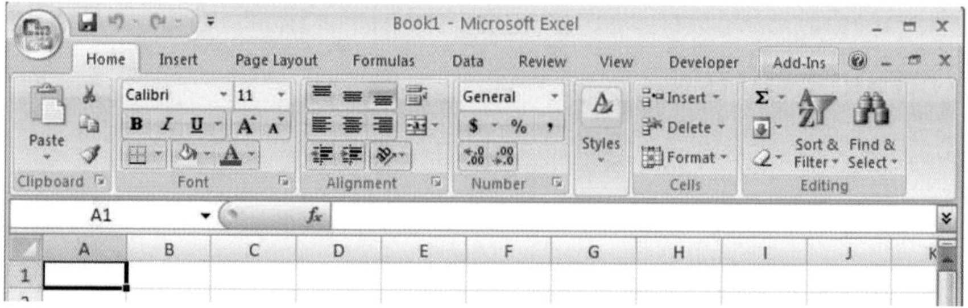

Fig. 1.2 Excel 2007 opens with the Home tab expanded into the Ribbon. Click the Add-Ins tab to get Fig. 1.3.

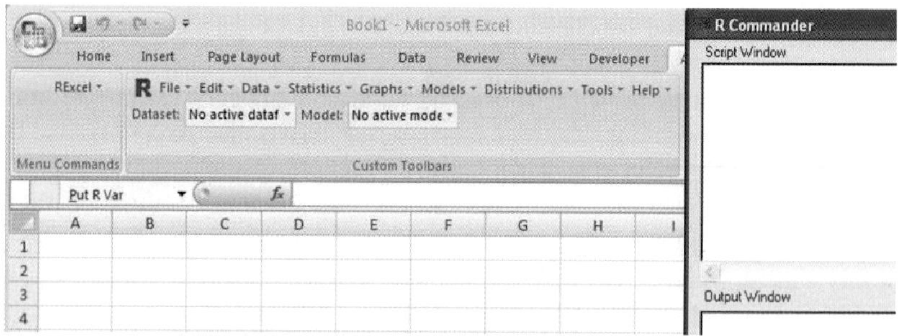

Fig. 1.3 The R Commander menu is now visible on the Excel 2007 Add-Ins Ribbon. The R Commander window has opened on the right.

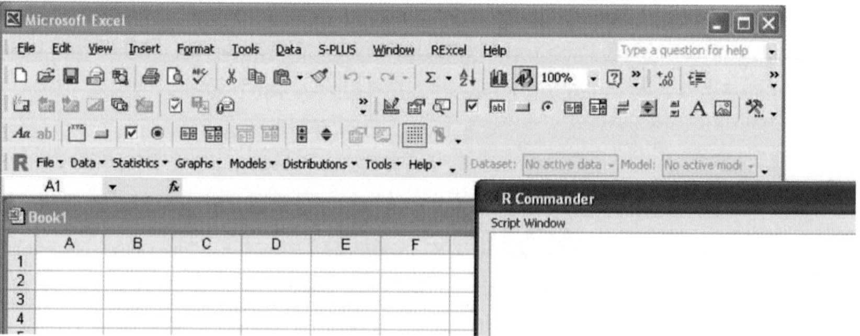

Fig. 1.4 Excel 2003 and 2002 open with the R Commander menu on the menu bar. The R Commander window has opened on the right.

1.2 Starting RExcel from a Running Excel Window

Sometimes we start Excel first, either by clicking the Excel icon or by double-clicking an `xls` or `xlsx` file. We then start RExcel and Rcmdr after the Excel session is running. There are two steps: RExcel ▶ R Start, followed by RExcel ▶ RCommander ▶ with Excel menus. See Figs. 1.5–1.9 for Excel 2007 and Figs. 1.10–1.12 for Excel 2003 and 2002.

1.2.1 Starting RExcel from a Running Excel 2007 Window

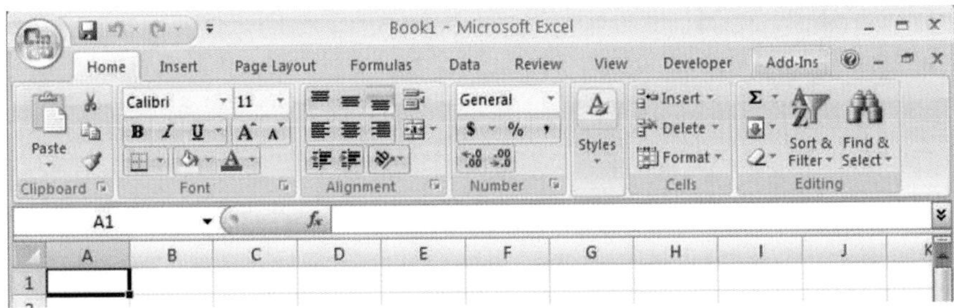

Fig. 1.5 Excel opens with the Home tab expanded into the Ribbon. Click the Add-Ins tab to get the RExcel menu in Fig. 1.6.

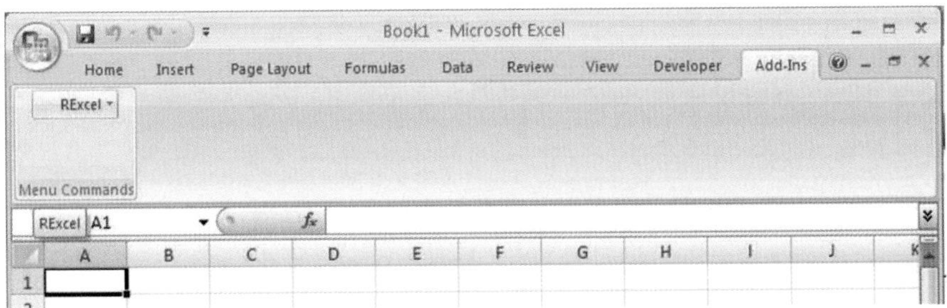

Fig. 1.6 The Add-Ins Ribbon opens with the Menu Commands box listing the installed add-ins. If you have additional add-ins installed, you may have additional menu items above or below the RExcel item. Click the RExcel item to get Fig. 1.7.

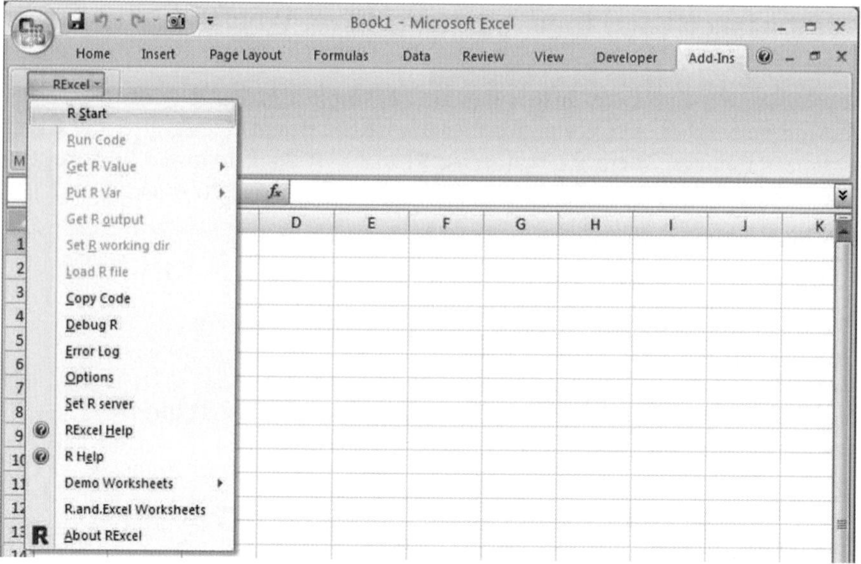

Fig. 1.7 Click R Start on the RExcel menu.

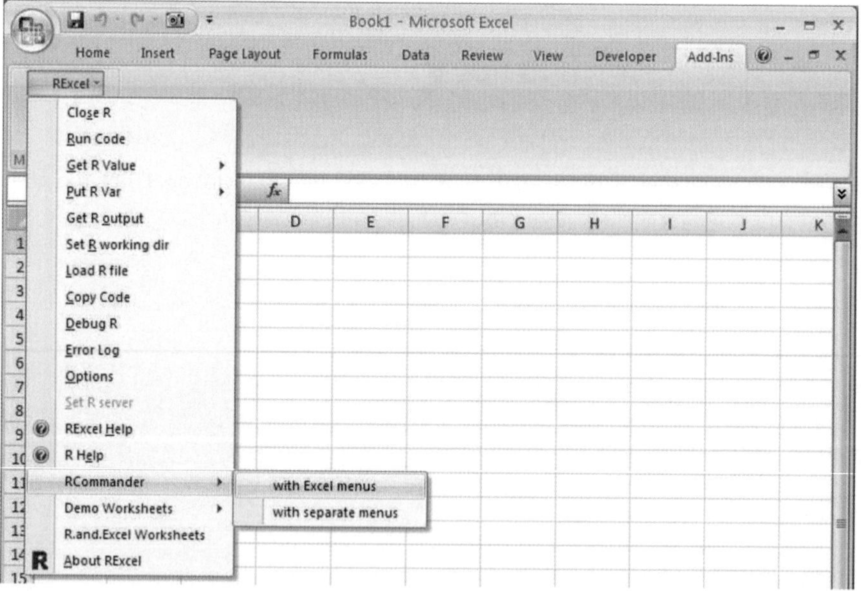

Fig. 1.8 There is no visible change after R has started. Click the RExcel item again, and then click the RCommander ► with Excel menus item to get Fig. 1.9.

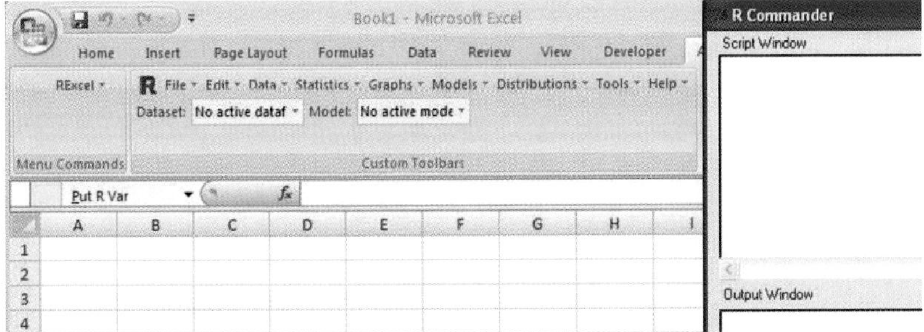

Fig. 1.9 The R Commander menu is now on the Excel Add-Ins Ribbon. The R Commander window has opened on the right.

1.2.2 Starting RExcel from a Running Excel 2003 Window

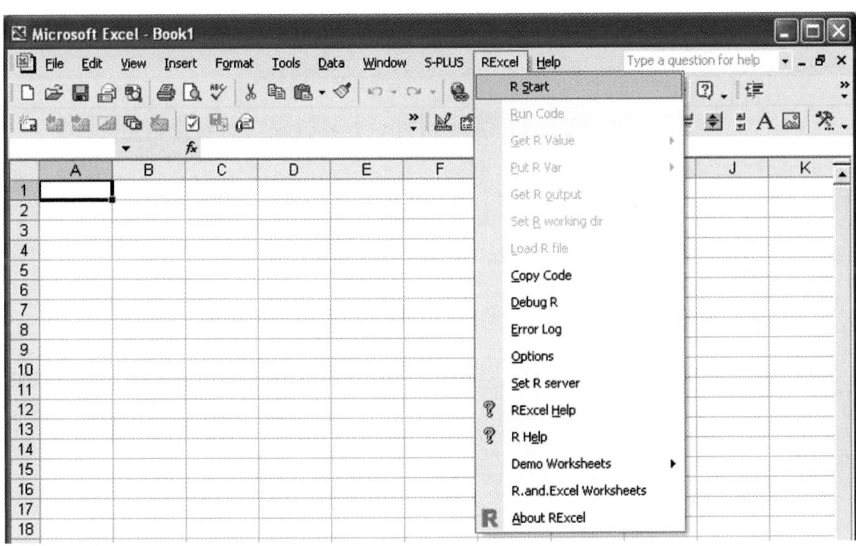

Fig. 1.10 In Excel 2003, click RExcel ▶ R Start.

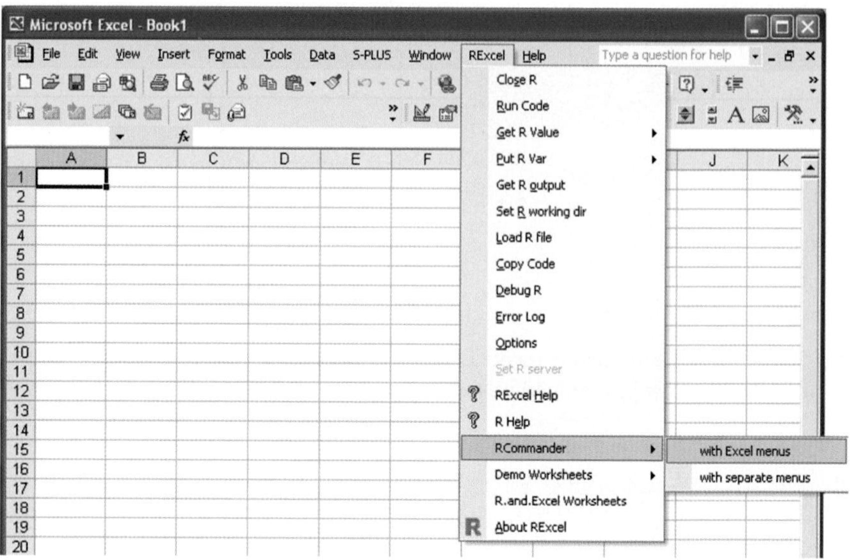

Fig. 1.11 There is no visible change after R has started. Click RExcel ► RCommander ► with Excel menus. This opens the Rcmdr window and places the Rcmdr menu on the Excel toolbar.

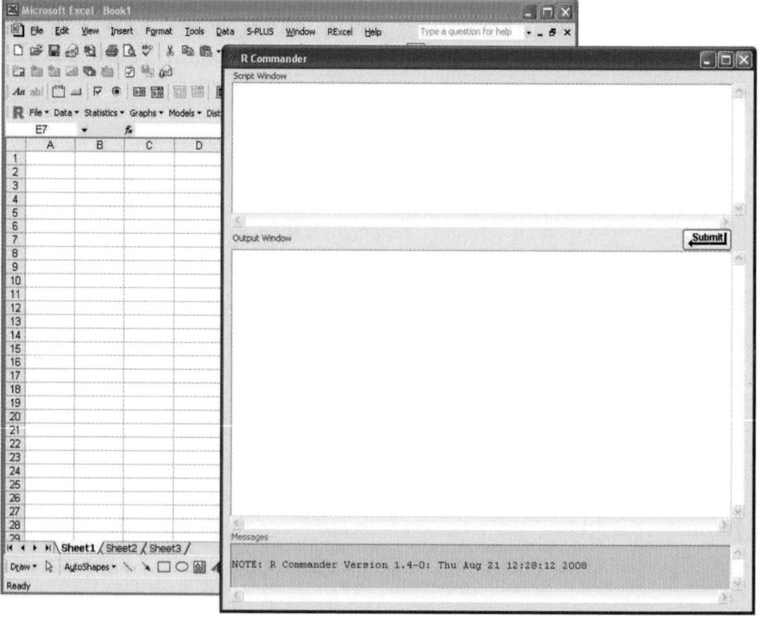

Fig. 1.12 Initial full-screen appearance of Excel 2003 with the Rcmdr window on the right. The RExcel menu item is on the main menu. The Rcmdr menu toolbar is on the main Excel toolbar. See Fig. 2.2 for more detail.

1.3 Starting R Commander Without Excel

Rcmdr was designed as a graphical interface to R for all operating systems on which R runs. The startup on Windows without Excel, or on Apple Macintosh (on which the interprocess communication method is different from Windows and therefore the RExcel interface doesn't work), or Unix-alikes (for which Excel isn't available) is described in this section.

When Rcmdr is started directly from R, the Rcmdr menu is on the R Commander window. When we start Rcmdr from Excel, we usually move the Rcmdr menu to the Excel window.

We illustrate starting Rcmdr from the RGui window on Windows. The startup is similar on Macintosh or Unix-alike.

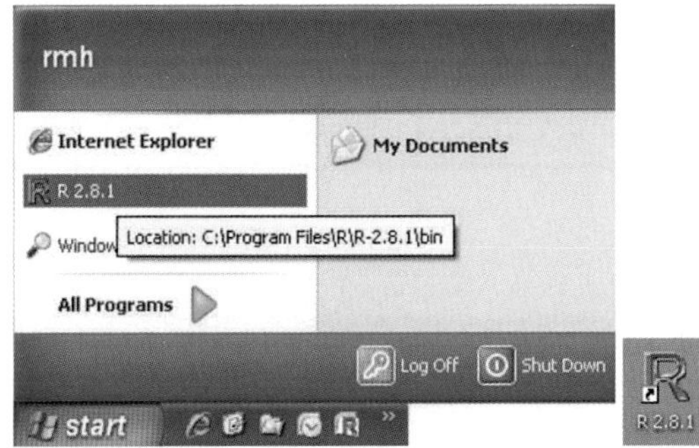

Fig. 1.13 Start R from the Start menu or from the R icon.

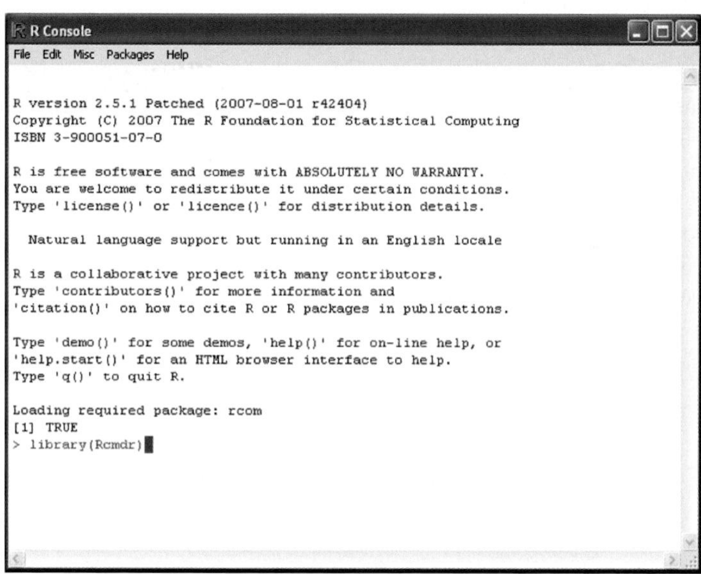

Fig. 1.14 Enter `library(Rcmdr)` in the R Console to open Rcmdr in Fig. 1.15.

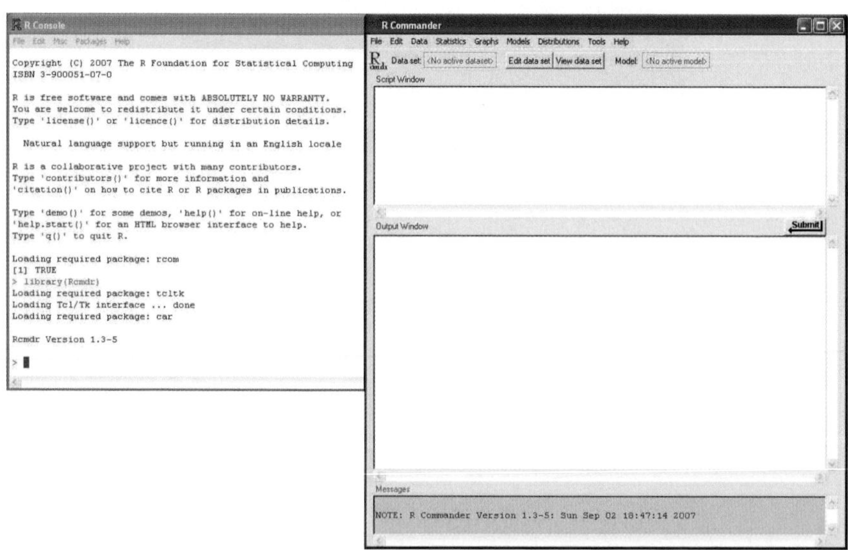

Fig. 1.15 The Rcmdr window opens with the Rcmdr menu. (When RExcel is active, we moved the Rcmdr menu to the Excel menu bar.) The Rcmdr menu in this location has exactly the same properties as the Rcmdr menu in Excel illustrated in Fig. 1.9.

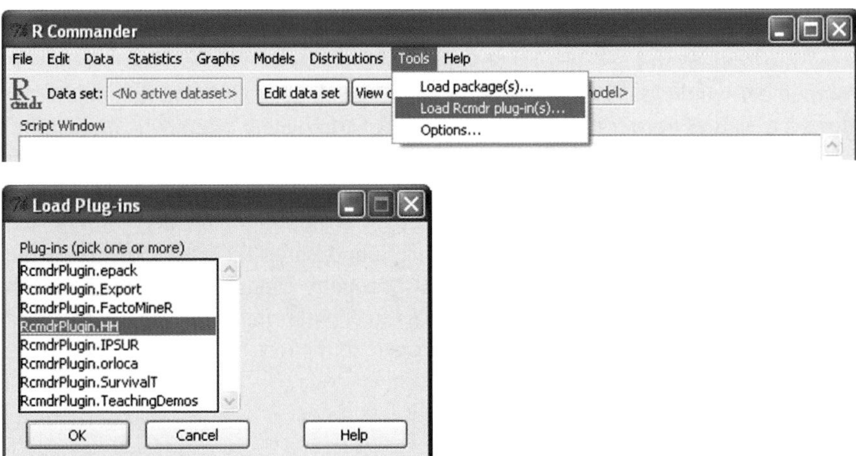

Fig. 1.16 On computers without Excel, we need to click the Tools ► Load Rcmdr plug-in(s)... and RcmdrPlugin.HH from the Rcmdr menu to get the additional HH [Heiberger, 2008a] menu items.

1.4 Window Arrangement

In our illustrations in Figs. 1.3, 1.4, 1.9, and 1.12, we show both the Excel and the R Commander windows. We recommend that they both be visible and that neither be allowed to entirely cover the other. When the R Commander window is hidden, the default behavior is that it does not automatically come to the top when the Rcmdr menu in Excel writes to it. Similarly, the Graphics window may be hidden. When a new graph is drawn, the Graphics window does not automatically come to the top. Should a window be hidden, it is easily found with the Taskbar or use of the Alt-Tab key. There is an option on RExcel ▶ Options to change the behavior. Check RCommander gets focus with output and then RExcel will bring either the Commander window or the Graphics window, as appropriate, to the top.

1.5 Graphics History

The R Graphics Device window has an option to record all graphs produced in a session. You can page up and down through the complete set. You may save them to a file. See Fig. 1.17 to see how to turn graphics history on.

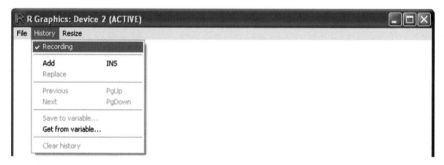

Fig. 1.17 We recommend you turn Graphics Device history on. From the Graphics Device menu, click History ▶ Recording to put the checkmark in place.

1.6 Quitting RExcel

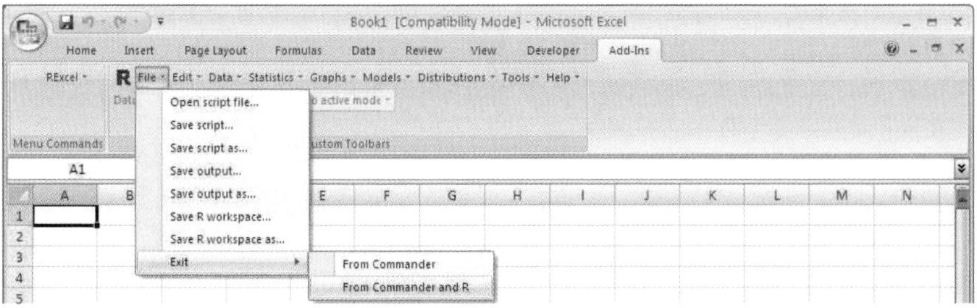

Fig. 1.18 When you have finished, quit R from the Rcmdr menu File ▶ Exit ▶ From Commander and R. Rcmdr will ask you to confirm quitting and about saving output and script files. Click OK to quit. You probably want to save the output. You might want to save the script file.

R will not ask about saving the Graphics window. You need to determine whether to save individual graphs. We recommend in Section 1.5 that you open the graphics window with recording on. This means you can page up and down through the graphs your created in the current session.

R will ask you about saving the workspace image. You will normally click No.

When you have quit R, then quit Excel. Excel will ask about saving changes you made to your workbooks. You shouldn't change textbook data files or workbooks that are part of the RExcel package. Whether you should save your own workbooks is your decision. It depends on whether the workbook is your primary data repository or just a scratchpad for calculations.

Chapter 2
Using RExcel and R Commander

Abstract We review the complete set of Rcmdr menu items, including both the action menu items and the active Dataset and model items. We illustrate the output graphs and tables associated with a least-squares fit. We show the R Commander window and the RGUI Console window.

2.1 Appearance

Users will normally have only one version of Excel installed on their computer. Most illustrations in this book use the most recent, Excel 2007. The RExcel behavior is identical in both Excel 2003 and Excel 2007. The Rcmdr behavior is identical in both Excel versions and without Excel.

The RExcel and Rcmdr menus in Excel 2007 (Fig. 2.1) and Excel 2003 (Fig. 2.2) and on the R Commander window (Fig. 2.3) have slightly different appearances.

The RExcel menu is an item on the Menu Commands box of the Add-Ins tab of Excel 2007. The RExcel menu is an item on the main menu of Excel 2003.

The Rcmdr menu is a toolbar on the Ribbon of the Add-Ins tab of Excel 2007 and is a toolbar on the main toolbar of Excel 2003. The Rcmdr menu is a toolbar on the Rcmdr window when Excel is not running.

The content and behavior of the RExcel menu in Fig. 2.4 are identical in both versions of Excel. The content and appearance of the Rcmdr menu are almost identical in all three settings. The Rcmdr ▸ Edit menu item does not appear in current releases of RExcel because it is not needed in the Excel setting. (It is shown on some of our earlier screenshots.) We display each item on the menus in the upcoming figures.

R.M. Heiberger, E. Neuwirth, *R Through Excel*, Use R,
DOI 10.1007/978-1-4419-0052-4_2,

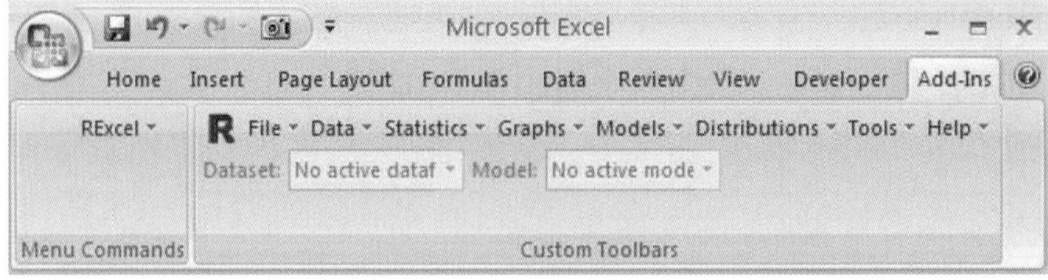

Fig. 2.1 RExcel and Rcmdr menus on the Add-Ins tab in Excel 2007.

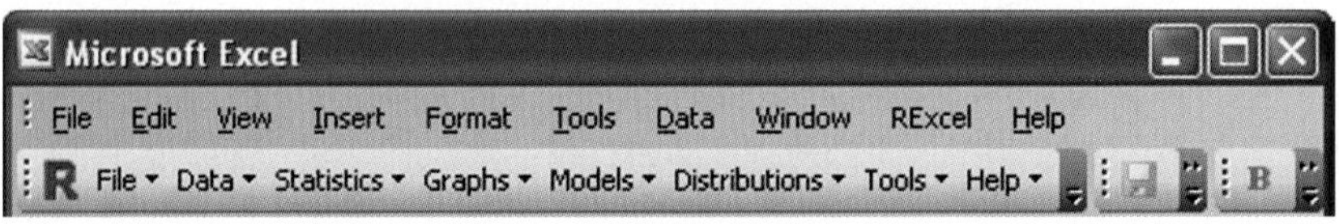

Fig. 2.2 RExcel and Rcmdr menus in Excel 2003.

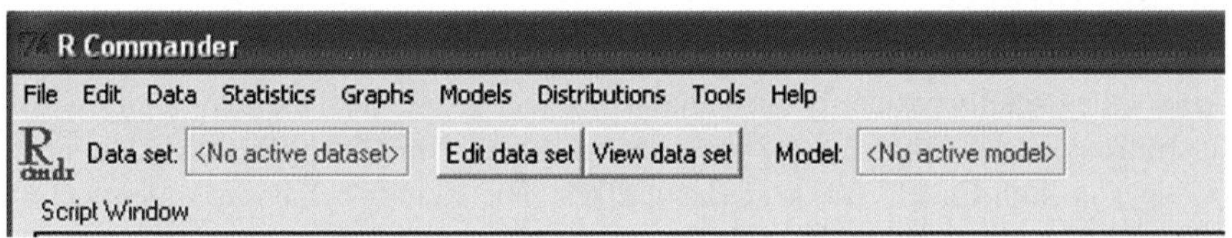

Fig. 2.3 Rcmdr menu on the R Commander window when Rcmdr has been started from RExcel by clicking the with separate menus menu item (see Fig. 1.11) or directly from R (see Fig. 1.15).

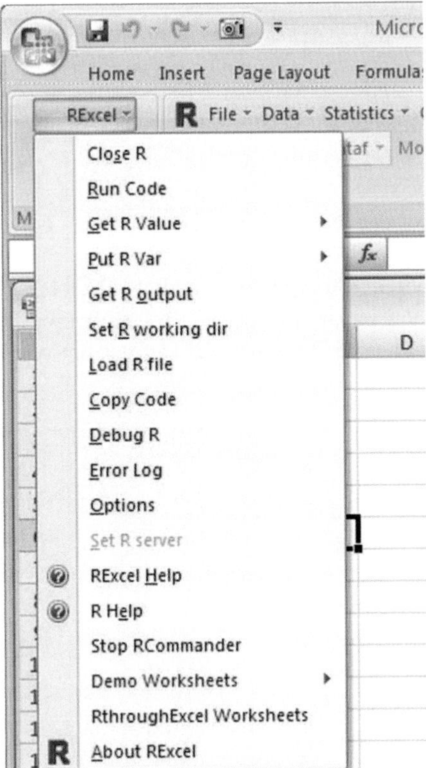

Fig. 2.4 RExcel menu. This is the main menu for starting and stopping the interface between Excel and R. This menu can also be used for communicating between R and Excel. We will usually use the Context menu (right-click menu) in Excel (Fig. 2.14) for communication between the two programs.

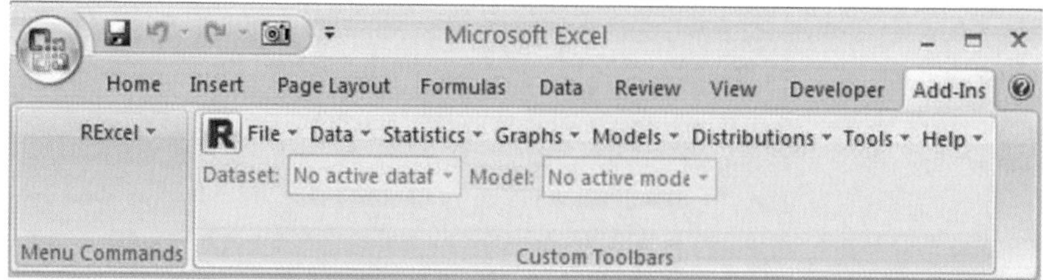

Fig. 2.5 **R** button. When you type commands to R directly (in either the Rcmdr script window or the R Console), as distinct from clicking in the Rcmdr menu in Excel, then Excel, R, and the Rcmdr menu can get out of phase. Clicking the **R** button resynchronizes them.

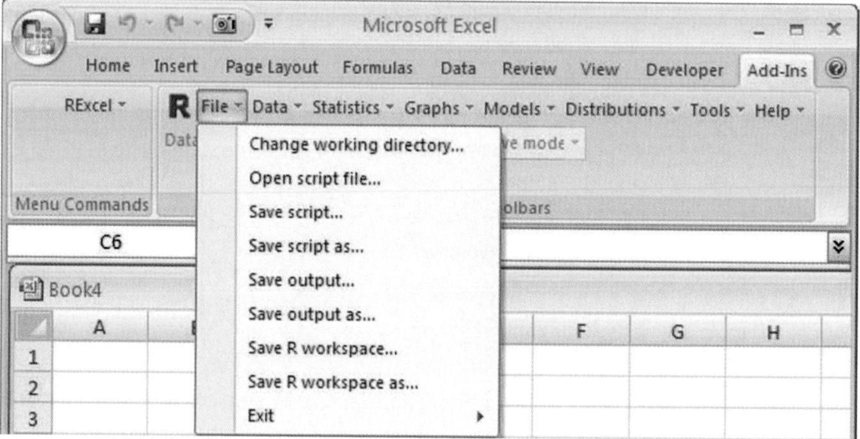

Fig. 2.6 Rcmdr File menu. We normally do not use this menu.

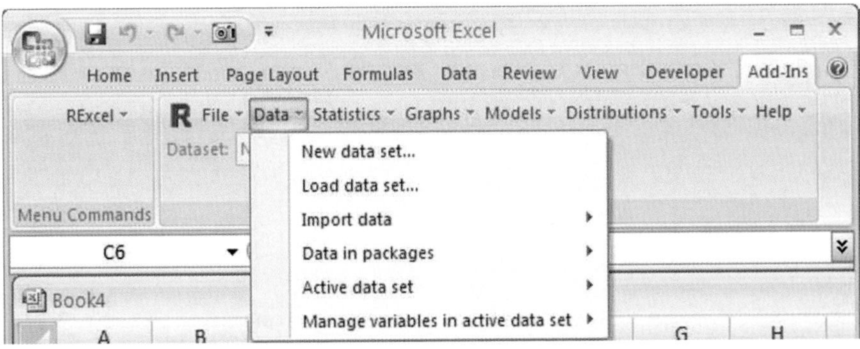

Fig. 2.7 Rcmdr Data menu. This menu is very helpful for bringing data into R and for restructuring the data after it is already in R.

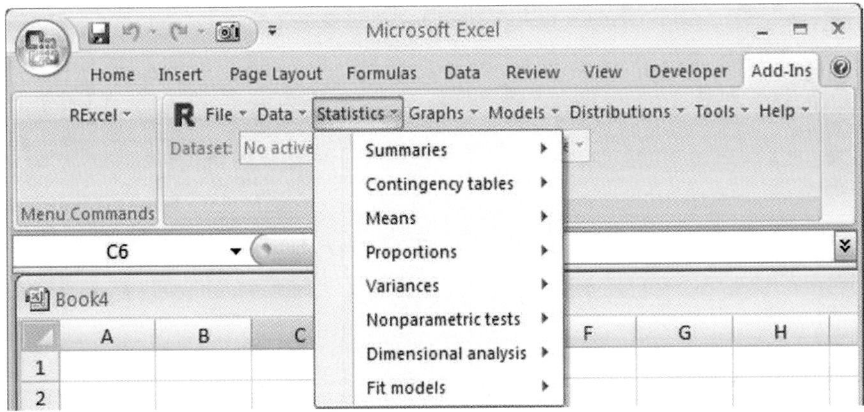

Fig. 2.8 Rcmdr Statistics menu. This is the workhorse menu for computations and analysis.

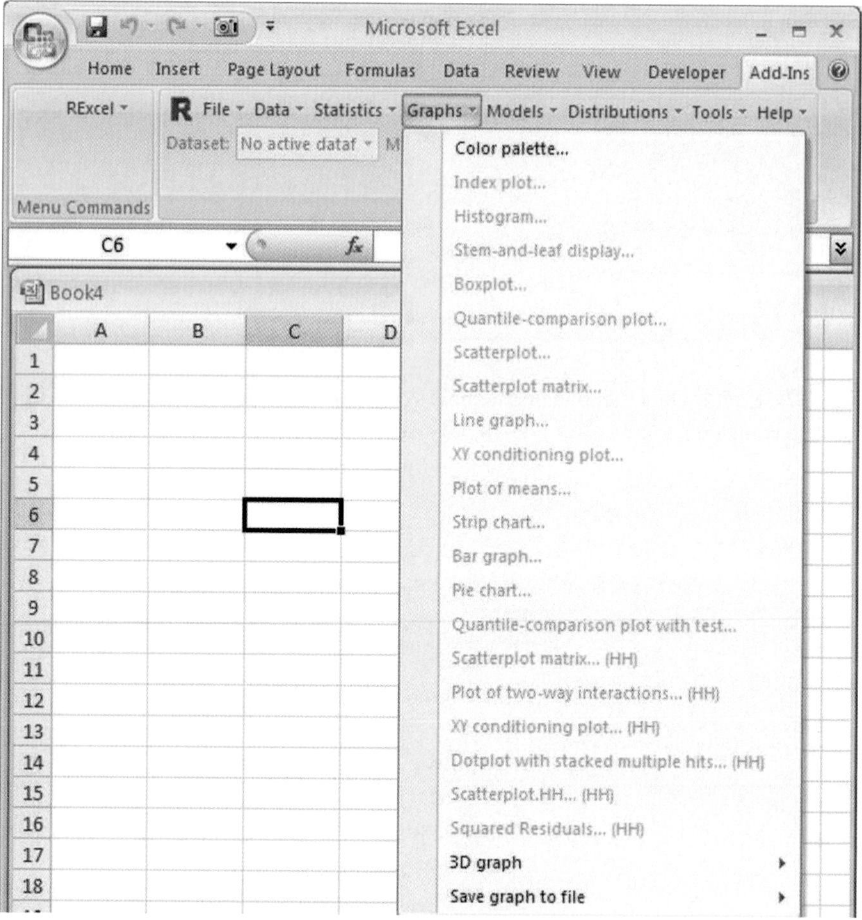

Fig. 2.9 Rcmdr Graphs menu. This is the workhorse menu for graphs.

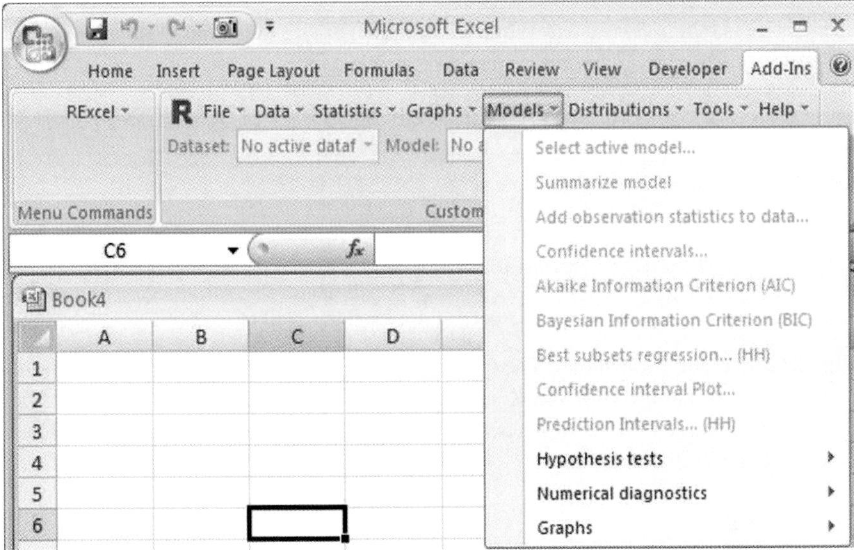

Fig. 2.10 Rcmdr Models menu. This menu allows follow-up display of results from analyses calculated in the Statistics menu.

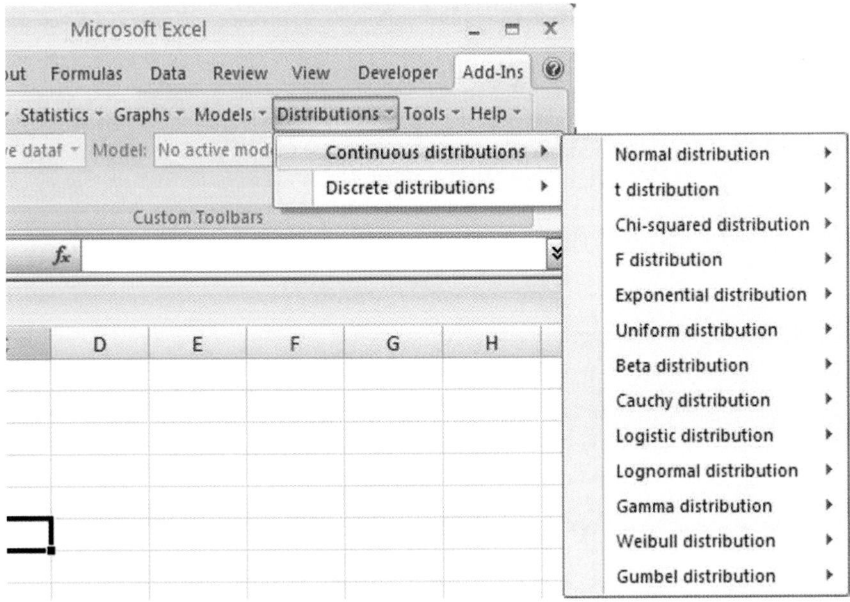

Fig. 2.11 Rcmdr Distributions menu. The normal, t, F, chi-squared, and other tables are accessible from the Continuous distributions menu shown here. The binomial and other tables are accessible from the Discrete distributions menu.

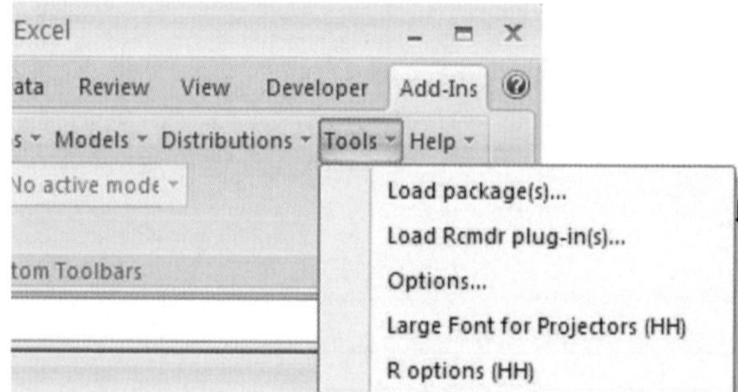

Fig. 2.12 Rcmdr Tools menu. The Options... item provides access to display options (font size, for example) for the Rcmdr window. Rcmdr plug-ins are a mechanism that permits people other than the author of Rcmdr to provide additional menu items on the Rcmdr menu bar.

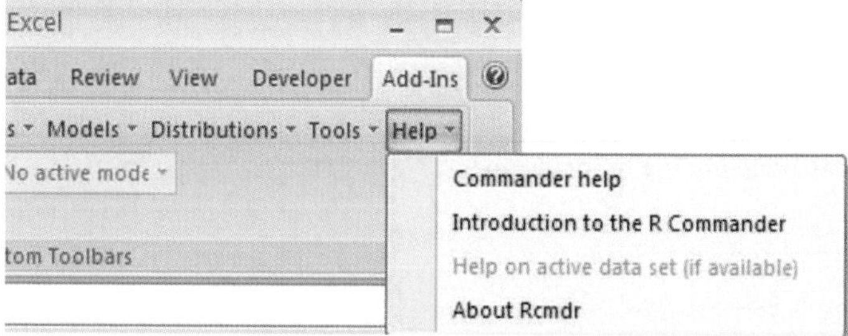

Fig. 2.13 Rcmdr Help menu. The Introduction to the R Commander is the best reference.

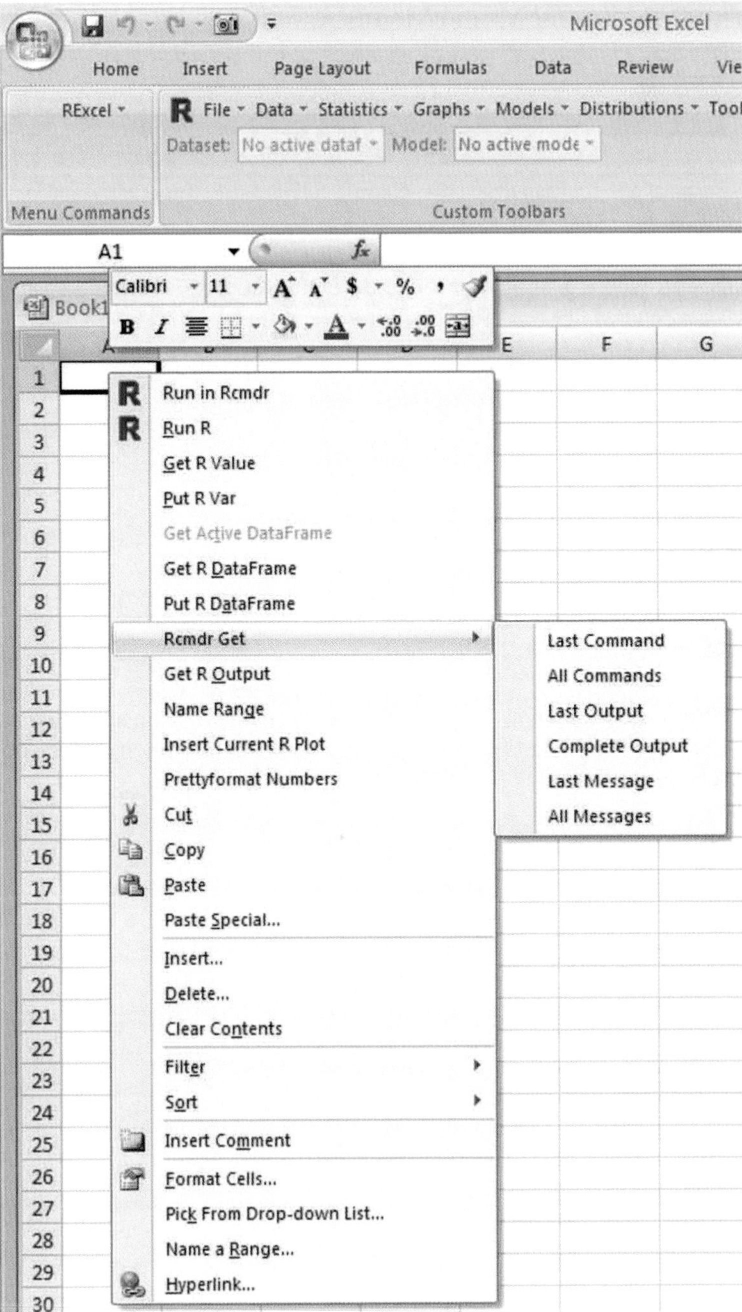

Fig. 2.14 Excel Context menu (right-click menu) displayed when RExcel is active and Rcmdr is loaded. This menu is the primary tool used to communicate between Excel and R.

2.2 The Dataset and Model Menus

In all previous figures (see Fig. 2.14, for example) the toolbar shows

This portion of the toolbar shows the Rcmdr active dataset and active model. Both initially show the value "not active".

When we work with a dataset, the active dataset is the one to which the menu commands are applied. In this section, we look at a dataset and model it with a simple least-squares fit.

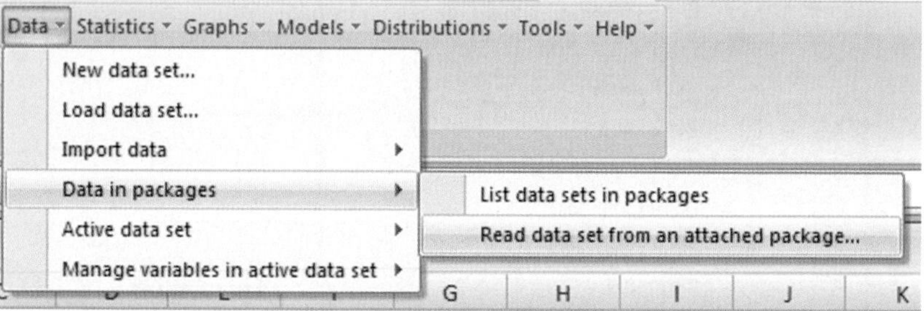

Fig. 2.15 R includes several datasets. We will make one of them active by clicking in the Rcmdr Data ▶ Data in packages ▶ Read data set from an attached package... menu. This opens the dialog box in Fig. 2.16.

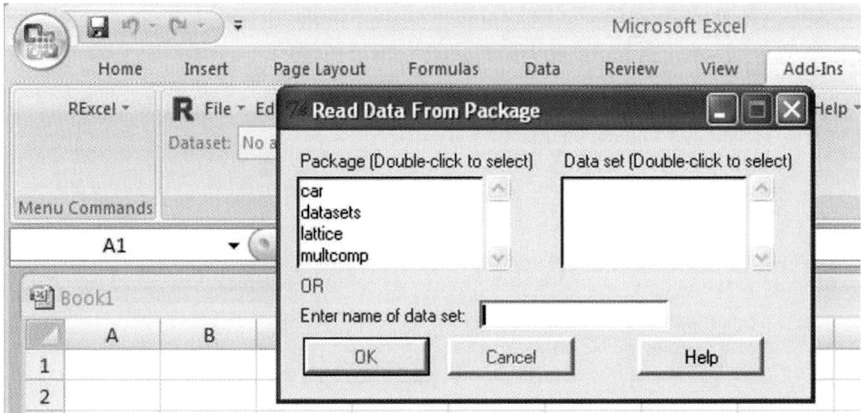

Fig. 2.16 R consists of a "base package" and many additional packages. The Read Data From Package menu shows those currently attached packages that include datasets.

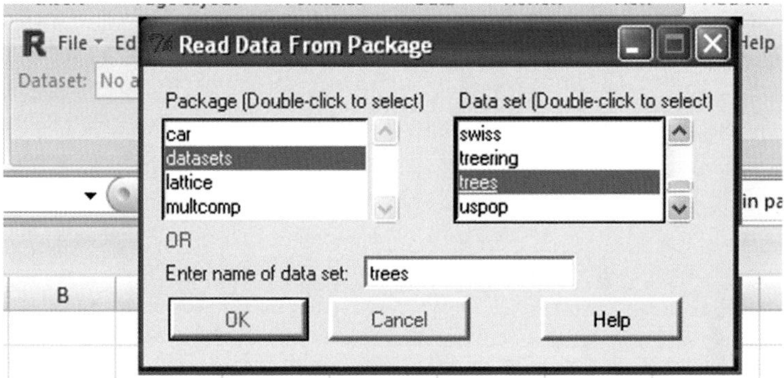

Fig. 2.17 Double-click a package name to put the list of datasets in the right-hand menu, double-click the trees dataset, and click OK.

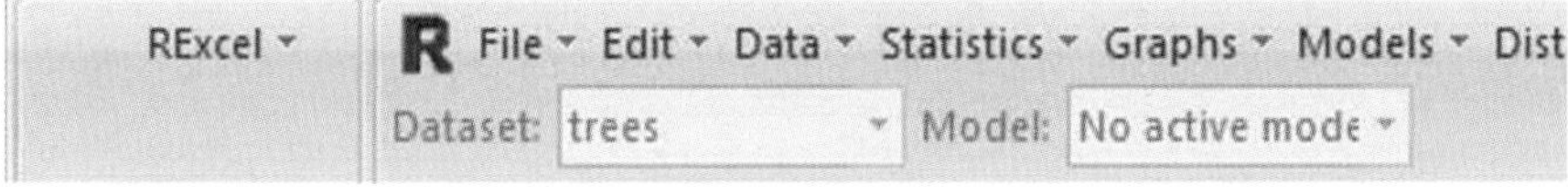

Fig. 2.18 The toolbar now shows trees as the active dataset.

We query R on the dataset by typing `?trees` in the Script Window and clicking the Submit button. R replies by displaying a help file. The screenshots of the query and the help file are shown in Fig. 2.29 and 2.30. The help file says the data is the

Girth, Height and Volume for Black Cherry Trees

Description:

This data set provides measurements of the girth, height and volume of timber in 31 felled black cherry trees. Note that girth is the diameter of the tree (in inches) measured at 4 ft 6 in above the ground. A data frame with 31 observations on 3 variables.

`[,1]` `Girth` numeric Tree diameter in inches
`[,2]` `Height` numeric Height in ft
`[,3]` `Volume` numeric Volume of timber in cubic ft

We need to look at the numbers in the dataset. The easiest way is to bring the numbers into Excel, using the technique described in Section 3.6.

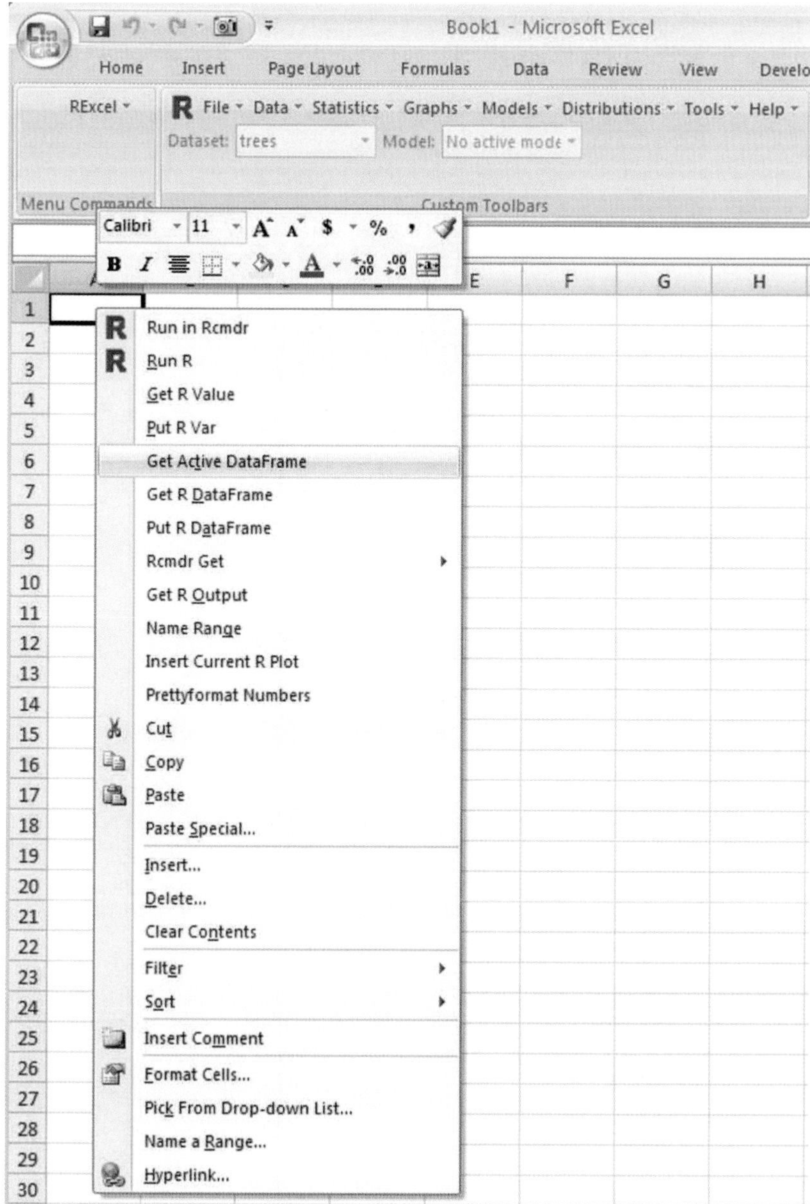

Fig. 2.19 Use the Context menu (right-click menu) to copy the active dataset named in the Dataset toolbar item into the Excel worksheet. We do so by activating an empty worksheet, clicking in cell A1 and then right-clicking Get Active DataFrame. The dataset will appear beginning with the highlighted cell. If you choose to bring data into an existing workbook, be careful about the choice of starting cell. There is no undo for this transfer.

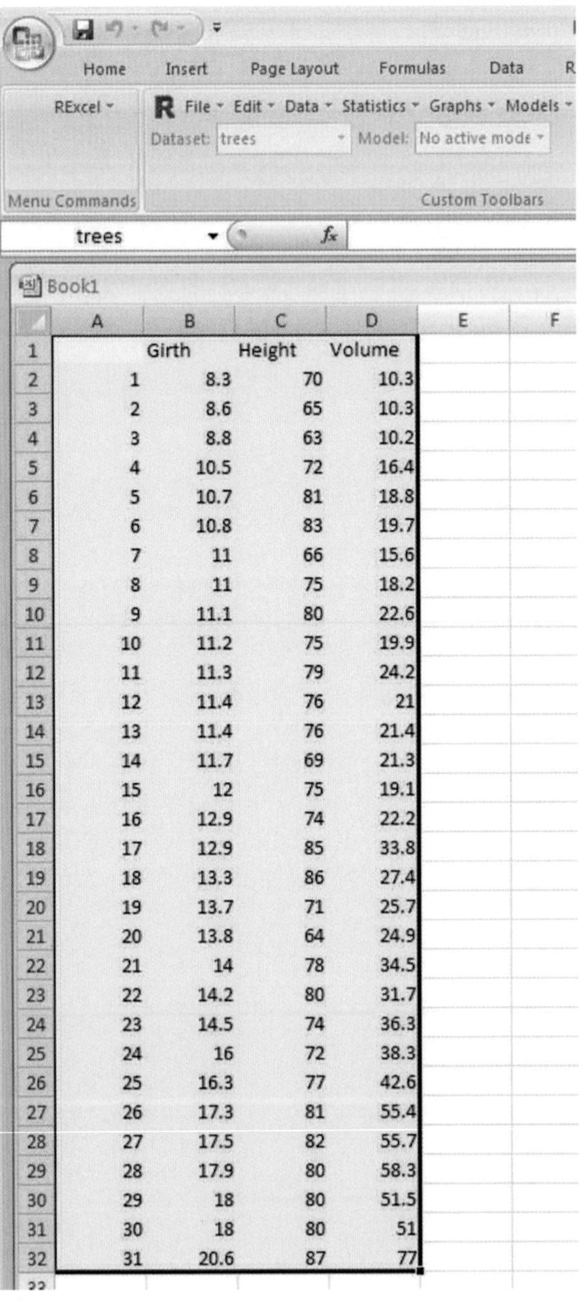

	Girth	Height	Volume
1	8.3	70	10.3
2	8.6	65	10.3
3	8.8	63	10.2
4	10.5	72	16.4
5	10.7	81	18.8
6	10.8	83	19.7
7	11	66	15.6
8	11	75	18.2
9	11.1	80	22.6
10	11.2	75	19.9
11	11.3	79	24.2
12	11.4	76	21
13	11.4	76	21.4
14	11.7	69	21.3
15	12	75	19.1
16	12.9	74	22.2
17	12.9	85	33.8
18	13.3	86	27.4
19	13.7	71	25.7
20	13.8	64	24.9
21	14	78	34.5
22	14.2	80	31.7
23	14.5	74	36.3
24	16	72	38.3
25	16.3	77	42.6
26	17.3	81	55.4
27	17.5	82	55.7
28	17.9	80	58.3
29	18	80	51.5
30	18	80	51
31	20.6	87	77

Fig. 2.20 The dataset is displayed in the worksheet. This dataset has four columns: the row name (in this example, a numerical index) and three variables. The region of the worksheet containing the dataset is colored and is given a name in the cell identifier box on the Excel toolbar.

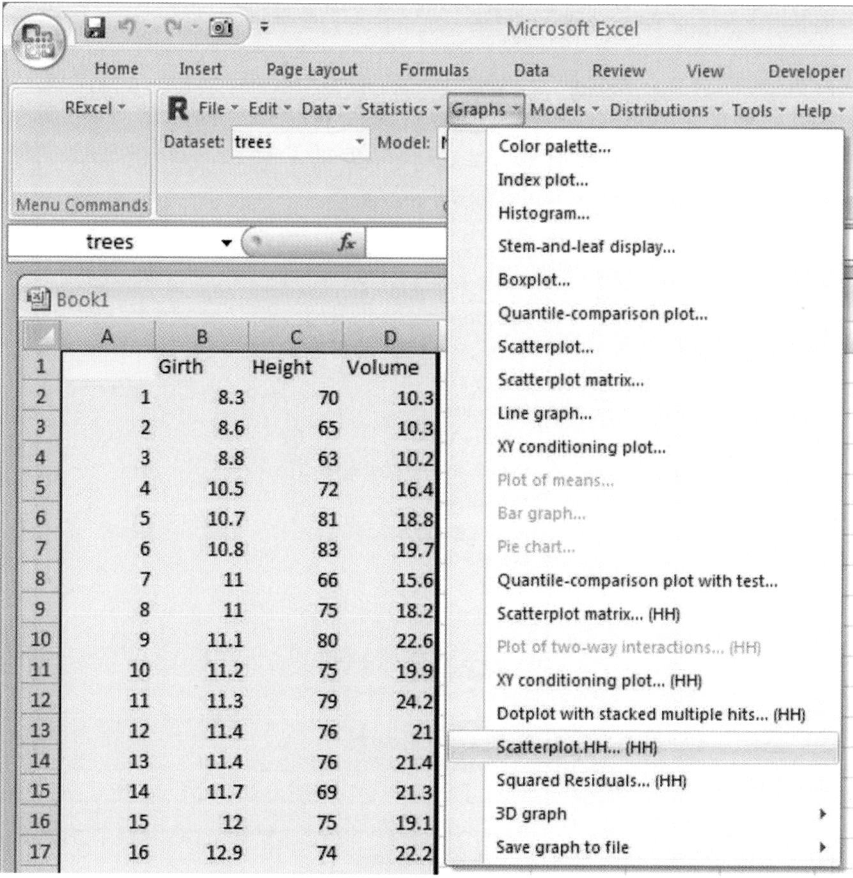

Fig. 2.21 Now that there is an active dataset, we can use the Graphs ▶ Scatterplot matrix... (HH) menu item. Menu items with ... indicate that the dialog box in Fig. 2.22 will ask for further information. The boldfaced menu items are the ones that make sense for the active dataset. The other items are grayed out.

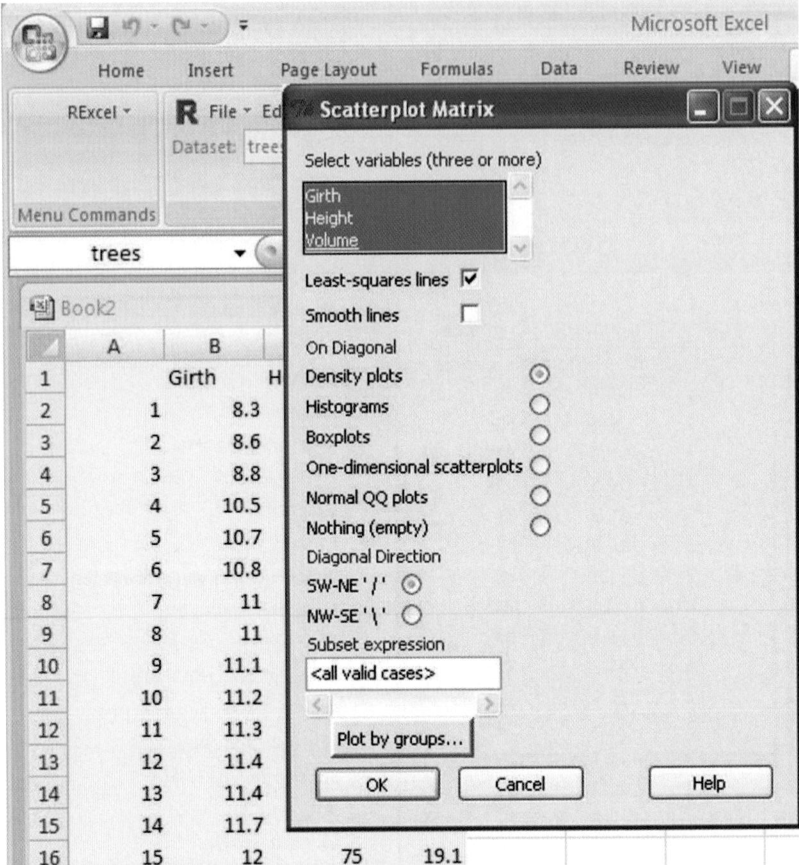

Fig. 2.22 Many of the menus in the Rcmdr dialog boxes include variable-selection dropdown boxes. When there is only one variable in the active dataset that meets the criterion, that variable is shown highlighted when the dialog box opens. When there are multiple variables, or when there is an optional variable selection, then no variables are shown highlighted when the dialog box opens. In this example, select all three variables, accept the defaults for the other items, and click OK.

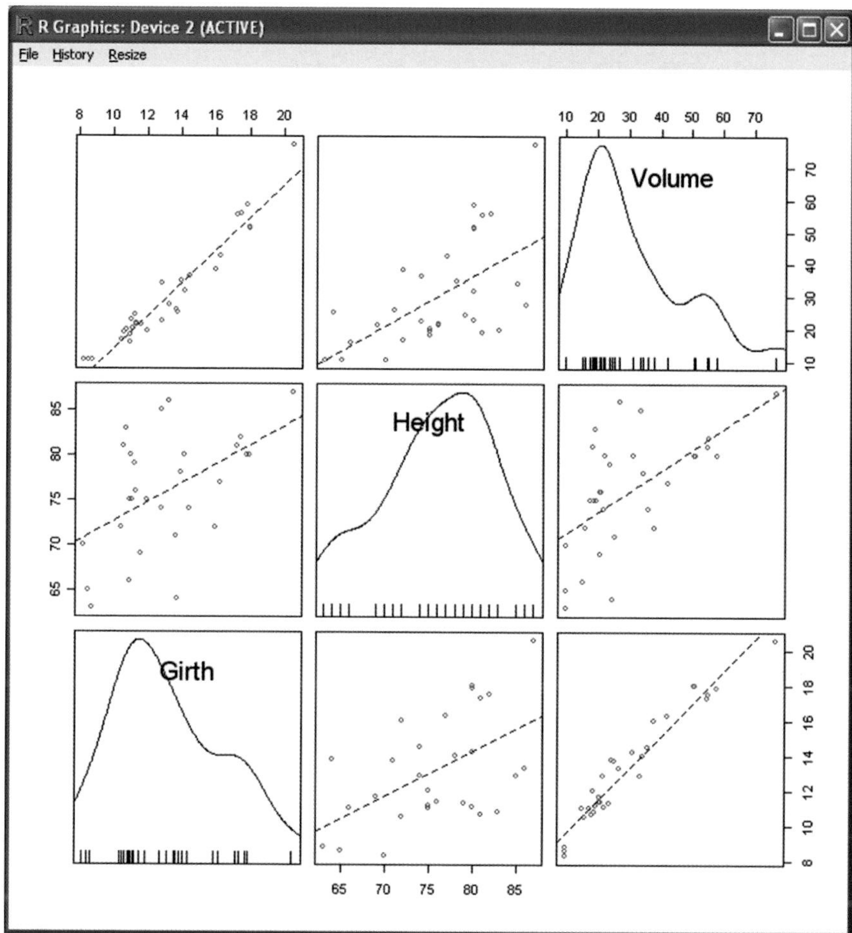

Fig. 2.23 The scatterplot matrix is a matrix of scatterplots of each variable plotted against the others. The sequence of variables normally starts at the lower left. Look at the plot of Volume $\sim$ Girth in the upper left panel and observe the linearity of the plot. This suggests a least-squares fit (see Chapter 8 for more information on least squares) might be appropriate. The scatterplot matrix displays on the main diagonal the estimated univariate densities for each of the variables. The notation $y \sim x$ means that the left variable is on the vertical axis and the right variable is on the horizontal axis. This notation is used throughout R to specify statistical models.

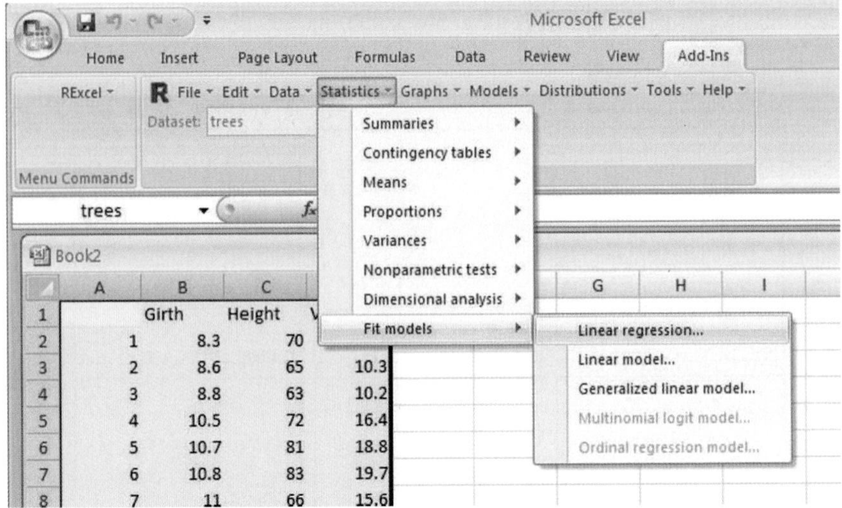

Fig. 2.24 Specify a least-squares fit on the active dataset by selecting the Statistics ► Fit models ► Linear regression... menu item.

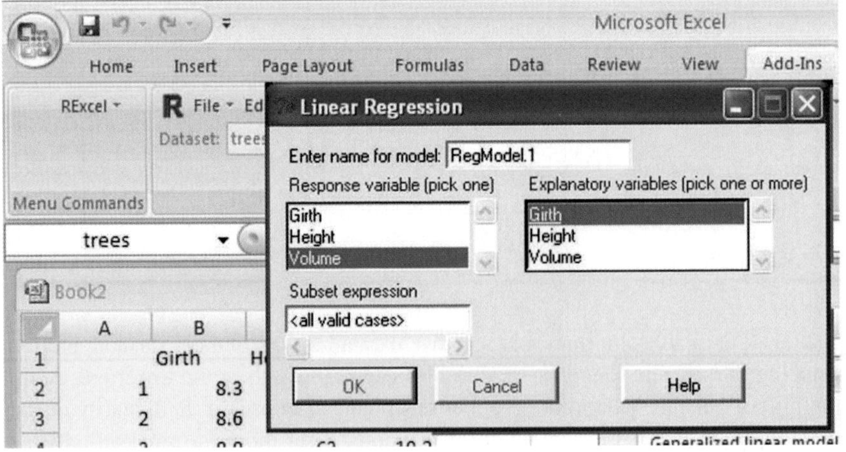

Fig. 2.25 The Linear Regression dialog box asks for a response variable, and we select the y-variable Volume from the Volume ~ Girth plot in Fig. 2.23. We select as Explanatory variable the x-variable Girth. Output from this dialog box is in Fig. 2.26. The dialog box also changes the active model as shown in Fig. 2.27.

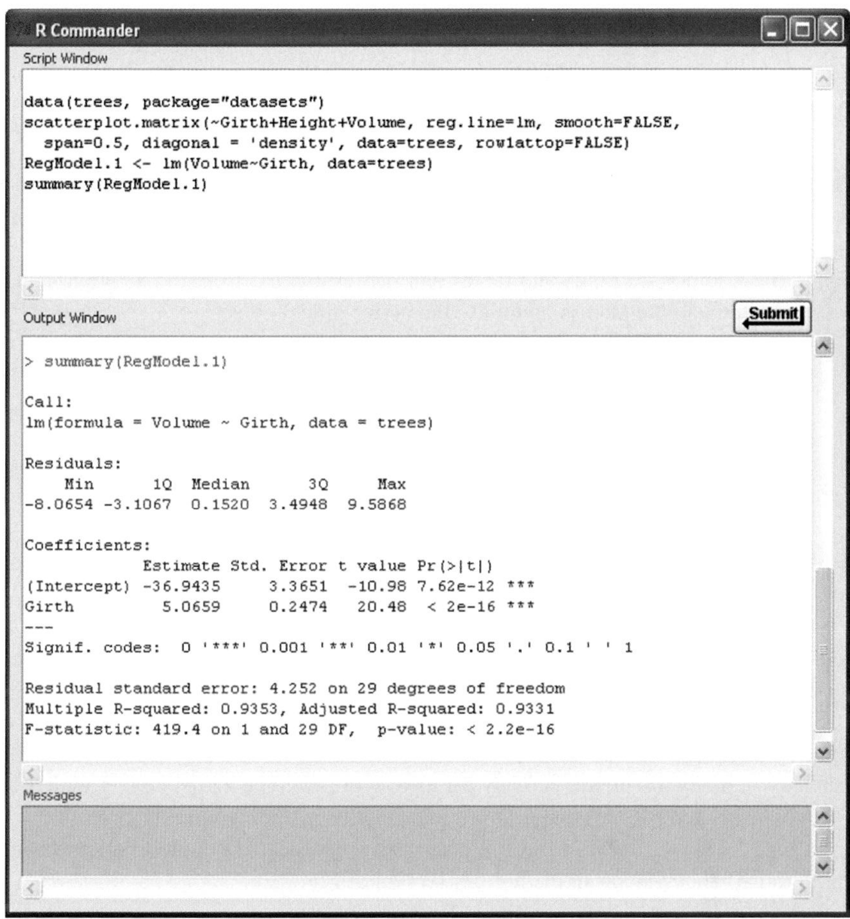

Fig. 2.26 The R Commander window shows the printed output from the dialog box in Fig. 2.25. The generated R code is in the top Script Window. The analysis object is given the name `RegModel.1`. The summary of the regression analysis in model `RegModel.1` is in the bottom Output Window. The coefficients of the least-squares line are displayed in the `coefficients` section of the output. The least-squares line is

$$\hat{y} = -36.9435 + 5.0659x$$

The least-squares line is displayed as the dotted line in the Volume ~ Girth panel on the plot in Fig. 2.23.

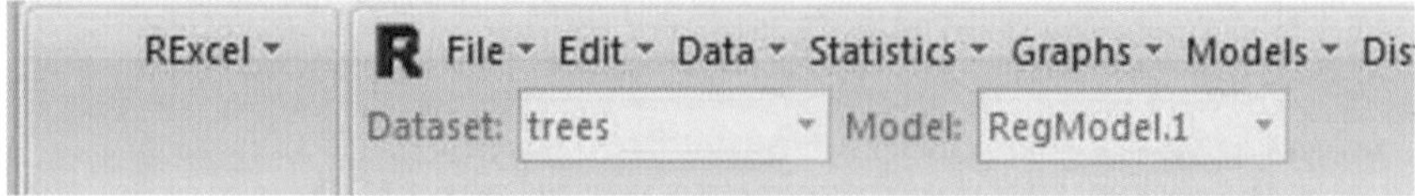

Fig. 2.27 The Model item in the Rcmdr menu now shows the name of the active regression analysis object `RegModel.1`. Compare to Fig. 2.18, where only the active dataset is displayed. The summary of the model object is automatically displayed in Fig. 2.26. Additional graphs and tables can be constructed from the active model. All menu items in the Models menu use the active model object.

2.3 R Console

R was originally designed as a command language; commands were typed into a text-based input area on the computer screen and the program responded with a written response to each command. The written response is usually a table. In this book, we normally do not use the command language directly. Occasionally, we need it; therefore, we give a small introduction here.

Start R as in Figs. 1.13 and 1.14. The R Console in Fig. 1.14 is essentially a typewriter window. The R Console opens with information and then a prompt mark, usually > , indicating that it is ready for us to type. We type a line, ending with the ↩ Enter key. Then R types one or more lines in return, ending with the prompt > .

In Fig. 2.28, we repeat in the R Console the regression example first shown in the Rcmdr Output Window in the bottom section of Fig. 2.26.

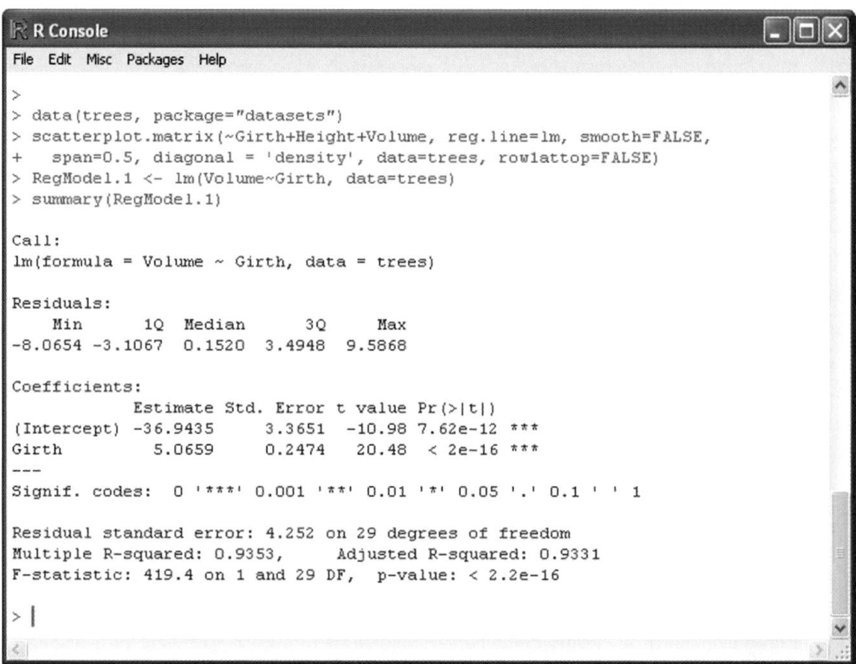

R Console
File Edit Misc Packages Help
>
> data(trees, package="datasets")
> scatterplot.matrix(~Girth+Height+Volume, reg.line=lm, smooth=FALSE,
+ span=0.5, diagonal = 'density', data=trees, row1attop=FALSE)
> RegModel.1 <- lm(Volume~Girth, data=trees)
> summary(RegModel.1)
Call:
lm(formula = Volume ~ Girth, data = trees)
Residuals:
Min 1Q Median 3Q Max
-8.0654 -3.1067 0.1520 3.4948 9.5868
Coefficients:
Estimate Std. Error t value Pr(>|t|)
(Intercept) -36.9435 3.3651 -10.98 7.62e-12 ***
Girth 5.0659 0.2474 20.48 < 2e-16 ***

Signif. codes: 0 '***' 0.001 '**' 0.01 '*' 0.05 '.' 0.1 ' ' 1
Residual standard error: 4.252 on 29 degrees of freedom
Multiple R-squared: 0.9353, Adjusted R-squared: 0.9331
F-statistic: 419.4 on 1 and 29 DF, p-value: < 2.2e-16
>

Fig. 2.28 Repeat of the regression analysis in Fig. 2.26. This figure is primarily a demonstration of the R Console window and only incidentally an illustration of the regression analysis. The R Console displays a prompt mark > indicating that it is ready for us to type. We type each line into the R Console window and end each line with an ↩ Enter keypress. After each *complete* line is typed, the R Console responds with a prompt > saying it is ready for a new line. After *incomplete* lines—in this example, the first line of the `scatterplot.matrix()` function call—the R Console responds with a continuation prompt + . The `data()` command produces no printed output. The `scatterplot.matrix()` command tells R to construct and display the plot in Fig. 2.23. The `summary()` command produces an output display, which is shown immediately after the command line and before the next prompt.

2.4 R Commander Window

The R Commander window is so named because it generates R commands from clicks on the menu. Let's look again at Fig. 2.26, this time focusing on the structure of the window.

In Figs. 2.15 and 2.18, we clicked menus and dialog boxes. The R Commander translated those clicks into the `data()` command in the Script Window in the top half of the R Commander window in Fig. 2.26. It also put the command in the Output Window in the bottom half of the R Commander window in Fig. 2.26 (it scrolled offscreen in this illustration).

In Figs. 2.21 and 2.22 we clicked menus and dialog boxes. The R Commander translated those clicks into the `scatterplot.matrix()` command in the Script Window. It also put the command in the Output Window. This command also scrolled offscreen in this illustration.

In Figs. 2.24–2.25 we clicked menus and dialog boxes. The R Commander translated those clicks into the `lm()` and `summary()` commands in the Script Window. It also put the command and its printed output in the Output Window.

The Script Window simulates a program file of commands that could be typed into the R Console. The Output Window simulates the R Console window.

It is possible, and sometimes useful, to type commands into the R Commander Script Window and submit them to the R Commander Output Window for execution. Just enter a complete command in the Script Window and click the Submit button. In Section 2.2, we showed the information in the help file for the `trees` dataset. In Section 2.5, as an example of typing into the R Commander window, we show screenshots of the query in Fig. 2.29 and the help file in Fig. 2.30.

2.5 R Help Files

All functions and datasets in R have a help file. Help files can be accessed by typing a query, for example, `?trees`, in the R Commander Script Window and then clicking the Submit button as shown in Fig. 2.29. In addition, all Rcmdr dialog boxes include a Help button that will open the appropriate help file.

Fig. 2.30 shows the help file for the `trees` dataset in the standard MS help format. R can present help files in other formats. See `?help` for more information. If the help files appear in some other format, you can force R to use the standard MS help format by entering `options(chmhelp=TRUE)` in the R Commander Script Window and then clicking the Submit button. You can also change the help file format from the RExcel ► Options dialog box.

Fig. 2.29 Type the help query `?trees` in the R Commander Script Window and leave the cursor on that line. Then click the Submit button. The R Commander copies the line to the Output Window and executes the line by opening the help file in Fig. 2.30 to a discussion of the trees dataset.

2.6 Messages from R, Rcmdr, or Excel

R and Excel are two different processes running on your computer. The RExcel interface coordinates communication between them. It is possible for them to get out of phase, particularly during startup. See Appendix B for remedies for some of the more likely problems.

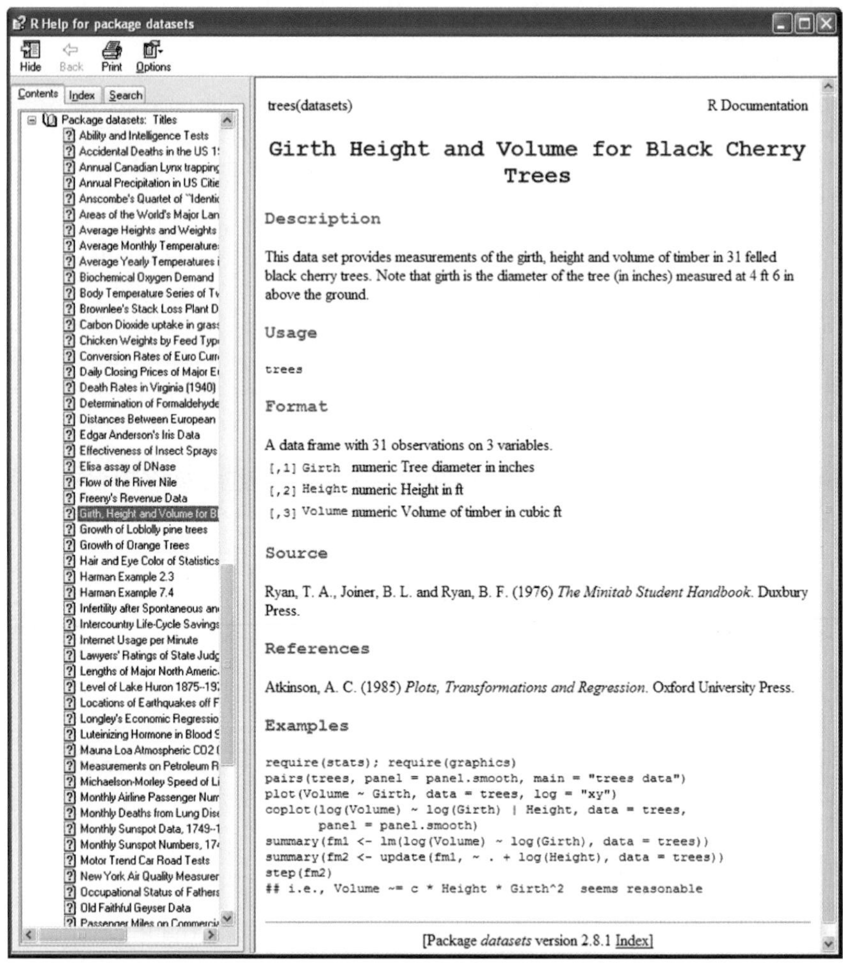

Fig. 2.30 This is an illustration of a help window in the standard MS help format. The right panel describes the dataset. The left panel opens to the table of contents for that help file. In this example, the help file contains descriptions of all the datasets included as part of base R.

Chapter 3
Getting Data into R

Abstract Datasets are frequently given as Excel worksheets. We must transfer them from Excel to R in order to place the variable names on the Rcmdr menu items. We show how to do the transfer for several different data structures. Sometimes datasets are given as ASCII text files. These too can be read into Excel and then transferred to R. Sometimes datasets are already in R. We can work with them directly, and we can display them in Excel by transferring the data the other direction from R to Excel.

3.1 Example Datasets

Datasets are frequently given as Excel worksheets. Most statistics texts, for example, include their example datasets in Excel workbooks. The usual method (if Excel is not started already) of bringing files into Excel is by double-clicking their file name in Windows Explorer.

For specificity in describing the transfer of the datasets to R, we include four example Excel workbooks in the RExcel ► RthroughExcel Worksheets menu item. Because these datasets are part of the R through Excel distribution, they are accessible from the RExcel menu instead of the usual Windows Explorer. We show how to access our example datasets in Figs. 3.1 and 3.2. Once opened, they are ordinary Excel worksheets.

R.M. Heiberger, E. Neuwirth, *R Through Excel*, Use R,
DOI 10.1007/978-1-4419-0052-4_3,

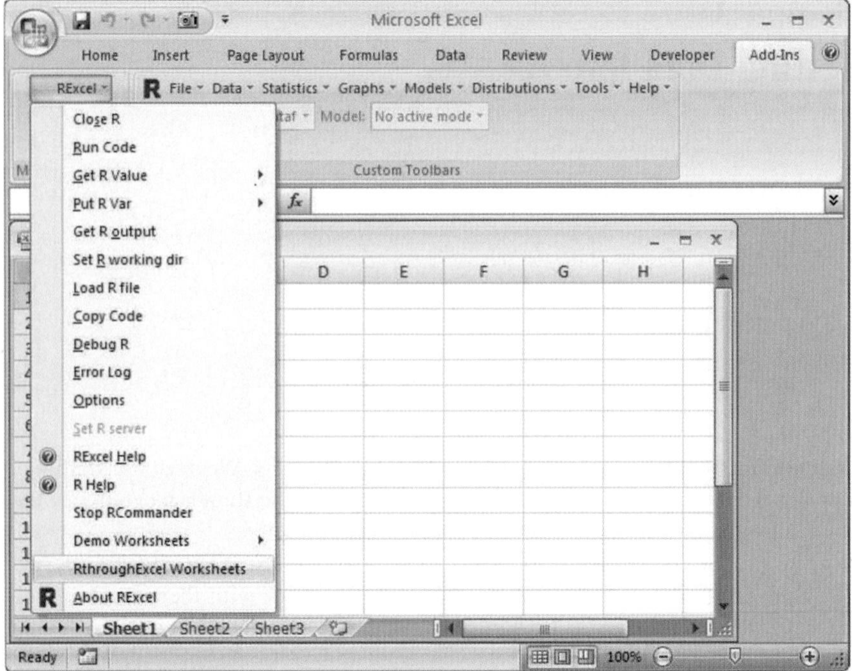

Fig. 3.1 Click in the RExcel ▶ RthroughExcel Worksheets menu item. This opens the workbook BookFilesTOC in Fig. 3.2.

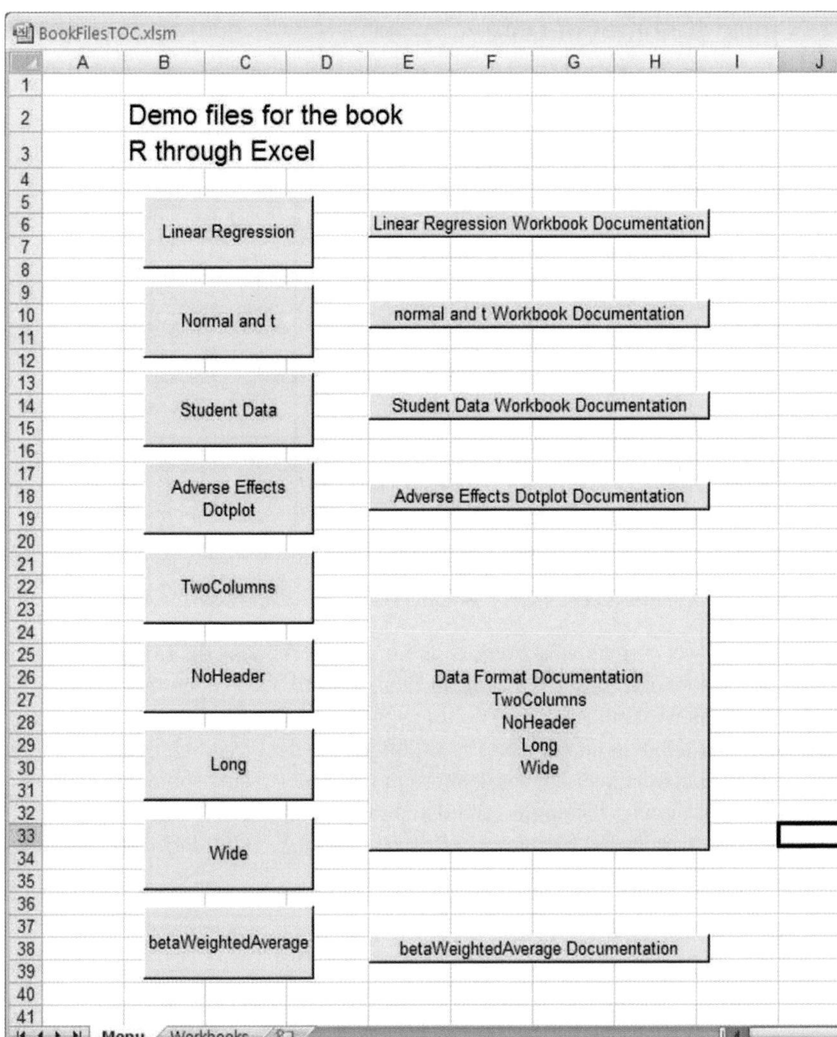

Fig. 3.2 The workbook titled Demo Files for the book R through Excel was opened in Fig. 3.1. The four example files we discuss in this chapter are accessed by clicking one of the buttons TwoColumns, NoHeader, Long, Wide. Click the TwoColumns button to open the TwoColumns workbook displayed in Fig. 3.3.

3.2 Named Columns of Data

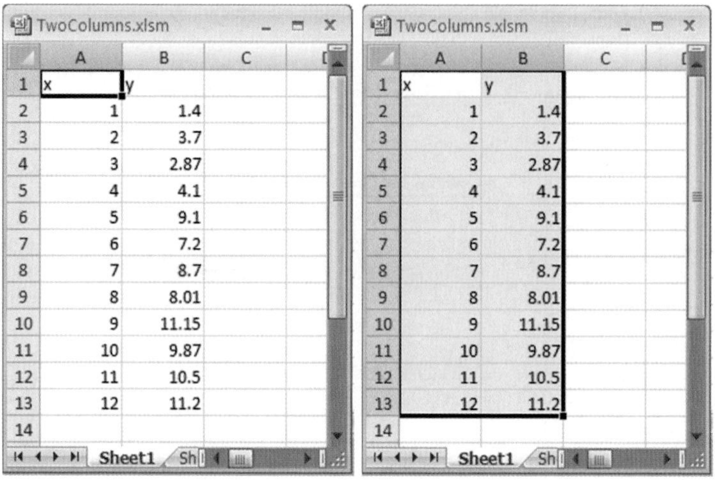

TwoColumns.xlsm

	A	B	C
1	x	y	
2	1	1.4	
3	2	3.7	
4	3	2.87	
5	4	4.1	
6	5	9.1	
7	6	7.2	
8	7	8.7	
9	8	8.01	
10	9	11.15	
11	10	9.87	
12	11	10.5	
13	12	11.2	
14			

Sheet1

TwoColumns.xlsm

	A	B	C
1	x	y	
2	1	1.4	
3	2	3.7	
4	3	2.87	
5	4	4.1	
6	5	9.1	
7	6	7.2	
8	7	8.7	
9	8	8.01	
10	9	11.15	
11	10	9.87	
12	11	10.5	
13	12	11.2	
14			

Sheet1

Fig. 3.3 The TwoColumns workbook is one of the workbooks distributed with the *R through Excel* book. Follow the steps in Figs. 3.1 and 3.2 to open this workbook. The TwoColumns workbook has two columns, with column names x and y in row 1 and numeric data values in rows 2–13. Highlight the data by clicking cell A1 and pressing the standard Excel keyboard shortcut Ctrl+shift+*. This shortcut highlights the smallest contiguous rectangle of cells containing the selected cell that is bordered (even at the corners) by empty cells or the worksheet borders only. The row containing the variable names is included.

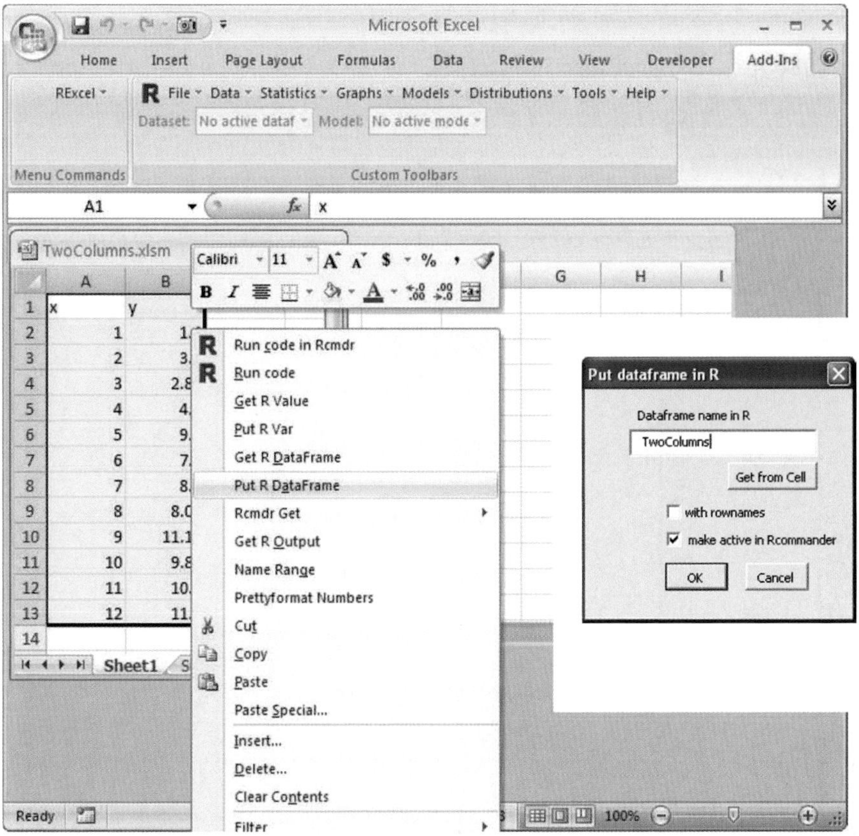

Fig. 3.4 Send the highlighted data, including the row containing the variable names, to R by (a) right-clicking Put R Dataframe and (b) accepting the suggested name in the dialog box and clicking OK. The suggested name is normally the base name of the Excel file, in this example TwoColumns.

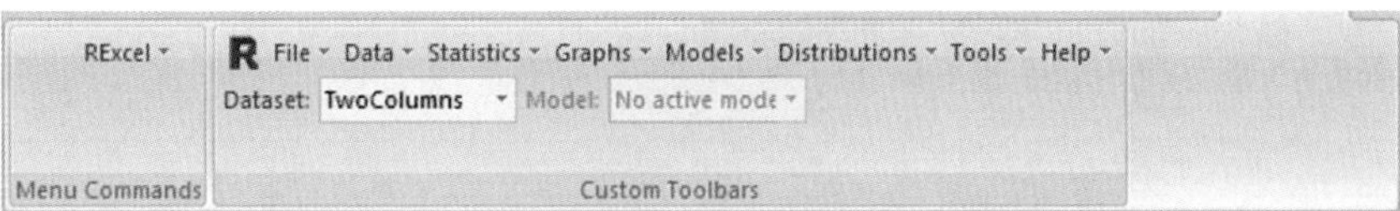

Fig. 3.5 The active dataset is now listed in the Rcmdr Dataset window as TwoColumns. Compare to the Dataset window in Fig. 3.4, where it says No active dataframe. One important consequence of Put R Dataframe is to make the transferred data into the active dataset and therefore make its variable names available in the Rcmdr menu items.

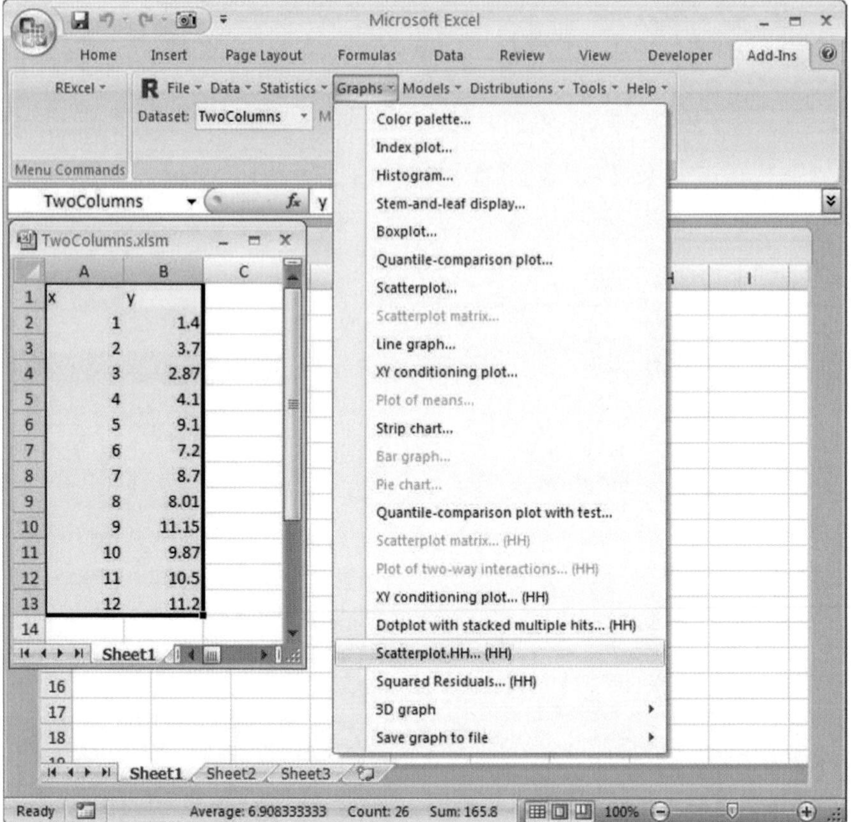

Fig. 3.6 We can now examine the data in the active dataset with the functions on the Rcmdr menus. We illustrate by plotting `y ~ x` . The formula notation says that `y`, the variable named on the left of the tilde "~", is to be plotted on the vertical axis and `x`, the variable named on the right of the tilde "~", is to be plotted on the horizontal axis. On the Rcmdr menu, click Graphs ► Scatterplot.HH... (HH) to get the dialog box in Fig. 3.7.

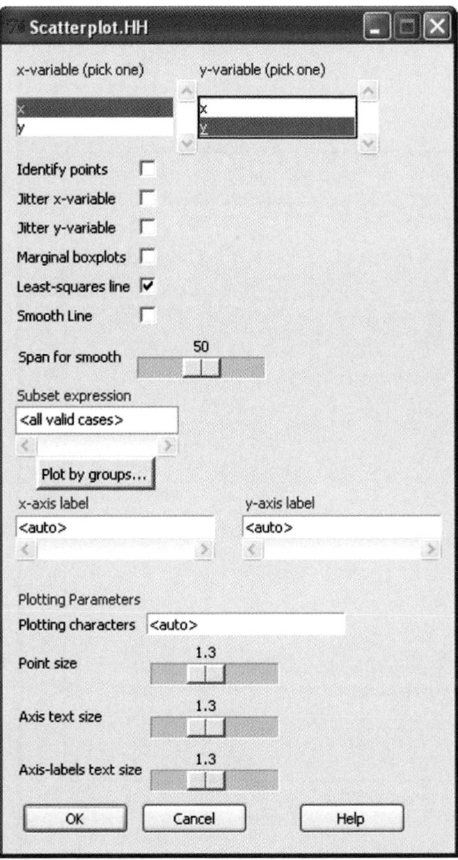

Fig. 3.7 This dialog box comes from Fig. 3.6. We click x in the x-variable selection box and y in the y-variable selection box. We accept the default values for all the other options in the dialog box. When we click OK, we get the graph in Fig. 3.8 and the generated statements in Fig. 3.9.

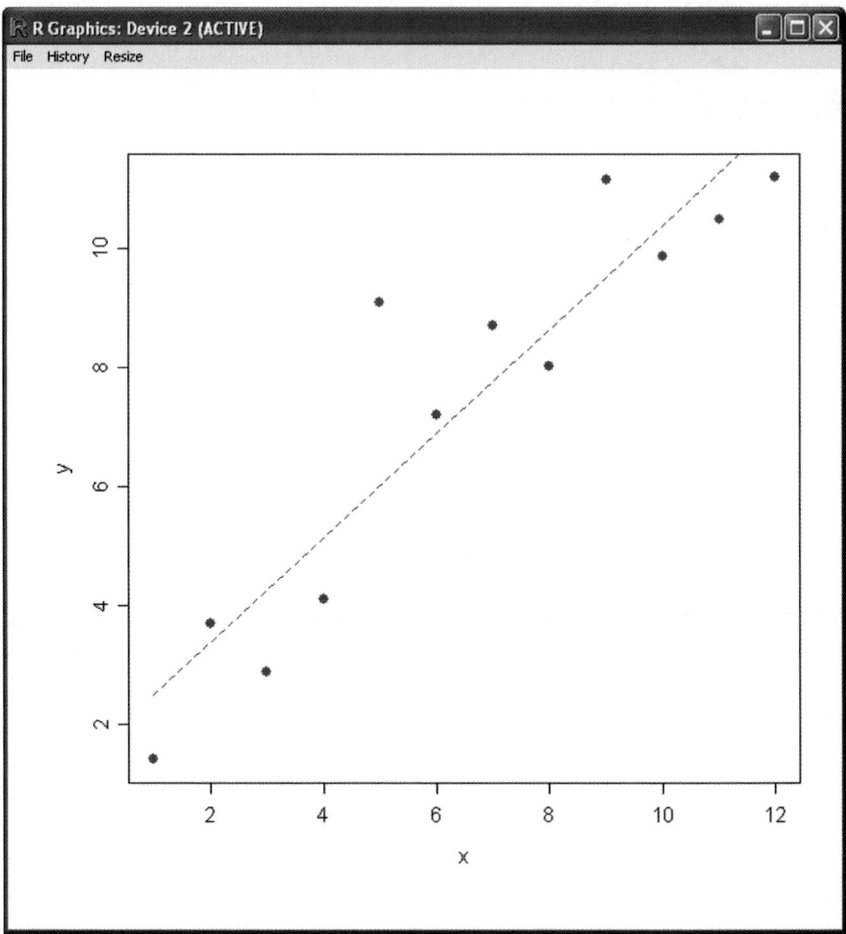

Fig. 3.8 This is the graph specified by the dialog box in Fig. 3.6. The points are specified by the x- and y-values in the rows of the dataset in Fig. 3.3. The line is the least-squares line, which we will discuss in Chapter 8.

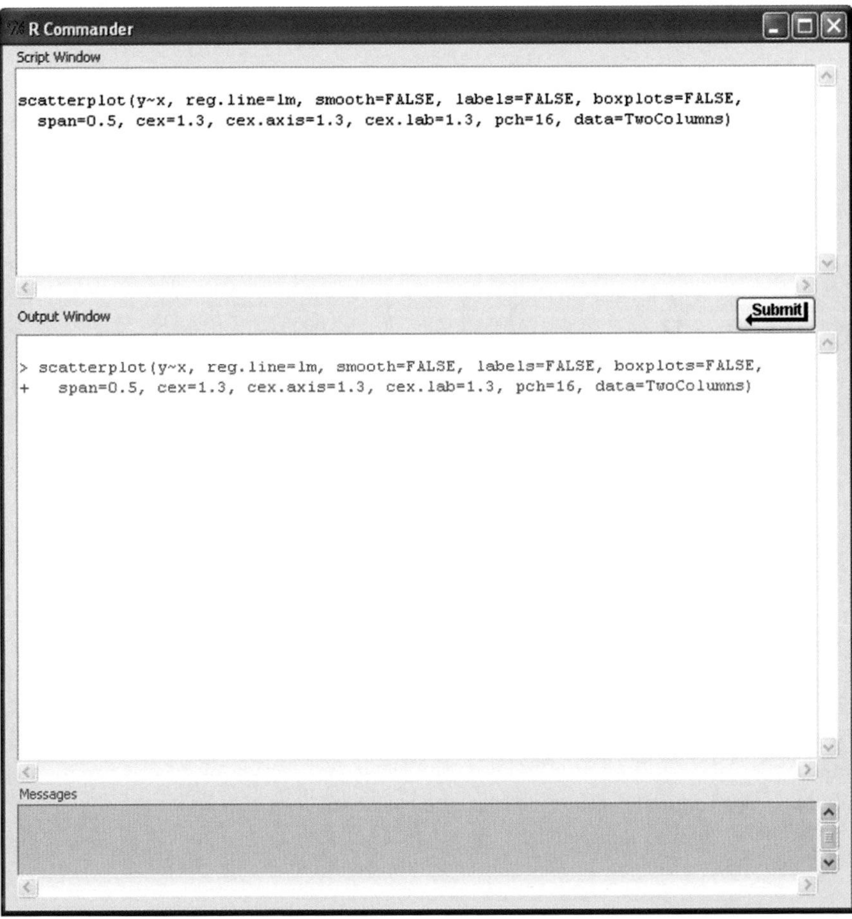

Fig. 3.9 Rcmdr works by translating the clicked items in the Rcmdr menu into statements in the R language. The generated statements are displayed in the Script Window of the R Commander window. The executed statements are displayed, along with any printed output, in the Output Window of the R Commander window.

3.3 Unnamed Columns of Data

a. Two columns, as opened.

NoHeader.xlsm

	A	B	C
1	1	1.4	
2	2	3.7	
3	3	2.87	
4	4	4.1	
5	5	9.1	
6	6	7.2	
7	7	8.7	
8	8	8.01	
9	9	11.15	
10	10	9.87	
11	11	10.5	
12	12	11.2	
13			
14			
15			

Sheet1 Sh

b. Row 1 highlighted.

NoHeader.xlsm

	A	B	C
1	1	1.4	
2	2	3.7	
3	3	2.87	
4	4	4.1	
5	5	9.1	
6	6	7.2	
7	7	8.7	
8	8	8.01	
9	9	11.15	
10	10	9.87	
11	11	10.5	
12	12	11.2	
13			
14			
15			

Sheet1 Sh

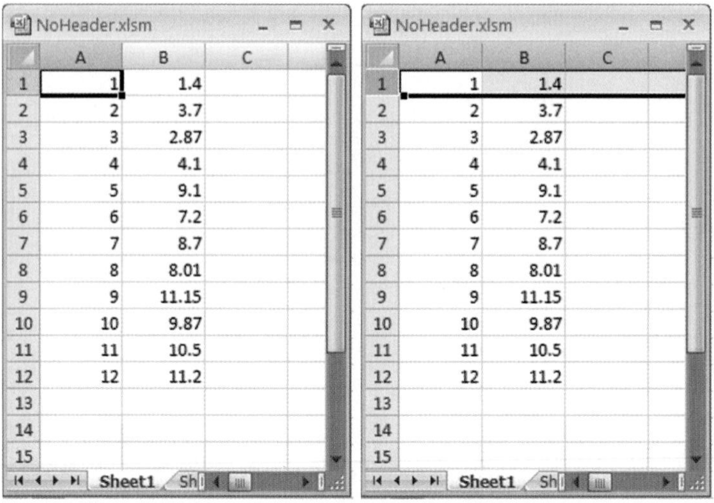

Fig. 3.10 The NoHeader workbook is one of the workbooks distributed with the *R through Excel* book. Follow the steps in Figs. 3.1 and 3.2 to open this workbook. The initial appearance is shown in Panel a. The NoHeader workbook has two unnamed columns. The numerical values are the same as in the TwoColumns workbook in Fig. 3.3. We need column names when we send the data to R. In Panel b, we highlight row 1 by clicking the row number column. We continue in Fig. 3.11.

a. Right-click ▶ Insert.

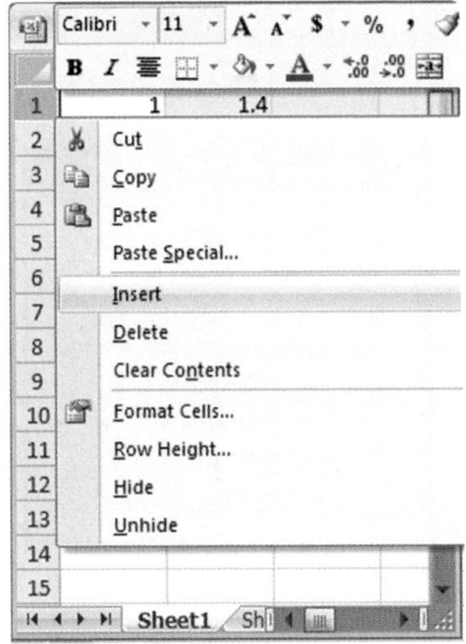

b. New, empty row 1.

c. Enter column names.

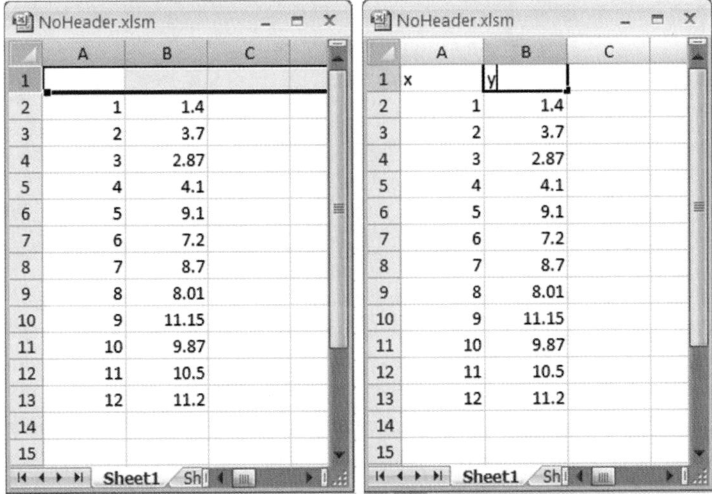

Panel b:

	A	B	C
1			
2	1	1.4	
3	2	3.7	
4	3	2.87	
5	4	4.1	
6	5	9.1	
7	6	7.2	
8	7	8.7	
9	8	8.01	
10	9	11.15	
11	10	9.87	
12	11	10.5	
13	12	11.2	
14			
15			

Panel c:

	A	B	C
1	x	y	
2	1	1.4	
3	2	3.7	
4	3	2.87	
5	4	4.1	
6	5	9.1	
7	6	7.2	
8	7	8.7	
9	8	8.01	
10	9	11.15	
11	10	9.87	
12	11	10.5	
13	12	11.2	
14			
15			

Fig. 3.11 Continuing from Fig. 3.10. In Panel a, we right-click the highlighted row number and click Insert. In Panel b, we now see a new blank row inserted in front of the previous row 1. In Panel c, we enter the column names in the newly inserted row 1. The worksheet now shows a labeled dataset that we can send to R, as in Fig. 3.12

a. Menu. b. Dialog box.

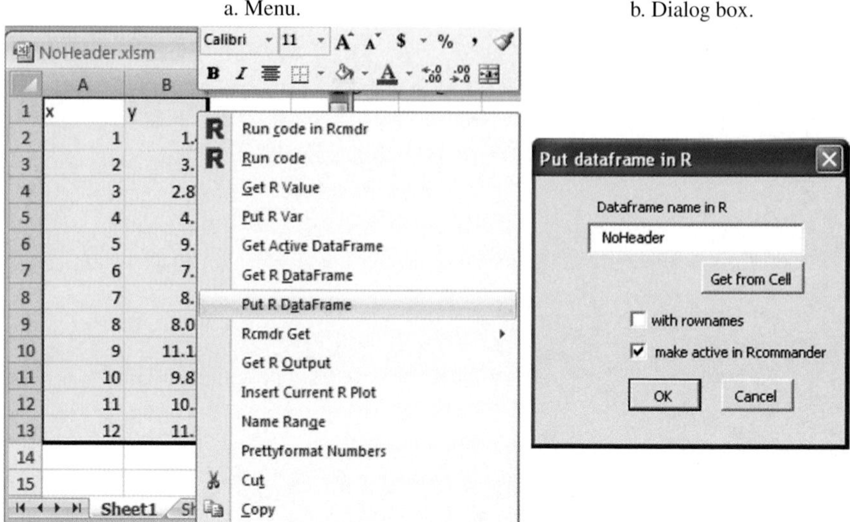

c. Ribbon with Rcmdr active dataset.

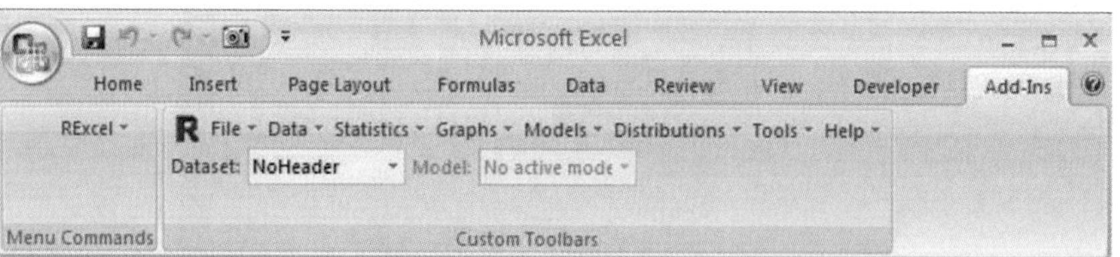

Fig. 3.12 Continuing from Fig. 3.11. a. Highlight the data, including the row containing the variable names, by clicking cell A1 and pressing the standard Excel keyboard shortcut Ctrl+shift+*. Then right-click Put R DataFrame to get the dialog box in Panel b. Accept the default dataframe name and click OK. In Panel c, we see that the active dataset is now listed in the Rcmdr Dataset window as NoHeader. The variable names in the dataset NoHeader are now available in the Rcmdr menu items.

3.4 Numeric Columns and Factor Columns

Long.xlsm

	A	B	C	D
1	y	group		
2	4.2	A		
3	5.2	A		
4	-2	A		
5	3.1	A		
6	2.3	A		
7	5.3	A		
8	6.3	A		
9	4	A		
10	5.1	A		
11	6.984	A		
12	8.2	A		
13	2.3	A		
14	10.2	B		
15	4.004	B		
16	3.7	B		
17	7.9	B		
18	9.3	B		
19	8.23	B		

Sheet1 Shee

Fig. 3.13 The Long workbook is one of the workbooks distributed with the *R through Excel* book. Follow the steps in Figs. 3.1 and 3.2 to open this workbook. The Long workbook has two columns. The y column contains numerical values of a response variable. The group column contains the level names for a factor. The workbook name Long is chosen to indicate that this data is stored in the *long* format, where all responses for all groups are in the same y column and the group membership is indicated by the levels in the group column. Compare the *long* format to the *wide* format in Fig. 3.16. The *Long* format is used by most of the modeling functions in R. In this figure, we have highlighted the data region, including the row containing the variable names, with the standard Excel keyboard shortcut Ctrl+shift+* and sent it to R with right-click Put R DataFrame to get Fig. 3.14.

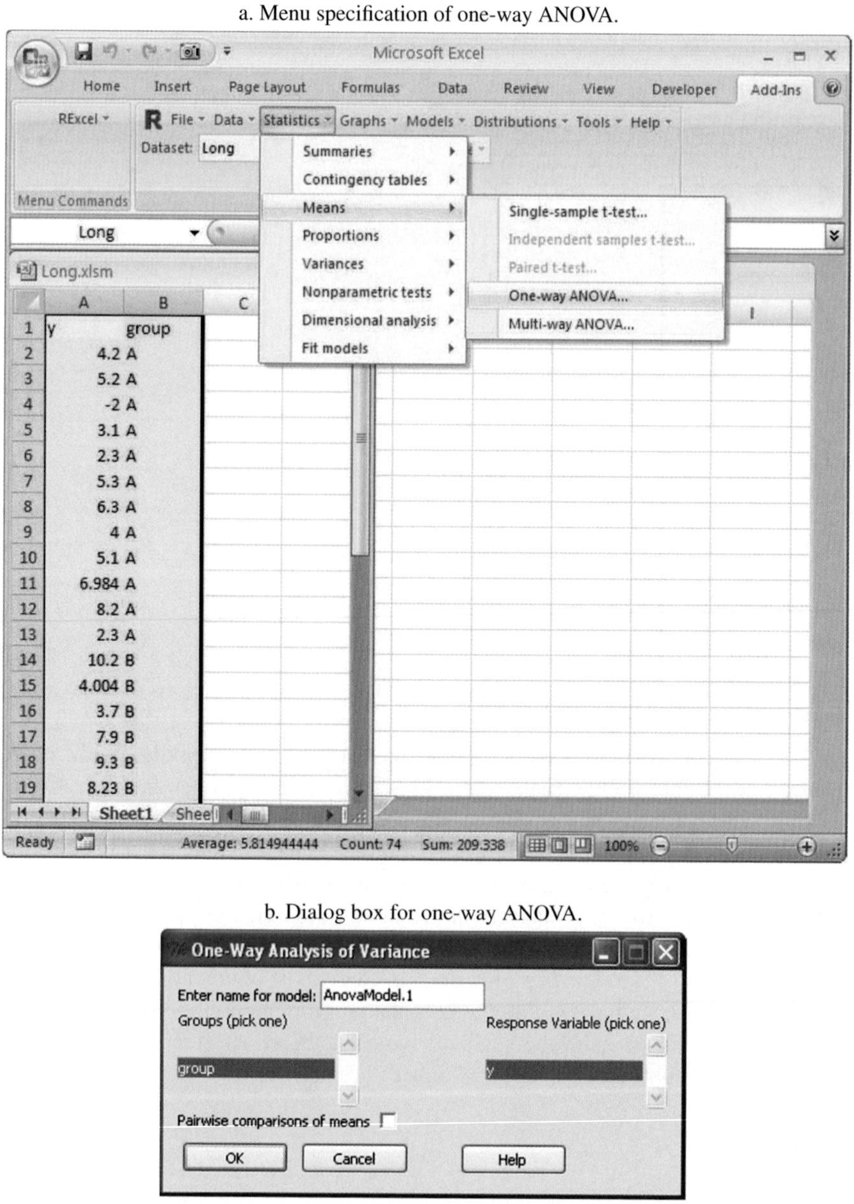

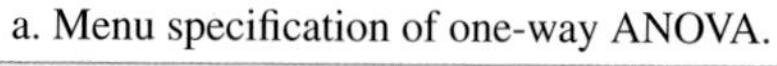

a. Menu specification of one-way ANOVA.

b. Dialog box for one-way ANOVA.

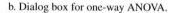

Fig. 3.14 The Long dataset was sent to R in Fig. 3.13. Here we specify a one-way analysis of variance (ANOVA) with the Rcmdr ► Statistics ► Means ► One-way ANOVA command. There are only one factor and one numeric variable in this dataset, so both selection boxes are highlighted when the dialog box opens. This dialog box specifies the tables in Fig. 3.15.

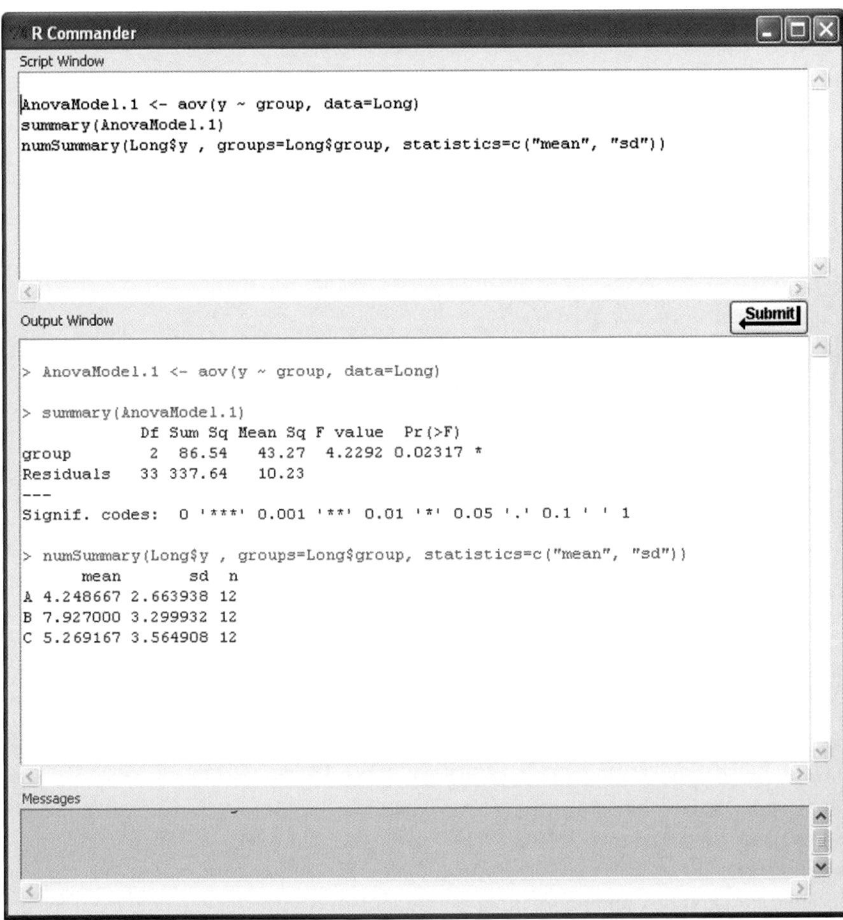

Fig. 3.15 Analysis of variance command lines generated by the R Commander. The Rcmdr Script Window shows the lines, and the Output Window shows the tabular output from running those lines.

3.5 Multiple Numeric Columns, One per Factor Level

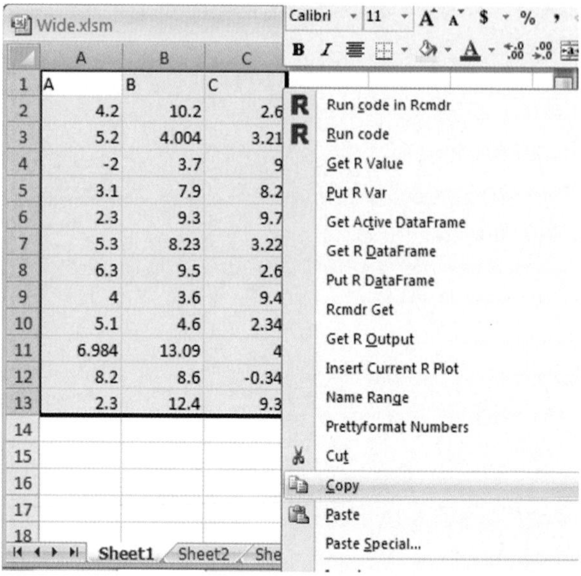

Wide.xlsm

	A	B	C
1	A	B	C
2	4.2	10.2	2.6
3	5.2	4.004	3.21
4	-2	3.7	9
5	3.1	7.9	8.2
6	2.3	9.3	9.7
7	5.3	8.23	3.22
8	6.3	9.5	2.6
9	4	3.6	9.4
10	5.1	4.6	2.34
11	6.984	13.09	4
12	8.2	8.6	-0.34
13	2.3	12.4	9.3

Sheet1 Sheet2 She

Run code in Rcmdr
Run code
Get R Value
Put R Var
Get Active DataFrame
Get R DataFrame
Put R DataFrame
Rcmdr Get
Get R Output
Insert Current R Plot
Name Range
Prettyformat Numbers
Cut
Copy
Paste
Paste Special...

Fig. 3.16 The Wide workbook is one of the workbooks distributed with the *R through Excel* book. Follow the steps in Figs. 3.1 and 3.2 to open this workbook. The initial appearance is shown in Panel a. Data about multiple groups is often stored in the *wide* format shown in the Wide workbook. The Wide workbook has three columns, one for each level of the group factor. To use data formatted this way in the one-way ANOVA and many other commands, it is necessary to reshape it to the long format. We do so by highlighting the data region, including the row containing the variable names, with the standard Excel keyboard shortcut Ctrl+shift+*. We then copy the data by right-clicking Copy, and we move to Fig. 3.17.

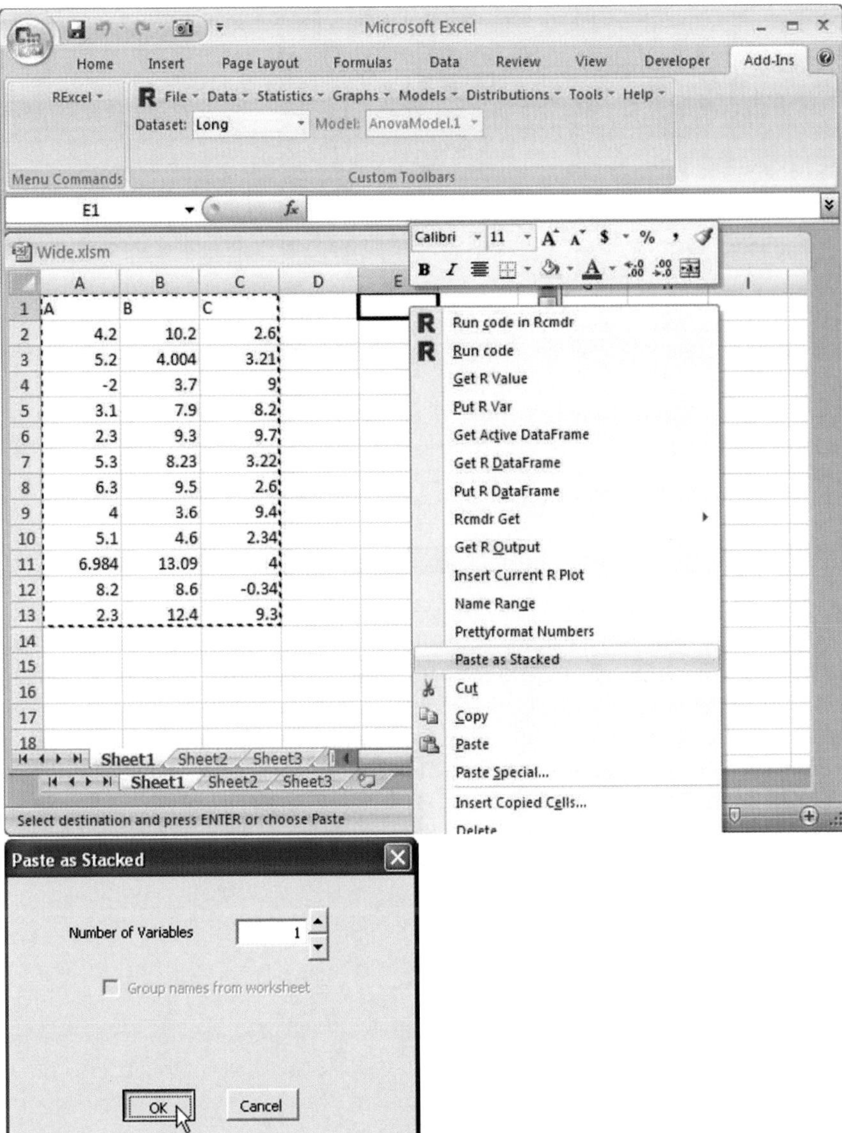

Fig. 3.17 We highlighted and right-click-Copyed the data in Fig. 3.16. Here, we place the cursor in cell E1, right-click Paste as Stacked, and click OK in the dialog box to produce the stacked formatting of the data in Fig. 3.18.

Wide.xlsm

	A	B	C	D	E	F
1	A	B	C		group	var
2	4.2	10.2	2.6		A	4.2
3	5.2	4.004	3.21		A	5.2
4	-2	3.7	9		A	-2
5	3.1	7.9	8.2		A	3.1
6	2.3	9.3	9.7		A	2.3
7	5.3	8.23	3.22		A	5.3
8	6.3	9.5	2.6		A	6.3
9	4	3.6	9.4		A	4
10	5.1	4.6	2.34		A	5.1
11	6.984	13.09	4		A	6.984
12	8.2	8.6	-0.34		A	8.2
13	2.3	12.4	9.3		A	2.3
14					B	10.2
15					B	4.004
16					B	3.7
17					B	7.9
18					B	9.3

Sheet1 Sheet2 Sheet3

Fig. 3.18 The region in cells E1:F37 is the stacked arrangement of the original data in cells A1:C13. cells F2:F13 in the var column are the numbers originally in cells A2:A13. The value A in cells E2:E13 indicate that these numbers are associated with the A level of the newly created factor group. Similarly, cells E14:F25 are the B level of the group factor and cells E26:F37 are the C level of the group factor. Column F is very difficult to read because the decimal points are not aligned. We repair that in Figs. 3.19 and 3.20.

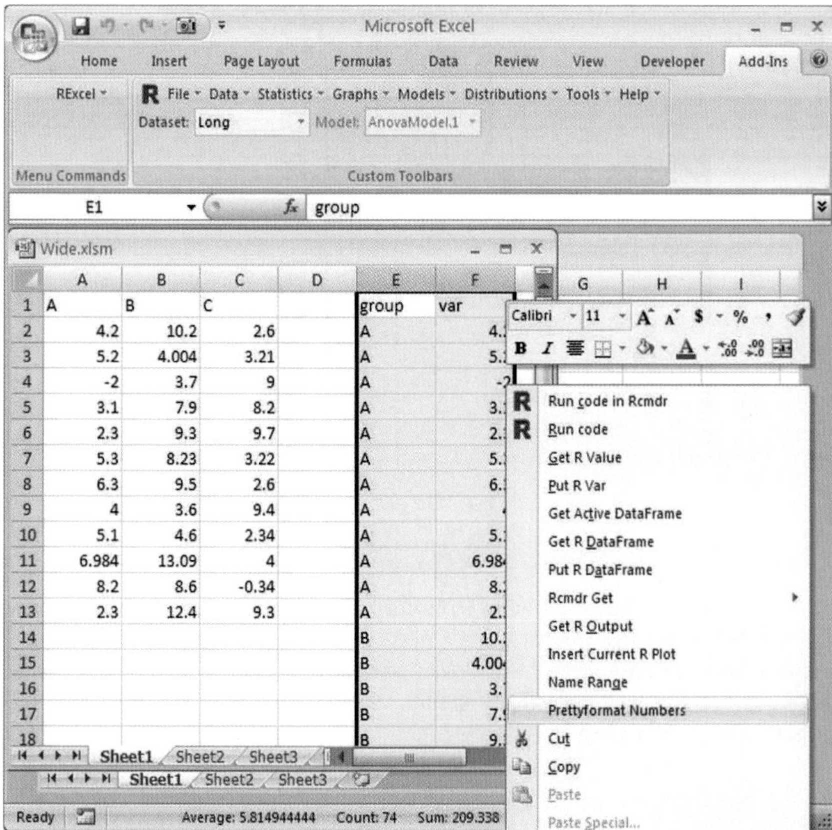

Fig. 3.19 Press the Esc key to remove the dotted line surrounding the original region A1:C13 in Fig. 3.18. Highlight cells E1:F37 and right-click Prettyformat Numbers to produce column F in Fig. 3.20.

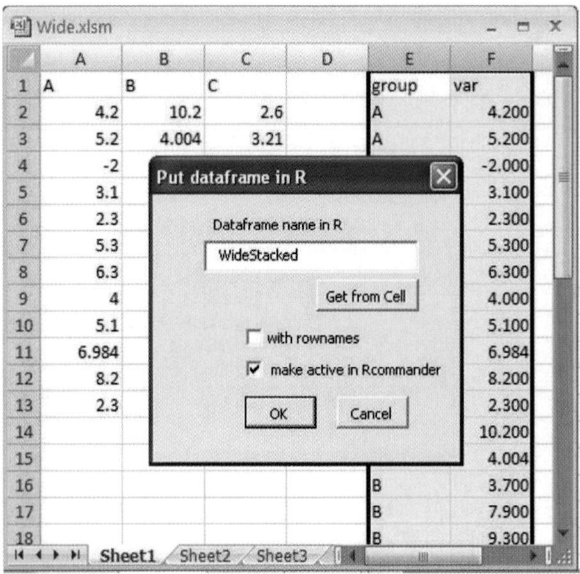

Fig. 3.20 The var column (column F) in the data from Fig. 3.19 is now formatted with aligned decimal points. Cells E1:F37 are still highlighted from Fig. 3.19. We can now right-click Put R DataFrame to send the data, with the new name WideStacked chosen to reflect the structural change, to R. The data becomes the active dataset as shown in Fig. 3.21.

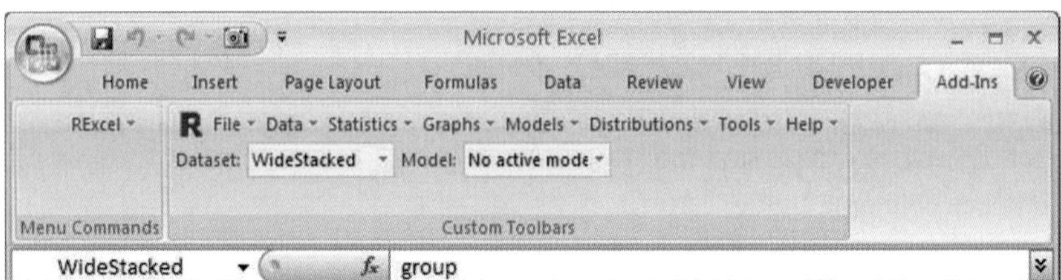

Fig. 3.21 Continuing from Fig. 3.20, the active dataset is now WideStacked. Since WideStacked is structured the same way as Long, we can continue with analyses similar to those shown in Figs. 3.14 and 3.15.

3.6 Transferring Data from R to Excel

In the previous sections, we illustrated the transfer of data from Excel to R. In this section, we illustrate the transfer of data from R to Excel. R and its many packages come with example datasets that are used in the R documentation and help files. They are easily accessed from the Rcmdr menu bar.

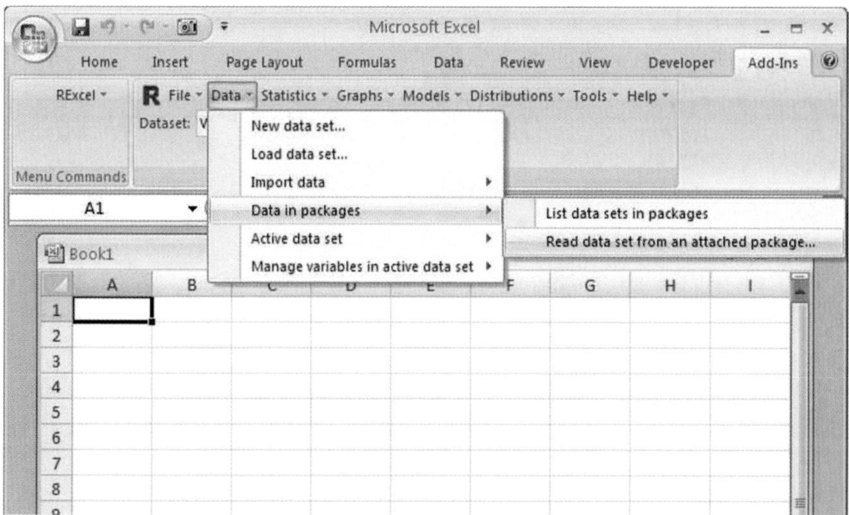

Fig. 3.22 Click on the Rcmdr ► Data ► Data in packages ► Read data set from an attached package... menu to get the dialog box in Fig. 3.23.

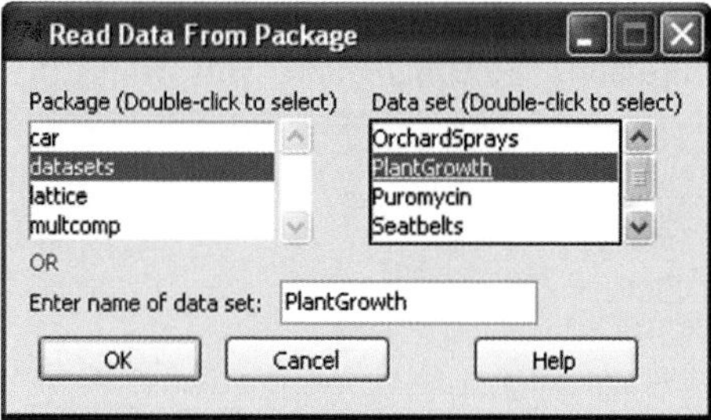

Fig. 3.23 This dialog box comes from Fig. 3.22. Double-click a package name, then double-click a dataset name, and then click OK. This selects a dataframe from an attached package, in this example, the PlantGrowth dataset from the datasets package. This makes the selected package the active dataset in the Rcmdr menu bar as shown in Fig. 3.24.

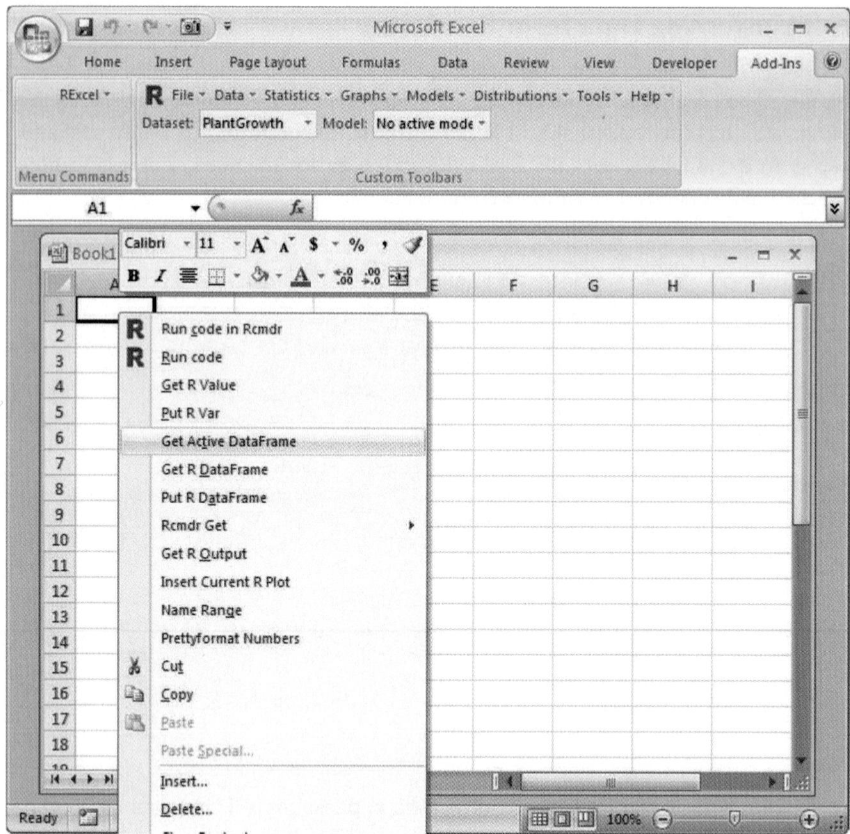

Fig. 3.24 In Fig. 3.22 we selected the PlantGrowth dataset as the active dataset, and we now see its name in the active dataset listing on the Rcmdr menu bar. The Rcmdr menu items now know about the variable names in this dataset. To see the dataset itself in Excel, we must get it from R. We do so by opening a new empty workbook, clicking in cell A1, and then right-clicking Get Active DataFrame. This brings the dataset into Excel as shown in Fig. 3.25.

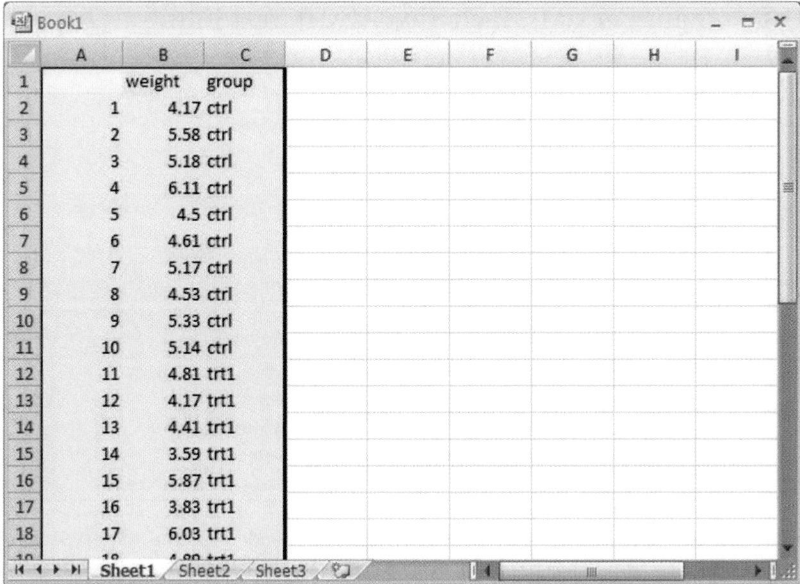

Fig. 3.25 This is the PlantGrowth data that we brought into Excel in Figs. 3.22 and 3.24.

3.7 Other Input Formats, Including ASCII Text Files

Datasets come in many formats. R and/or Excel can read most of them. We show the menu locations of the data import functions in both systems.

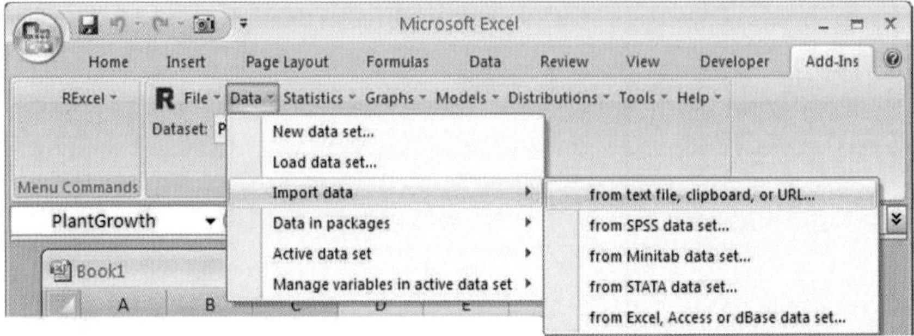

Fig. 3.26 To read data directly into R, we can use the Rcmdr ► Data ► Import data ► menu. We show one more step here, the from text file, clipboard, or URL... item. Once the dataset is in R, we can access it using the techniques illustrated in Section 3.6.

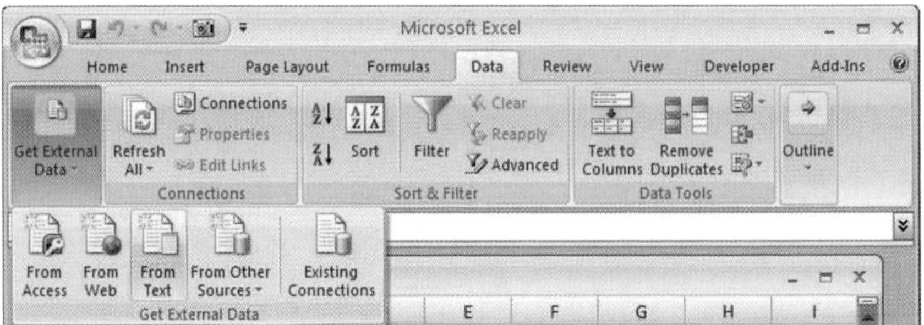

Fig. 3.27 To read data directly into Excel, we can use the Excel Data ► Get External Data menu. We show one more step here, the From Text item. Once the dataset is in Excel, we can access it using the techniques illustrated in Sections 3.2–3.5.

Chapter 4
Normal and t Distributions

Abstract The normal and t distributions are heavily used in statistical analysis. The normal and t-tables on the Rcmdr menu can be used to look up probabilities p given quantiles (z- or t-values), or quantiles (z or t) corresponding to known p-values. Some of these probability functions are also available in Excel (as part of the Analysis toolpack), but the R functions are more versatile and more precise.

The tables can also be used to explore the relationship between an observed mean $\bar{x}$ of n observations and its standard deviation s by using the standardized normal $z = \bar{x}/s_{\bar{x}}$ where the sample standard error of the mean is given by $s_{\bar{x}} = s/\sqrt{n}$.

Graphical displays can be used to explore the Type I and II errors associated with hypothesis tests and to explore the effect of sample size on the width of a confidence interval. We can access the graphs from the menus and also from an Excel workbook described in Chapter 5 that communicates with the R process.

4.1 Accessing R Functions with the Rcmdr Menus

The standard normal and t-tables can be accessed directly from the menus. Figs. 4.1, 4.2, and 4.3 show how to use the menu to find critical values given the p-values. Figs. 4.4, 4.5, and 4.6 show how to use the menu to find p-values given the observed value of the statistic.

R.M. Heiberger, E. Neuwirth, *R Through Excel*, Use R,
DOI 10.1007/978-1-4419-0052-4_4,

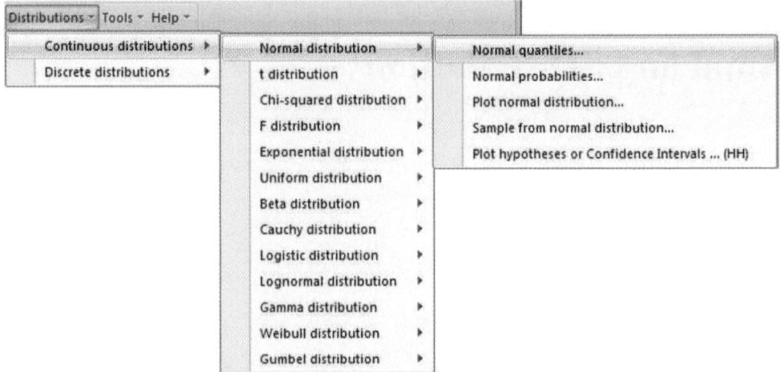

Fig. 4.1 The Normal quantiles... menu item requests the dialog box in Fig. 4.2 in which to specify the probabilities. This is the inverse use of the normal table.

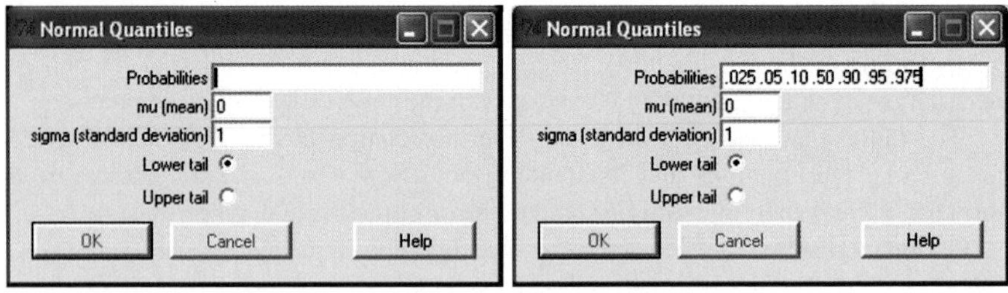

Fig. 4.2 Given a probability value $p = 0.95$, the normal quantile is $z = 1.96$. A list of several probabilities can be entered into the dialog box. The box defaults to Standard Normal (mean 0 and standard deviation 1). The user can specify other values for the mean and standard deviation. The left dialog box is the initial appearance. The right dialog box is the same box after we filled in some probabilities.

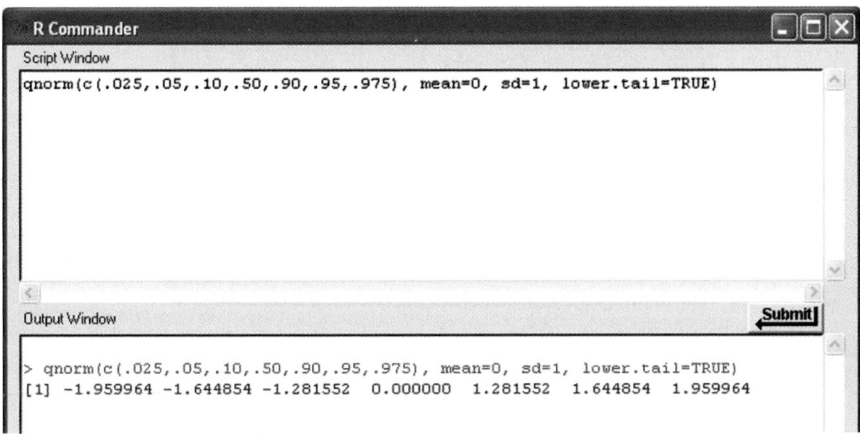

Fig. 4.3 The Rcmdr generates an R statement and displays the generated statement in the Script Window. The quantiles are displayed in the Output Window.

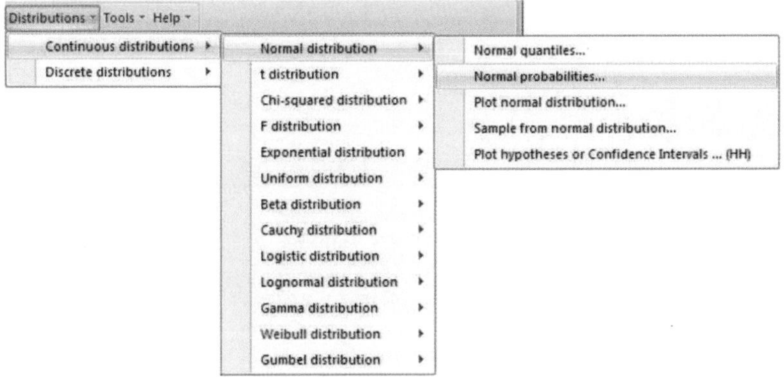

Fig. 4.4 The Normal probabilities... menu item requests the dialog box in Fig. 4.5 in which to specify the quantiles. This is the forward use of the normal table.

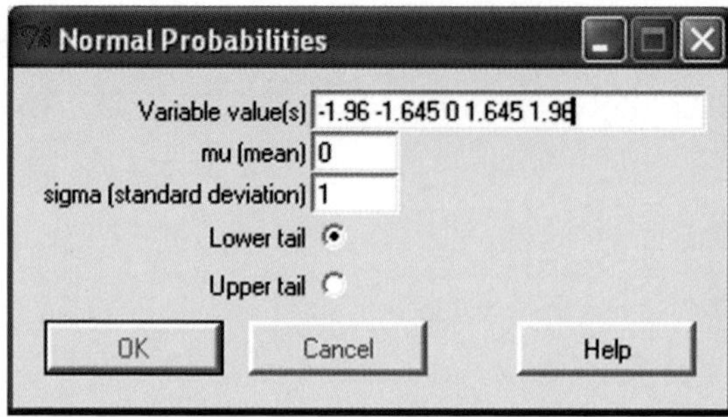

Fig. 4.5 Given the normal quantile $z = 1.96$, the probability value is $p = 0.95$. A list of several quantiles can be entered into the dialog box. We filled in some quantiles.

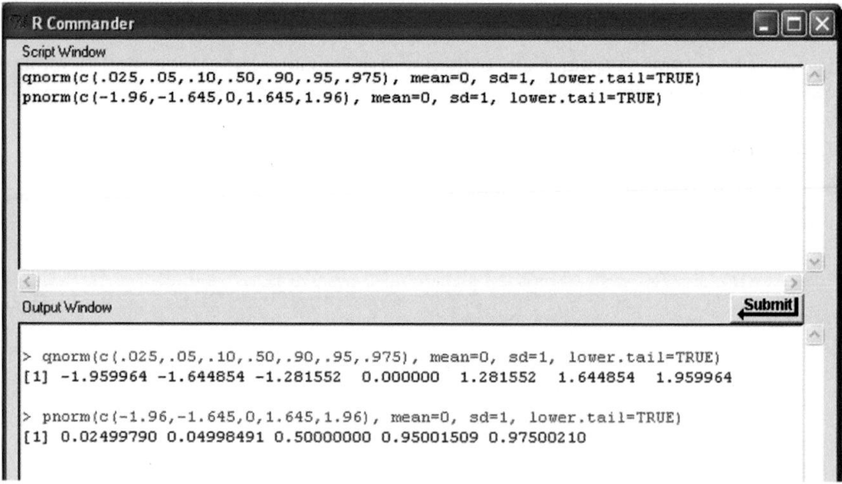

Fig. 4.6 Rcmdr generates an R statement and displays the generated statement in the Script Window. The probabilities are displayed in the Output Window. Both the Script and Output windows accumulate during the session. They can be saved at the end for a complete record of the day's activity.

The identical procedures work for the t distribution (and the other distributions listed on the pull-out menu). We illustrate here for the t distribution on 5 degrees of freedom.

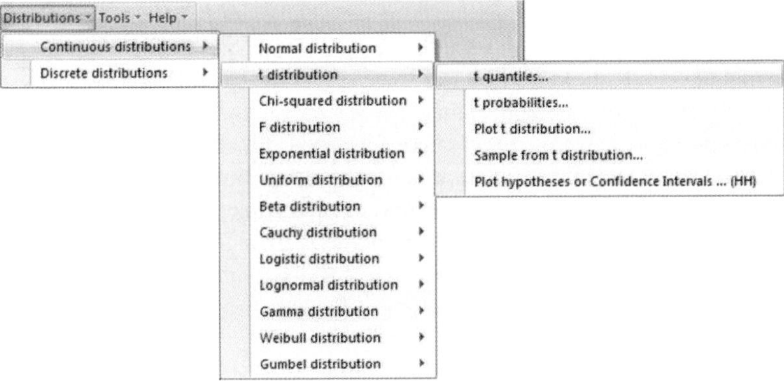

Fig. 4.7 Click the distribution menu item.

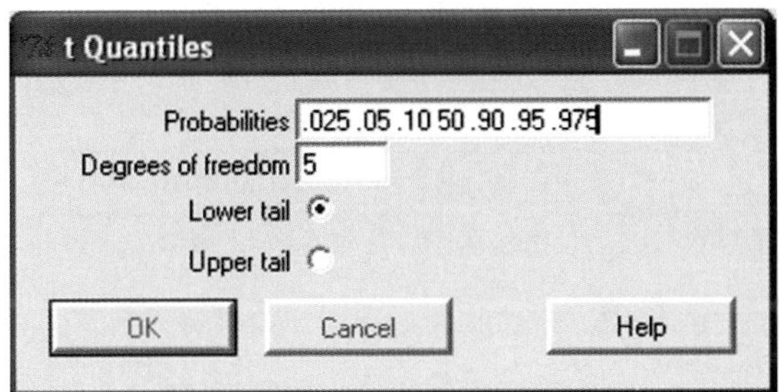

Fig. 4.8 Fill in the dialog box with some probability values and the degrees of freedom.

```
> qt(c(.025,.05,.10,.50,.90,.95,.975), df=5, lower.tail=TRUE)
[1] -2.570582 -2.015048 -1.475884  0.000000  1.475884  2.015048  2.570582
```

Fig. 4.9 The quantiles are displayed in the Output Window.

4.2 Accessing R Functions from Within Excel Cells

RExcel can access R functions from inside Excel workbook cells. This ability places the entirety of R's capabilities inside the spreadsheet automatic recalculation model.

We illustrate this feature by getting numerical values calculated in R into spreadsheet cells. In Figs. 4.2–4.4, we used the Rcmdr menus and dialog boxes to access the normal table in R. In Figs. 4.10–4.13, we repeat the calculations, this time placing the R function calls inside the spreadsheet recalculation model.

RExcel provides a set of Excel sheet functions, functions that can be written in an Excel cell. The RApply function is an Excel function that takes two or more arguments. The first argument is the name of an R function as a text string. The remaining arguments are references to regions of Excel cells. RApply calls the R function with the values of the referenced cells as its arguments.

In Fig. 4.10, we show the Excel worksheet formula

```
=RApply("qnorm",A4)
```

in cell B4. The argument string is constructed by ordinary Excel text commands and clicking commands. The value in cell A4 (currently 0.025) will be sent to R to be evaluated as the argument of the qnorm function. This has the same effect as typing "qnorm(0.025)" into the R Console or the Rcmdr Script Window. This is the notation in R for the probability statement: Find z such that $\text{Prob}(Z < z) = 0.025$ from the standard normal distribution. The RApply command receives the numerical answer $z = -1.960$ back from R, and displays it in cell B4 in Fig. 4.11.

INDEX ▾ × ✓ fx =RApply("qnorm",A4)

Book1

	A	B	C	D
1	enter	calculate		
2	p-values	quantiles		
3	in Excel	in R		
4	0.025	=RApply("qnorm",A4)		
5	0.050			
6	0.100			
7	0.500			
8	0.900			
9	0.950			
10	0.975			

Fig. 4.10 Open a new workbook. Place probability values in cells A4:A10. Enter the formula `=RApply("qnorm",A4)` into cell B4. The blue A4 in the formula bar and the blue-outlined cell A4 in the worksheet indicate that the formula in cell B4 depends on the value in cell A4. Press Enter and continue on to Fig. 4.11.

3	in Excel	in R
4	0.025	-1.960
5	0.050	
6	0.100	
7	0.500	
8	0.900	
9	0.950	
10	0.975	

Fig. 4.11 Press Enter in Fig. 4.10, and the formula in B4 is evaluated to show the numerical value −1.960.

3	in Excel	in R
4	0.025	-1.960
5	0.050	
6	0.100	
7	0.500	
8	0.900	
9	0.950	
10	0.975	

Fig. 4.12 We use standard Excel techniques to extend the formula in Figs. 4.10 and 4.11 to additional z-values. Grab the fill handle in the lower right corner of cell B4 and drag it down to fill cells B5:B10. The cell references will be automatically updated as shown in Fig. 4.13.

3	in Excel	in R
4	0.025	-1.960
5	0.050	-1.645
6	0.100	-1.282
7	0.500	0.000
8	0.900	1.282
9	0.950	1.645
10	0.975	1.960

Fig. 4.13 After the formula in cell B4 in Fig. 4.12 has been copied to cells B5:B10, all cells are immediately evaluated and the resulting z-values are displayed in cells B4:B10, for each probability in cells A4:A10.

Many more examples, including some elaborate ones, of getting calculated values from R into Excel are in the Worksheet functions demo [Neuwirth et al., 2008] on the RExcel menu as shown in Fig. 4.14.

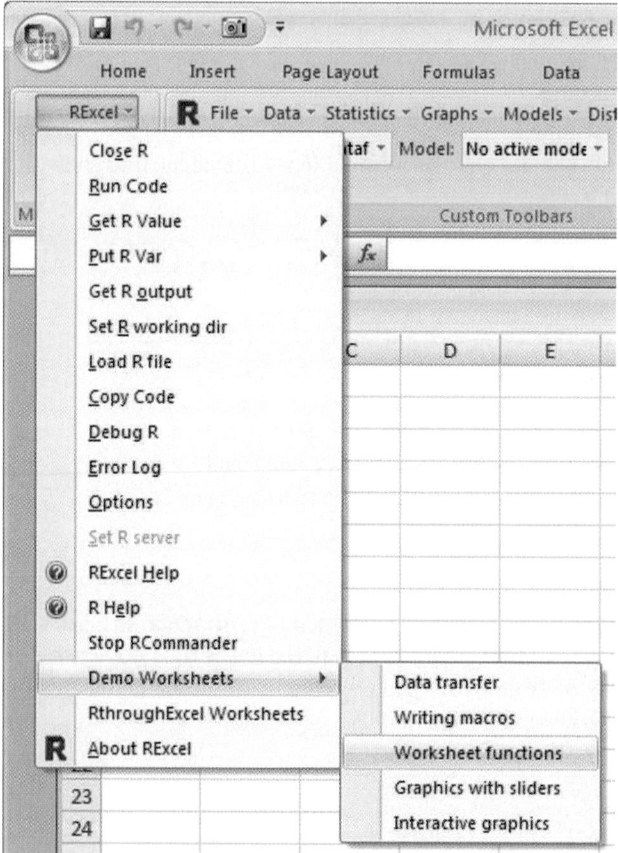

Fig. 4.14 The RExcel ▶ Demo Worksheets ▶ Worksheet functions menu item opens a workbook that lists and illustrates the RExcel functions used in the communication between R and Excel.

The workbooks distributed with this book, available on the RExcel ▶ RthroughExcel Worksheets menu item, are constructed with the functions described in the Worksheet functions demo. Two of the workbooks will be discussed in Chapter 5 and Chapter 9. If the RthroughExcel Worksheets menu item is missing, see step 4 of Section A.3.3.

4.3 Graphical Displays of the Standard Normal Distribution

Graphical displays of the density function of the normal and t distributions are important to understanding the distributions. There are two access points to the graphical displays, the menu and the Excel workbook. In both, we highlight regions associated with a range of z-values, and report the probability (area) of the region. We illustrate menu access here. We illustrate access from an Excel workbook in Chapter 5.

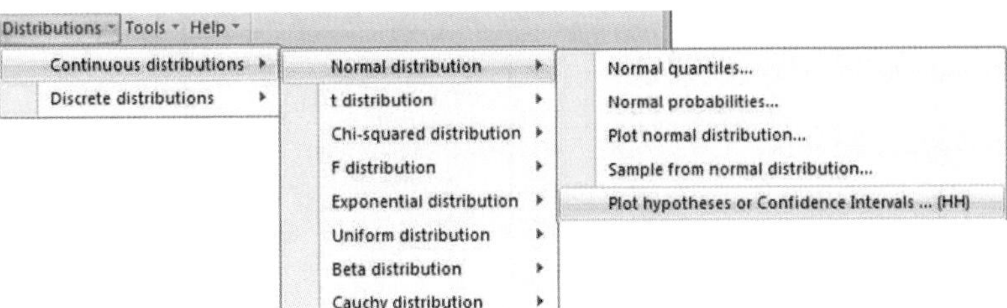

Fig. 4.15 Click the Distributions ▶ Continuous distributions ▶ Normal distribution ▶ Plot hypotheses or Confidence Intervals ... (HH) menu item. This brings up the dialog box in Fig. 4.16.

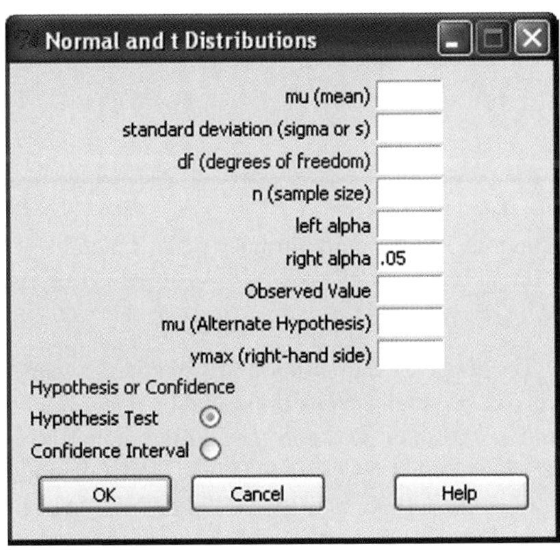

Fig. 4.16 Normal and t Distributions dialog box from the Plot hypotheses or Confidence Intervals ... (HH) menu item. Missing mu and sigma values default to 0 and 1, appropriate for the standard normal. We specify right alpha for a one-sided $\alpha = 0.05$ test. Click OK to get Fig. 4.17.

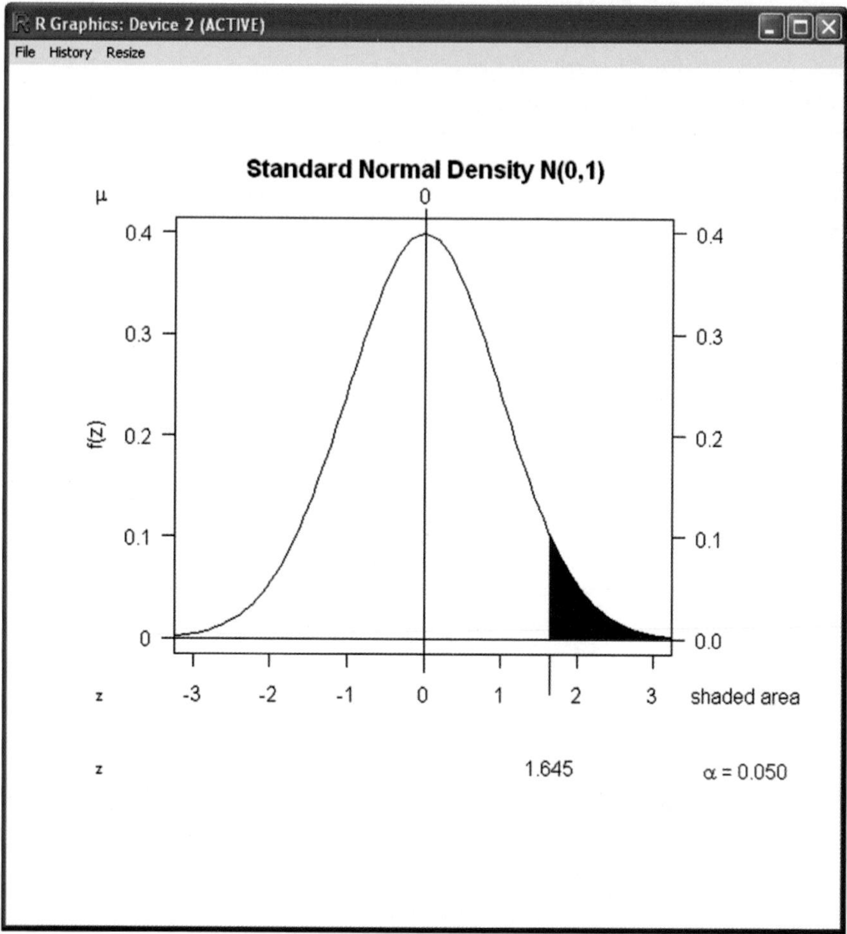

Fig. 4.17 This is the familiar standard normal density function

$$f(z) = \frac{1}{\sqrt{2\pi}} e^{-\frac{1}{2}z^2}$$

with two z-scales. The ticks on the abscissa are standard z-values. The long tick leading to the lower set of labels shows the critical value $z_{\text{crit}} = z_{.05} = 1.645$ that corresponds to the $\alpha = 0.05$ that was specified in the dialog box. The area to the right of the critical value $z_{\text{crit}} = 1.645$ is shaded blue, and the numerical value of the area, $\alpha = \text{Prob}(Z > 1.645) = 0.05$, is displayed in the right margin. There are two scales on the abscissa. For the standard normal, both show the same values.

Paperback

Subtotal	$56.15
Shipping & Handling	$1.99
Order Total	$58.14
Paid via Visa	$58.14
Balance Due	$0.00

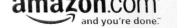

This shipment completes your order.

Have feedback on how we packaged your order? Tell us at www.amazon.com/packaging.

(1 of 1)

SDJIK80pSR

18/DJIK80pSR/-1 of 1-//1M/std-n-us/4989200/0818-01:00/0816-22:29 V3

amazon.com
and you're done.

amazon.com

Billing Address:

Tim Haifley
2255 Starbright Drive
San Jose, CA 95124
United States

Shipping Address:

Tim Haifley
2255 Starbright Drive
San Jose, CA 95124
United States

Returns Are Easy!

Visit http://www.amazon.com/returns to return any item -including gifts- in unopened or original condition within 30 days for a full refund (other restrictions apply)

Your order of July 24, 2009 (Order ID:002 – 6336605 – 9979440)

Qty Item

4.4 Significance Level, Rejection Region, and Type I Error

In this chapter, we discuss tests only for the location parameter of a model, specifically for the mean. There are other tests, to be addressed later, for standard deviation and other parameters of a model.

A typical homework exercise is as follows:

> We have an experiment from a normally distributed population with
>
> $$H_0\colon\ \mu = \mu_0 = 150$$
> $$H_1\colon\ \mu > 150$$
>
> We know $\sigma = 20$. We have observed $\bar{x}_{\text{obs}} = 160$ as the mean of $n = 25$ observations. Test at $\alpha = 0.05$. Determine the critical value. Under the alternate assumption that the population mean $\mu_1 = 165$, what is the probability of the Type II error and what is the power of the test? The answer is displayed in Figs. 4.18–4.22.

The statement $\alpha = 0.05$ means that we are willing to take the risk, with probability α, of making a Type I Error. A Type I error is a decision to reject the null hypothesis, even when it is a correct description of the world. In Fig. 4.17, we calculated the $\alpha = 0.05$ critical value of the standard normal (with mean 0 and standard deviation 1) as $z_{\text{crit}} = z_{.05} = 1.645$. This is the value of z for which $\text{Prob}(Z > z_{\text{crit}} = 1.645) = 0.05$.

We translate the problem statement from the data scale into the standard normal scale by writing

$$z_{\text{obs}} = \frac{\bar{x}_{\text{obs}} - \mu}{\sigma/\sqrt{n}} \tag{4.1}$$

Then we can determine a critical value x_{crit} in the $\bar{x}$ scale by

$$\begin{aligned}
\alpha &= \text{Prob}\left(\text{reject } H_0 \mid H_0 \text{ is true}\right) \\
&= \text{Prob}\left(z_{\text{obs}} > z_{.05} = 1.645\right) \\
&= \text{Prob}\left(\frac{\bar{x}_{\text{obs}} - \mu}{\sigma/\sqrt{n}} > 1.645 \;\middle|\; \mu = \mu_0 = 150\right) \\
&= \text{Prob}\left(\bar{x}_{\text{obs}} > 150 + 1.645 \times 20/\sqrt{25} = 156.579 = \bar{x}_{\text{crit}}\right.
\end{aligned} \tag{4.2}$$

The arithmetic of Equation (4.2) is illustrated by the dialog box in Fig. 4.18 and the graph in Fig. 4.19.

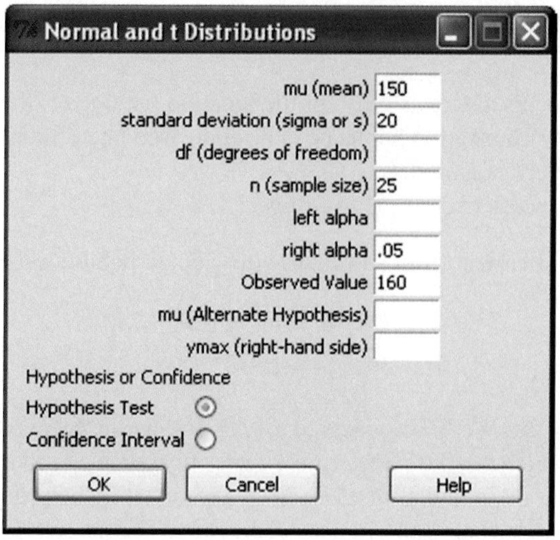

Fig. 4.18 Normal and t Distributions dialog box from the Plot hypotheses or Confidence Intervals ... (HH) menu item. The values illustrated are all taken from the homework specification. Click OK to get Fig. 4.19. The figure shows the specification for the test of the null hypothesis against the general location alternative.

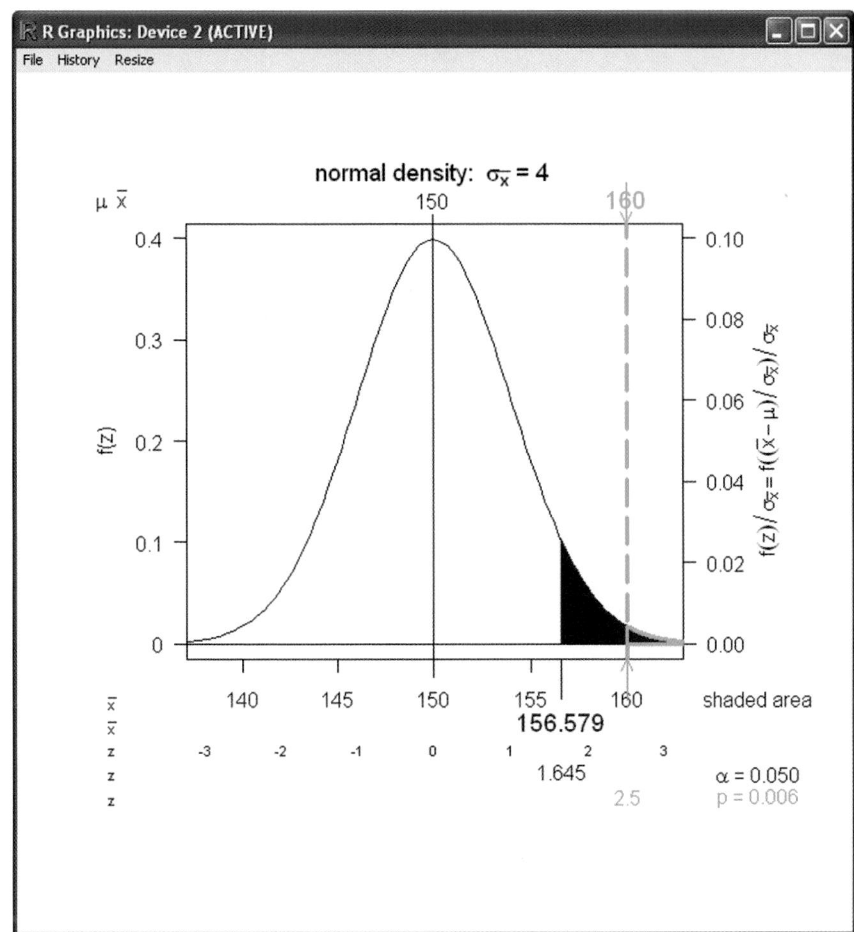

Fig. 4.19 This figure shows the graphics window created by the dialog box in Fig. 4.18. The blue-shaded area is the rejection region. The $\bar{x}$ scale is in data units. The z scale is in standard error units. The critical value shown in blue in the $\bar{x}$ scale, corresponding to $z_{\text{crit}} = 1.645$, is $\bar{x}_{\text{crit}} = 156.579$. The green vertical line shows the observed sample mean $\bar{x}_{\text{obs}} = 160$ in data units, and the corresponding $z_{\text{obs}} = 2.5 = (\bar{x}_{\text{obs}} - \mu_0)/\sigma_{\bar{x}} = (160 - 150)/4$ in the z scale. The green-outlined area indicates the area associated with the p-value for the test $p = \text{Prob}(Z > z_{\text{obs}})$, and the p-value itself is shown in the margin as $p = 0.006$. The left axis is marked in standard normal density units and is paired with the z-axis labels. The right axis is marked in data-scaled density units and is paired with the $\bar{x}$-axis labels. The area under the curve corresponds to probability and is the same using either set of axis pairs.

4.5 Type II Error and Power

Once we have determined a critical value ($\bar{x}_{\text{crit}} = 156.579$ in Fig. 4.19) based on the null hypothesis and the significance level, we can ask questions about the effectiveness of the test in rejecting the null hypothesis for specified values of the alternative. Specifically, we define

$$\beta = \beta(\mu_1) = \text{Prob}(\bar{x} < \bar{x}_{\text{crit}} \mid \mu = \mu_1) \tag{4.3}$$

$$\text{power}(\mu_1) = 1 - \beta(\mu_1) = \text{Prob}(\bar{x} \geq \bar{x}_{\text{crit}} \mid \mu = \mu_1) \tag{4.4}$$

Equation (4.3) is read: "Beta (β) equals the probability that the observed $\bar{x}$ is less than the critical value of $\bar{x}$ conditional on the true mean having value μ_1". Therefore, β is the probability of not rejecting H_0, conditional on the value μ_1. In this example, when the population mean is $\mu_1 = 165$, then not rejecting H_0 (that the population mean is $\mu_0 = 155$) is an error. The Type II Error β is a function of the specified alternative mean μ_1. Not all texts make the dependence of β on μ_1 explicit.

Power is the complement of the Type II Error. Equation (4.4) is read: "The power of the test against the alternative hypothesis that the true mean has value μ_1 is the probability that the observed $\bar{x}$ is greater than or equal the critical value of $\bar{x}$ conditional on the true mean having value μ_1". Therefore, power is the probability of rejecting H_0, conditional on the value μ_1. A high power implies a high "detection rate" for situations where H_0 is not true. In this example, when the population mean is $\mu_1 = 165$, then rejecting H_0 is the correct decision.

The notation for "conditional" is a vertical bar "|". It is neither a forward slash "/" nor a backslash "\", both of which are meaningful symbols and mean something else.

In Figs. 4.20–4.22, for this example, that becomes

$$\beta = \beta(\mu = 165) = \text{Prob}(\bar{x} < 156.579 \mid \mu = 165) = 0.0176 \tag{4.5}$$

and

$$\begin{aligned} \text{power}(\mu_1 = 165) &= \text{Prob}(\bar{x} \geq 156.579 \mid \mu = 165) \\ &= 1 - \beta(\mu_1 = 165) = (1 - 0.0176) = 0.9824 \end{aligned} \tag{4.6}$$

Both terms, Type II Error and power, are used. They carry the same information.

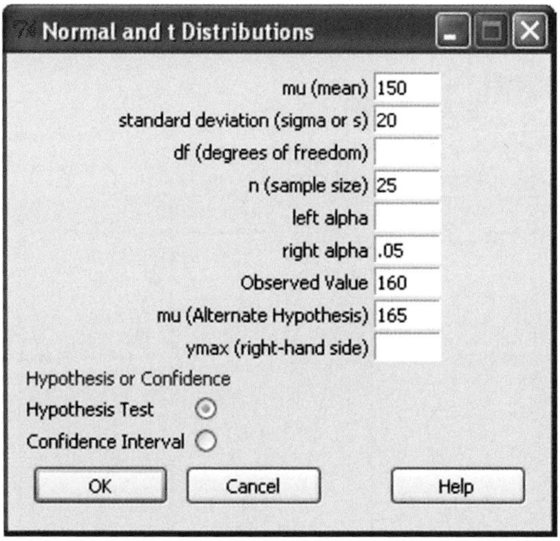

Fig. 4.20 Normal and t Distributions dialog box from the Plot hypotheses or Confidence Intervals ... (HH) menu item. The values illustrated are all taken from the homework example in Section 4.4. The alternate hypothesis value of $\mu = 165$ is used to calculate the power against this specific alternative value. Click OK to get Fig. 4.21 and then Fig. 4.22.

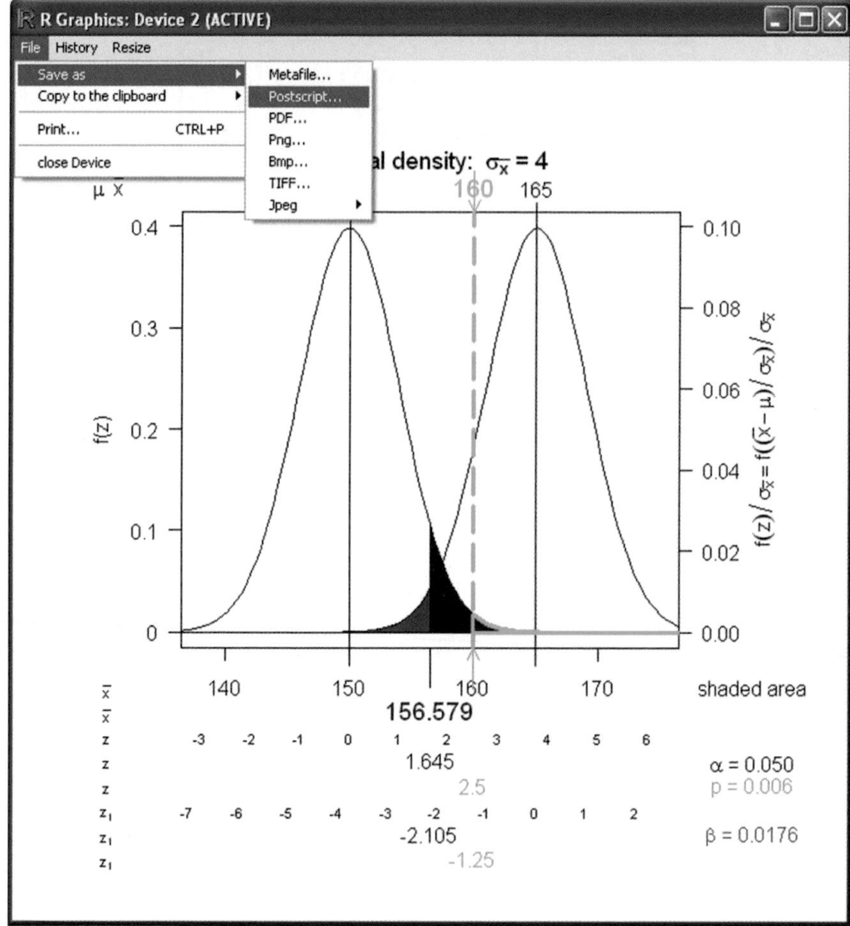

Fig. 4.21 This figure shows the graphics window created by the dialog box in Fig. 4.20. We discuss the content of the graph in Fig. 4.22 and in the accompanying text. The graph itself, not the window containing the graph, is displayed and discussed in a report on the study.

Here, we discuss saving the graph into a file. The graphics window, is a computational intermediate and is never displayed in a report. Compare the quality of the reproduction of the window in Fig. 4.21 and of the graph in Fig. 4.22. We have been using `png` graphs for the screenshots. `png` is a bit-mapped format, which means the individual dots on the screen are saved. Magnifying a screenshot gives bigger dots, not better resolution.

Reproduction of a graph for a report should use a vector-graphics format, a format in which information about which line or character is to be plotted has been saved. We saved this graph in the PostScript vector-graphics format using the File ▶ Save as ▶ PostScript... menu item, as illustrated. MS Word users will normally use the File ▶ Save as ▶ Metafile... menu item or, equivalently the Ctrl-w key.

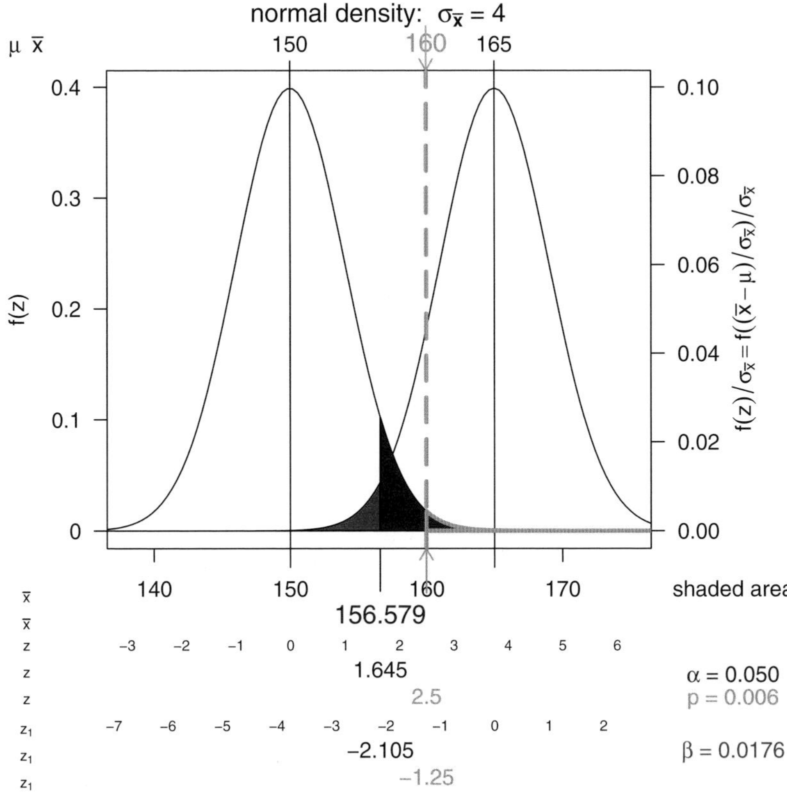

Fig. 4.22 This figure shows the *graph* that was created in the graphics device window of Fig. 4.21. The *window* titlebar and menus are not part of the graph and are not displayed here. The graph, not a picture of a window containing a graph, is what belongs in your report. Vector formats, such as Windows Metafile or PostScript, have superior resolution. When a vector-graphics image is magnified, the graph will be redrawn to take advantage of the higher resolution. See Section 4.6 for a discussion of graphical file formats.

After discussing these technical details let's look at the graph itself. The graph displayed here is a variant of the normal plot in Fig. 4.17. The standard error for this example is

$$\sigma_{\bar{x}} = \frac{\sigma}{\sqrt{n}} = \frac{20}{\sqrt{25}} = 4$$

The left curve is centered at the null hypothesis $\mu_0 = 150$. The right curve is centered at the alternate hypothesis $\mu_1 = 165$. The green vertical line is the location of the observed sample mean. See the text for further details on this graph.

Fig. 4.22 was created by the dialog box in Fig. 4.20. The critical feature of this graph is the sizes of the blue- and red-shaded areas. The blue-shaded area shows α, the probability of the Type I Error, the probability of incorrectly rejecting a true null hypothesis. The red-shaded area shows $\beta(\mu_1)$, the probability of the Type II Error, the probability of not rejecting the null hypothesis when the null is false and the true mean is μ_1.

The left curve is centered at the null hypothesis $\mu_0 = 150$ and is identical to the curve shown in Fig. 4.19. The blue-shaded area is the area to the right of $\bar{x}_{\text{crit}} = 156.579$ and under the left curve. Equivalently, it is the area to the right of $z_{\text{crit}} = 1.645$ and under the left curve. Its numerical value $\alpha = \text{Prob}(Z > 1.645) = 0.05$ is displayed in the right margin of the axis. The blue-shaded area is the probability of the Type I Error, the probability of rejecting the null hypothesis when it is actually true.

The right curve is centered at the alternative hypothesis $\mu_1 = 165$. The red-shaded area is the area to the left of $\bar{x}_{\text{crit}} = 156.579$ and under the right curve. We show an additional horizontal axis, the z_1-axis, in Fig. 4.22. The z_1-axis is measured in standard error units $\sigma_{\bar{x}} = \frac{\sigma}{\sqrt{n}}$ centered on the alternative hypothesis. When the alternative is true, the z_1-axis is in standard normal units. The red-shaded area is the area to the left of $z_{1c} = -2.105$ and under the right curve. Its numerical value $\beta = \text{Prob}(Z_1 < -2.105) = 0.0176 = \beta(\mu_1 = 165)$ is displayed in the right margin of the axis. The red-shaded area is the probability of the Type II Error, the probability that a true mean of $\mu_1 = 165$ will not be detected by the test. The complement of the red-shaded area under the right curve is the power of the test $\text{power}(\mu_1 = 165) = 1 - \beta(\mu_1 = 165) = (1 - 0.0176) = 0.9824$. Power measures the probability that a true mean of $\mu_1 = 165$ will be detected by the test.

The green vertical line is the location of the observed sample mean. The observed mean in data units $\bar{x}_{\text{obs}} = 160$ is shown in the $\bar{x}$-axis label at the top of the graph. The observed mean in null hypothesis units $z_{\text{obs}} = 2.5$ is in the bottom z-axis label. The observed mean in alternate hypothesis units $z_{1,\text{obs}} = -1.25$ is in the bottom z_1-axis label. In this example, the vertical line for the observed sample mean is in the rejection region of the test. The green-outlined area is the area to the right of $z_{\text{obs}} = 2.5$ and its numerical value $p = \text{Prob}(Z > 2.5) = 0.006$.

There are nine sets of abscissa axis labels, one above the graph and eight below the graph.

The $\bar{x}$-axis labels are in the scale of the observed data. The z-axis labels are scaled in standard error units centered at the null hypothesis

$$z = \frac{\bar{x} - \mu_0}{\sigma_{\bar{x}}}$$

The z_1-axis labels are scaled in standard error units centered at the alternative hypothesis

$$z_1 = \frac{\bar{x} - \mu_1}{\sigma_{\bar{x}}}$$

The top axis of each type shows evenly spaced values defining the scale.

The middle z-axis label shows the critical value $z_{\text{crit}} = z_{.05} = 1.645$ specified in the dialog box. The bottom $\bar{x}$-axis shows the same critical value in $\bar{x}$ units:

$$\bar{x}_{\text{crit}} = \mu_0 + 1.645 \times \sigma_{\bar{x}} = 150 + 1.645 \times 4 = 156.58$$

The middle z_1-axis label shows the same critical value in standard error units centered at the alternative hypothesis:

$$z_{1c} = \frac{\bar{x}_{\text{crit}} - \mu_1}{\sigma_{\bar{x}}} = \frac{156.58 - 165}{4} = -2.105$$

There are two ordinate scales. The left scale is in standard normal $f(z)$ units. The right scale is in data units

$$g(\bar{x}) = f(\frac{\bar{x} - \mu}{\sigma_{\bar{x}}})/\sigma_{\bar{x}}$$

4.6 Displaying Graphs

Screenshots, such as Fig. 4.21 and many of the illustrations in this book, use bitmapped graphics. The individual dots on the screen are saved. Magnifying a screenshot gives bigger dots, not better resolution. We use screenshots to illustrate what the image on the computer screen looks like.

Reproduction of a graph for a report, for example, Fig. 4.22, uses a vector-graphics format, a format in which information about which line or character is to be plotted has been saved. When a vector-graphics image is magnified, the graph will be redrawn to take advantage of the higher resolution. We use vector graphics to show the graph of our data in the best resolution for the presentation medium we will use. Printed graphs on paper have much higher resolution than dots on a screen can provide.

Compare, for example, the smoothness of the curves in Figs. 4.21 (bitmapped) and 4.22 (vector graphics) to see the difference. Similarly, the tick labels in the screenshot of Fig. 4.21 are granular, and the tick marks in the graph in Fig. 4.22 are smooth.

MS Word users normally use the `wmf` (Windows metafile) format, a vector-graphics format. Graphs can be copied from the R Grapics Device window as a `wmf` either with the menu as shown in Fig. 4.21 or with Ctrl-w, and can then be pasted into MS Word with Ctrl-v. MS Word users should not copy an R graph with Ctrl-c, as that uses the lower-resolution `bmp` (Bitmap) format.

We used the `ps` (PostScript) [Adobe Systems Incorporated, 1999] format, another vector-graphics format, for Fig. 4.22 and other figures. PostScript works smoothly with the LaTeX Document Preparation System [Lamport, 1986] in which this book was written.

Chapter 5
Normal and t Workbook

Abstract The normal and t distributions discussed in Chapter 4 can be explored dynamically with the normal.and.t workbook. This workbook uses Excel's automatic recalculation mode to change the R graph as numerical values or control tools are changed in the workbook. A short discussion of how it works appears in Section 5.5. The workbook directly accesses the same R functions that the dialog box in Fig. 4.16 uses.

5.1 Standard Normal and t Distributions

The normal.and.t.dist workbook [Heiberger and Neuwirth, 2008] allows us to explore the Normal and t distributions dynamically. Fig. 5.1 shows the screenshots of the menus that open the workbook in Fig. 5.2.

R.M. Heiberger, E. Neuwirth, *R Through Excel*, Use R,
DOI 10.1007/978-1-4419-0052-4_5,

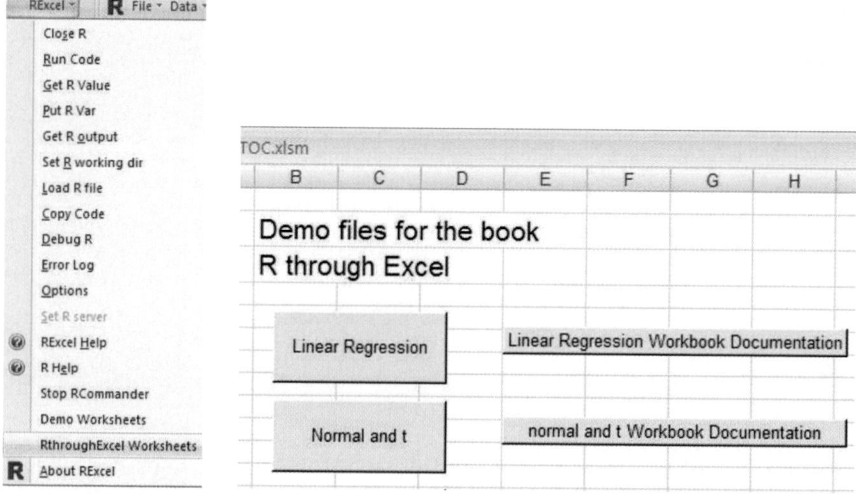

Fig. 5.1 Open the normal.and.t.dist workbook by clicking on RExcel ► RthroughExcel Worksheets. This opens an Excel workbook BookFilesTOC with the names of the workbooks for this book. Click on normal.and.t. The full BookFilesTOC is shown in Fig. 3.2. (If the RthroughExcel Worksheets menu item is missing, see step 4 in Section A.3.3.)

normal.and.t.xlsm

	A	B	C	D	E	F	G	H	I	J	K
1			Show					critical values		probability	
2	Optional user input		Slider		on Graph			left	right	right-sided	observation
3	μ_0	0	☐		Display		σ				1.000
4	μ_1		☐								
5	z		☐				z scale		1.645		
6	σ	1					α		0.0500	0.0500	
7	n										
8	v										
9											
10	☐ α left	☑ α right	α:	◉ prob or hypoth							
11		0.050	0.050	○ confidence interval							
12											
13											
14											
15	Optional user-specified										
16	display parameters										
17	z-range										
18	horizontal min		} Copy current horizontal range								
19	horizontal max										
20	g($\bar{x}$) min				☑ graph on Top						
21	g($\bar{x}$) max		} Copy current g($\bar{x}$) range			Reset					

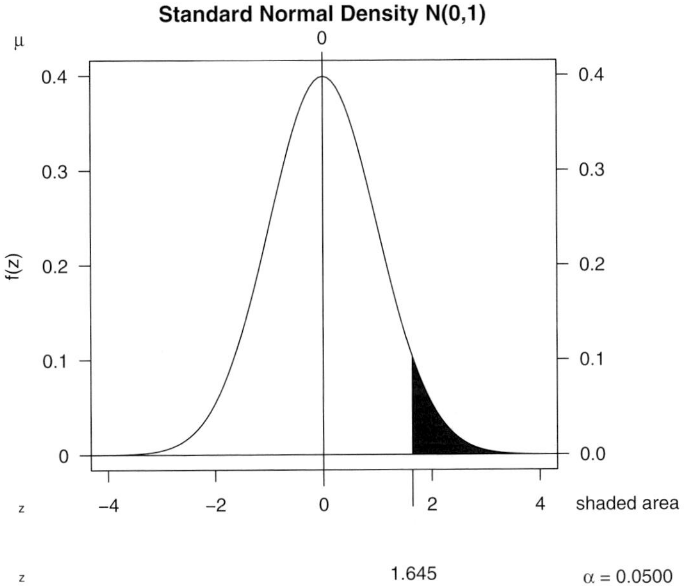

Fig. 5.2 Workbook `normal.and.t.dist.xlsm` opens to Standard Normal with one-sided $\alpha = 0.05$. The user controls the graph by entering numbers in the shaded cells, checking checkboxes, and moving the sliders. Numerical output values are displayed in cells G1:K13 and on the graph in the R graphics window. The workbook uses the normal table when the ν (degrees of freedom) field is empty. It uses the appropriate t distribution when the ν field contains a positive integer.

normal.and.t.xlsm

	A	B	C	D	E	F	G	H	I	J	K
1			Show					critical values		probability	
2	Optional user input		Slider		on Graph			left	right	right-sided	observation
3	μ_0	0	☐		Display		σ				1.000
4	μ_1		☐								
5	z		☐				z scale		1.440		
6	σ	1					α		0.0750	0.0750	
7	n										
8	v										
9											
10	☐ α left	☑ α right	α:	◉ prob or hypoth							
11		0.075	0.075	○ confidence interval							
12		< >									
13											
14											
15	Optional user-specified										
16	display parameters										
17	z-range										
18	horizontal min		} Copy current horizontal range								
19	horizontal max										
20	$g(\bar{x})$ min				☑ graph on Top						
21	$g(\bar{x})$ max		} Copy current $g(\bar{x})$ range			Reset					

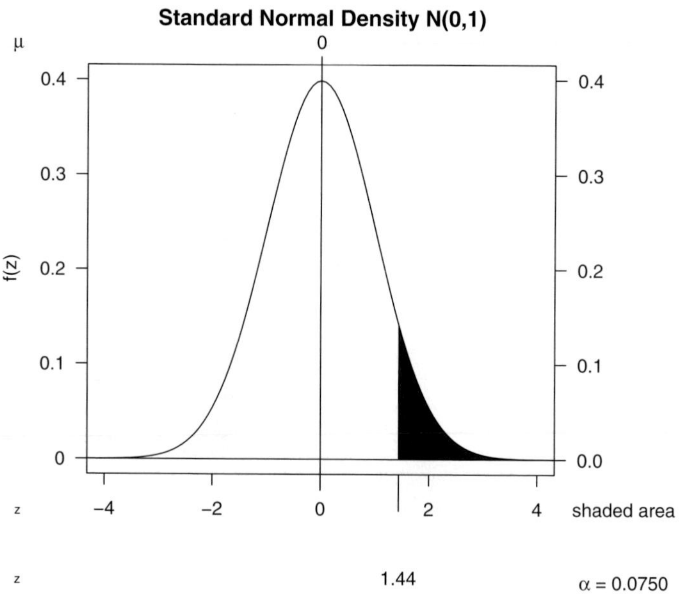

Fig. 5.3 Adjust the significance level α (with scroll bar α right) to show one-sided $\alpha = 0.075$.

normal.and.t.xlsm

	A	B	C	D	E	F	G	H	I	J	K
1			Show					critical values		probability	
2	Optional user input		Slider		on Graph			left	right	right-sided	observation
3	μ_0	0	☐		Display		s				1.000
4	μ_1		☐								
5	t		☐				t scale		1.699		
6	s	1					α		0.0750	0.0750	
7	n										
8	ν	5									
9											
10	☐ α left	☑ α right	α:	◉ prob or hypoth							
11		0.075	0.075	○ confidence interval							
12		< >									
13											
14											
15	Optional user-specified										
16	display parameters										
17	z-range										
18	horizontal min		} Copy current horizontal range								
19	horizontal max										
20	g($\bar{x}$) min				☑ graph on Top						
21	g($\bar{x}$) max		} Copy current g($\bar{x}$) range			Reset					

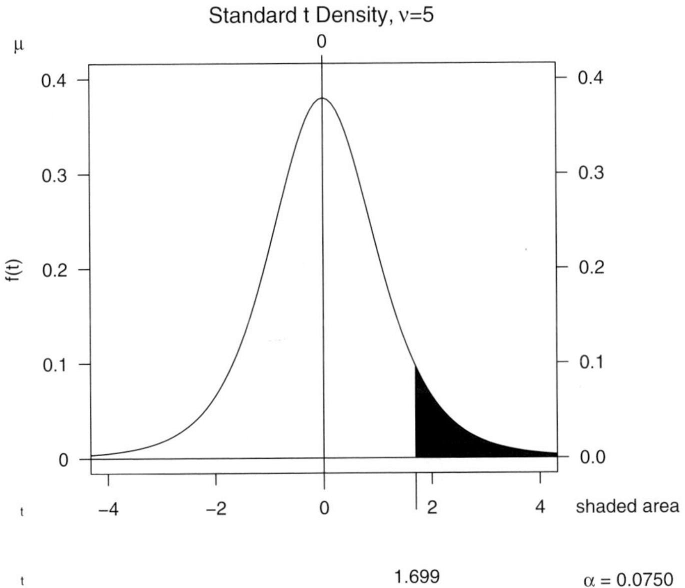

Fig. 5.4 When the degrees of freedom are not missing, the graph displays a *t* distribution, in this case with 5 degrees of freedom and showing one-sided $\alpha = 0.075$.

A comparison of Figs. 5.3 and 5.4 shows important differences between the normal distribution and the t distribution. The t_5 distribution is differently shaped than the normal. The maximum value of the density curve at $t = 0$ is smaller than the normal curve at $z = 0$, and the body of the curve is wider. The value of the density at $t = 4.32$, where the graph is truncated, is larger than for the normal at $z = 4.32$. The $\alpha = 0.075$ critical value for the t_5 distribution is larger than the $\alpha = 0.075$ critical value for the normal. Some of the highlighted area for the t_5 distribution is offscreen to the right. It would be necessary to change the xmin and xmax values to see more of the highlighted area.

5.2 Relation Between α and z

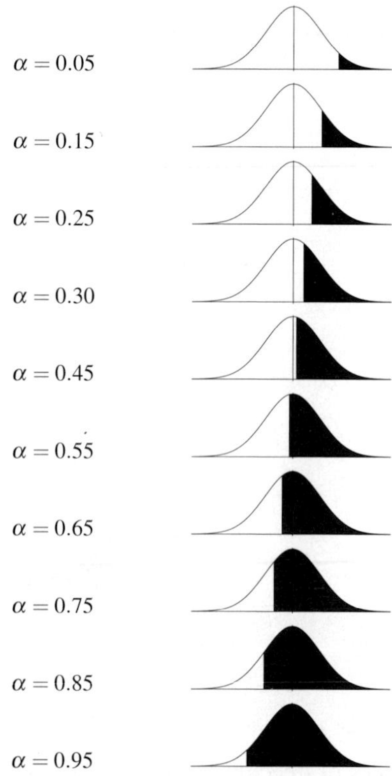

Fig. 5.5 Derivatives in Action. Using the Fig. 5.2 setup, press and hold the left arrow on the α-right slider and watch the progress of the blue rejection region as α increases. It's right-left motion noticeably slows down near the middle of the null-hypothesis distribution (near $z = 0$). The terminator is moving proportionally to probability units, not z units, and the probability units are much closer together in z-coordinates near the mean of the normal density function.

5.3 Normal Tests, Type II Error, and Power

1. Construct a one-sided test with $\alpha = 0.05$ of

   H_0: $\mu = \mu_0 = 0$

   H_1: $\mu > \mu_0 = 0$

   in a situation where $n = 1$ and we know $\sigma = 1$.
   α is called the *probability of the Type I Error*. A *Type I Error* means that the null hypothesis is rejected when the null hypothesis is true.

   a. Answer (algebra)
      Find the critical value X_{crit} such that $P(\bar{x} > \bar{X}_{\text{crit}} \mid \mu = 0) = 0.05$.

$$
\begin{aligned}
.05 &= P(\ \bar{x} && > \bar{X}_{\text{crit}} && \mid \mu = 0) \\
&= P((\bar{x} - \mu)/\sigma_{\bar{x}} && > (\bar{X}_{\text{crit}} - 0)/1 && \mid \mu = 0) \\
&= P(\quad z && > \bar{X}_{\text{crit}} &&) \\
&= P(\quad z && > z_{.05} &&) \\
&= P(\quad z && > 1.645 &&)
\end{aligned}
$$

      We have determined that $\bar{X}_{\text{crit}} = 1.645$. In this example, with $\mu = 0$ and $\sigma = 1$, we found $\bar{X}_{\text{crit}} = z_{.05}$. Equality is not the case for other values of μ and σ.

   b. Answer (workbook)
      We can calculate the numerical value $\bar{X}_{\text{crit}}$ with the normal.and.t workbook in Fig. 5.6, which in turn generates the graph in Fig. 5.7. Four numbers and one side are mentioned in the problem statement for part 1. All are entered into the workbook:

Parameter	α	μ_0	n	σ	Side
Value	0.05	0	1	1	right
Workbook cell	B11	B3	B7	B6	check B10 and uncheck A10

2. From part 1 we have a test:
Reject the null hypothesis if the observed $\bar{X} > X_{\text{crit}} = 1.645$.
What is the probability $1-\beta = 1-\beta(\mu_1)$ of rejecting the null hypothesis when the true value of population mean $\mu = \mu_1 = 2.5$? Equivalently, what is the probability $\beta = \beta(\mu_1)$ of NOT rejecting the null hypothesis when the true value of population mean $\mu = \mu_1 = 2.5$? The number β is called the *probability of the Type II Error*. The *Type II Error* means that the null hypothesis is not rejected when the null hypothesis is false. The probability $\beta = \beta(\mu_1)$ is a function of the alternative hypothesis value μ_1. The dependence on μ_1 is not always stated explicitly.

   a. Answer (algebra)
   Evaluate $1-\beta = P(\bar{x} > \bar{X}_{\text{crit}} | \mu = 2.5)$.

$$\begin{aligned}
&= P(\ \bar{x} && > \bar{X}_{\text{crit}} && \mid \mu = \mu_1) \\
&= P(\ \bar{x} && > 1.645 && \mid \mu = 2.5) \\
&= P((\bar{x}-\mu)/\sigma_{\bar{x}} && > (1.645-2.5)/1 && \mid \mu = 2.5) \\
&= P(\quad z && > -0.855 &&) \\
&= 0.8038
\end{aligned}$$

   We have determined that $1-\beta = 0.8038$; therefore, $\beta = 1-(1-\beta) = 0.1962$.

   b. Answer (workbook)
   We can calculate the numerical values β and $1-\beta$ with one additional entry on the normal.and.t workbook in Fig. 5.6. We enter $\mu_1 = 2.5$ into cell B4. $\beta = 0.1962$ is displayed in cell J12. Power = $1-\beta = 0.8038$ is displayed in cell J13.
   The red-shaded region in Fig. 5.7, with area $\beta = 0.1962$, is to the left of the critical value $X_{\text{crit}} = 1.645$ and under the normal curve centered at $\bar{x} = \mu_1 = 2.5$. Power against the alternative $\mu = \mu_1 = 2.5$ is illustrated as the complement of the red-shaded area under the normal curve centered at $\bar{x} = \mu_1 = 2.5$.

normal.and.t.xlsm

	A	B	C	D	E	F	G	H	I	J	K
1			Show					critical values		probability	
2	Optional user input		Slider		on Graph			left	right	right-sided	observation
3	μ_0	0	☐		Display		$\sigma_{\bar{x}}$				1.000
4	μ_1	2.5	☑	< >	Display		$\bar{x}$ scale		1.6449		
5	$\bar{x}$		☐				z scale		1.645		
6	σ	1					α		0.0500	0.0500	
7	n	1									
8	ν										
9											
10	☐ α left	☑ α right	α:	◉ prob or hypoth							
11		0.050	0.050	○ confidence interval			z_1 for H_1		-0.855		
12		< >					β			0.1962	
13							power			0.8038	
14											
15	Optional user-specified										
16	display parameters										
17	z-range										
18	horizontal min		} Copy current horizontal range								
19	horizontal max										
20	$g(\bar{x})$ min				☑ graph on Top						
21	$g(\bar{x})$ max		} Copy current $g(\bar{x})$ range			Reset					

Fig. 5.6 For part 1, the specified $\alpha = 0.05$ level is placed in cell B11 and is displayed again in cell I6. The calculated numerical value from the normal table $z_{.05} = 1.645$ is in cell I5. The calculated numerical value of $\bar{X}_{\text{crit}}$ is in cell I4.

For part 2, μ_1 is entered into cell B4 and the checkbox in cell C4 is checked. $\beta = 0.1962$ is displayed in cell J12. Power = $1 - \beta = 0.8038$ is displayed in cell J13.

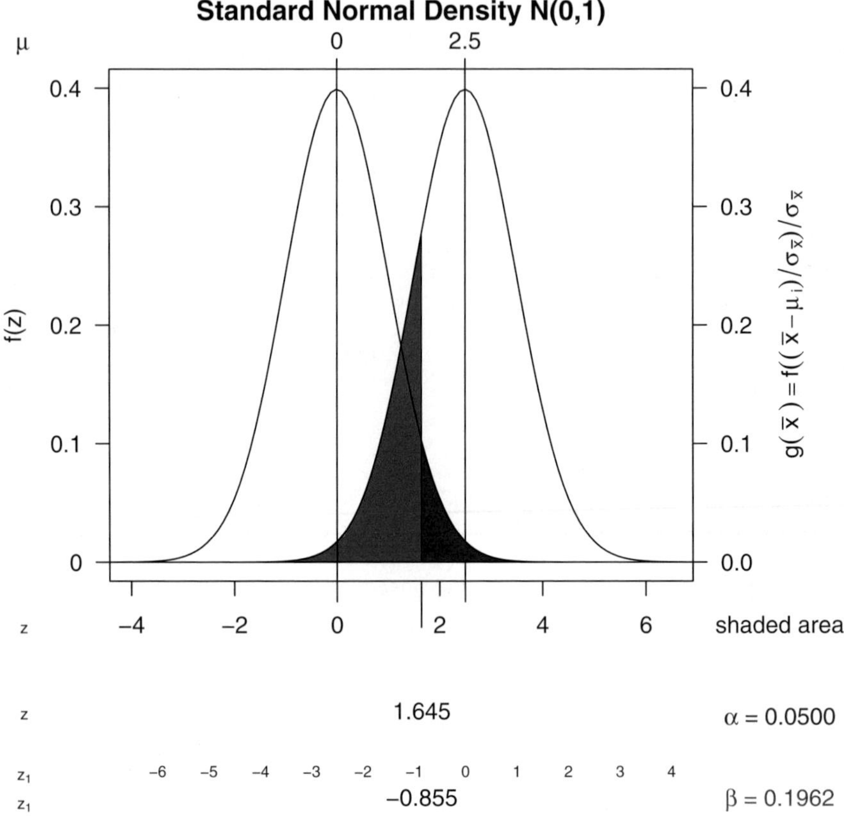

Fig. 5.7 The answer to part 1 is illustrated by the blue-shaded region. The blue-shaded region, with area $\alpha = 0.05$, is to the right of the critical value $X_{\text{crit}} = 1.645$ and under the normal curve centered at $\bar{x} = \mu_0 = 0$.

The answer to part 2 is illustrated by the red-shaded region. The red-shaded region, with area $\beta = 0.1962$, is to the left of the critical value $X_{\text{crit}} = 1.645$ and under the normal curve centered at $\bar{x} = \mu_1 = 2.5$. On the z_1-axis we see that the critical value in z_1 units is $z_1 = -0.855$. Power against the alternative $\mu = \mu_1 = 2.5$ is illustrated as the complement of the red-shaded area under the normal curve centered at $\bar{x} = \mu_1 = 2.5$.

5.4 Significance, Rejection Region, and Power—Continued

In Sections 4.4 and 4.5, we illustrated significance, rejection region, and power with graphs specified using the Normal and t Distribution dialog box. Here, we continue with the same example, this time specifying the graphs with the worksheet. We illustrate the specification in Fig. 5.8. The graph itself is displayed in Fig. 5.9.

normal.and.t.xlsm

	A	B	C	D	E	F	G	H	I	J	K
1			Show					critical values		probability	
2	Optional user input		Slider		on Graph			left	right	right-sided	observation
3	μ_0	150	☐		Display		$\sigma_{\bar{x}}$				4.000
4	μ_1	165	☐				$\bar{x}$ scale		156.58		160
5	$\bar{x}$	160	☑	< >	Display		z scale		1.645		2.500
6	σ	20					α		0.0500	0.0500	
7	n	25									
8	ν						z for p value H_0		2.500		
9							p value H_0			0.0062	
10	☐ α left	☑ α right	α:	◉ prob or hypoth							
11		0.050	0.050	○ confidence interval							
12		< >									
13											
14											
15	Optional user-specified										
16	display parameters										
17	z-range										
18	horizontal min	134	} Copy current horizontal range								
19	horizontal max	181									
20	$g(\bar{x})$ min		} Copy current $g(\bar{x})$ range		☑ graph on Top						
21	$g(\bar{x})$ max					Reset					

Fig. 5.8 Specification by worksheet of the typical homework exercise introduced in Section 4.4. We set the null μ_0- and alternative μ_1-values and the observed mean $\bar{x}$ by typing into cells B3:B5. The observed mean line is displayed by checking the checkbox in cell C5. The worksheet displayed here specifies the graph we display in Fig. 5.9. We set the horizontal limits, the sample size n, and the known population standard deviation $\sigma =$ std.dev by typing them into the workbook cells. In this example, with known standard deviation, we leave the degrees of freedom field empty.

We need to set the horizontal limits because their default values are based on the initially entered values μ_0, μ_1, and $\bar{x}$. We will be changing μ_1 as part of the discussion of Type II Error. Changes in values made by typing numbers in the μ_0, μ_1, and $\bar{x}$ cells change the horizontal limits. Changes in values made by adjusting the scrollbars do not change the horizontal limits.

We do not need to set the $g(\bar{x})$-limits, because we will not be changing σ or n in this discussion. See Section 5.7 for an example where it is imperative to set the $g(\bar{x})$-limits.

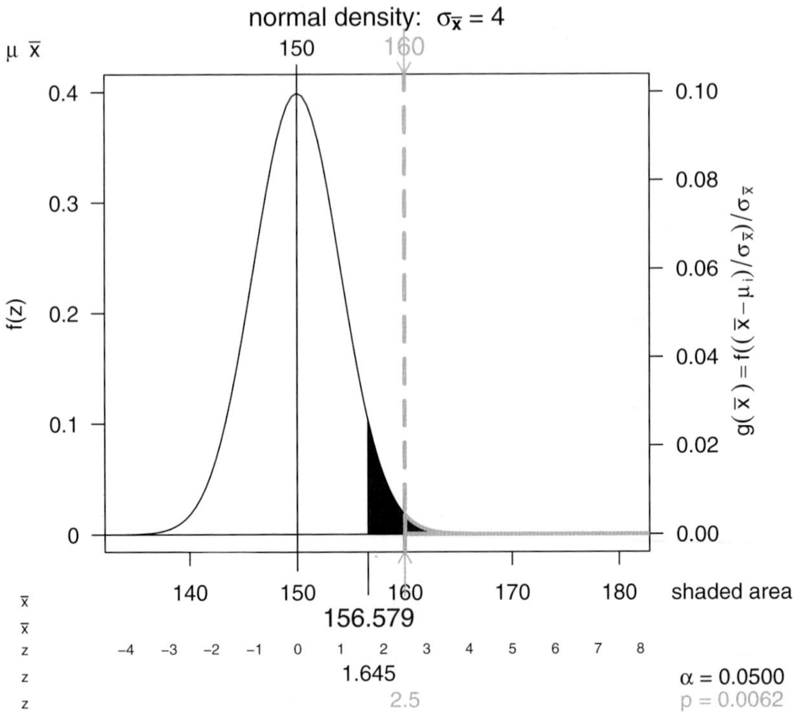

Fig. 5.9 Plot of null hypothesis and observed mean. This figure is specified by the worksheet in Fig. 5.8. This figure is almost identical to Fig. 4.19 specified by the the Normal and t Distribution dialog box in Fig. 4.18. Here, we allowed additional space on the right because we know we will need it for the alternative hypothesis that we saw in Figs. 4.21 and 4.22 and will see again in Fig. 5.10.

normal.and.t.xlsm

	A	B	C	D	E	F	G	H	I	J	K
1			Show					critical values		probability	
2	Optional user input		Slider		on Graph			left	right	right-sided observation	
3	μ_0	150	☐		Display		$\sigma_{\bar{x}}$				4.000
4	μ_1	165	☑		Display		$\bar{x}$ scale		156.58		160
5	$\bar{x}$	160	☑		Display		z scale		1.645		2.500
6	σ	20					α		0.0500	0.0500	
7	n	25									
8	ν						z for p value H_0		2.500		
9							p value H_0			0.0062	
10	☐ α left	☑ α right	α:	◉ prob or hypoth							
11		0.050	0.050	○ confidence interval			z_1 for H_1		-2.105		-1.250
12							β			0.0176	
13							power			0.9824	
14											
15	Optional user-specified										
16	display parameters										
17	z-range										
18	horizontal min	134	} Copy current horizontal range								
19	horizontal max	181									
20	$g(\bar{x})$ min		} Copy current $g(\bar{x})$ range		☑ graph on Top						
21	$g(\bar{x})$ max					Reset					

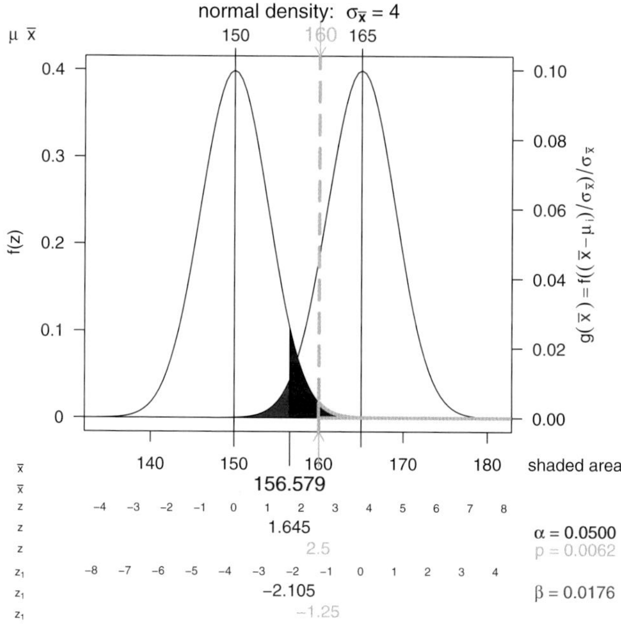

Fig. 5.10 We continue with the example in Figs. 5.8 and 5.9. Evaluate the power at the alternative hypothesis mean $\mu_1 = 165$. Check the checkbox in cell C4 to display the alternative distribution on the graph. When the checkbox is checked, the scroll bar can be used to dynamically adjust the value of μ_1. In this figure, we set the alternative mean to $\mu_1 = 165$ and see that $\beta(\mu_1 = 165) = 0.0176$ and power$(\mu_1 = 165) = (1 - 0.0176) = 0.9824$. This figure is identical to Fig. 4.22.

normal.and.t.xlsm

	A	B	C	D	E	F	G	H	I	J	K
1			Show					critical values		probability	
2	Optional user input		Slider		on Graph			left	right	right-sided	observation
3	μ_0	150	☐		Display		$\sigma_{\bar{x}}$				4.000
4	μ_1	155	☑		Display		$\bar{x}$ scale		156.58		160
5	$\bar{x}$	160	☑		Display		z scale		1.645		2.500
6	σ	20					α		0.0500	0.0500	
7	n	25									
8	ν						z for p value H_0		2.500		
9							p value H_0			0.0062	
10	☐ α left	☑ α right	α:	◉ prob or hypoth							
11		0.050	0.050	○ confidence interval			z_1 for H_1		0.395		1.250
12							β			0.6535	
13							power			0.3465	
14											
15	Optional user-specified										
16	display parameters										
17	z-range										
18	horizontal min	134	} Copy current horizontal range								
19	horizontal max	181									
20	$g(\bar{x})$ min		} Copy current $g(\bar{x})$ range		☑ graph on Top						
21	$g(\bar{x})$ max					Reset					

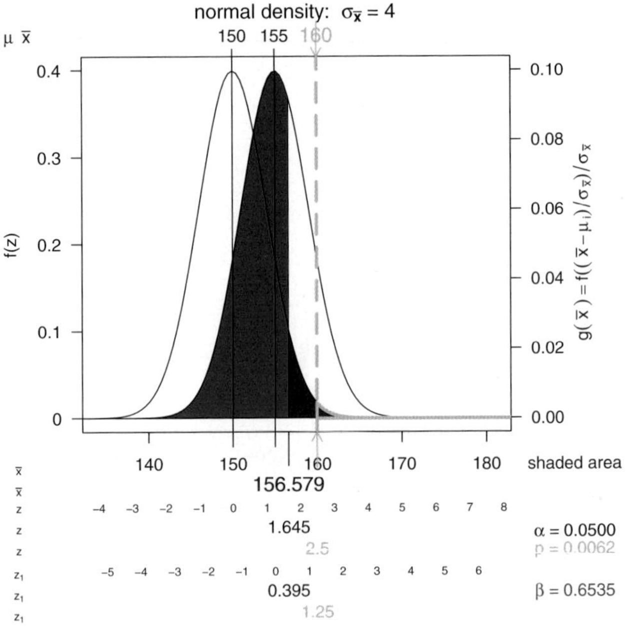

Fig. 5.11 In this figure, we set the alternative mean to $\mu_1 = 155$ and see that $\beta(\mu_1 = 155) = 0.6535$ and power$(\mu_1 = 155) = (1 - 0.6535) = 0.3465$.

5.5 How Does the Normal and t Workbook Work?

The normal.and.t workbook gives a user in Excel control over a complex graph constructed in R. It does so by placing the R functions inside the standard Excel automatic recalculation model. When a user changes a cell in the Excel workbook, a call to a graph in R is automatically generated using the revised data values in the cell.

Cells A1:K21 are designed for user input and output. This workbook contains several shaded data entry fields and several standard Excel checkboxes and sliders for user control. It contains a region in cells G1:K13 for numerical output. It produces a graph in the R Graphics window.

The communication between R and Excel is done in the offscreen sections of the workbook, using the REval function (introduced in Section 4.2) and several related functions, particularly RCallA. The workbook collects all inputs to R in cells AF1:AG28. In cell AF30, RCallA constructs a call to an R function using the name of the function and an argument constructed from the values of the input Excel cells. The workbook uses REval to collect all the outputs from R in cells AM1:AN20. The automatic updating process then copies those values to the display region in cells G1:K13.

When the workbook detects that the user has changed a cell, either by typing into one of the shaded fields or by using a checkbox or slider, it automatically updates all cells that depend on the value of the changed cell. Automatic updating is the defining feature of spreadsheets. Cell AF30 contains a call to an R function normal.and.t.dist with all the values that are currently in the workbook. When cell AF30 detects that one of the data entry cells has been changed, it automatically issues a new call to the normal.and.t.dist function in R with the revised argument values. The normal.and.t.dist function calls the same normal.curve and related functions that are accessed by the menu items described in Section 4.3.

5.5.1 Input Fields

These numbers completely specify the statistical problem.

Means: $\mu_0, \mu_1, z, t, \bar{x}$. Values *typed* into the entry fields B3:B5 are used to set the horizontal limits on the graph and to set the range of the sliders in cells D3:D5. Moving the sliders to change the values displayed in cells B3:B5 does not change the range of the sliders, nor does it change the horizontal limits on the graph. The checkboxes in cells C3:C5 hide or show the sliders and determine whether the associated values will be displayed on the graph. The label in cell A5 is either z or t, as appropriate for the degrees of freedom, when the sample size in cell B7 is empty. The label in cell A5 is $\bar{x}$ when a sample size is entered in cell B7.

Standard error: σ or s, n. The standard error $\sigma_{\bar{x}}$ or $s_{\bar{x}}$ is calculated from these values and is displayed in cell K3. When both fields are empty (use the Delete key), the standard normal or standard t distribution is displayed. The label in cell A5 changes to either z or t, as appropriate for the degrees of freedom.

Degrees of freedom: ν. Blank (use the Delete key) means the standard deviation σ is known, the label in cell A6 is σ, and the normal distribution is used. A positive integer means the standard deviation s was determined from the data, the label in cell A6 is s, and the t distribution with ν degrees of freedom is used. Various labels in cells G3:G13 are adjusted accordingly.

Hypothesis test or confidence interval. Check one of the option buttons. The graph for hypothesis tests is centered on the μ_0-value. The graph for confidence intervals is centered on the $\bar{x}$-value. Various labels in cells G3:G13 are adjusted accordingly.

Significance or confidence level: α. The significance level is α. The confidence level is $1 - \alpha$. Sidedness is determined by checking the α left and/or α right checkboxes. The α displayed in cell C11 is the sum of the values in cells A11:B11. When α left is checked, the "α left from right scrollbar?" checkbox appears in cell A13. Check it (the default) for symmetric two-sided tests or intervals. Uncheck it for independent control on each of the sides.

5.5.2 Display Parameters

These values give the user control over the use of the plotting region in the graph. They override the default calculations of the horizontal and vertical limits. They do not affect the numerical values on the graph or in the Output region of the workbook.

z-range. The horizontal limits of the graph default to z standard errors below $\min(\mu_0, \mu_1, \bar{x})$ and z standard errors above $\max(\mu_0, \mu_1, \bar{x})$.

horizontal limits. Optionally override default values. Used when comparing, for example, the effect of different alternatives μ_1, or to see the effect of different potentially observed values $\bar{x}$. Visual comparability requires the same x limits.

$g(\bar{x})$ limits. Optionally override default values. Used when comparing the effect of changing standard error $\sigma_{\bar{x}}$ (usually by changing either σ or n). Visual comparability requires the same $g(\bar{x})$ limits. See Section 5.7 for an example.

5.5.3 Numerical Output

All numerical values used in the construction of the graph are displayed.

Label. The displayed results and their labels change as a function of the values in the input fields.

Critical values. The critical values are displayed in as many scales as are appropriate, chosen from $z, z_1, t, t_1, \bar{x}$. Left and right significance levels are shown.

Probability. As appropriate, chosen from α, p, β, power $= 1 - \beta$.
Observed value. The observed value is displayed in as many scales as are appropriate, chosen from $z, z_1, t, t_1, \bar{x}$. The standard error is also shown in this column.

5.6 Confidence Intervals

This is a typical confidence interval homework exercise:

> For a sample of size $n = 50$ from a population whose standard deviation is known to be $\sigma = 25$, and for which the observed sample mean is $\bar{x} = 100$, estimate the population mean with 90% confidence.

The terminology "two-sided 90% confidence interval" means that the normal curve has been partitioned into three sections, with probability 0.90 in the center and probability 0.05 on each side.

$$\begin{aligned} \alpha &= 1 - 0.90 = 0.10 \\ \alpha/2 &= 0.05 \\ z_{\alpha/2} &= z_{.05} = 1.645 \end{aligned}$$

5.6.1 Algebra

The interval estimate is centered on the observed sample mean and has a width that is based on the standard error of the mean and on the tabled values of the normal distribution.

Then

$$\begin{aligned} 90\%\text{CI}(\mu) &= \bar{x} \pm z_{\alpha/2}\,(\sigma/\sqrt{n}) \\ &= 100 \pm 1.645\,(25/\sqrt{50}) \\ &= 100 \pm 5.815 \\ &= (94.185, 105.815) \end{aligned}$$

Sometimes the interval is denoted by its endpoints:

LCL = 94.18 and UCL = 105.82

where LCL means "lower confidence level" and UCL means "upper confidence level."

5.6.2 Workbook

normal.and.t.xlsm

	A	B	C	D	E	F	G	H	I	J	K
1			Show					90% conf limits		probability	
2	Optional user input		Slider		on Graph			left	right	two-sided	observation
3	μ_0	0	☐				$\sigma_{\bar{x}}$				3.536
4	μ_1	0	☐				$\bar{x}$ scale	94.185	105.82		100
5	$\bar{x}$	100	☑		Display		z scale	-1.645	1.645		0.000
6	σ	25					1-Confidence	0.0500	0.0500	0.1000	
7	n	50					confidence level			0.9000	
8	ν										
9											
10	☑ α left	☑ α right	α:	○ prob or hypoth							
11	0.050	0.050	0.100	◉ confidence interval							
12											
13	☑ α left from right scrollbar?										
14											
15	Optional user-specified										
16	display parameters										
17	z-range										
18	horizontal min	90	} Copy current horizontal range								
19	horizontal max	110									
20	$g(\bar{x})$ min		} Copy current $g(\bar{x})$ range		☑ graph on Top						
21	$g(\bar{x})$ max					Reset					

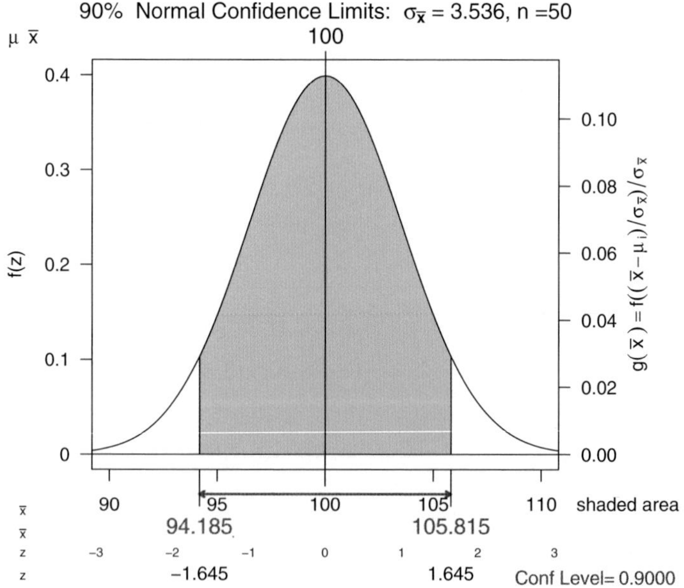

Fig. 5.12 On the normal.and.t workbook, click confidence interval, set x.min=90, x.max=110, n=50, σ=25, click both α checkboxes, click α left from right scrollbar?, accept the default for α right = 0.050, click the $\bar{x}$ checkbox in cell C5, and set $\bar{x} = 100$.

5.7 Scaling to Keep Constant Area

The default vertical scaling for the normal and t density plots uses the entire vertical space of the panel. The vertical scale has the maximum value of normalized density $f(z)$, $f(0) = 0.3989423$, near the top of the panel. The right-hand scale, in $g(\bar{x}) = f((x-\mu)/\sigma_{\bar{x}})/\sigma_{\bar{x}}$ units, varies as a function of $\sigma_{\bar{x}}$, which in turn depends on the sample size n. When the sample size changes, as in the left column of Fig. 5.14, the graphs have a constant numerical area (in probability units), but varying visual area (in square inches or cm^2). We maintain a constant visual area, as well as a constant numerical area, by specifying the range on the right-hand axis. In the right column of Fig. 5.14, the graphs have a constant visual area because all three panels have the same specified min and max values on the right-hand $g(\bar{x})$-axis. We illustrate the specification in the workbook excerpts in Fig. 5.13.

a. $g(\bar{x})$ min = , $g(\bar{x})$ max = , $n =$

normal.and.t.xlsm

	A	B
7	n	
18	x.min	-4
19	x.max	4
20	f(x) min	
21	f(x) max	

b. $g(\bar{x})$ min = , $g(\bar{x})$ max = , $n = 4$

normal.and.t.xlsm

	A	B
7	n	4
18	x.min	-4
19	x.max	4
20	f(x) min	
21	f(x) max	

c. $g(\bar{x})$ min = , $g(\bar{x})$ max = , $n = 16$

normal.and.t.xlsm

	A	B
7	n	16
18	x.min	-4
19	x.max	4
20	f(x) min	
21	f(x) max	

d. $g(\bar{x})$ min = 0, $g(\bar{x})$ max = 1.6, $n =$

normal.and.t.xlsm

	A	B
7	n	
18	x.min	-4
19	x.max	4
20	f(x) min	0
21	f(x) max	1.6

e. $g(\bar{x})$ min = 0, $g(\bar{x})$ max = 1.6, $n = 4$

normal.and.t.xlsm

	A	B
7	n	4
18	x.min	-4
19	x.max	4
20	f(x) min	0
21	f(x) max	1.6

f. $g(\bar{x})$ min = 0, $g(\bar{x})$ max = 1.6, $n = 16$

normal.and.t.xlsm

	A	B
7	n	16
18	x.min	-4
19	x.max	4
20	f(x) min	0
21	f(x) max	1.6

Fig. 5.13 Display parameters in normal.and.t workbook that specify the scaling in Fig. 5.14. We specify the vertical range in $g(\bar{x}) = f(z)/\sigma_{\bar{x}}$ units in cells B20:B21. For constant σ, we control $\sigma_{\bar{x}} = \sigma/\sqrt{n}$ by specifying n in cell B7. In all six panels, we control $x_{\text{min}} = 4$ and $x_{\text{max}} = 4$ in cells B18:B19.

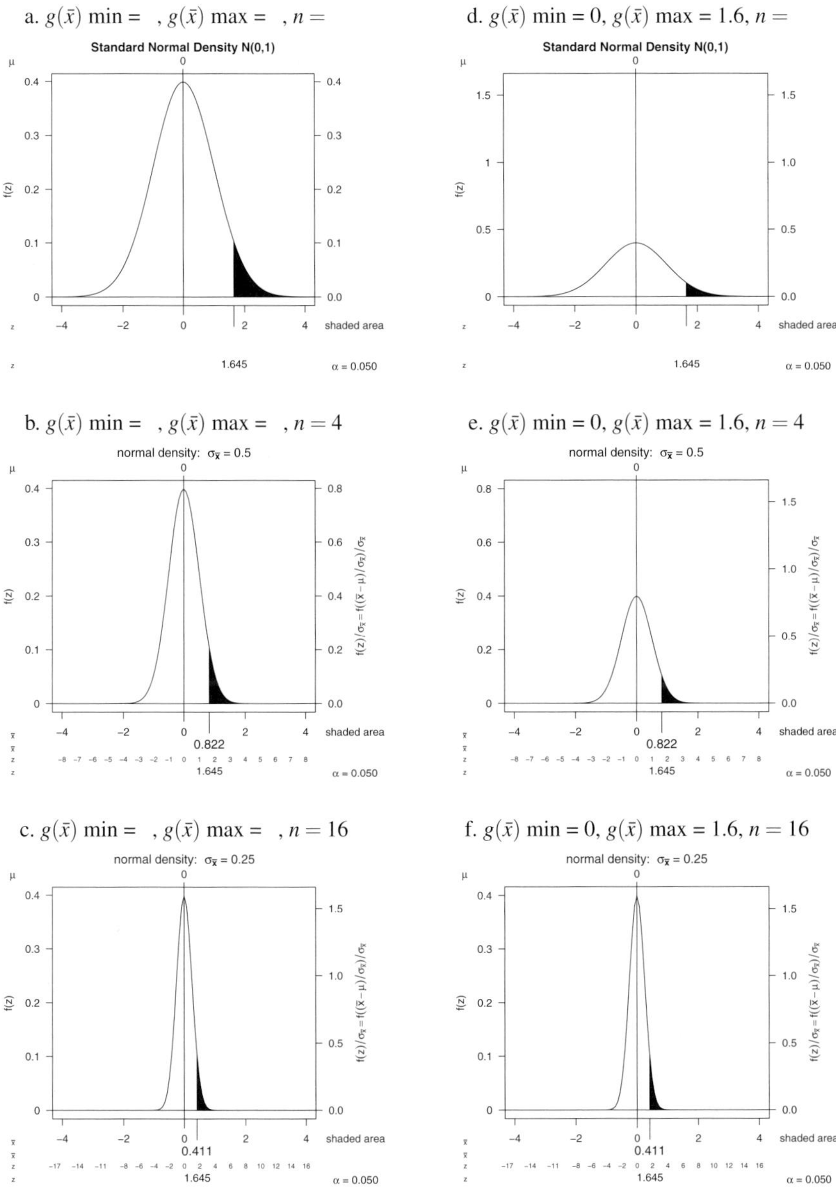

Fig. 5.14 The areas under the curve are numerically the same for all graphs in both columns because all six panels have the same vertical scaling on the $f(z)$-axis on the left [the maximum value is always $f(0) = 0.3989423$]. The areas are visually different in the left column, because each of Panels a, b, and c has a different vertical range on the $g(\bar{x}) = f(z)/\sigma_{\bar{x}}$-axis on the right. The areas are visually the same in the right column because all three Panels d, e, and f have an identical vertical range on the $g(\bar{x}) = f(z)/\sigma_{\bar{x}}$-axis on the right. The specification of vertical range is shown in Fig. 5.13. In all six panels, we control $x_{\min} = 4$ and $x_{\max} = 4$.

5.8 Normal Approximation to the Binomial

This is an example of an extended use of the normal.and.t workbook.

The normal approximation to the binomial sets $z = p/\sqrt{(p(1-p)/n)}$. We can use the confidence interval setting to display how the width of a specified size confidence interval gets narrower as we move away from $p = 0.5$.

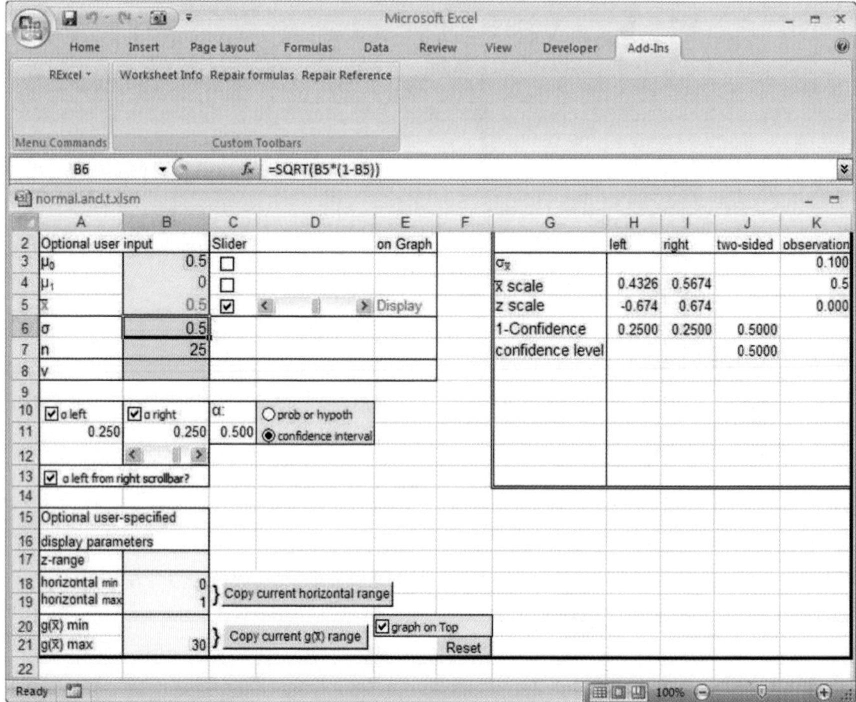

Fig. 5.15 Turn on the x̄ slider and enter $\mu_0 = 0.5$, $\mu_1 = 0$, $\bar{x} = 0.5$. These three numbers set the scale and initialize the sliders. Set the horizontal range of the plot with the values horizontal min to 0 and horizontal max to 1. Set the $g(\bar{x})$ max to 30. Set the standard deviation to $\sqrt{p(1-p)}$ using the Excel formula =SQRT(B5*(1-B5)) as shown in the Excel formula box. Enter the sample size n $= 25$. Set the display to confidence interval. Click the checkboxes to show the x̄ slider and turn off the other two sliders. Set both α-levels to 0.250. This sets the central portion of the displayed confidence interval to 50%. These settings specify the graph in Fig. 5.16.

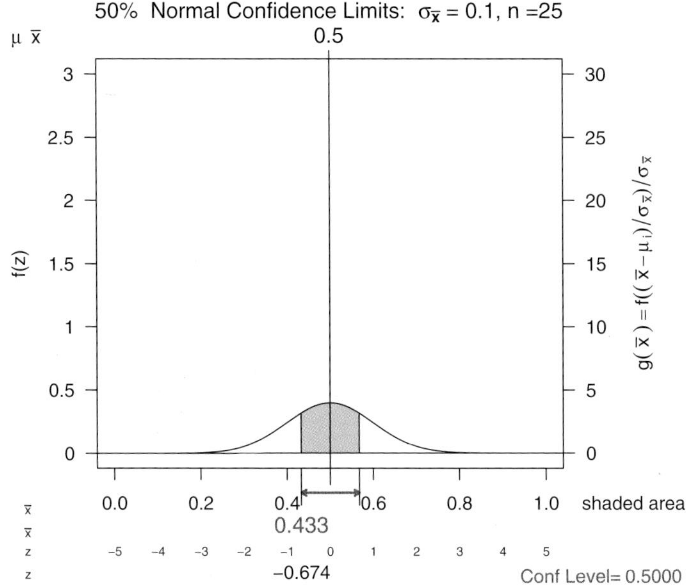

Fig. 5.16 Graph of normal approximation to the binomial as specified in Fig. 5.15. When $p = 0.50$ and $n = 25$, the 50% confidence limits are $p \pm z_{.025}\sqrt{(p \times p/n)} = .5 \pm 0.6744898 \times 0.5/5 = (0.432551, 0.567449)$.

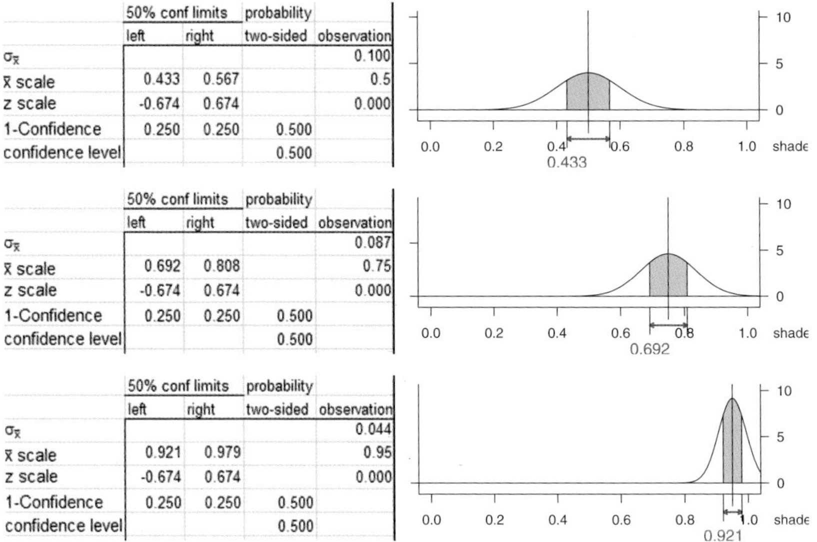

	50% conf limits		probability	
	left	right	two-sided	observation
$\sigma_{\bar{x}}$				0.100
x̄ scale	0.433	0.567		0.5
z scale	-0.674	0.674		0.000
1-Confidence	0.250	0.250	0.500	
confidence level			0.500	

	50% conf limits		probability	
	left	right	two-sided	observation
$\sigma_{\bar{x}}$				0.087
x̄ scale	0.692	0.808		0.75
z scale	-0.674	0.674		0.000
1-Confidence	0.250	0.250	0.500	
confidence level			0.500	

	50% conf limits		probability	
	left	right	two-sided	observation
$\sigma_{\bar{x}}$				0.044
x̄ scale	0.921	0.979		0.95
z scale	-0.674	0.674		0.000
1-Confidence	0.250	0.250	0.500	
confidence level			0.500	

Fig. 5.17 Now, as we scroll the x̄ slider in Fig. 5.15, we see that the width of the 50% range is widest at the center and narrowest at the extremes of the range.

Chapter 6
t-Tests

Abstract The t-test is used for the mean of a normal distribution with estimated standard deviation s, or for comparing the means of two normal distributions.

We will look at several datasets, graphically and numerically, and focus on two types of questions.

Testing: We have null (H_0) and alternative (H_1) hypotheses about the true value μ of the mean of the population from which the data was drawn. We wish to test whether there is enough evidence to reject the null hypothesis. The possible answers to the test are "reject the null hypothesis" or "do not reject the null hypothesis." The possible answers do not contain any numbers.

The null hypothesis is a statement about the world. It might be a true statement. It might be a false statement. The phrase "reject the null hypothesis" means the evidence from the data suggests that the null hypothesis is a false statement.

Estimation: We have some data, and we wish to estimate the location of the population mean μ. We estimate the location with a confidence interval with a specified confidence level. Frequently, the level is 95%. The answer is an interval, a set of two numbers. The interval is written in the form

$$95\%\text{CI}(\mu) = (L, U) \tag{6.1}$$

where the numbers L and U stand for "lower bound" and "upper bound," respectively. The interval is written as a set of parentheses with the smaller number on the left, the larger number on the right, and a comma separating them.

R.M. Heiberger, E. Neuwirth, *R Through Excel*, Use R,
DOI 10.1007/978-1-4419-0052-4_6,

6.1 Data—Canned Vegetables

The initial dataset we look at is similar to examples in an introductory text. We have a claim that the average weight of canned vegetables in cans marked 16 ounces is actually 15.75 ounces or less. If the claim is sustained, the company is subject to regulatory action for false advertising. The contents of $n = 12$ cans are weighed. The resulting values are

15.13 15.31 15.72 16.51 16.02 16.19 15.73 15.90 15.78 16.05 15.75 15.77

We begin by entering the data into a new workbook in Fig. 6.1.

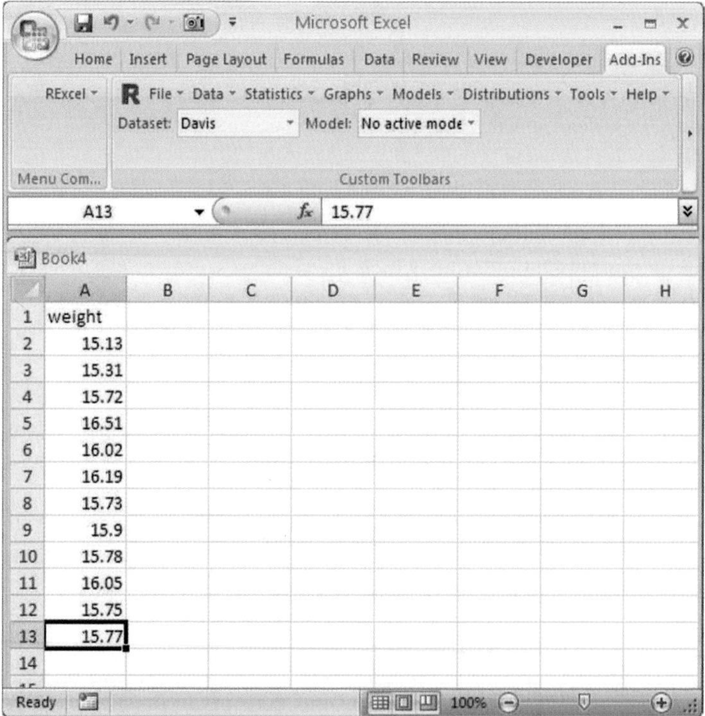

Fig. 6.1 Row 1 contains the variable name weight, and rows 2–13 contain the observed values. Notice that the decimal points are not aligned. Specifically, the number 15.9 in cell A9 has only one digit after the decimal point while all the other numbers have two digits after the decimal. Unaligned decimal points make it difficult to read a column of numbers. We will repair this in Figs. 6.2 and 6.3.

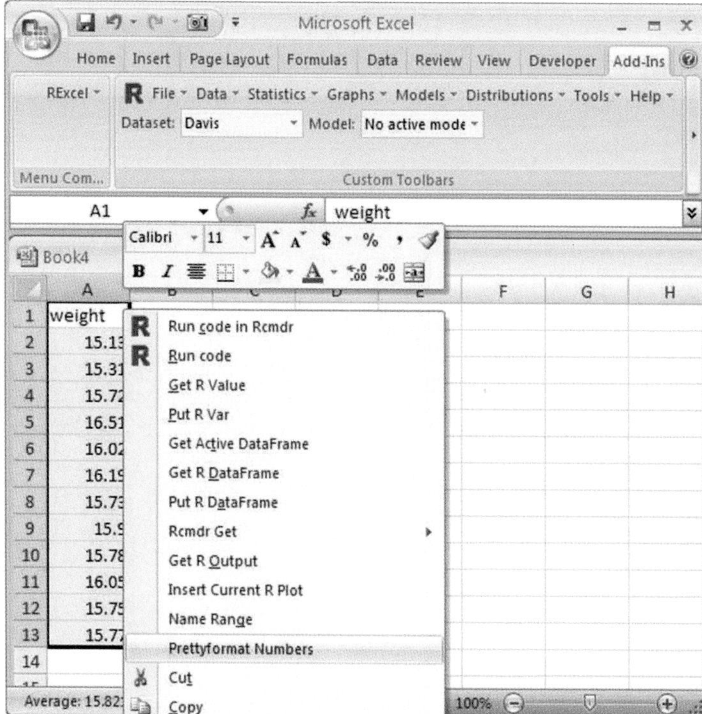

Fig. 6.2 Highlight the region A1:A13 containing the data—including the variable name. Right-click Prettyformat Numbers to align the decimal points, as seen in Fig. 6.3.

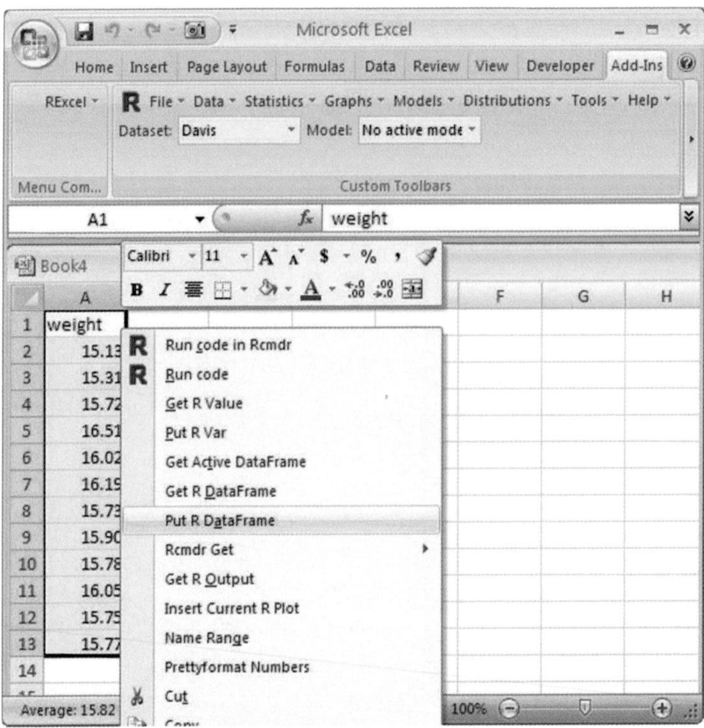

Fig. 6.3 Now that the decimal points are aligned, we can continue. We send the data from Excel to R, using the the technique detailed in Section 3.2. The data is already highlighted from Fig. 6.2. We right-click Put R Dataframe to get the dialog box in Fig. 6.4.

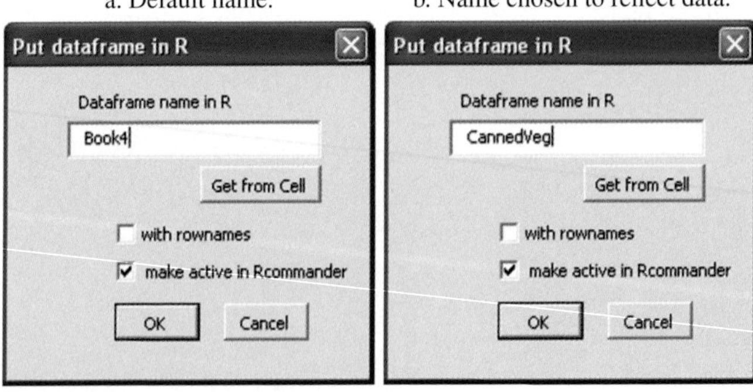

Fig. 6.4 Dialog box for Put dataframe in R. The default name Book4 in Panel a is not descriptive of this dataset. We change the name in Panel b to CannedVeg and click OK. All menu items on the Rcmdr menu refer to variables that are columns in the active dataframe.

6.1.1 *Plot the Data*

We show several different types of graphs for looking at measured data: the histogram, the dotplot, and the boxplot.

6.1.1.1 Histogram

a. Menu.

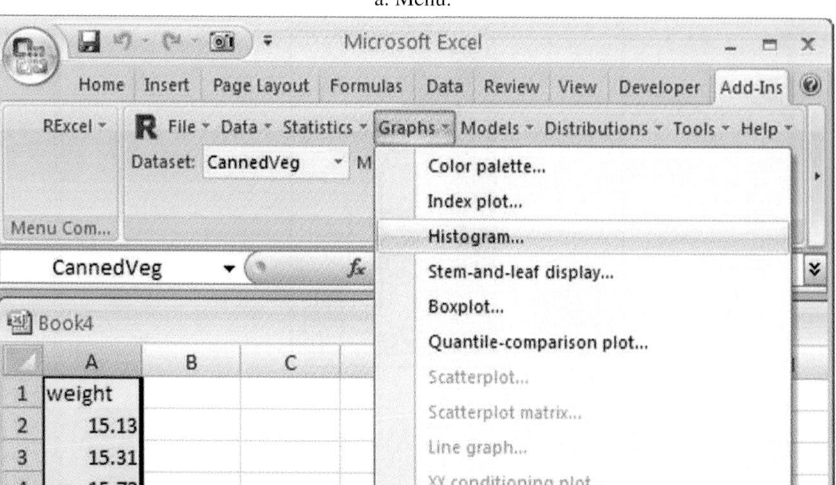

b. Dialog box.

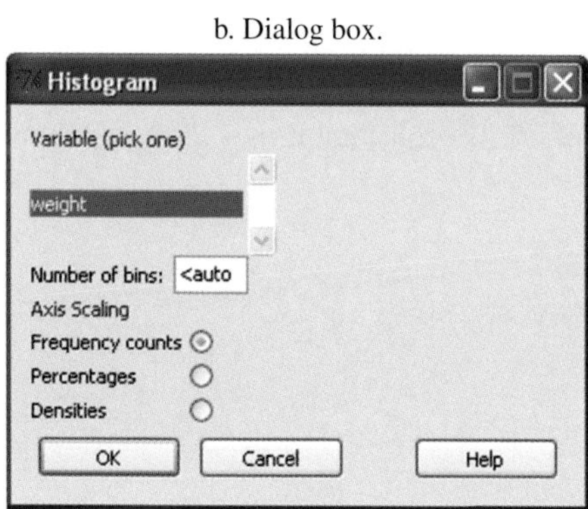

Fig. 6.5 The active dataset is now listed as CannedVeg. The Rcmdr menu items will now know the variable names in this dataset. We graph the data, with a histogram in this case, by clicking in Panel a on the Rcmdr menu Graphs ▶ Histogram... and in Panel b accepting the defaults in the Histogram dialog box. The histogram is shown in Fig. 6.6.

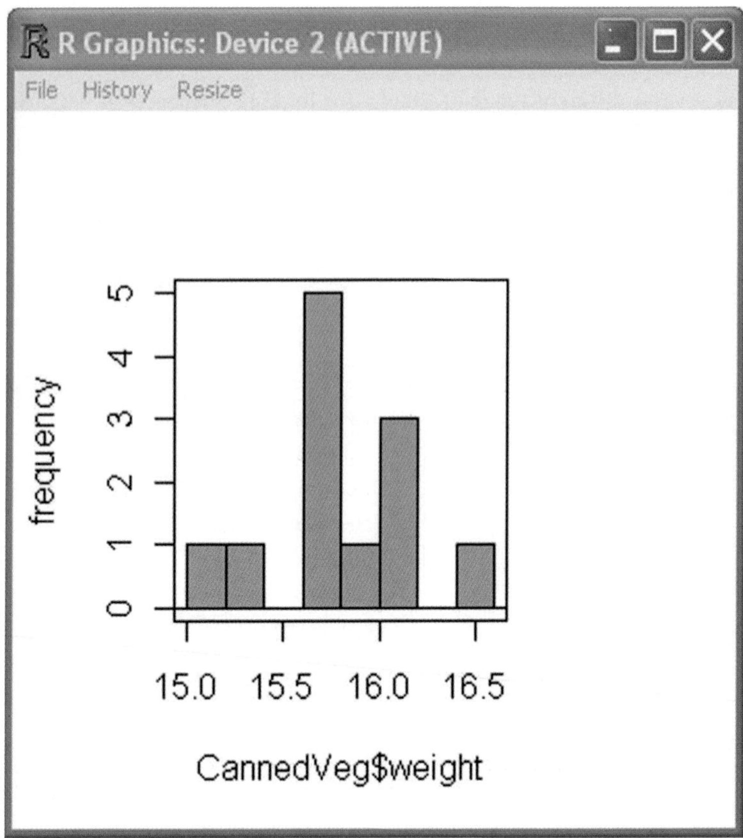

Fig. 6.6 The histogram constructed by the menu and dialog box of Fig. 6.5. The graph of the weight variable shows the numbers to be centered at a value smaller than the labeled value of 16. We can't tell if they are smaller enough to need to take regulatory action.

6.1.1.2 Dotplot

a. Menu.

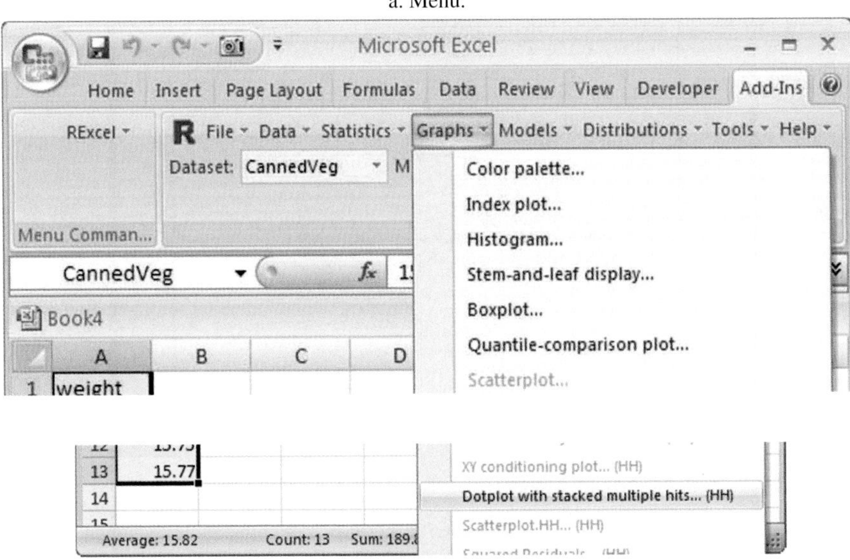

b. Dialog box.

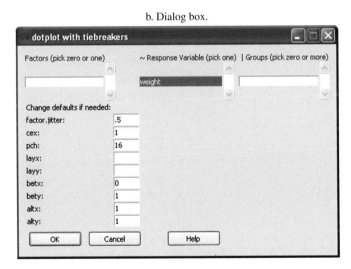

Fig. 6.7 Specification of the dotplot with the Graphs ► Dotplot with stacked multiple hits... menu item. The plot is shown in Fig. 6.8.

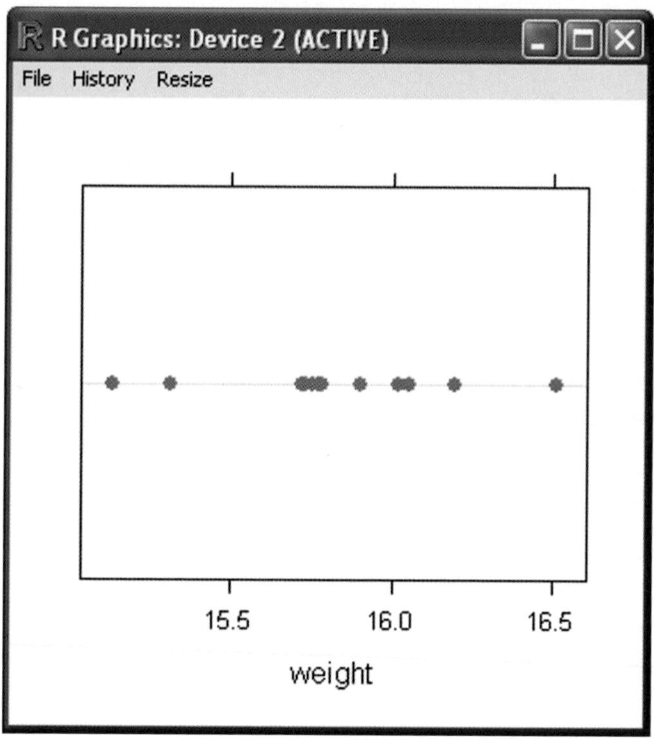

Fig. 6.8 Dotplot specified in Fig. 6.7. The dotplot shows each individual point. The points close together in the center of the plot give a direct impression of density. The center of the plot is at a value smaller than the labeled value of 16.

6.1.1.3 Boxplot

a. Menu.

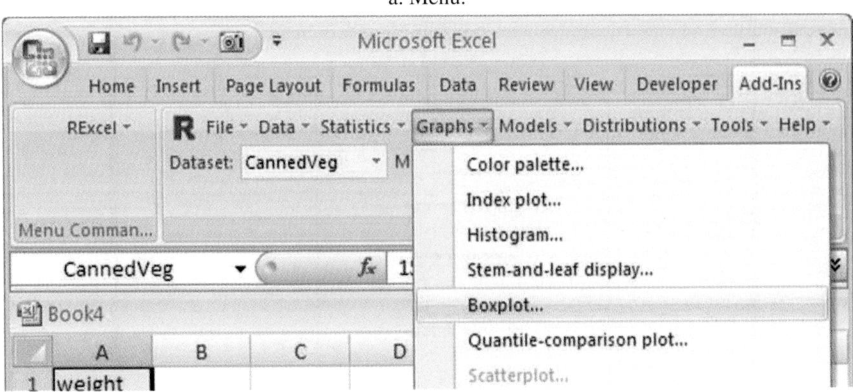

b. Dialog box.

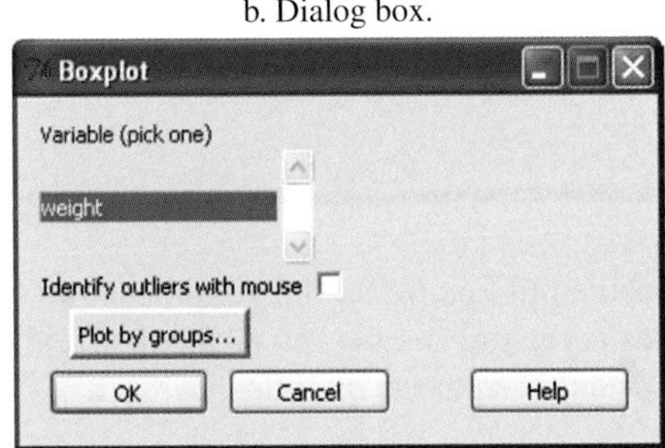

Fig. 6.9 Specification of the boxplot with the Graphs ► Boxplot... menu item. The plot is shown in Fig. 6.10.

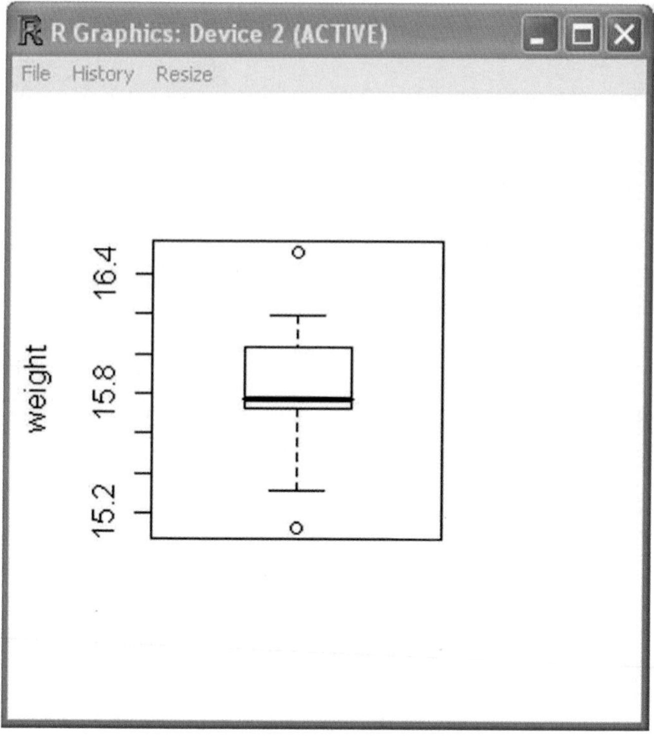

Fig. 6.10 Boxplot specified in Fig. 6.10. The boxplot shows the median as a horizontal line, the quartiles at the top and bottom of the box, and two outliers at more than 1.5 interquartile distances from the quartiles.

6.1.2 Calculate the t-Test

a. Menu.

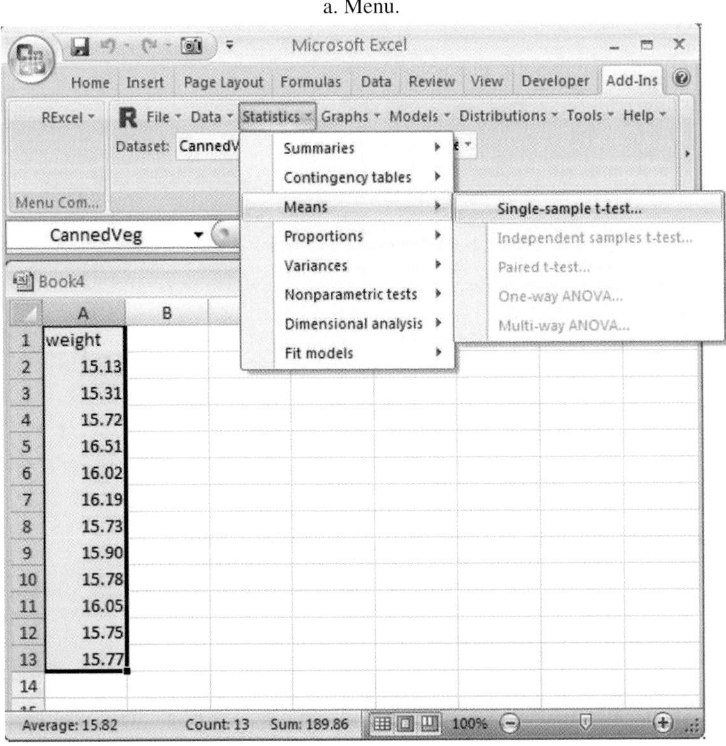

b. Dialog box.

Single-Sample t-Test
Variable (pick one)
weight
Alternative Hypothesis
Population mean = mu0 Null hypothesis: mu = 15.75
Population mean < mu0 Confidence Level: .95
Population mean > mu0
OK Cancel Help

Fig. 6.11 For this example, the null hypothesis is $\mu = 15.75$ and the alternative hypothesis is $\mu < 15.75$. We specify the t-test with the Statistics ► Means ► Single sample t-test... menu and dialog. In Panel b, the variable name is automatically highlighted because it is the only variable name in the dataset. We must type the null hypothesis value mu=15.75. We must click on the alternative hypothesis Population mean < mu0. Then click OK. This produces the tabular output in Fig. 6.12.

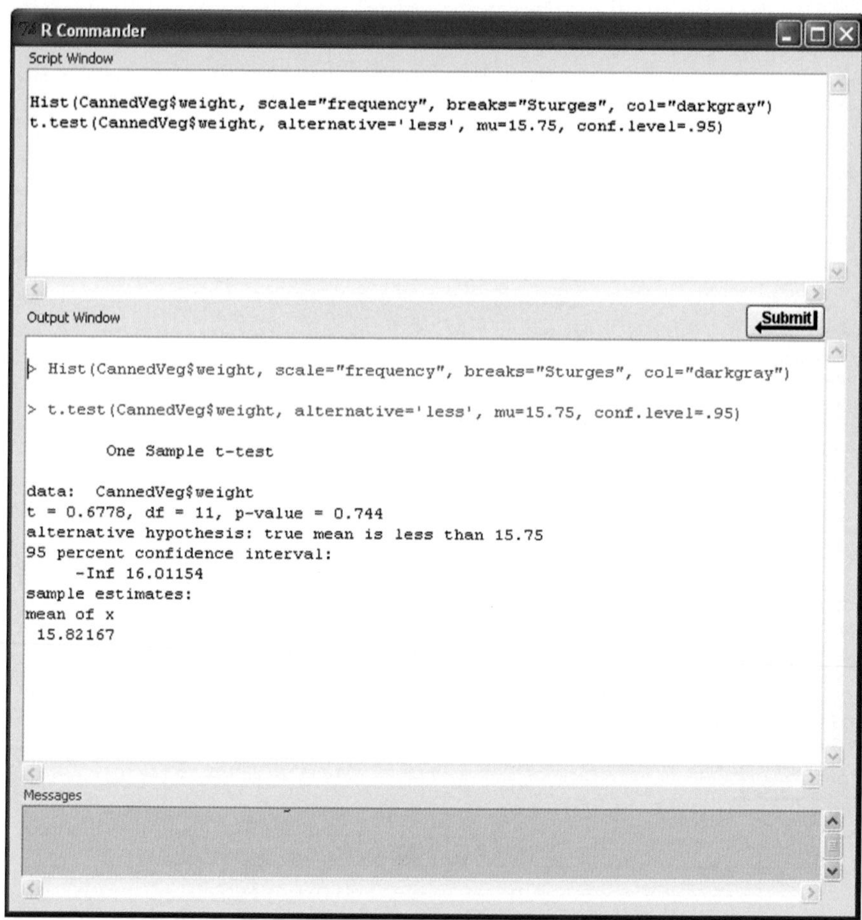

Fig. 6.12 *t*-test output from the menu and dialog box in Fig. 6.11. The R commands generated from the dialog box are displayed in the Script Window, the top half of the Commander window, and the executed command and output are in the Output Window, the bottom half of the Commander window. The observed $\bar{x} = 15.822$ is larger than the hypothesized value $\mu_0 = 15.75$ (we rounded the observed mean to one more digit than in the data; see the discussion on rounding in the Notes to Readers section). We are not in the rejection region and hence do not reject the null hypothesis. We will act as if the null hypothesis is true, and we will not take regulatory action. We draw the graph of the result of this test in Figs. 6.13–6.16.

6.1.3 Plot the *t*-Test

a. Menu.

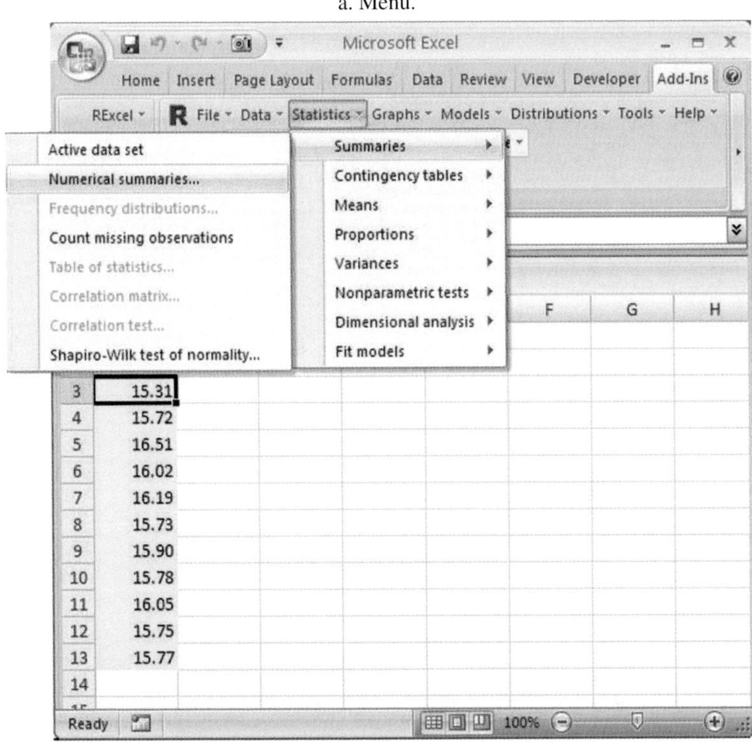

b. Dialog box.

Numerical Summaries

Variables (pick one or more)

weight

Mean ☑

Standard Deviation ☑

Quantiles ☑ quantiles: 0, .25, .5, .75, 1

Summarize by groups...

OK Cancel Help

Fig. 6.13 Drawing the graph requires the sample standard deviation. We calculate the summary statistics, including the sample standard deviation, with the Rcmdr Statistics ▸ Summaries ▸ Numerical Summaries... menu item and its dialog box. For this example, accept the defaults in the dialog box.

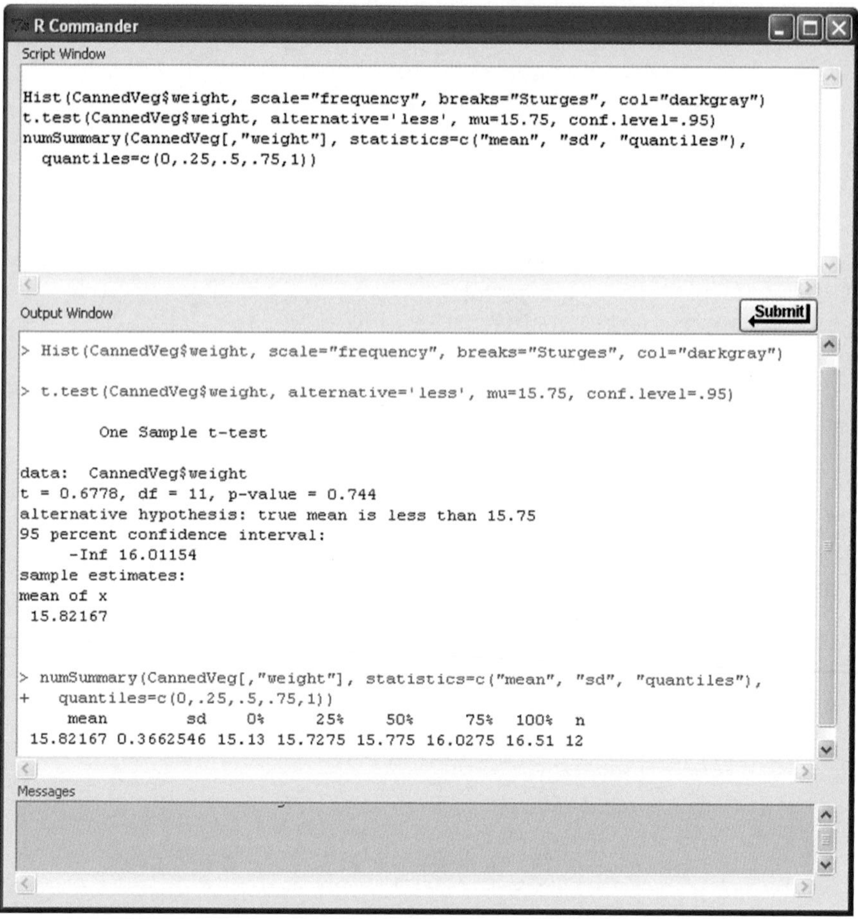

Fig. 6.14 The printed output in the Commander window shows the standard deviation to be sd = 0.3662546. We pick up the standard deviation value with the mouse and paste it into the dialog box in Fig. 6.15b. Alternatively, we could have used an Excel sheet function =RApply("sd", A2:A13), which returns the value 0.366254589 into its cell, and copied that value into the dialog box.

a. Menu.

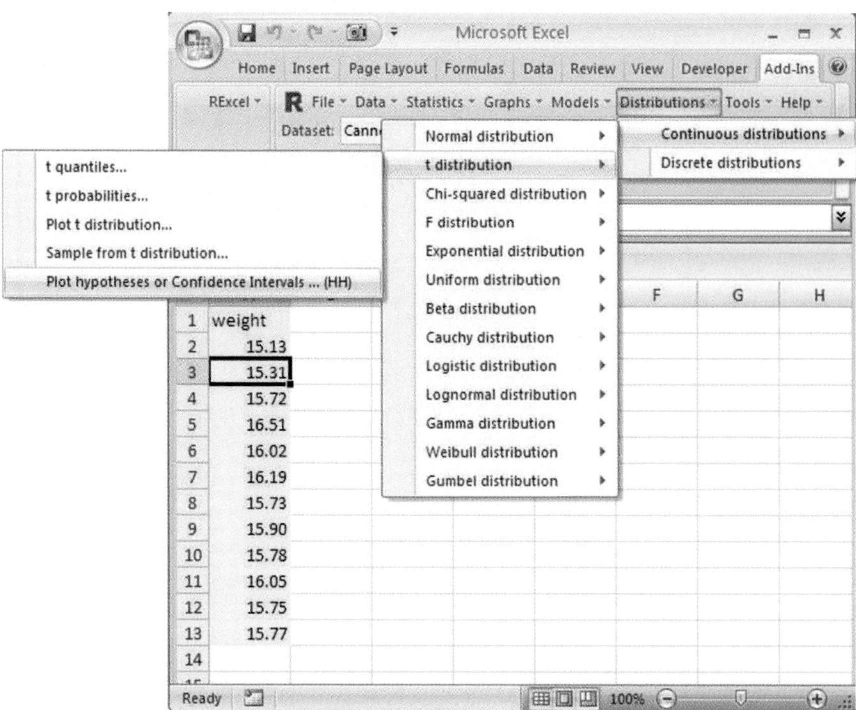

b. Dialog box.

Normal and t Distributions
mu (mean) 15.75
standard deviation (sigma or s) .36625
df (degrees of freedom) 11
n (sample size) 12
left alpha .05
right alpha
Observed Value 15.8216
mu (Alternate Hypothesis)
ymax (right-hand side)
Hypothesis or Confidence
Hypothesis Test
Confidence Interval
OK Cancel Help

Fig. 6.15 We can now specify the plot of the t-test as introduced in Section 4.4. The dialog box is the same for the normal and t distributions. In this example, we fill in the degrees of freedom box to inform the dialog box that this is a t distribution. The plot is in Fig. 6.16.

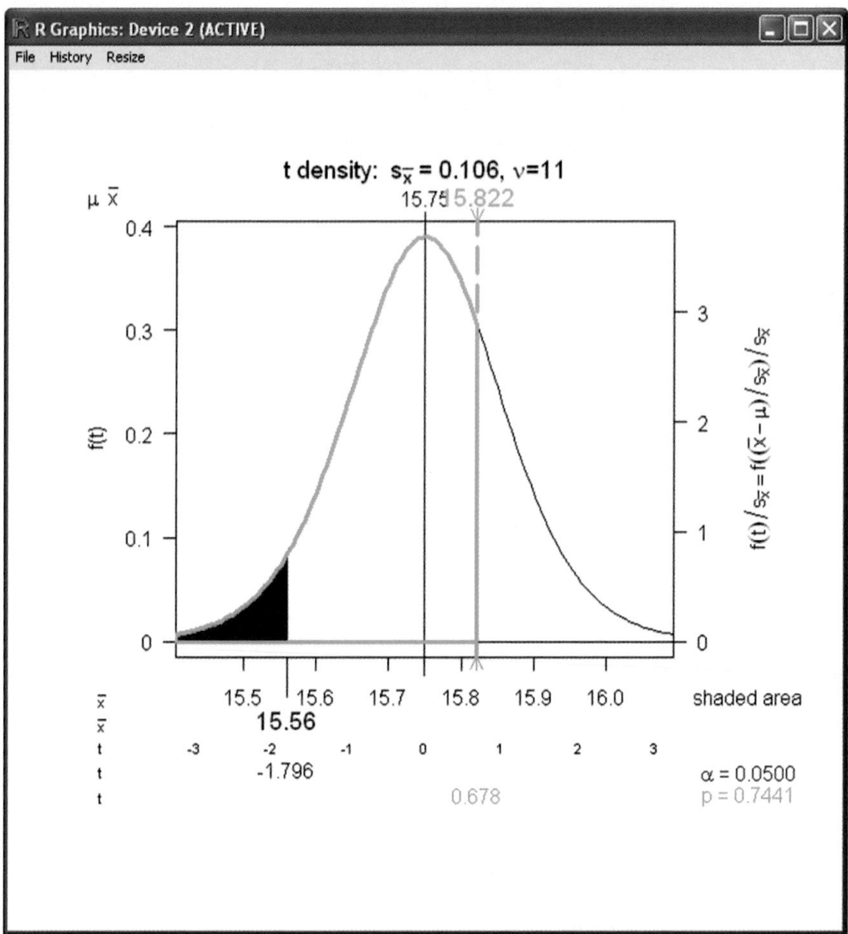

Fig. 6.16 Plot of the t-test in Fig. 6.12. The observed value $\bar{x} = 15.822$ is to the right of the null hypothesis $\mu_0 = 15.75$; hence, the green-outlined area representing the p-value is large, in this case $p = 0.7441$. The standard error of the mean, shown on the plot as $s_{\bar{x}} = 0.106$, was calculated as $s/\sqrt{n} = 0.3662546/\sqrt{12} = 0.1057286$ and rounded to three digits.

6.2 Data—Heights

The second dataset we look at is the Davis dataset containing the heights and weights of a group of men and women engaged in regular exercise. We will bring it into R and Excel using the technique introduced in Section 3.6, look at the numbers themselves, at several plots of the numbers, and ask several questions of the data about the heights of the subjects.

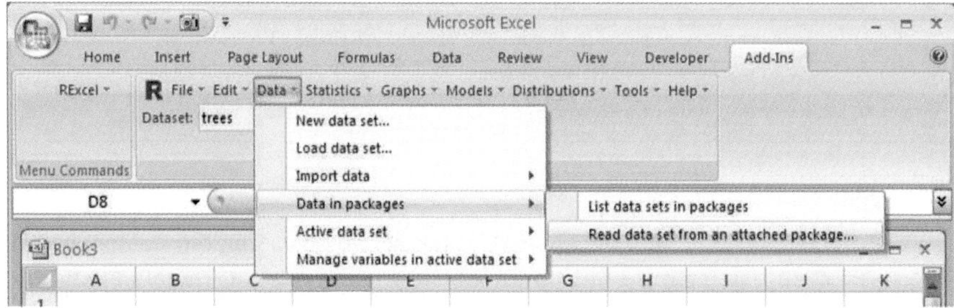

Fig. 6.17 Click the Data ► Data in packages ► Read data set from an attached package... menu item.

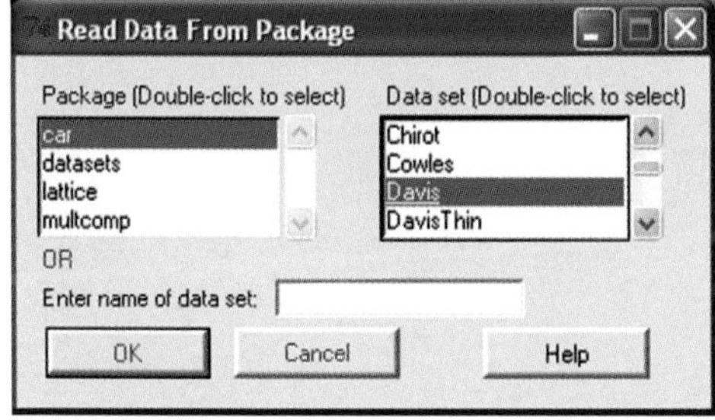

Fig. 6.18 Highlight the package and the dataset names. Click OK.

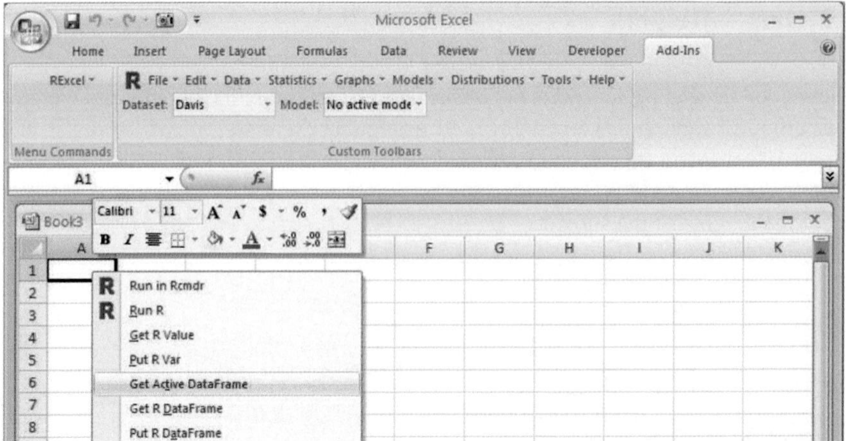

Fig. 6.19 The dataset name now appears as the active dataset in the Dataset box in the Rcmdr menu bar. To bring it into Excel, we highlight a cell (here A1) and use the right-click Get Active DataFrame menu item.

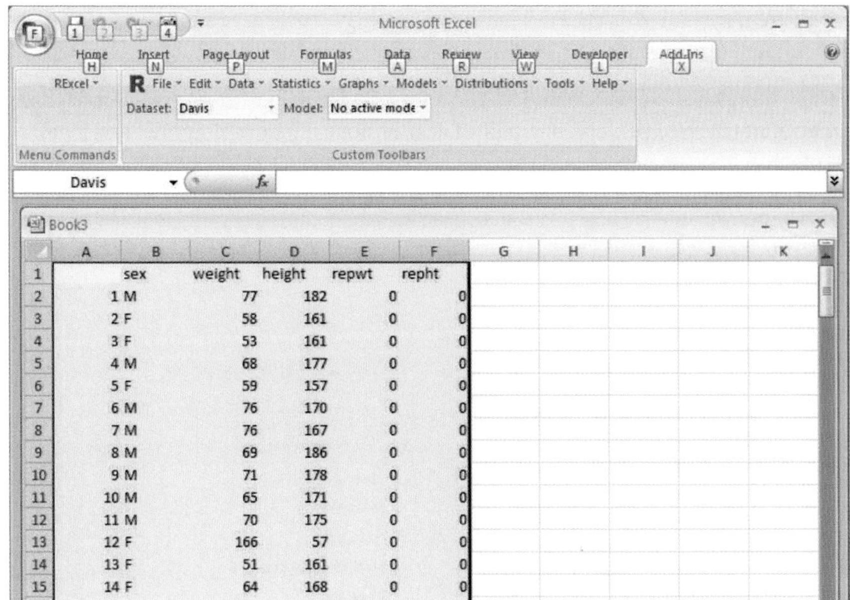

Fig. 6.20 The dataset is displayed in Excel. Its region is highlighted and its name now appears in the Excel `Name Box`, immediately above cell `A1`. We look at the numbers and immediately see that case 12 is an anomaly. It looks like the height and weight fields may have been interchanged. We will need to go back to the data source to confirm this.

6.2.1 Plots

We need to plot the data, conditioned on the classification factor sex, before doing any arithmetic. We will look at a pair of scatterplots, a pair of dotplots, and a pair of boxplots.

6.2.1.1 Scatterplots

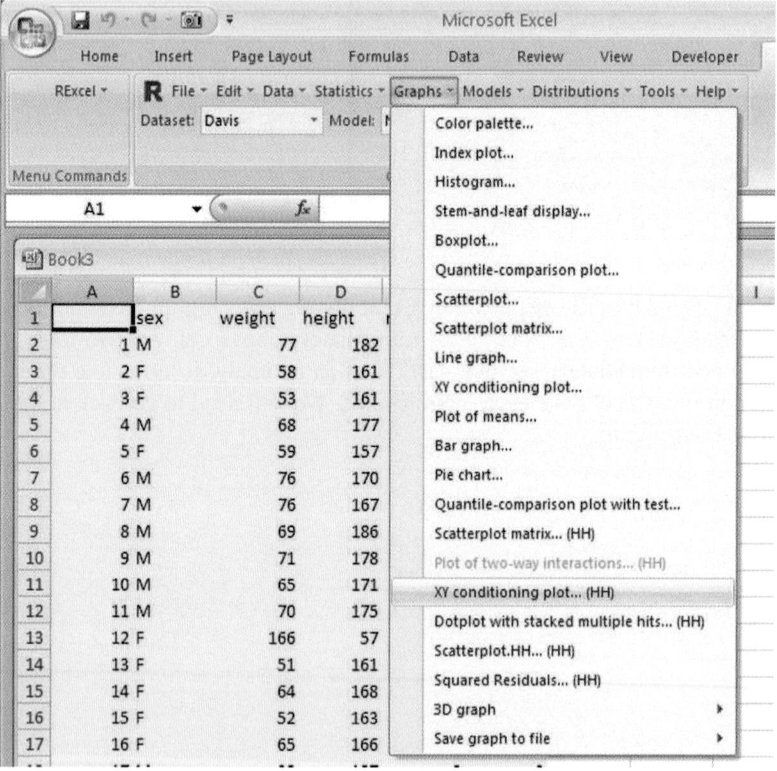

Fig. 6.21 We need to plot the data before doing any arithmetic. Use the

Graphs ► XY conditioning plot . . . (HH)

menu item.

XY Conditioning Plot

Explanatory variables (pick one or more)
height
repht
repwt
weight

Response variables (pick one or more)
height
repht
repwt
weight

Conditions '|' (pick zero or more)
sex

Groups 'groups=' (pick zero or more)
sex

Options
Automatically draw key
Different panels for different y~x combinations

X-Axis Scales in Different Panels
Identical
Free
Same range

Y-Axis Scales in Different Panels
Identical
Free
Same range

Layout
number of columns:
number of rows:

OK Cancel Help

Fig. 6.22 Click the explanatory variable height, the response variable weight, and the conditions variable sex. Then click OK.

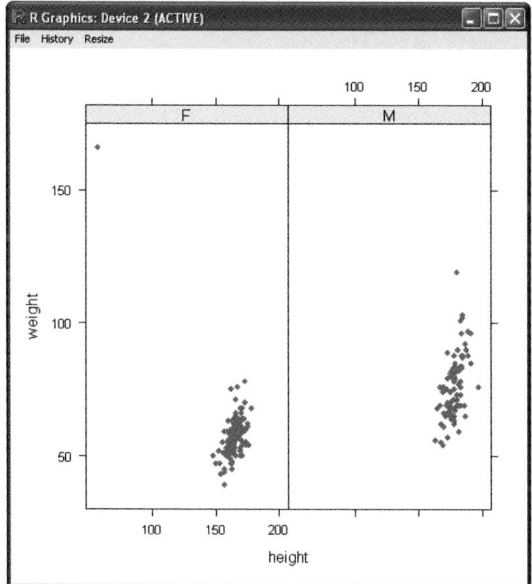

Fig. 6.23 Conditioning on the sex variable gave us a pair of coordinated plots. We see the anomalous observation by itself in the upper left-hand corner of the F panel.

6.2.1.2 Dotplots

dotplot with tiebreakers
Factors (pick zero or one)
sex
~ Response Variable (pick one)
height
repht
repwt
weight
| Groups (pick zero or more)
sex
Change defaults if needed:
factor.jitter: .5
cex: 1
pch: 16
layx:
layy:
betx: 0
bety: 1
altx: 1
alty: 1
OK
Cancel
Help

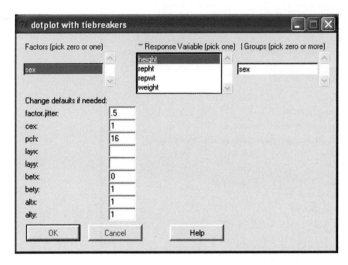

Fig. 6.24 Click the Graphs ▶ Dotplot with stacked multiple hits ... (HH) to get this dialog box. Click height as the response variable and sex as the factor to get Fig. 6.25.

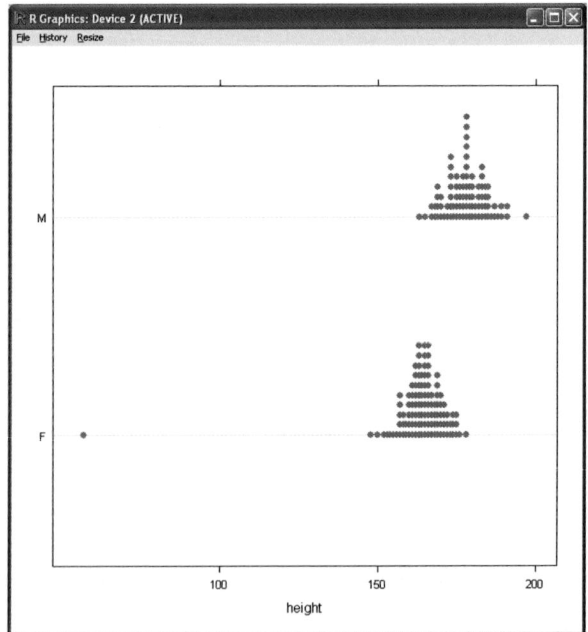

Fig. 6.25 This plot was specified in Fig. 6.24. That anomalous point in the Female heights is very visible as a lone point on the left side of the graph. We will put it aside in Section 6.2.5 and study the remaining points.

6.2.1.3 Boxplots

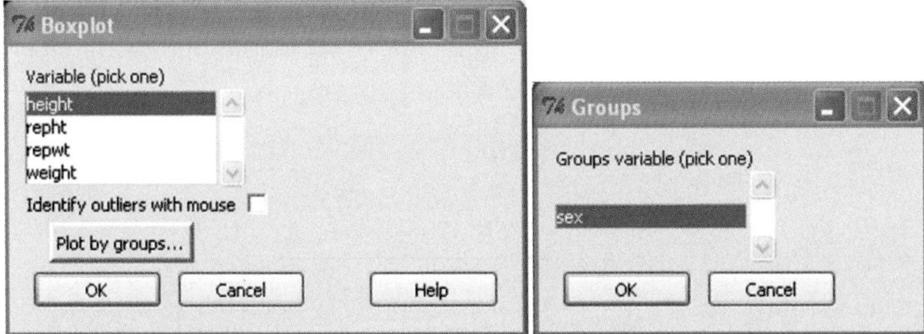

Fig. 6.26 Click the Graphs ► Boxplot... to get the first dialog box. Click Plot by groups... to get the second dialog box. Clicking OK gives Fig. 6.27.

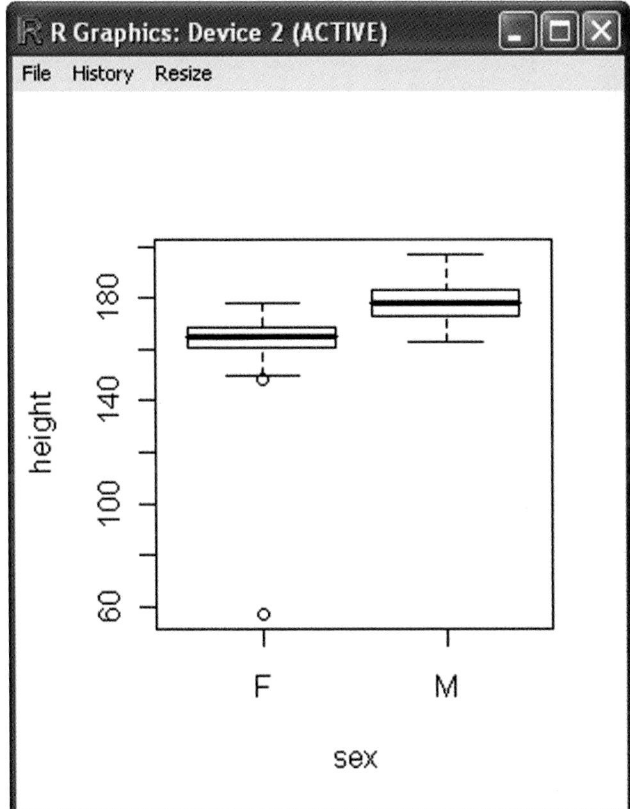

Fig. 6.27 This plot was specified in Fig. 6.26. That anomalous point in the Female heights is very visible as an outlier far below the box and whiskers. We will put it aside in Section 6.2.5 and study the remaining points.

6.2.1.4 Bar Graph for Frequencies

Factors require a different type of graph than measured variables. Here we show a bar graph for the sex factor. We plot the number of F observations and the number of M observations.

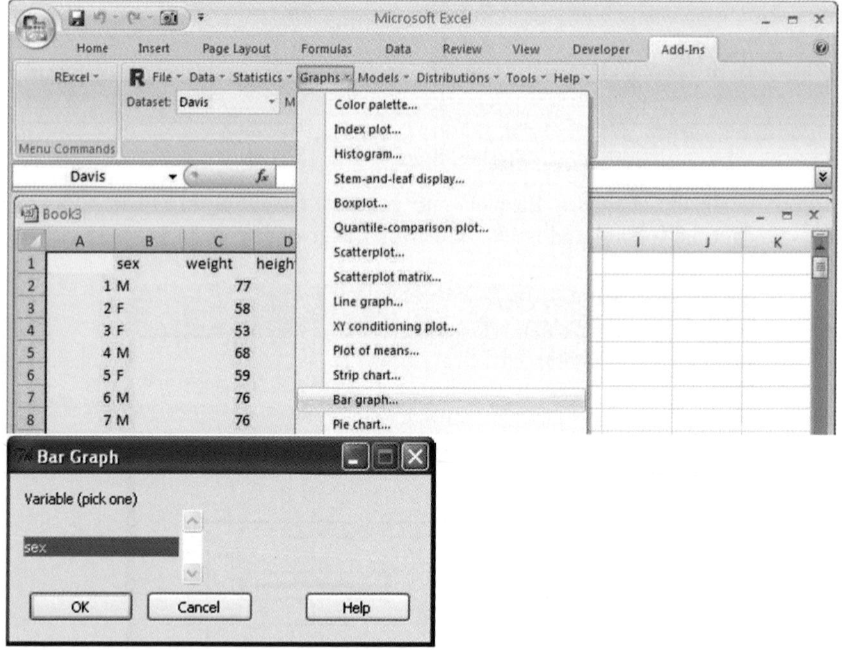

Fig. 6.28 Click the Graphs ▶ Bar graphs... to get the dialog box. This specification gives the bar graph in Fig. 6.29.

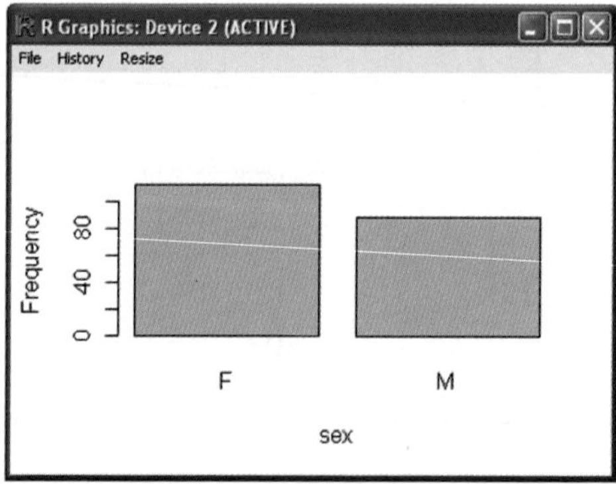

Fig. 6.29 This plot was specified in Fig. 6.28. The plot shows the number of F and M observations in the dataset.

6.2.2 Summary Statistics

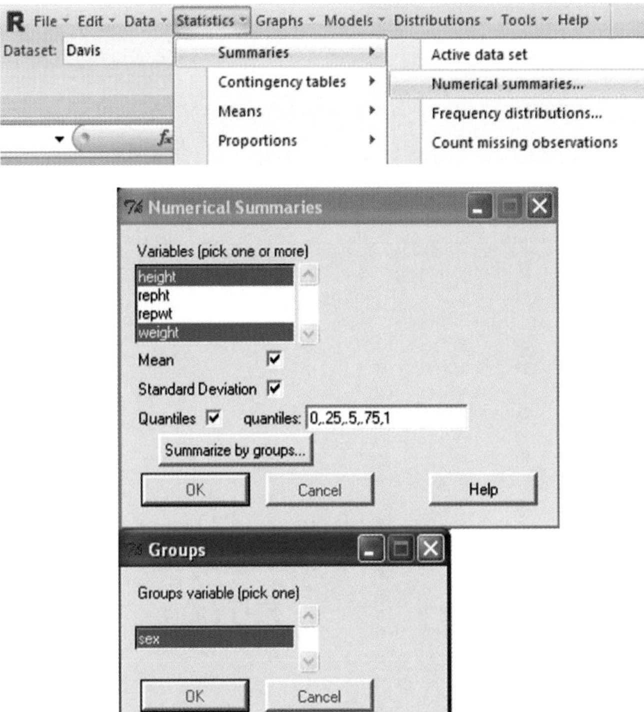

Fig. 6.30 We will look at the summary statistics with the Statistics ► Summaries ► Numerical summaries... menu item. We click the height and weight variables in the dialog box, click the Summarize by groups... button, and select the sex variable. Click OK twice.

Output Window

```
> numSummary(Davis[,c("height", "weight")], groups=Davis$sex, statistics=c("mean

Variable: height
      mean        sd  0% 25% 50% 75% 100%   n
F 163.7411 11.643925  57 161 165 169  178 112
M 178.0114  6.440701 163 173 178 183  197  88

Variable: weight
      mean       sd 0%   25% 50% 75% 100%   n
F 57.86607 12.38314 39 52.75  56  62  166 112
M 75.89773 11.89034 54 67.75  75  83  119  88
```

Fig. 6.31 The tabular summary is in the Output Window of the R Commander window.

6.2.3 Subsetting the Data for Males

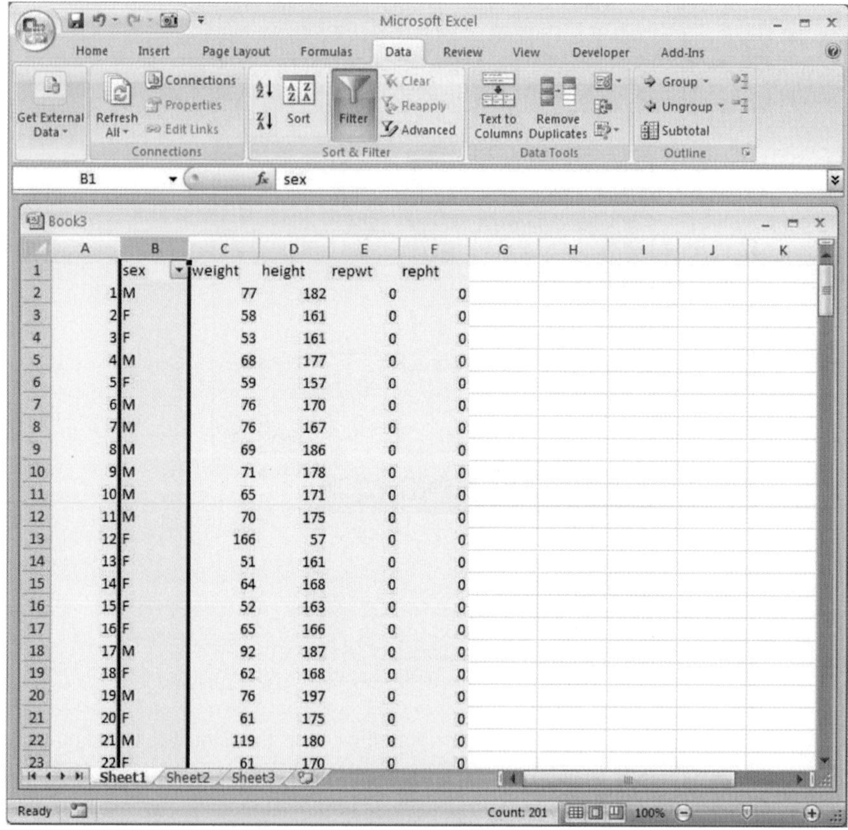

	A	B	C	D	E	F
1		sex	weight	height	repwt	repht
2	1	M	77	182	0	0
3	2	F	58	161	0	0
4	3	F	53	161	0	0
5	4	M	68	177	0	0
6	5	F	59	157	0	0
7	6	M	76	170	0	0
8	7	M	76	167	0	0
9	8	M	69	186	0	0
10	9	M	71	178	0	0
11	10	M	65	171	0	0
12	11	M	70	175	0	0
13	12	F	166	57	0	0
14	13	F	51	161	0	0
15	14	F	64	168	0	0
16	15	F	52	163	0	0
17	16	F	65	166	0	0
18	17	M	92	187	0	0
19	18	F	62	168	0	0
20	19	M	76	197	0	0
21	20	F	61	175	0	0
22	21	M	119	180	0	0
23	22	F	61	170	0	0

Fig. 6.32 Initially, we look at the two groups individually. We illustrate how to look at the males. Click column B containing the sex variable. On the Excel Data tab, click the Filter icon. This places a selection arrow in cell B1.

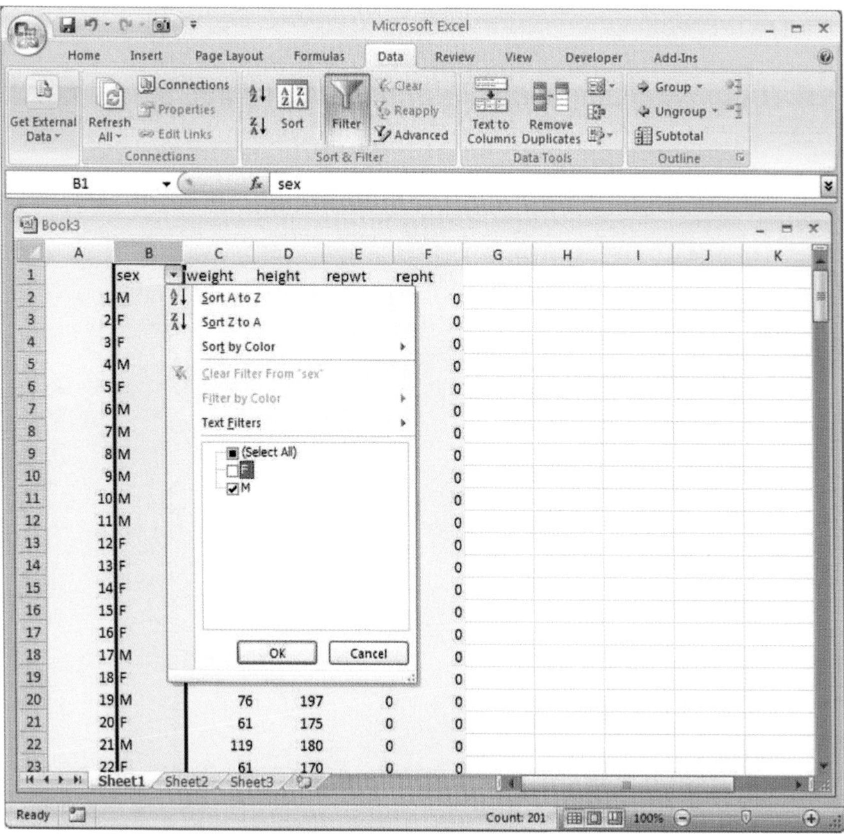

Fig. 6.33 Click the arrow, and then uncheck F and click OK.

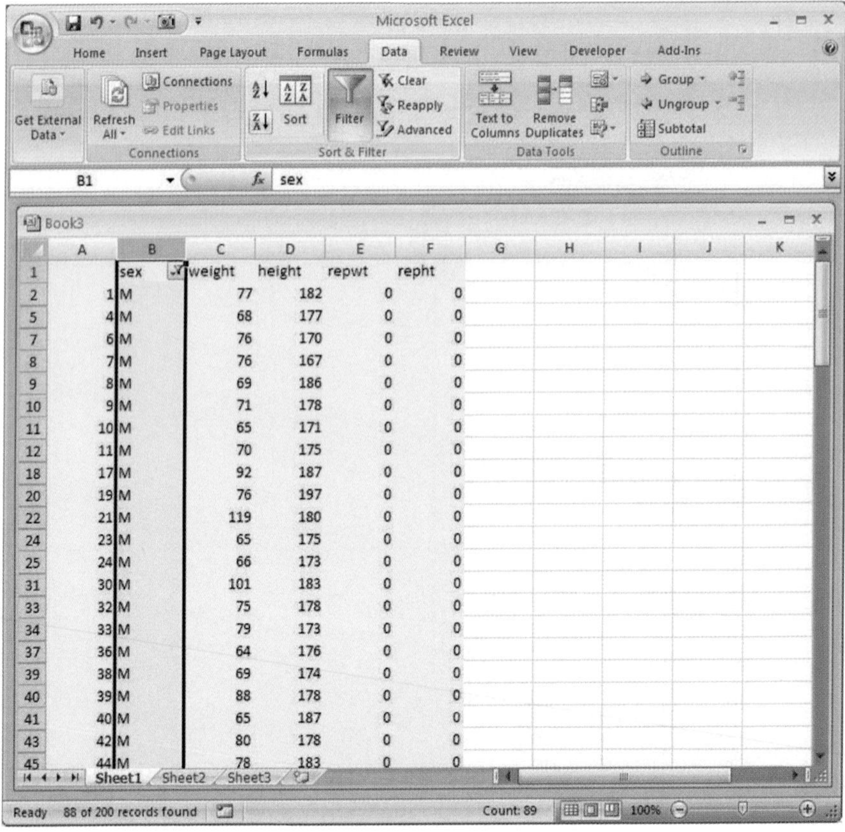

Fig. 6.34 Only the male data values are displayed.

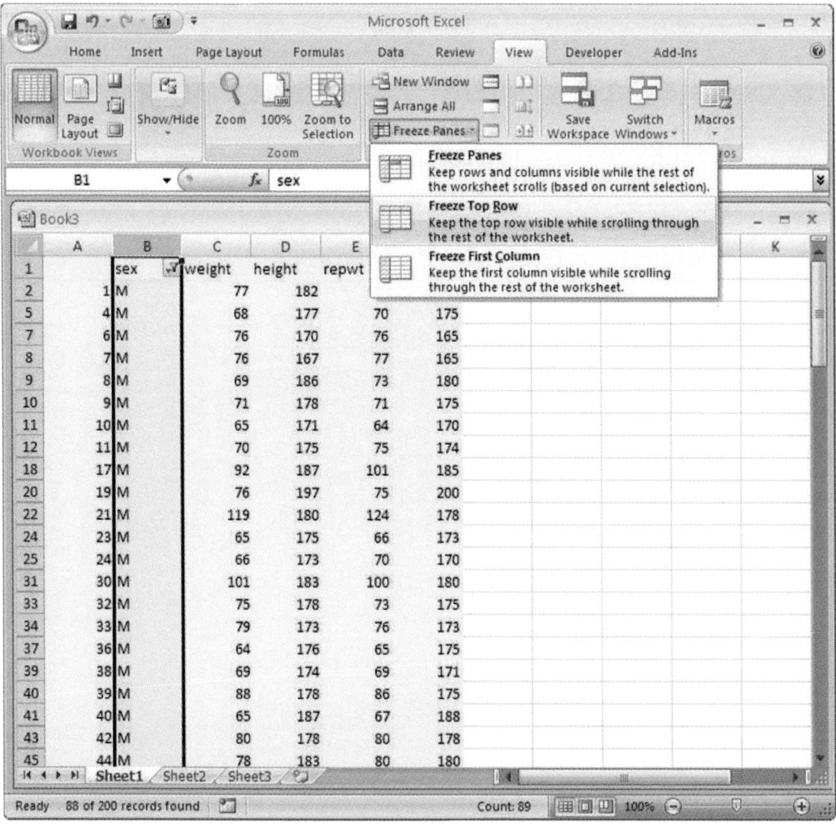

Fig. 6.35 We will need to scroll down the data, but first we will freeze the top pane so the column names stay visible. On the Excel View tab, click Freeze Panes ▸ Freeze Top Row.

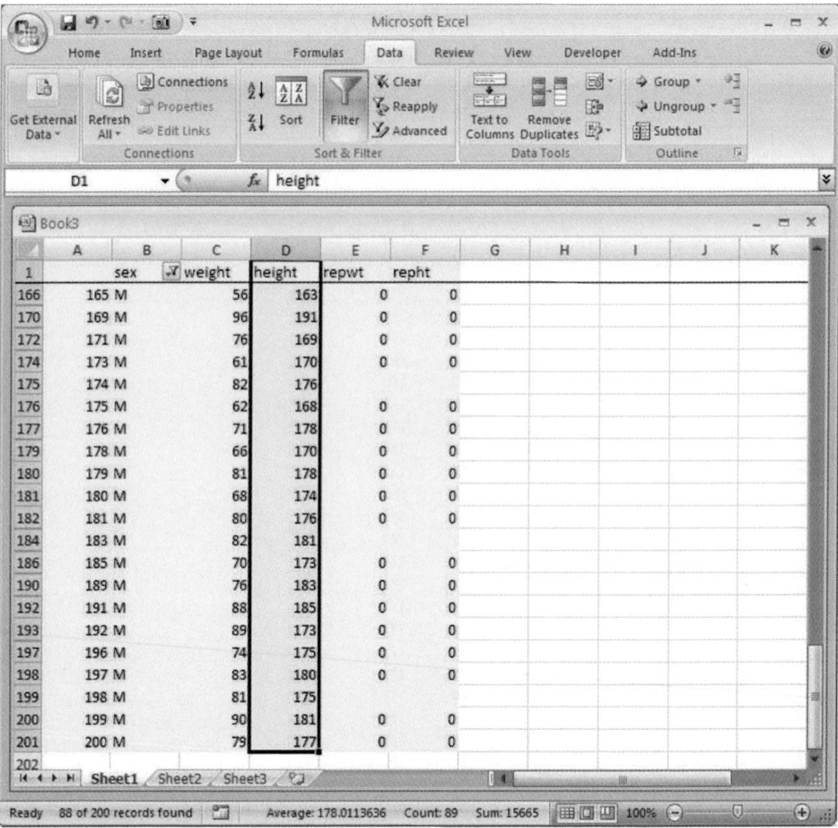

Fig. 6.36 The top row is now always visible. Put the cursor on cell D1 (the variable name for height), and press Shift-Control-↓ to highlight the height column (of only male heights).

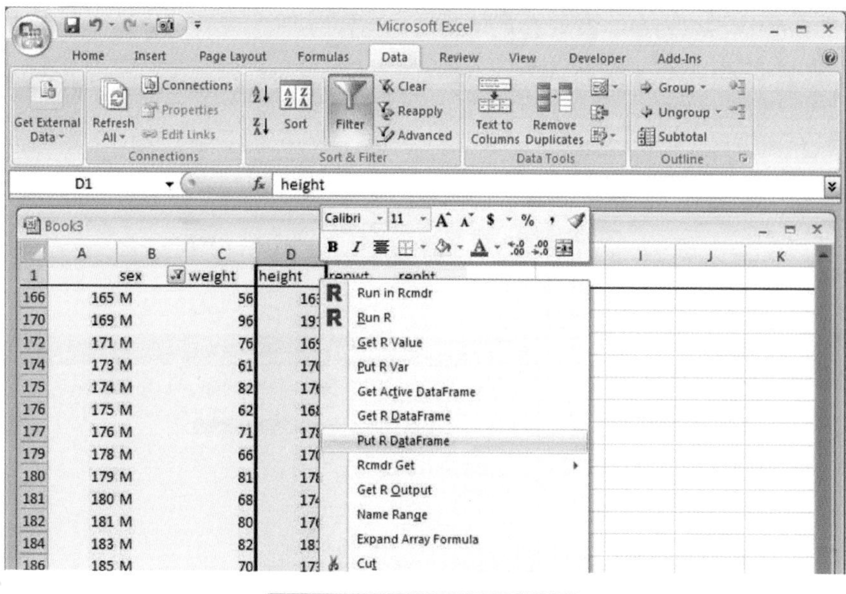

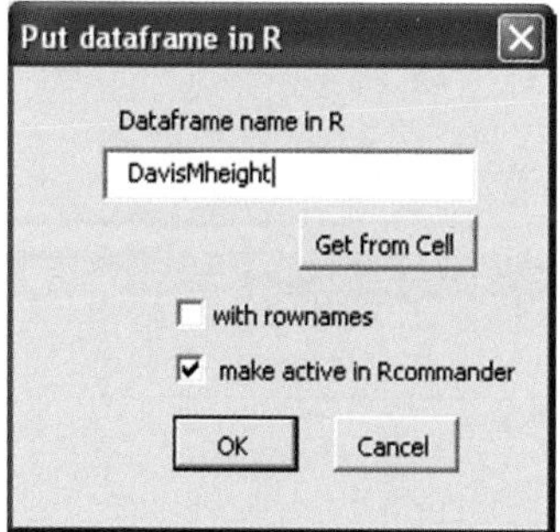

Fig. 6.37 Right-click Put R DataFrame. Enter the dataframe name DavisMheight. This dialog box constructs a dataframe in R consisting of the male heights and makes it the active dataset in the Rcmdr window. All menu items on the Rcmdr menu refer to variables that are columns in the active dataframe.

6.2.4 One-Sample t-Test for Males

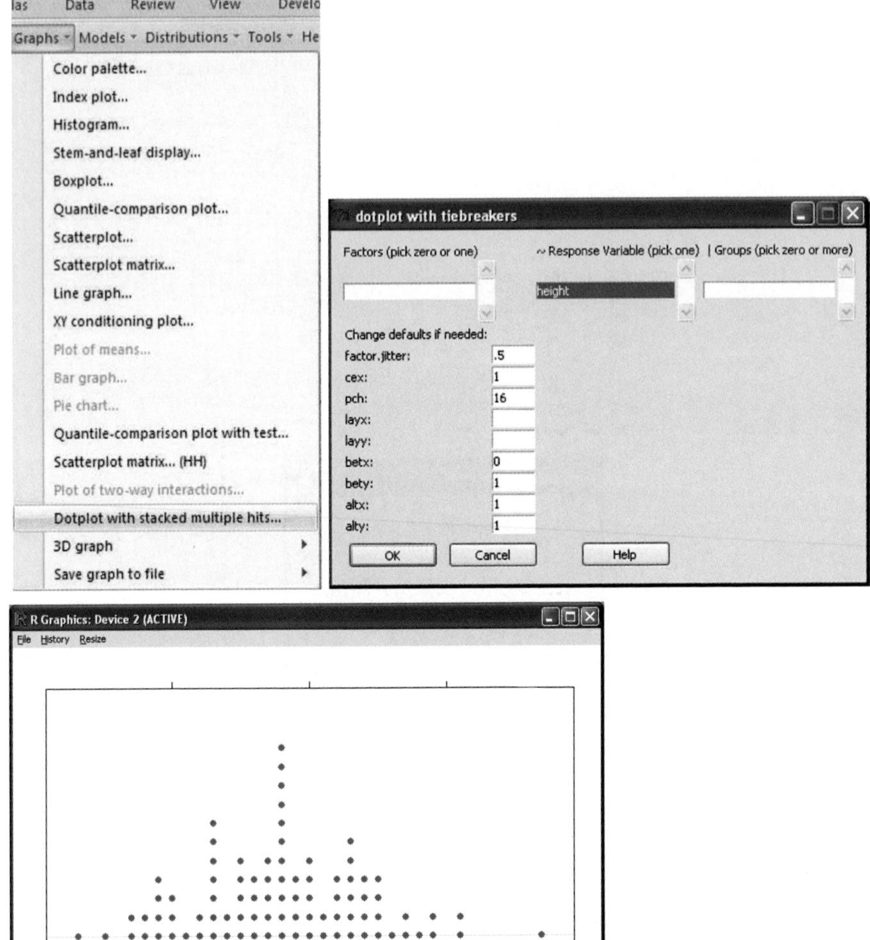

Fig. 6.38 Dotplot of the male heights.

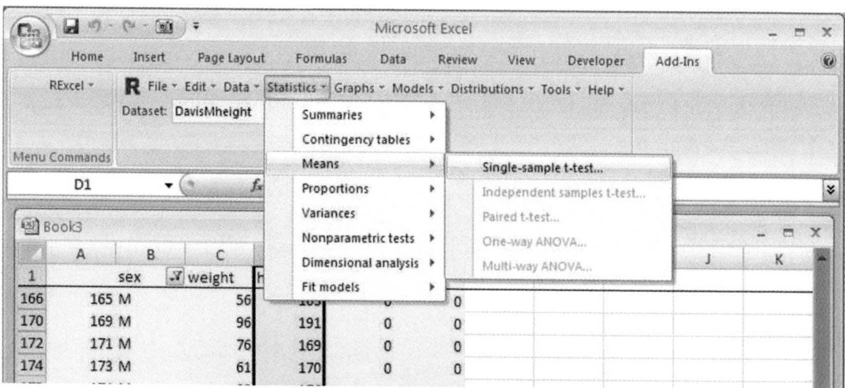

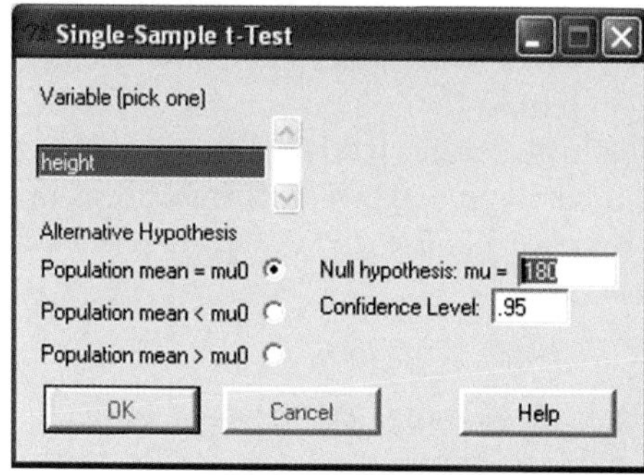

Fig. 6.39 We are ready to do the arithmetic of the t-test of the null hypothesis $H_0\colon \mu = 180$. Use the Statistics ▸ Means ▸ Single-sample t-test... menu item. Fill in the Null hypothesis: mu=180 and accept the other defaults.

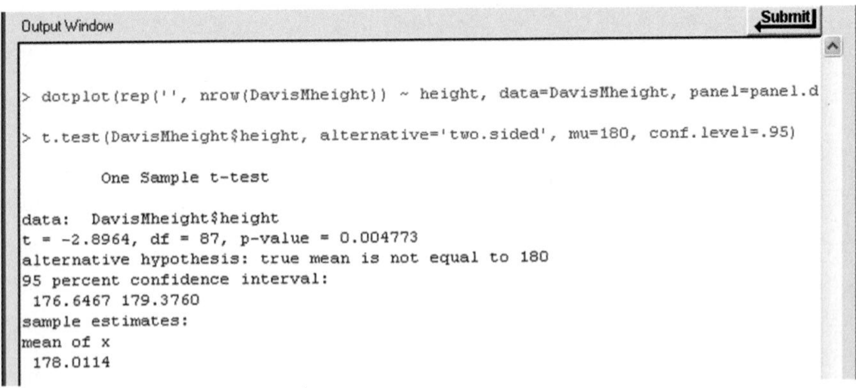
Output Window
Submit
```
> dotplot(rep('', nrow(DavisMheight)) ~ height, data=DavisMheight, panel=panel.d

> t.test(DavisMheight$height, alternative='two.sided', mu=180, conf.level=.95)

        One Sample t-test

data:  DavisMheight$height
t = -2.8964, df = 87, p-value = 0.004773
alternative hypothesis: true mean is not equal to 180
95 percent confidence interval:
 176.6467 179.3760
sample estimates:
mean of x
 178.0114
```

Fig. 6.40 The output answers two distinct questions. Usually, only one of them is meaningful in a problem setting.

The t-value -2.8964 with p-value 0.004773 answers the question about the null hypothesis. Since the observed $p = 0.004773$ is much less than the α level of the test (not stated here, so we usually use $\alpha = 0.05$), we reject the null hypothesis.

The confidence interval is

$$95\%\text{CI}(\mu) = (176.6467, 179.3760)$$

This answers the question about estimating the value of the true mean of the population from which the data was drawn.

6.2.5 Two-Sample t-Test Comparing Males and Females

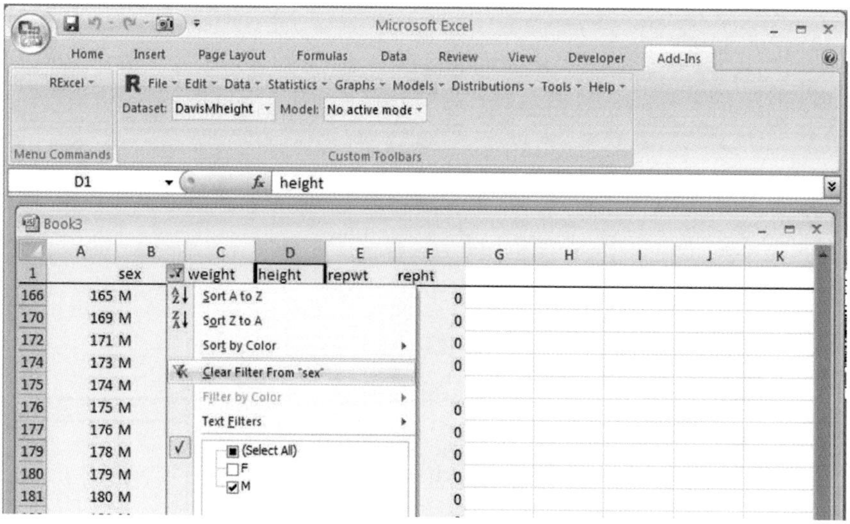

Fig. 6.41 Clear the filter by clicking on the filter arrow.

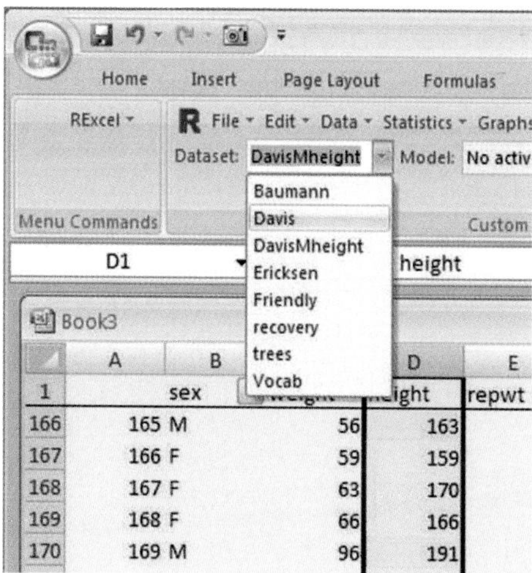

Fig. 6.42 Click the dropdown Dataset box, and restore Davis as the active dataset.

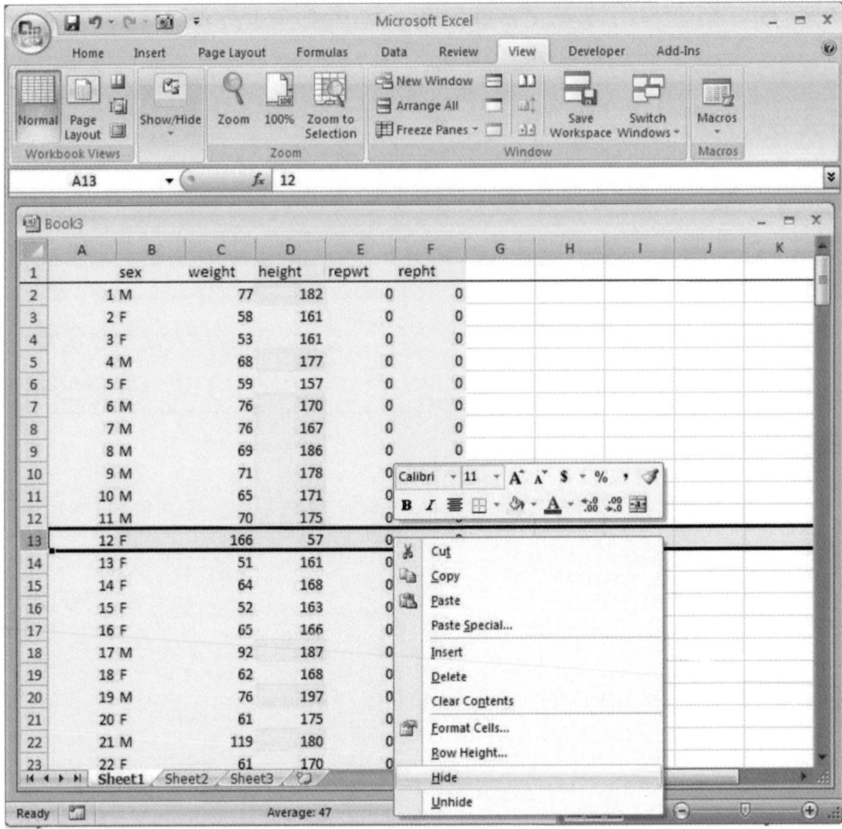

Fig. 6.43 Click the row (in the row number area) containing the anomalous observation and right-click Hide.

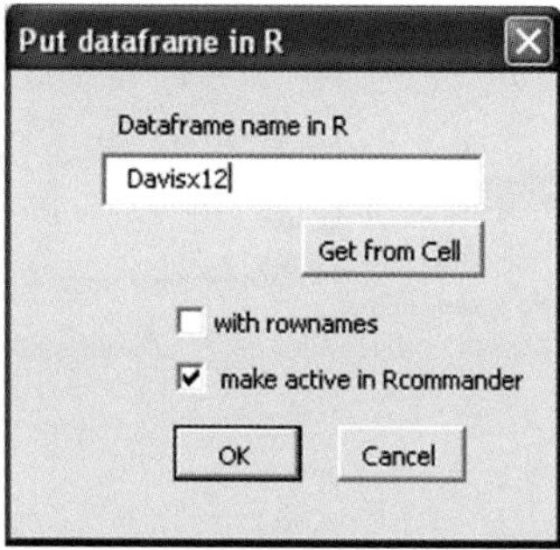

Fig. 6.44 Highlight the dataset with the hidden row in Excel using Shift-Control-* and right-click Put R DataFrame. Name it Davisx12. All menu items on the Rcmdr menu refer to variables that are columns in the active dataframe.

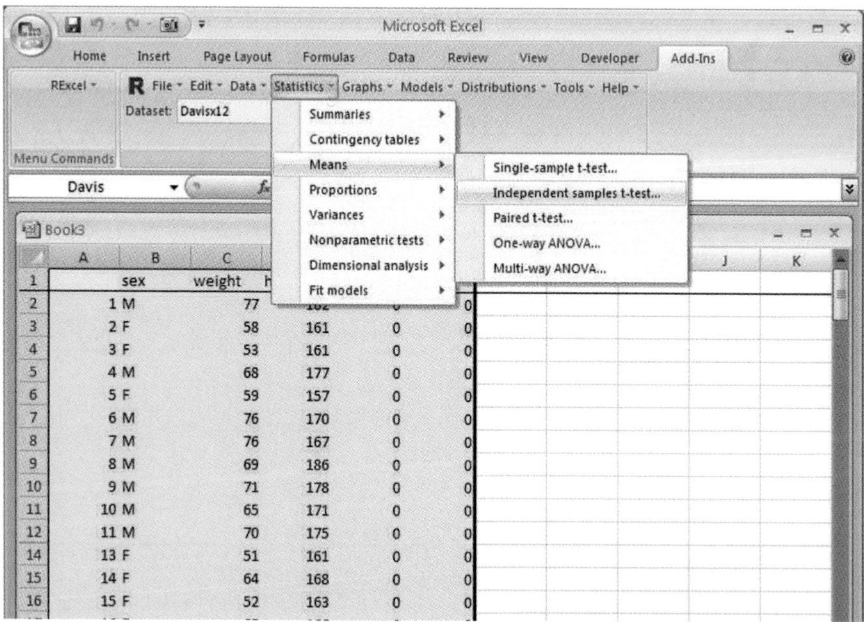

Fig. 6.45 The anomalous row is now hidden in the Davisx12 dataset. Note that the row numbers go from 12 directly to 14. The height variable contains heights for both males and females. The groups are distinguished by the value of the sex variable. We specify the independent samples t-test with the Statistics ► Means ► Independent samples t-test... menu item.

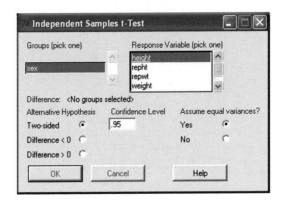

Fig. 6.46 Specify the Response variable as height and the Groups variable as sex. We take the default alternative hypothesis as Two-sided, the default 95% confidence level, and check Yes to use the equal-variances formulas. Click OK.

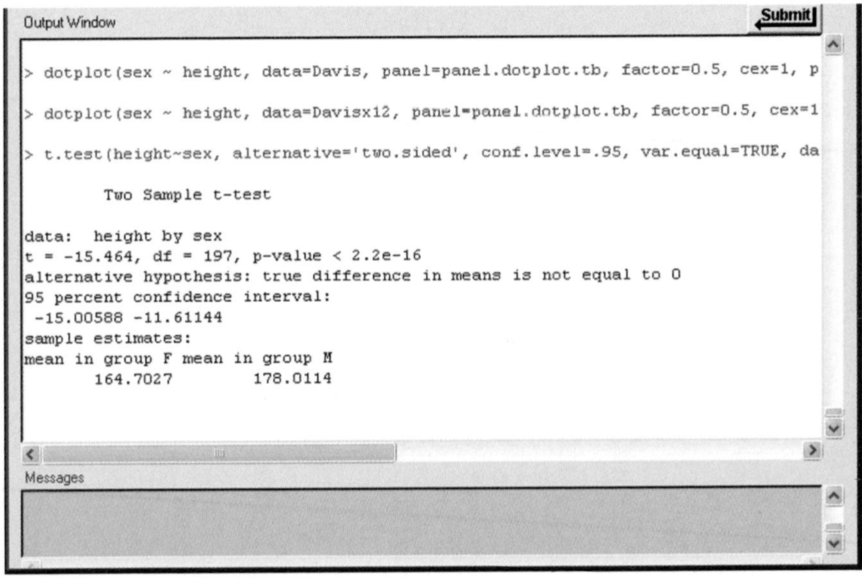


```
> dotplot(sex ~ height, data=Davis, panel=panel.dotplot.tb, factor=0.5, cex=1, p

> dotplot(sex ~ height, data=Davisx12, panel=panel.dotplot.tb, factor=0.5, cex=1

> t.test(height~sex, alternative='two.sided', conf.level=.95, var.equal=TRUE, da

        Two Sample t-test

data:  height by sex
t = -15.464, df = 197, p-value < 2.2e-16
alternative hypothesis: true difference in means is not equal to 0
95 percent confidence interval:
 -15.00588 -11.61144
sample estimates:
mean in group F mean in group M
       164.7027        178.0114
```

Fig. 6.47 The t-test output is in the Output Window of the Rcmdr window. Two different questions are answered in the output listing.

The test of the null hypotheses $H_0\colon \mu_F = \mu_M$ vs the alternative hypothesis $H_0\colon \mu_F \neq \mu_M$ has $t = -15.464$ with $p < 2.2 \times 10^{-16}$. We can reject the null hypothesis.

The 95% confidence interval for the difference of the population means is given by the interval $(-15.00588, -11.61144)$.

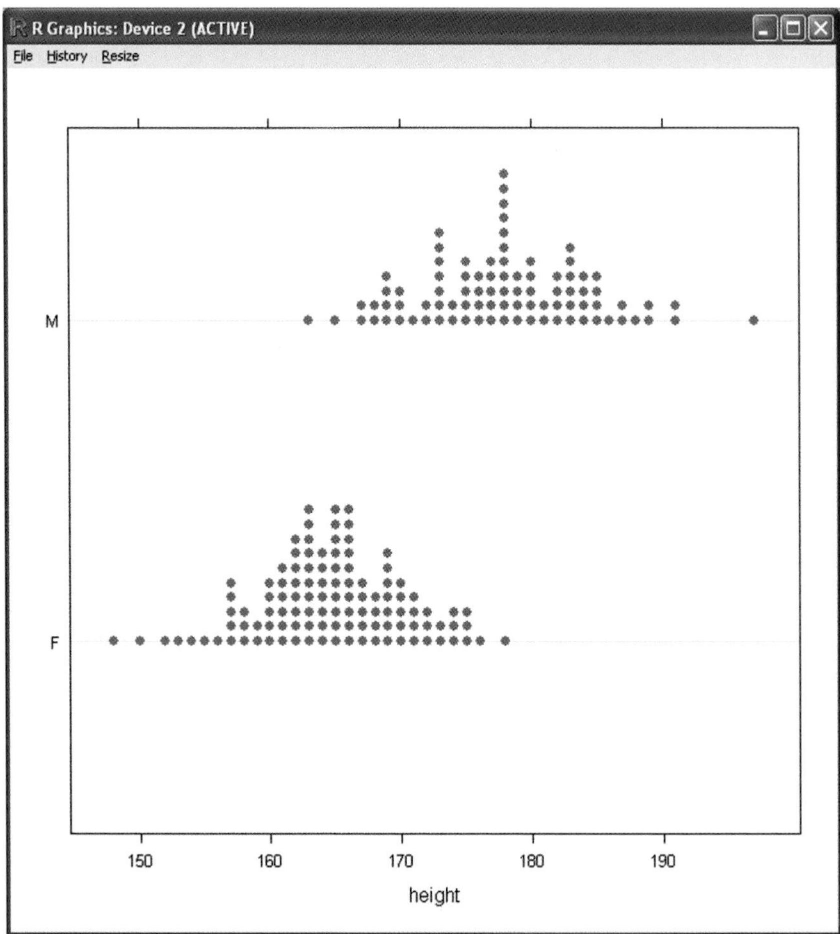

Fig. 6.48 Draw the same plot as in Figs. 6.24 and 6.25 to get this figure. Now we see clearly that the male population has a distribution with a higher mean than the female population.

6.3 Matched Pairs t-Test

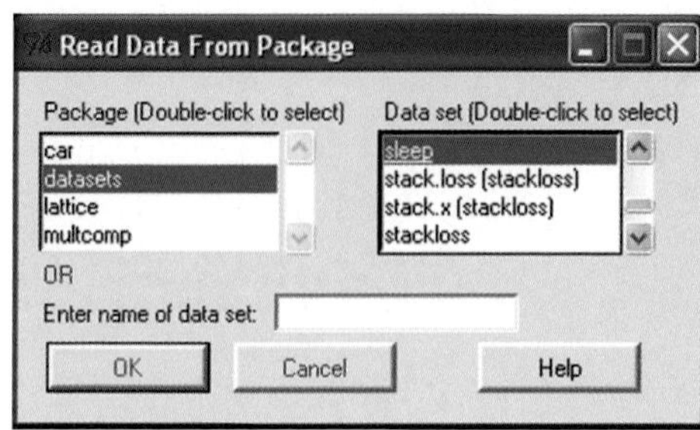

Fig. 6.49 We will look at the sleep dataset to study matched pairs. The dataset shows the effect of two soporific drugs (measured as increase in hours of sleep compared to control) on 10 patients. Each subject was measured twice, once on each of the drugs. We are interested in the difference between the two drugs.

On the Rcmdr menu, click the

Data ► Data in packages ► Read data set from an attached package...

menu item to open this dialog box. Double-click the package datasets and the dataset sleep. Click OK.

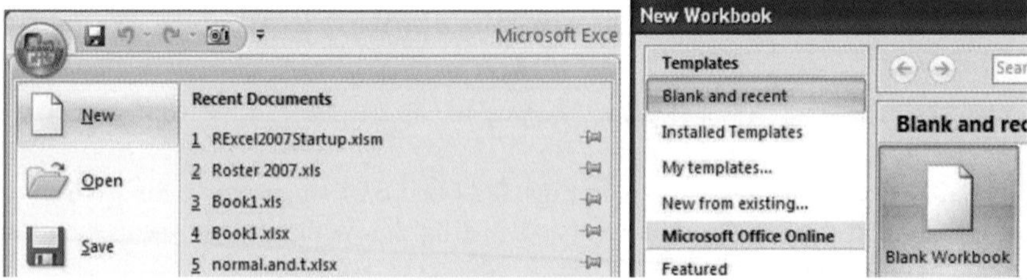

Fig. 6.50 Open a new Excel workbook in which to display the data.

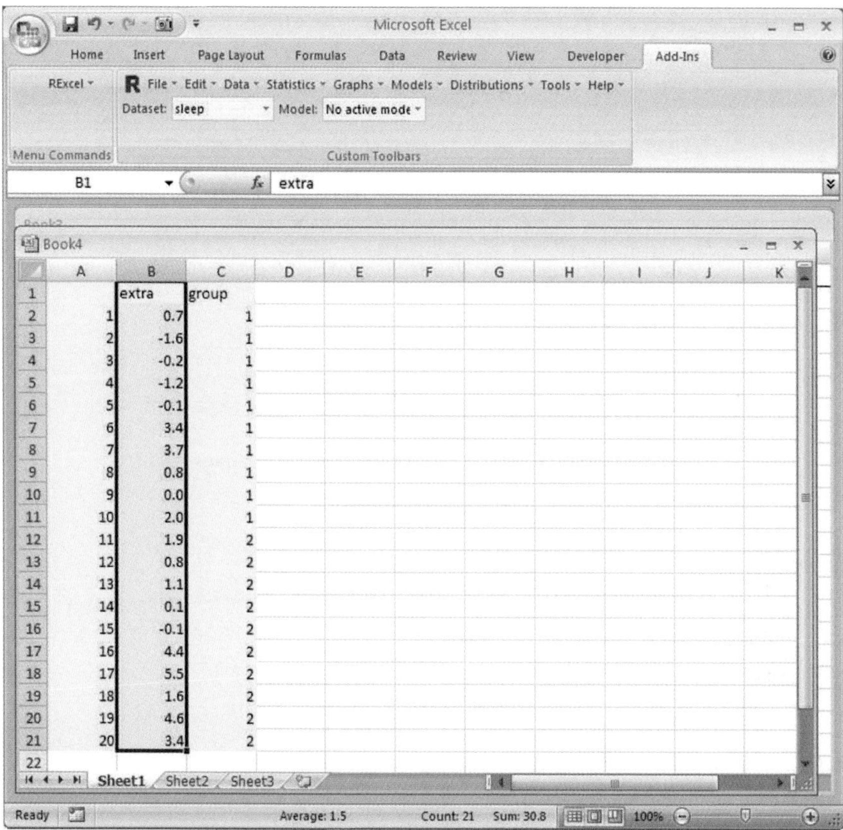

Fig. 6.51 In the new workbook, place the cursor in cell A1 and right-click Get Active DataFrame to bring the data into Excel. The default format for the extra column was unaligned. Therefore, we aligned it to one decimal position with the right-click Prettyformat Numbers menu item.

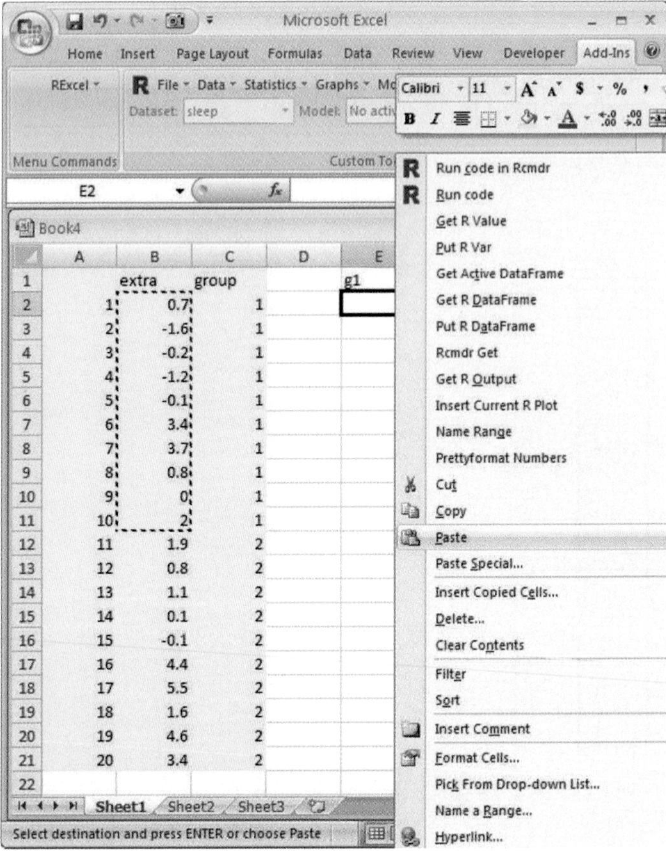

Fig. 6.52 It is usually easier to work with paired data when it is stored in a wide format, as in Section 3.5. The individual subjects in the study take the role of the factor used in the illustration in Section 3.5. We reshape it manually. In cell E1, type the new column name g1. Then highlight the first group of data in cells B2:B11, copy it with right-click Copy, and paste it into a block beginning in cell E2. Similarly, copy cells B12:B21 into cells F2:F11 to get Fig. 6.53.

a. Enter formula.

Book4

	A	B	C	D	E	F	G
1		extra	group		g1	g2	g1mg2
2	1	0.7	1		0.7	1.9	=E2-F2
3	2	-1.6	1		-1.6	0.8	
4	3	-0.2	1		-0.2	1.1	
5	4	-1.2	1		-1.2	0.1	
6	5	-0.1	1		-0.1	-0.1	
7	6	3.4	1		3.4	4.4	
8	7	3.7	1		3.7	5.5	
9	8	0.8	1		0.8	1.6	
10	9	0.0	1		0.0	4.6	
11	10	2.0	1		2.0	3.4	
12	11	1.9	2				
13	12	0.8	2				
14	13	1.1	2				
15	14	0.1	2				
16	15	-0.1	2				
17	16	4.4	2				
18	17	5.5	2				
19	18	1.6	2				
20	19	4.6	2				
21	20	3.4	2				
22							

Sheet1 Sheet2 Sheet3

b. Pull down fill handle.

E	F	G
g1	g2	g1mg2
0.7	1.9	-1.2
-1.6	0.8	-2.4
-0.2	1.1	-1.3
-1.2	0.1	-1.3
-0.1	-0.1	0.0
3.4	4.4	-1.0
3.7	5.5	-1.8
0.8	1.6	-0.8
0.0	4.6	-4.6
2.0	3.4	-1.4

c. Add id variable.

E	F	G	H
g1	g2	g1mg2	id
0.7	1.9	-1.2	1
-1.6	0.8	-2.4	2
-0.2	1.1	-1.3	3
-1.2	0.1	-1.3	4
-0.1	-0.1	0.0	5
3.4	4.4	-1.0	6
3.7	5.5	-1.8	7
0.8	1.6	-0.8	8
0.0	4.6	-4.6	9
2.0	3.4	-1.4	10

Fig. 6.53 With paired data, we are usually interested in computing a difference value for each pair. We use Excel's arithmetic for the differences. In Panel a, enter the command =E2-F2 in cell G2. In the Panel b, we grab the fill handle of cell G2 and drag it down to G11. Together, these steps produce column G in Panel c. The difference column g1mg2 has mostly negative values with one zero value. In Panel c, we add an id variable in column H to use as an explanatory variable in the plot to be defined in Figs. 6.54 and 6.55 We right-click Put R DataFrame the highlighted region E1:H11 with the name sleep2col.

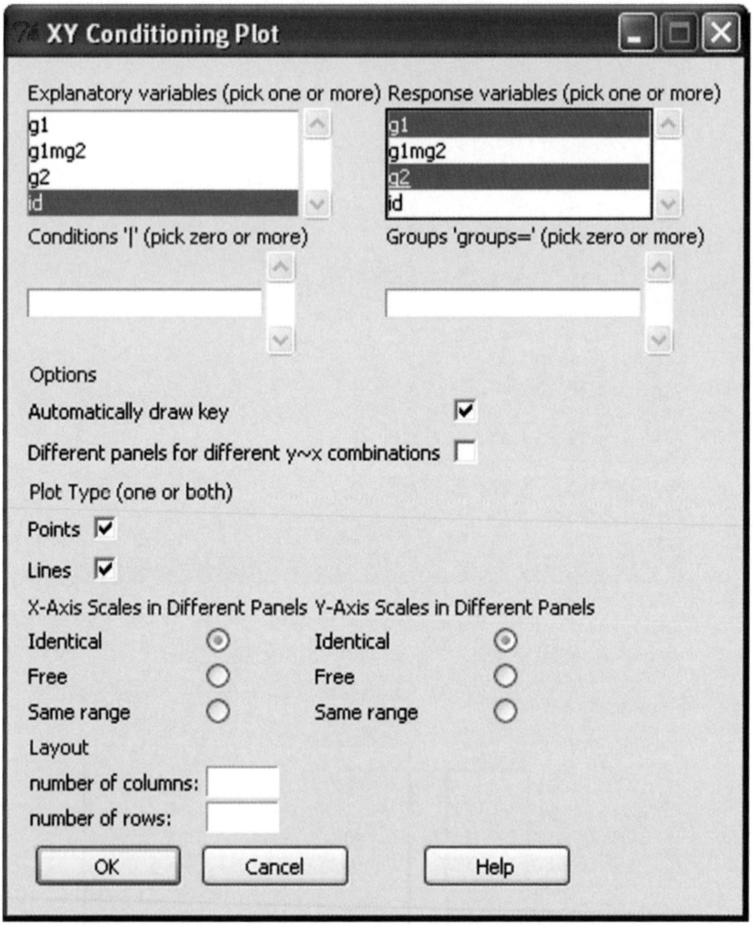

Fig. 6.54 We plot both obervations on the vertical axis against the id on the horizontal axis. Use the Graphs ► XY Conditioning Plot... (HH) menu item to get the dialog box. Specify id as the explanatory variable and both g1 and g1 as response variables (use control-click for the second variable). Check both Points and Lines. This produces Fig. 6.55.

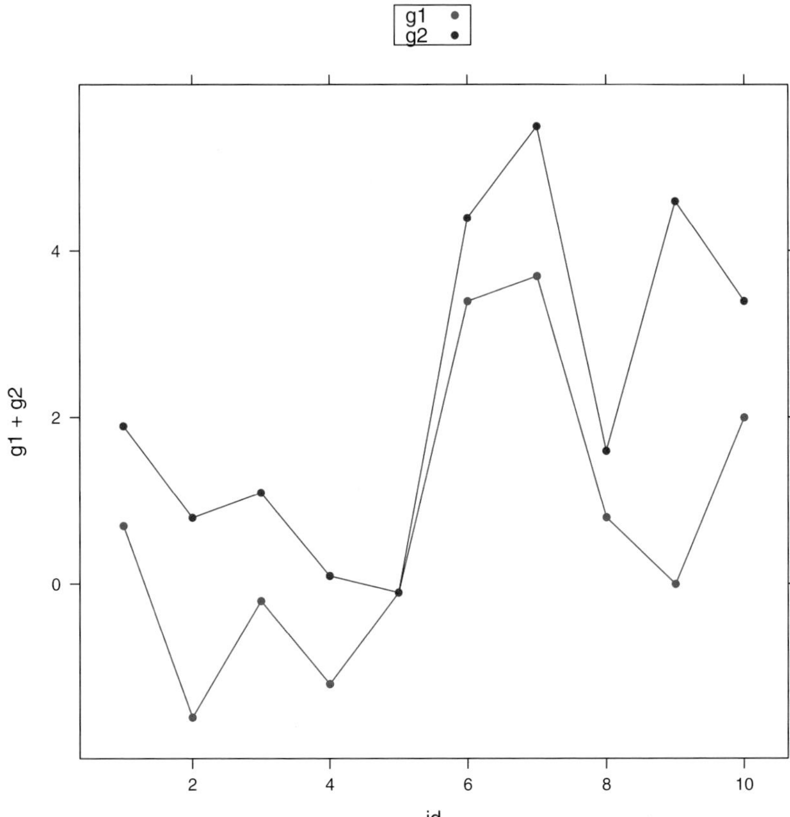

Fig. 6.55 This plot is specified by the dialog box in Fig. 6.54. This dataset is grouped by id, with each id measured at both group = 1 and group = 2. For almost every id, group 2 (the red circles) has a higher value on the vertical axis (variable extra in the original dataset) than does group 1 (the blue circles).

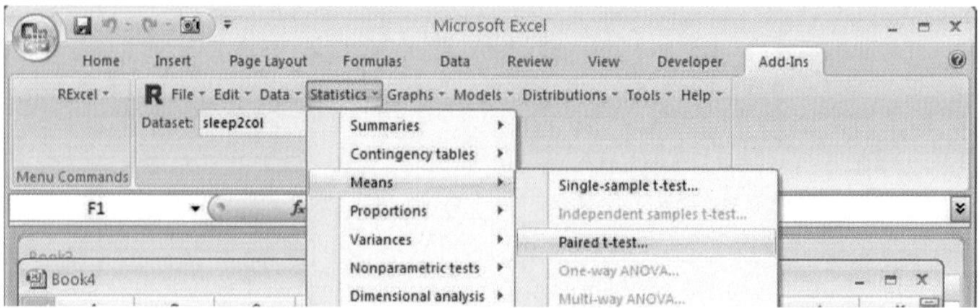

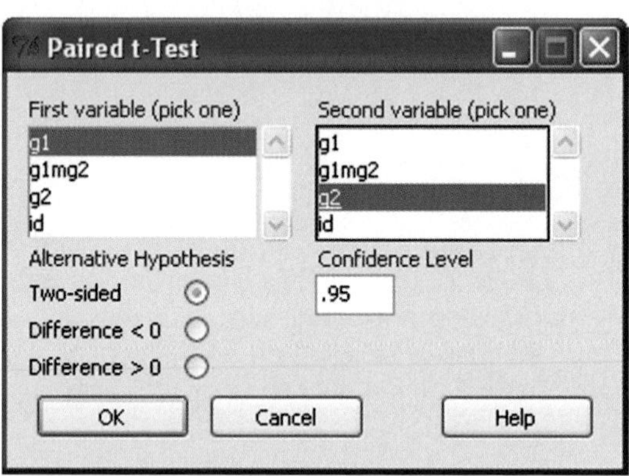

Fig. 6.56 Specify the paired t-test of the variables g1 and g2.

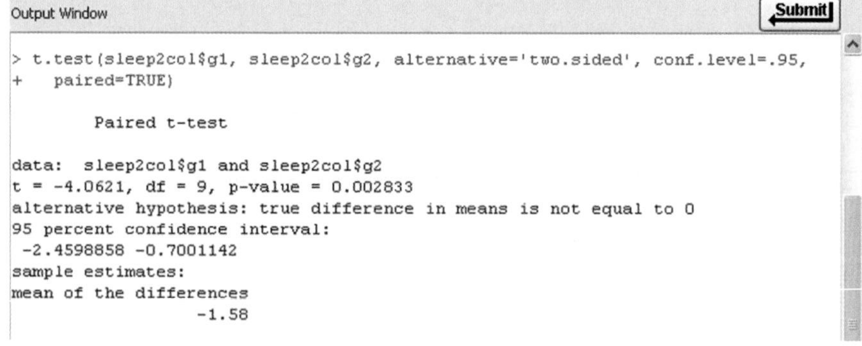

Fig. 6.57 The null hypothesis that the differences of the pairs have mean 0 is rejected with a p-value of 0.002833.

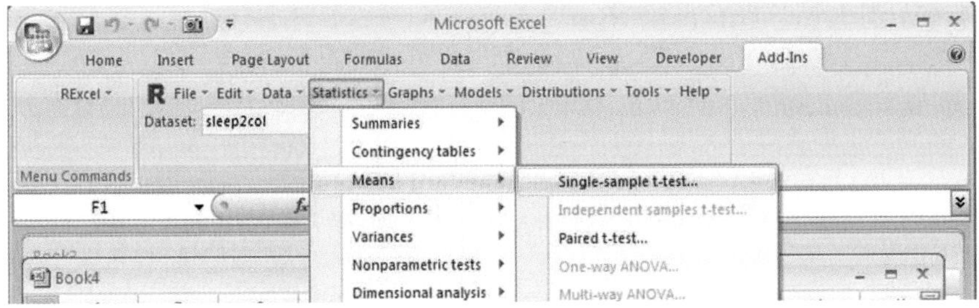

Single-Sample t-Test

Variable (pick one)

g1
g1mg2
g2
id

Alternative Hypothesis

Population mean = mu0 Null hypothesis: mu = 0.0

Population mean < mu0 Confidence Level: .95

Population mean > mu0

OK Cancel Help

Fig. 6.58 Specify the single-sample t-test of the difference g1mg2 = g1 − g2. The t-values and p-values in Fig. 6.59 are identical to those in Fig. 6.57.

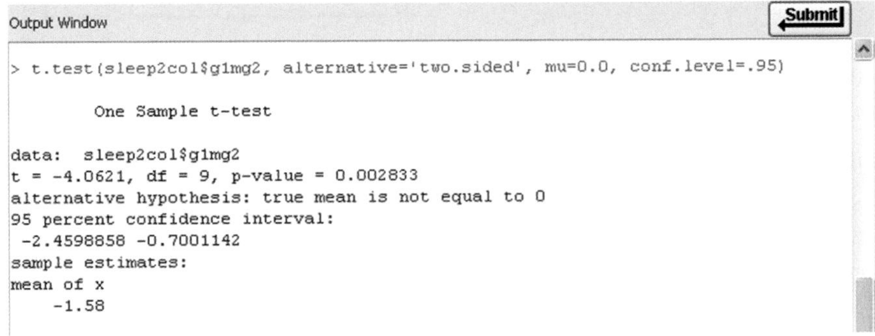
Output Window

Submit

```
> t.test(sleep2col$g1mg2, alternative='two.sided', mu=0.0, conf.level=.95)

        One Sample t-test

data:  sleep2col$g1mg2
t = -4.0621, df = 9, p-value = 0.002833
alternative hypothesis: true mean is not equal to 0
95 percent confidence interval:
 -2.4598858 -0.7001142
sample estimates:
mean of x
    -1.58
```

Fig. 6.59 The null hypothesis that the set of differences of the pairs have mean 0 is rejected with a p-value of 0.002833.

6.4 Confidence Interval Plot

Problem statement:

We have an observed $\bar{x} = 10$ and sample standard deviation $s = 4$ from a sample of size $n = 18$. Display a 95% two-sided confidence interval for estimating the population mean.

6.4.1 *Confidence Intervals with the* normal and t *Worksheet*

The normal.and.t.dist worksheet introduced in Chapter 5 allows us to explore the Normal and t distributions dynamically. Open the worksheet by clicking on RExcel ► RthroughExcel.Worksheets (as shown in Fig. 5.1) and then click on normal.and.t.

normal.and.t.xlsm

	A	B	C	D	E	F	G	H	I	J	K
1			Show					95% conf limits		probability	
2	Optional user input		Slider		on Graph			left	right	two-sided	observation
3	μ_0	0	☐		Display		$s_{\bar{x}}$				0.943
4	μ_1	0	☐				$\bar{x}$ scale	8.011	11.989		10
5	$\bar{x}$	10	☑		Display		t scale	-2.110	2.110		0.000
6	s	4					1-Confidence	0.025	0.025	0.050	
7	n	18					confidence level			0.950	
8	v	17									
9											
10	☑ α left	☑ α right	α:	○ prob or hypoth							
11	0.025	0.025	0.050	● confidence interval							
12											
13	☑ α left from right scrollbar?										
14											
15	Optional user-specified										
16	display parameters										
17	z.range										
18	x.min	7.15	Copy current x range								
19	x.max	12.85									
20	f(x) min		Copy current f(x) range							☑ graph on Top	
21	f(x) max									Reset	

prob and hypoth

Fig. 6.60 On the normal.and.t worksheet, set the values for $\bar{x} = 10, s = 4, n = 18, \nu = 17$, check α left, α right, and α left from right scrollbar?, slide the α right scrollbar to 0.25, and check confidence interval. This specification is sufficient to illustrate the problem statement. To scale the graph in Fig. 6.61 to exactly match the specification in the dialog box in Fig. 6.62, we also set horizontal min to 7.15 and horizontal max to 12.85.

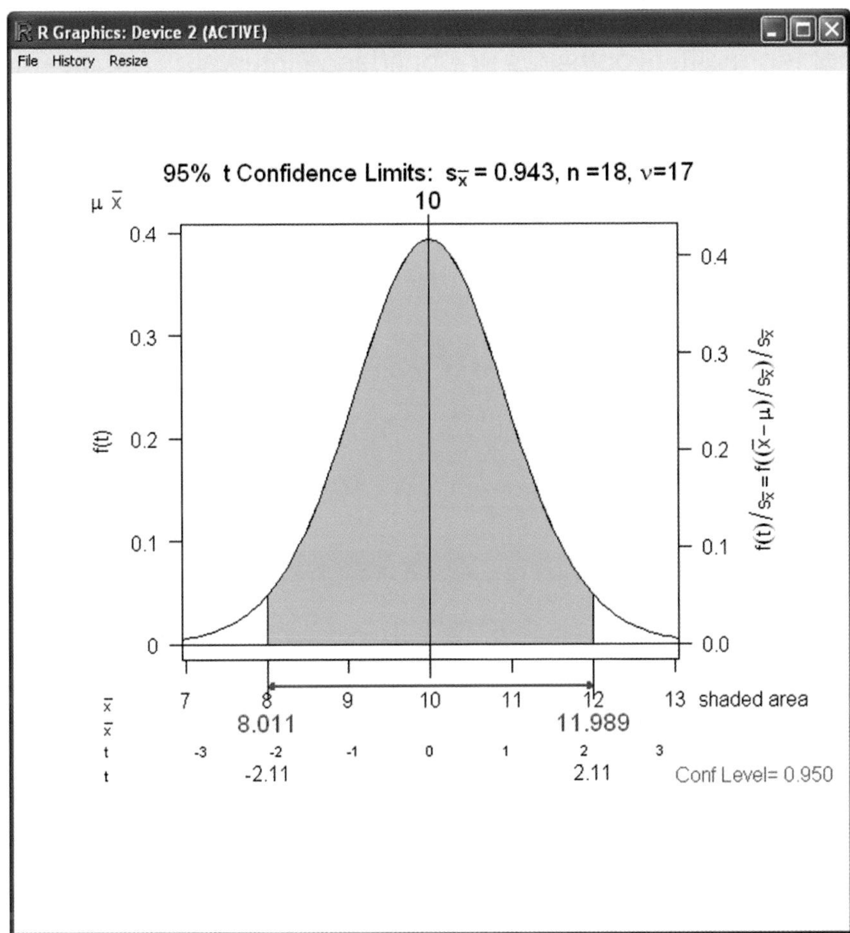

Fig. 6.61 The graph is centered at $\bar{x} = 10$, with the central 95% of the area colored green to show the confidence level (Conf Level = 0.950). The confidence interval (8.011, 11.989) is indicated with a double-headed arrow as the range of the $\bar{x}$-axis between the lower (LCL = 8.011) and upper (UCL = 11.989) confidence limits. This graph can be specified with either the worksheet in Fig. 6.60 or the dialog box in Fig. 6.62.

6.4.2 *Confidence Intervals with the* Plot [normal|t] hypotheses or Confidence Intervals... *Menus*

The Plot hypotheses or Confidence Intervals... (HH) menu is accessible from either the normal or t distribution menus.

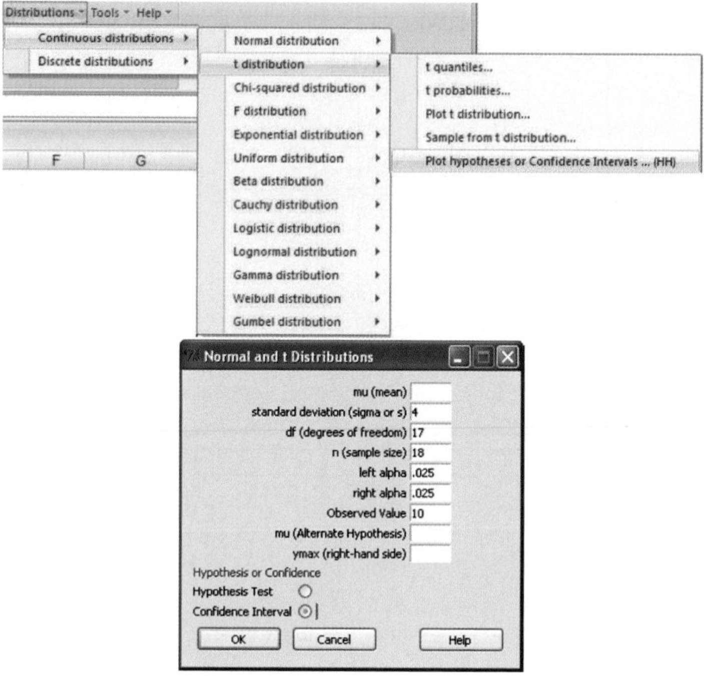

Fig. 6.62 On the Rcmdr menu, click

Distributions ► Continuous distributions ► t distribution ► Plot hypotheses or Confidence Intervals... (HH)

to get the dialog box for the Normal and t distribution plot. Fill in the numerical values from the problem specification or, in other examples, from the summary information. Check Confidence Interval. This specification is another way to produce the graph in Fig. 6.61.

6.5 Hypothesis Plot and Confidence Interval Plot from Summary Information

We continue with the example in Fig. 6.31. The tabular summary is repeated in Fig. 6.63.

Output Window Submit

```
> numSummary(Davis[,c("height", "weight")], groups=Davis$sex, statistics=c("mean

Variable: height
      mean        sd  0% 25% 50% 75% 100%   n
F 163.7411 11.643925  57 161 165 169  178 112
M 178.0114  6.440701 163 173 178 183  197  88

Variable: weight
      mean       sd 0%   25% 50% 75% 100%   n
F 57.86607 12.38314 39 52.75  56  62  166 112
M 75.89773 11.89034 54 67.75  75  83  119  88
```

Fig. 6.63 The tabular summary of the Davis height and weight data is repeated from Fig. 6.31. The mean, standard deviation, and sample size for both variables, grouped by sex, are shown. A two-sided, one-sample t-test for this data is shown in Fig. 6.40. We will construct a t hypothesis plot of the male heights using the summary information.

6.5.1 Hypothesis Plots with the Plot hypotheses and Confidence Intervals *Menu and Workbook*

The Plot hypotheses or Confidence Intervals... (HH) menu and dialog box are accessible from either the normal or t distribution menus. The dialog box, for a normal distribution with α on the right, is illustrated in Figs. 4.18 and 4.19.

The Excel Workbook normal.and.t was introduced in Chapter 5.

The illustrations in this section show how to use both the dialog boxes and the normal.and.t workbook to illustrate a two-sided t-test and the two-sided t-confidence interval using summary information that was previously calculated.

6.5.2 Hypothesis Plot

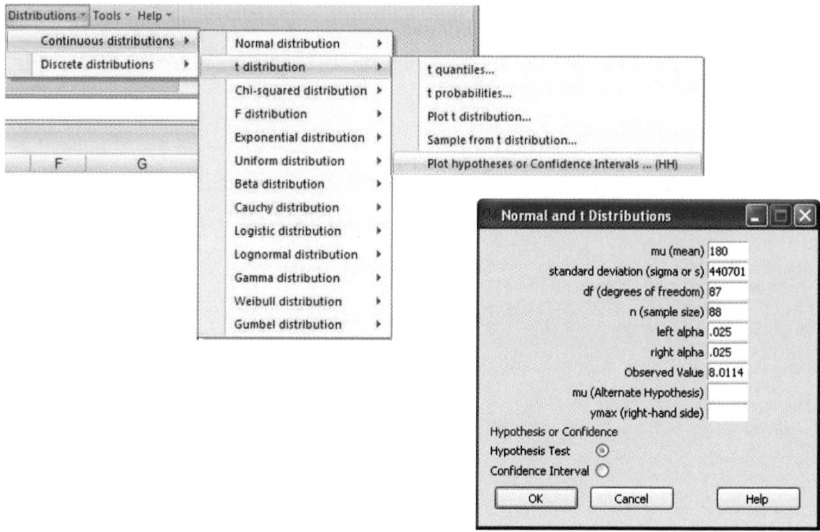

Fig. 6.64 Menu and dialog box specification of Fig. 6.66 using the summary information in Fig. 6.63.

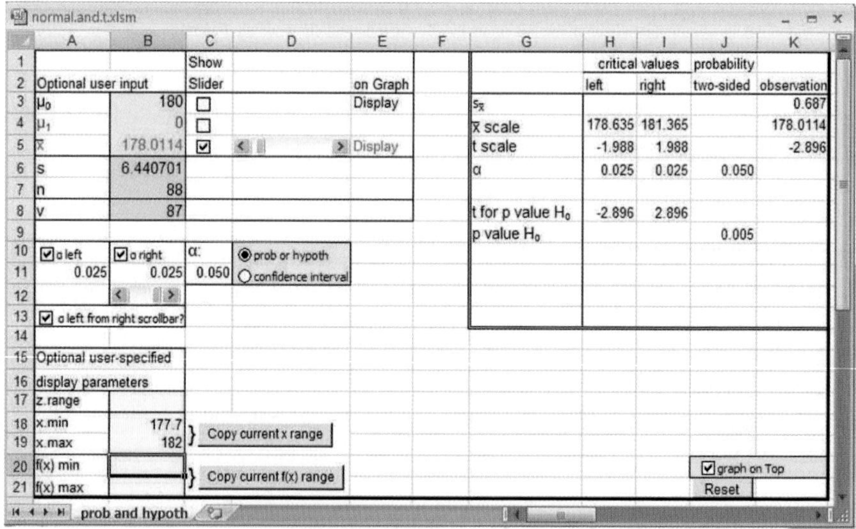

Fig. 6.65 Workbook specification of Fig. 6.66 using the summary information in Fig. 6.63. The horizontal min and horizontal max values are there solely to make the scaling identical to the scaling from the dialog box.

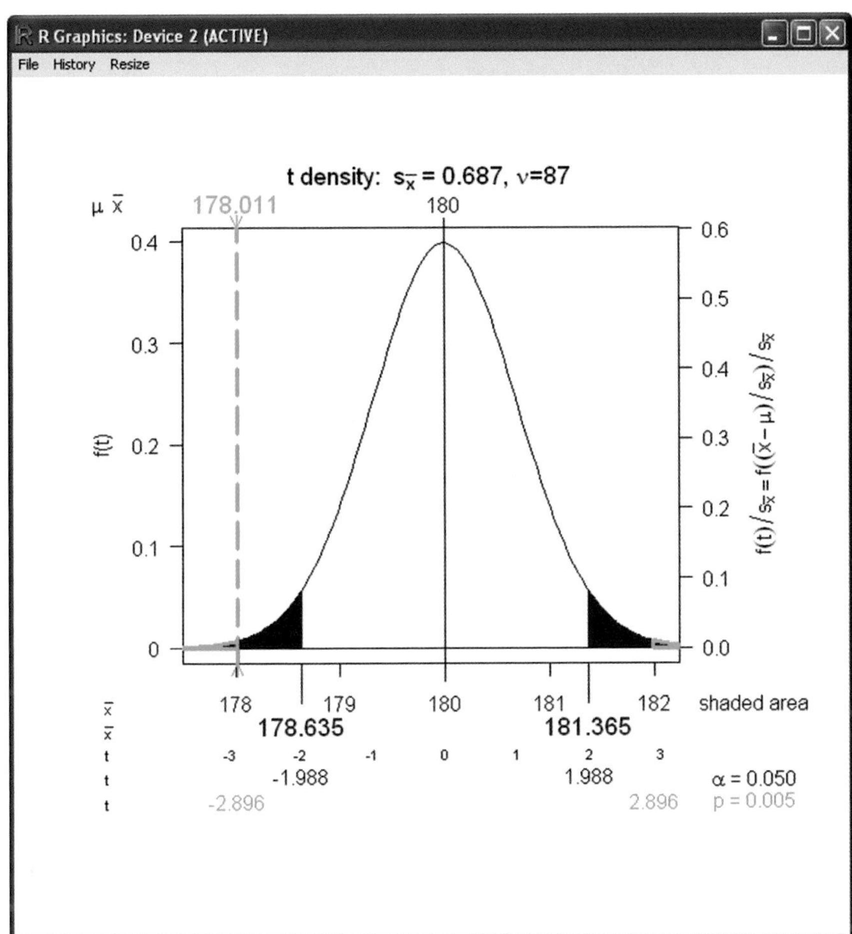

Fig. 6.66 This figure is produced by either Fig. 6.64 or 6.65. The observed value $\bar{x} = 178.011$ is in the left rejection region. The p-value ($p = 0.005$) is calculated from both the left green-outlined area and the right green-outlined area. The critical values for the test are displayed in large blue $\bar{x}$ units and in smaller black t_{87} units. The observed $t = -2.896$ agrees with the value we saw in Fig. 6.40.

6.5.3 Confidence Interval Plot

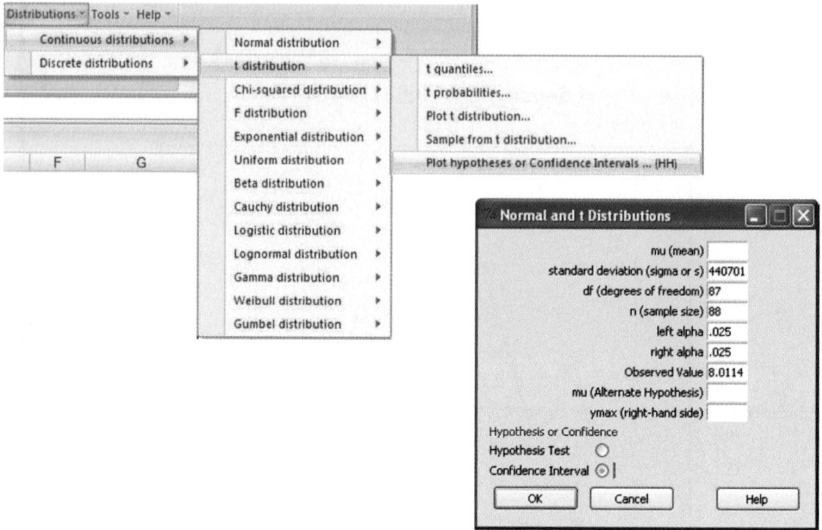

Fig. 6.67 Menu and dialog box specification of Fig. 6.69 using the summary information in Fig. 6.63.

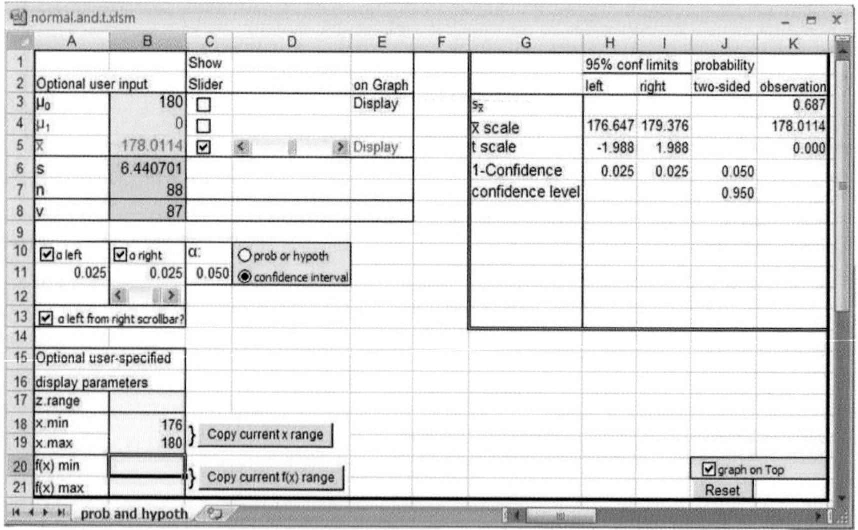

Fig. 6.68 Workbook specification of Fig. 6.69 using the summary information in Fig. 6.63. The horizontal min and horizontal max values are there solely to make the scaling identical to the scaling from the dialog box.

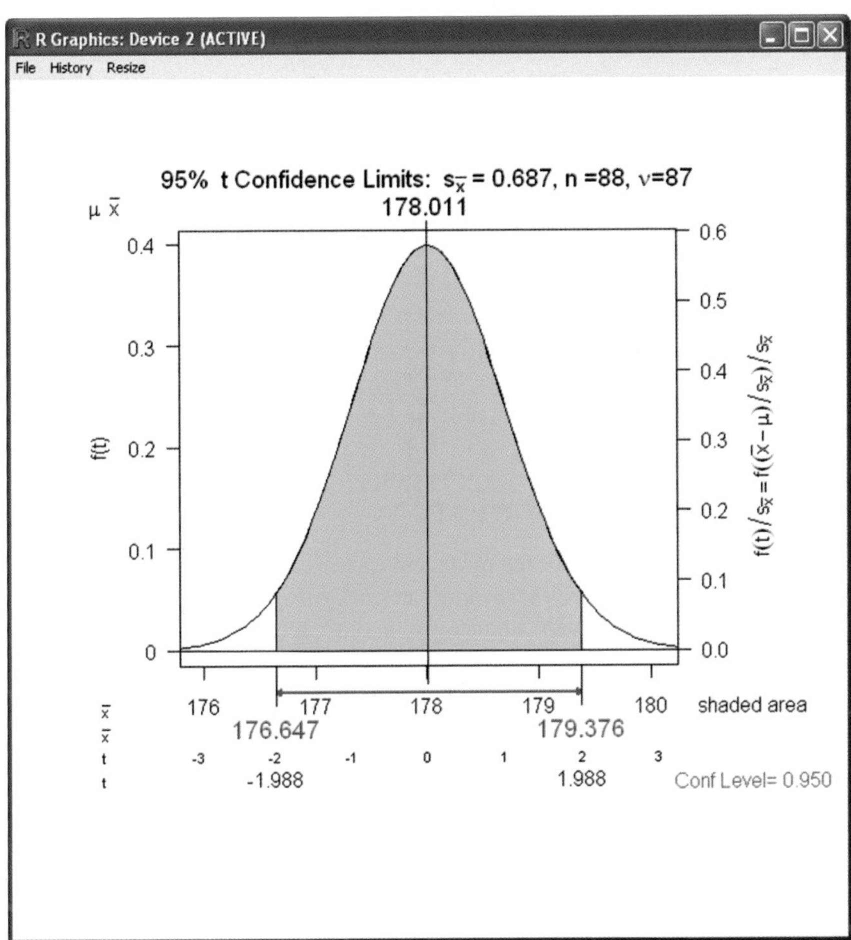

Fig. 6.69 This figure is produced by either Fig. 6.67 or 6.68. The confidence interval, indicated by the horizontal two-headed arrow, is centered on the observed value $\bar{x} = 178.011$. The green shading has area equal to the confidence level 0.95 = 95%. The lower and upper bounds of the confidence interval (176.647, 179.376) are displayed in large green $\bar{x}$ units and in smaller black t_{87} units. The confidence bounds agree with the values we found in Fig. 6.40.

6.6 Alternate Styles for the Calculation of Confidence Intervals

The t-test dialog box and the normal and t worksheets can be used in many apparently different situations, as illustrated in earlier sections. In this section, we show the reason that these situations all lead to the same graph is that they are fundamentally variations on the same formula. For specificity, we do so with an example of a two-sample normal test of the differences of two means.

Assume X and Y are normally distributed random variables with means

	Mean	Standard deviation	Variance	Sample size
X	$\mu_X = 18$	$\sigma_X = 3$	$\sigma_X^2 = 3^2 = 9$	$n_X = 10$
Y	$\mu_Y = 15$	$\sigma_Y = 3$	$\sigma_Y^2 = 3^2 = 9$	$n_Y = 10$

Calculate the probability that $\bar{X} > \bar{Y}$, $P(\bar{X} > \bar{Y})$.

We use the basic formula for the mean and variance of the sum of two independent normals. If X and Y are *independent* normally distributed random variables with means μ_X and μ_Y and with variances σ_X^2 and σ_Y^2, then

$$\mu_{X+Y} = E(X+Y) = E(X) + E(Y) = \mu_X + \mu_Y \quad (6.2)$$

$$\sigma_{X+Y}^2 = \text{var}(X+Y) = \text{var}(X) + \text{var}(Y) = \sigma_X^2 + \sigma_Y^2 \quad (6.3)$$

Note that this formula for variances is true only in the special case that X and Y are independent. The more general formula for variances has a covariance term $2\,\text{cov}(X,Y)$.

6.6.1 Recommended Style

We recommend defining and using a new symbol, W. This style simplifies the appearance of the calculation and makes it clearer how to generalize to other examples.

1. Identify the information in the problem statement.

$$\begin{aligned} \mu_X &= 18 \\ \mu_Y &= 15 \\ \sigma_X &= 3 \\ \sigma_Y &= 3 \\ n_X &= 10 \\ n_Y &= 10 \end{aligned}$$

2. Define the new variable, $W = \bar{X}_X - \bar{X}_Y$. Find the mean and standard deviation of W.
   Then, from Equation (6.2), we see

$$\begin{aligned}
\mu_W &= E(W) \\
&= E(\bar{X}_X - \bar{X}_Y) \\
&= E(\bar{X}_X) - E(\bar{X}_Y) \\
&= \mu_X - \mu_Y \\
&= 18 - 15 \\
&= 3
\end{aligned}$$

   and from Equation (6.3), we see

$$\begin{aligned}
\sigma_W^2 &= V(W) \\
&= V(\bar{X}_X - \bar{X}_Y) \\
&= V(\bar{X}_X) + V(\bar{X}_Y) + 0 \\
&= \frac{\sigma_X^2}{n_X} + \frac{\sigma_Y^2}{n_Y} \\
&= \frac{3^2}{10} + \frac{3^2}{10} \\
&= 1.8 \\
\sigma_W &= 1.341641
\end{aligned}$$

   The mean μ_W and standard deviation σ_W are used in the formula in the next step and in the dialog box in Fig. 6.70.
3. The assignment is to calculate

$$\begin{aligned}
&P(\bar{X}_X > \bar{X}_Y) \\
&= P(\bar{X}_X - \bar{X}_Y > 0) \\
&= P(W > 0)
\end{aligned}$$

   We now use the ordinary formula and dialog box, along with μ_W and σ_W, to complete the calculation.

$$\begin{aligned}
&= P\left(\frac{W - \mu_W}{\sigma_W} > \frac{0 - 3}{\sqrt{1.8}}\right) \\
&= P(Z > -2.236068) \\
&= 0.9873263
\end{aligned}$$

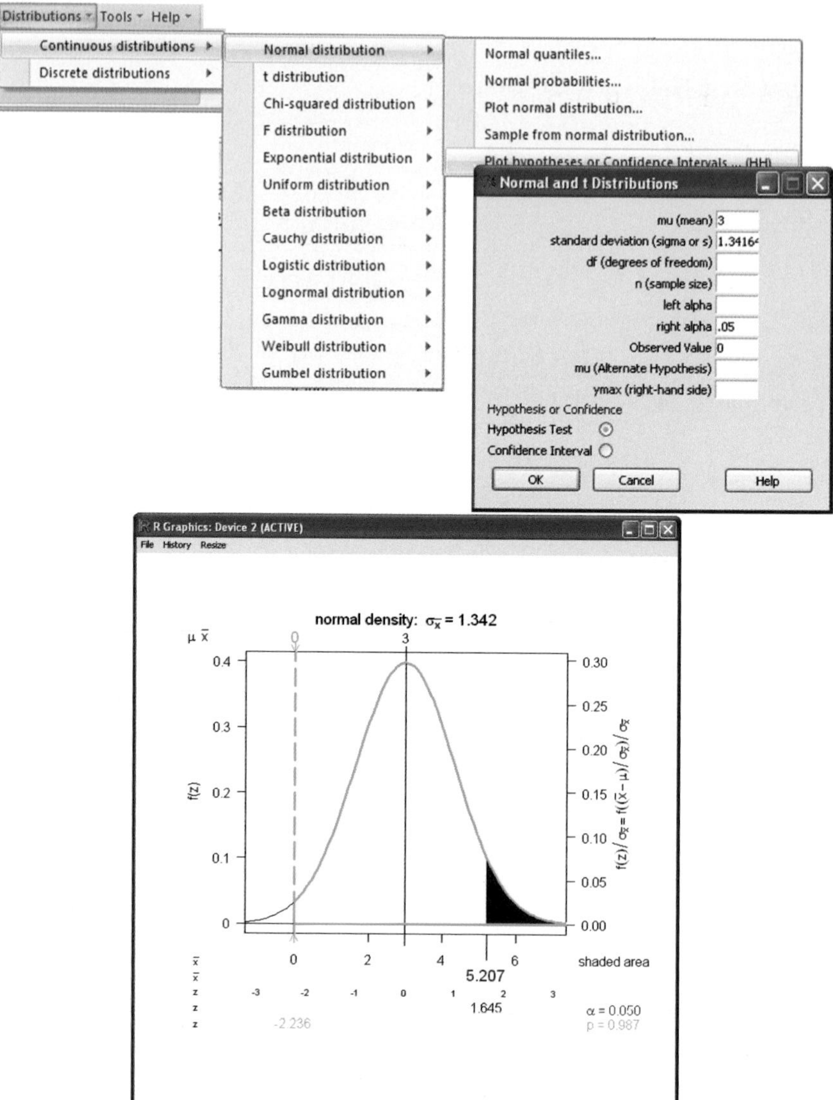

Fig. 6.70 Menu: Distributions ► Continuous distributions ► Normal distribution ► Plot hypotheses or Confidence Intervals . . . (HH)
The numerical answer to the exercise is identified as $p = 0.987$ and is illustrated as the green-outlined area to the right of $\bar{x} = 0$ and the right of $z = -2.236$. The $\bar{x}$-scale is called W in the algebraic expansion. μ_W and σ_W are entered into the dialog box.

6.6.2 Not Recommended Style

The näive formula treats the problem as a special case with its own unique formula.

$$
\begin{aligned}
P(\bar{X}_X - \bar{X}_Y > 0) &= P\left(\frac{(\bar{X}_X - \bar{X}_Y) - (\mu_X - \mu_Y)}{\sqrt{\dfrac{\sigma_X^2}{n_X} + \dfrac{\sigma_Y^2}{n_Y}}} > \frac{0 - (18 - 5)}{\sqrt{\dfrac{3^2}{10} + \dfrac{3^2}{10}}}\right) \\
&= P(Z > -2.24) \\
&= 0.5 + P(0 < Z < 2.24) \\
&= 0.5 + 0.4875 \\
&= 0.9875
\end{aligned}
$$

This formula gets the same answer as the recommended style. It is, after all, doing the same arithmetic. The difficulty with this style, and the reason we don't recommend it, is that the simplicity of the standard phrase

$$\frac{W - \mu_W}{\sigma_W}$$

is not instantly visible. Several clear steps, as in Section 6.6.1, are always to be preferred to one complex step, as in Section 6.6.2.

Chapter 7
One-Way ANOVA

Abstract One-way ANOVA (analysis of variance) is a technique that generalizes the two-sample t-test to three or more samples. We test the hypotheses (specified here for $k = 6$ samples) about population means μ_j:

$$H_0\colon \mu_1 = \mu_2 = \mu_3 = \mu_4 = \mu_5 = \mu_6$$
$$H_1\colon \text{Not all } \mu_j \text{ are equal } (j = 1{:}6)$$

The test is based on the observed sample means $\bar{x}_j$.

7.1 Data

We will explore ANOVA with an example from the chickwts dataset that is distributed with R. From the help file ?chickwts:

> An experiment was conducted to measure and compare the effectiveness of various feed supplements on the growth rate of chickens. Newly hatched chicks were randomly allocated into six groups, and each group was given a different feed supplement. Their weights in grams after six weeks are given along with feed types.

R.M. Heiberger, E. Neuwirth, *R Through Excel*, Use R,
DOI 10.1007/978-1-4419-0052-4_7,

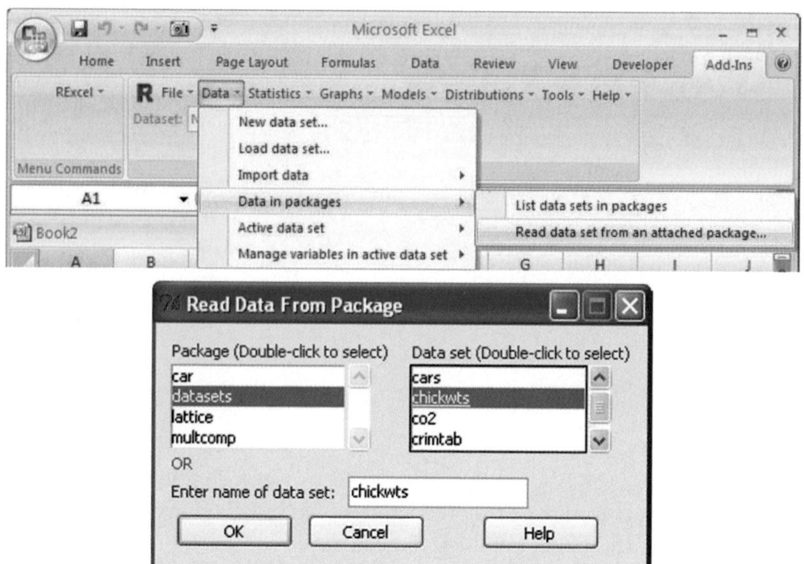

Fig. 7.1 Use the

Data ► Data in packages ► Read data set from an attached package...

menu item. Double-click to select the datasets package, double-click again to select the chickwts dataset, and then click OK.

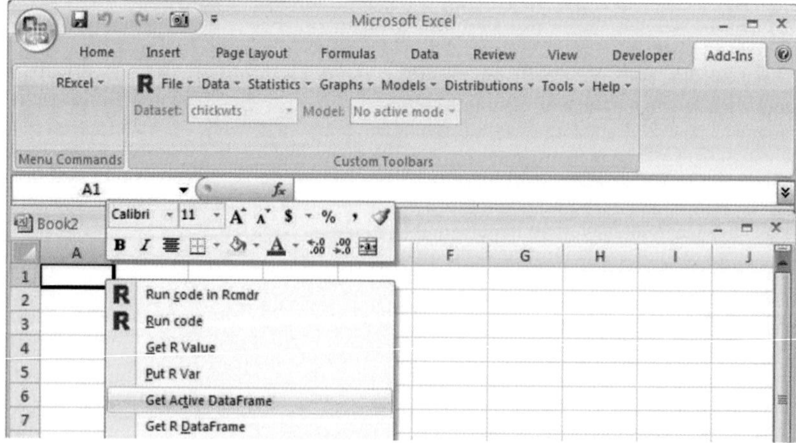

Fig. 7.2 chickwts is now listed as the active dataset on the Rcmdr menu. All menu items on the Rcmdr menu refer to variables that are columns in the active dataframe. Put the cursor in cell A1 of a new workbook and use the right-click Get Active DataFrame menu item to get the chickwts data into the Excel worksheet, where we can look at it.

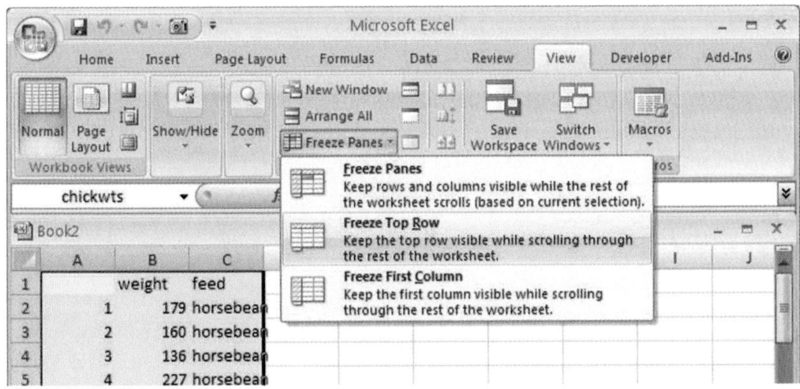

Fig. 7.3 Freeze the top row of the worksheet. This makes the variable names always visible, even if we are scrolled down to high-numbered rows. Click the Excel View tab, and then click the Freeze Panes ► Freeze Top Row menu item. Then click the Excel Add-Ins tab to get back to the Rcmdr menu.

Book2 Width: 8.43 (64 pixels)

	A	B	C
1		weight	feed
2	1	179	horsebea
3	2	160	horsebea
4	3	136	horsebea
5	4	227	horsebea
6	5	217	horsebea
7	6	168	horsebea
8	7	108	horsebea
9	8	124	horsebea
10	9	143	horsebea
11	10	140	horsebea
12	11	309	linseed
13	12	229	linseed
14	13	181	linseed
15	14	141	linseed

Sheet1 Sheet2 Sheet3

Fig. 7.4 Notice that the top row is underlined, indicating that the top row is now frozen. Also, note that column C is not quite as wide as the word horsebean. We widen the column by placing the cursor on the boundary between the column names C and D and then double-clicking. We see the wider column in Fig. 7.9.

7.2 Plots

Before doing any arithmetic or statistical analysis on the data, it is important to look at it with several graphs. We show two types of graphs, the dotplot and the boxplot.

7.2.1 Dotplot

The dotplot shows one dot for each observation, plotted on a vertical scale for the data value and on a horizontal scale for the groups.

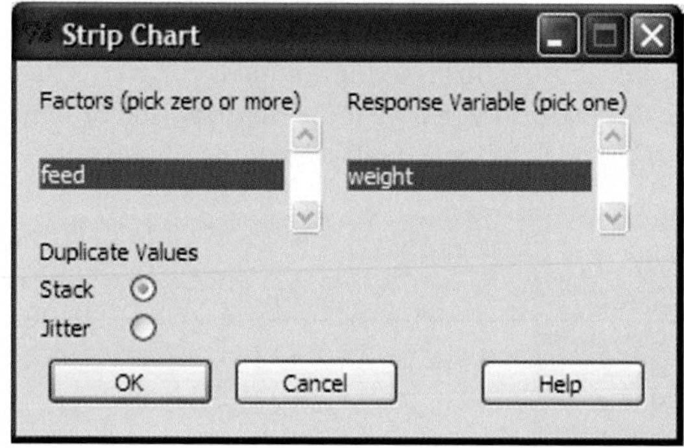

Fig. 7.5 Click the Graphs ▸ Strip chart... to get this dialog box. There is only one factor and one continuous variable in the chickwts dataset so we can accept the defaults. Click OK to get Fig. 7.6.

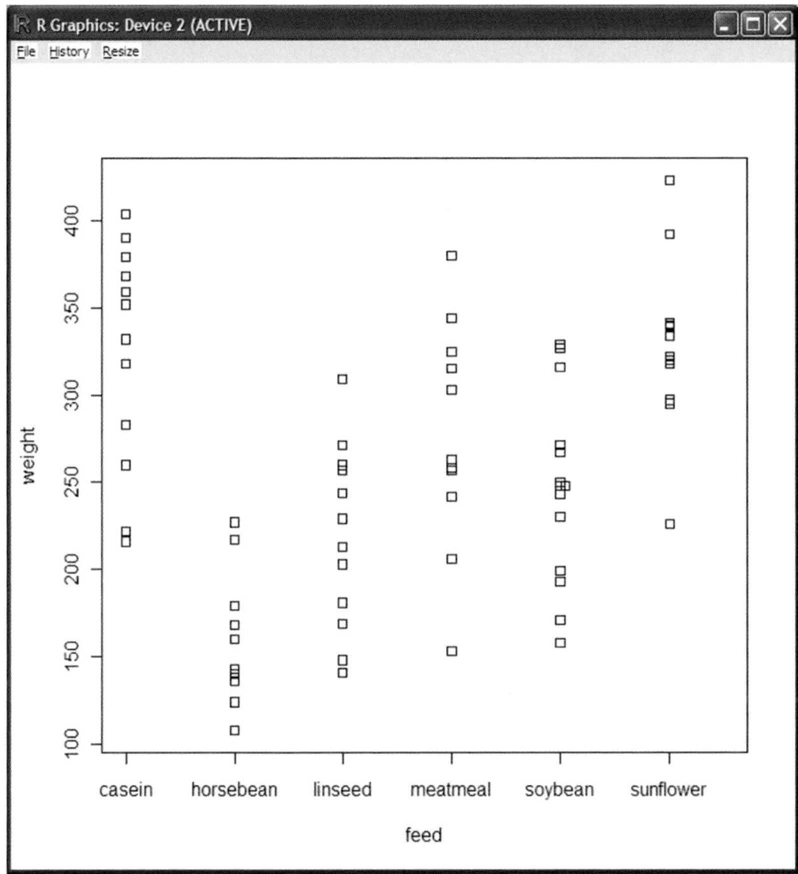

Fig. 7.6 Each of the six feeds is displayed in its own column. The vertical axis shows the response variable weight. Each point is one observation. Visually, two feeds (sunflower and casein) have higher means than the other four. Three feeds (soybean, meatmeal, and linseed) have very similar ranges.

7.2.2 Boxplot

The boxplot shows a summary of a variable's values, consisting of the basic order statistics: median, quartiles, minimum, maximum. Calculate these order statistics by ordering the data values from smallest to largest and counting. The median is the middle observation. The quartiles are half way from the end points to the median. See the help file `?boxplot.stats` for details. Each box shows its group's median in the center. The bottom and top lines of the central box are at the first and third quartiles. If there are no outliers (defined in a moment), the whiskers go out to the minimum and maximum of the data. If there are outliers, the program defines the *fences* as 1.5 interquartile ranges out from the quartiles. The whiskers go out to the last point inside the fence. Points beyond the fences are individually plotted. Outliers are points that are noticebly smaller or larger than the remaining points, as measured on a scale defined by the distance between the first and third quartiles. There is no implication that they are necessarily incorrect. Existence of outliers often indicates that the data do not come from a normal distribution. Sometimes it is a consequence of a large number of observations.

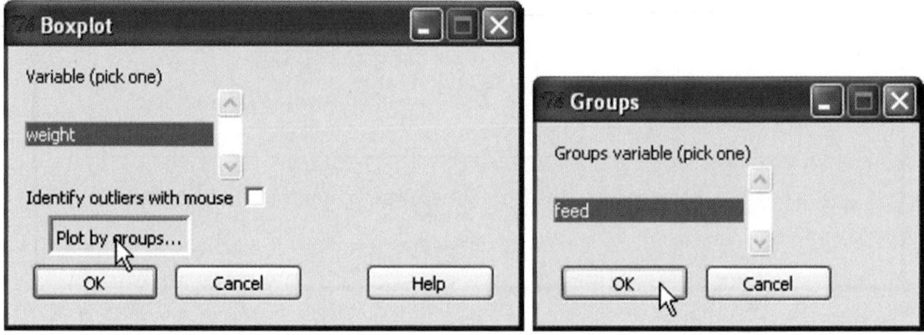

Fig. 7.7 Use the Graphs ▸ Boxplot... menu item. Click Plot by groups... to specify parallel boxplots of the six groups.

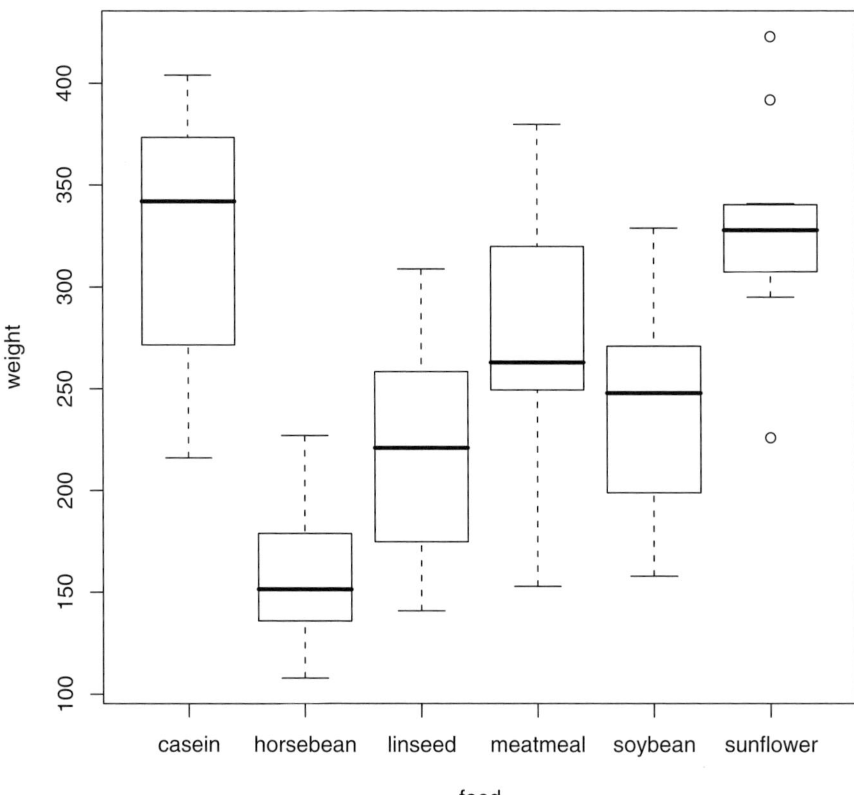

Fig. 7.8 In this plot, the response variable weight is on the vertical axis. There is one box for each feed. As in Fig. 7.6, we see that two feeds (sunflower and casein) have higher medians (boxplots use order statistics, hence medians not means) than the other four. Three feeds (soybean, meatmeal, and linseed) have very similar ranges. We need to look (in Section 7.3) at the arithmetic of the analysis of variance (ANOVA) to determine if the visible differences in the observed $\bar{x}_j$-values and medians are an indicator of real differences in the population means μ_j.

7.3 ANOVA Specification

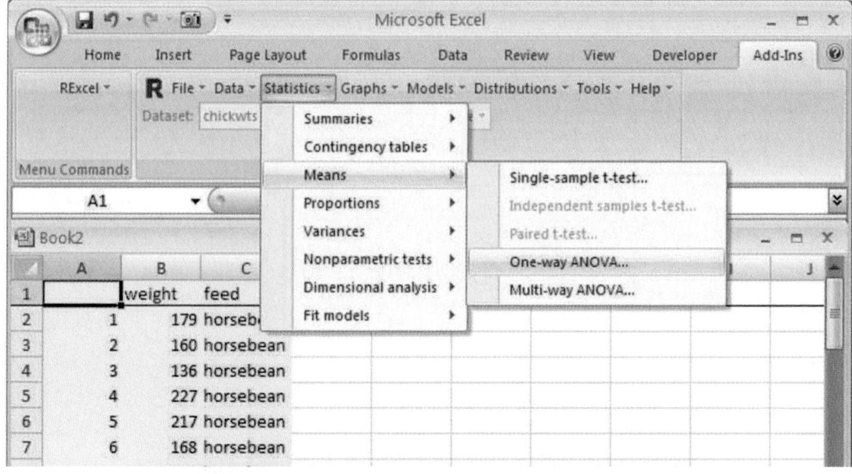

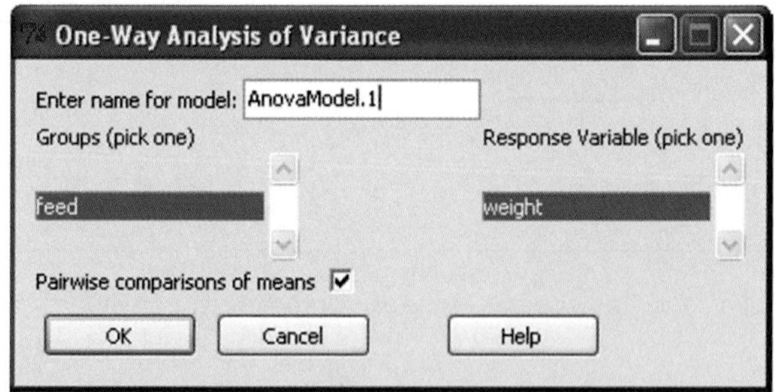

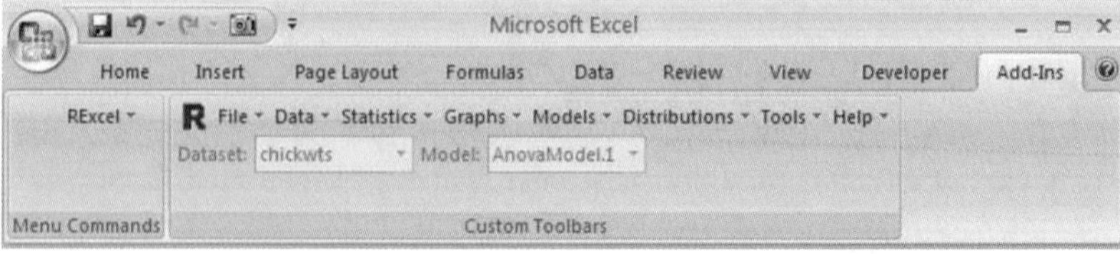

Fig. 7.9 Use the Statistics ► Means ► One-way ANOVA... menu item to get the ANOVA dialog box. Specify feed as the group variable and weight as the response variable. In this example, with only one numeric variable and one factor, the variables are initially highlighted. Check the Pairwise comparison of means checkbox. This dialog box sets the active model to AnovaModel.1 and produces the output in Table 7.1 and Fig. 7.13.

Table 7.1 This is the complete tabular output from the dialog box in Fig. 7.9. We illustrate it here to show that the simple command in Fig. 7.9 produces many subtables and graphs, all of which must be read and interpreted. We will print in a full-size font and discuss each subtable and graph individually.

```
> AnovaModel.1 <- aov(weight ~ feed, data=chickwts)

> summary(AnovaModel.1)
            Df Sum Sq Mean Sq F value    Pr(>F)
feed         5 231129   46226  15.365 5.936e-10 ***
Residuals   65 195556    3009
---
Signif. codes:  0 '***' 0.001 '**' 0.01 '*' 0.05 '.' 0.1 ' ' 1

> numSummary(chickwts$weight , groups=chickwts$feed, statistics=c("mean",
+   "sd"))
               mean       sd  n
casein     323.5833 64.43384 12
horsebean 160.2000 38.62584 10
linseed    218.7500 52.23570 12
meatmeal   276.9091 64.90062 11
soybean    246.4286 54.12907 14
sunflower 328.9167 48.83638 12

> .Pairs <- glht(AnovaModel.1, linfct = mcp(feed = "Tukey"))

> confint(.Pairs)

 Simultaneous Confidence Intervals

Multiple Comparisons of Means: Tukey Contrasts


Fit: aov(formula = weight ~ feed, data = chickwts)

Estimated Quantile = 2.9361
95% family-wise confidence level


Linear Hypotheses:
                           Estimate  lwr       upr
horsebean - casein == 0    -163.3833 -232.3381  -94.4286
linseed - casein == 0      -104.8333 -170.5791  -39.0876
meatmeal - casein == 0      -46.6742 -113.8976   20.5491
soybean - casein == 0       -77.1548 -140.5090  -13.8006
sunflower - casein == 0       5.3333  -60.4124   71.0791
linseed - horsebean == 0     58.5500  -10.4047  127.5047
meatmeal - horsebean == 0   116.7091   46.3441  187.0741
soybean - horsebean == 0     86.2286   19.5502  152.9069
sunflower - horsebean == 0  168.7167   99.7619  237.6714
meatmeal - linseed == 0      58.1591   -9.0643  125.3825
soybean - linseed == 0       27.6786  -35.6756   91.0328
sunflower - linseed == 0    110.1667   44.4209  175.9124
soybean - meatmeal == 0     -30.4805  -95.3668   34.4058
sunflower - meatmeal == 0    52.0076  -15.2158  119.2310
sunflower - soybean == 0     82.4881   19.1339  145.8423


> old.oma <- par(oma=c(0,5,0,0))

> plot(confint(.Pairs))

> par(old.oma)

> remove(.Pairs)
```

7.4 ANOVA Table and F-Test

The ANOVA (analysis of variance) table is the first section of the output from the One-Way Analysis of Variance dialog box in Table 7.1. We repeat it in Table 7.2 as it appears in the Rcmdr Output Window and in Table 7.3 as it is normally reformatted in a table in a report.

Table 7.2 ANOVA table as displayed in the Rcmdr listing in Fig. 7.1. The p-value of 5.936×10^{-16} is significant at any reasonable level of significance.

```
> AnovaModel.1 <- aov(weight ~ feed, data=chickwts)

> summary(AnovaModel.1)
            Df Sum Sq Mean Sq F value    Pr(>F)
feed         5 231129   46226  15.365 5.936e-10 ***
Residuals   65 195556    3009
---
Signif. codes:  0 '***' 0.001 '**' 0.01 '*' 0.05 '.' 0.1 ' ' 1
```

Table 7.3 ANOVA table from the Rcmdr listing in Fig. 7.1 and Table 7.2 reformatted as it is normally displayed in a printed report.

Analysis of variance table for response: count

Source	Degrees of freedom	Sum of squares	Mean square	F-value	p-value	
Feed	5	231129	46226	15.365	5.936×10^{-10}	***
Residuals	65	195556	3009			
Total	70	426685				

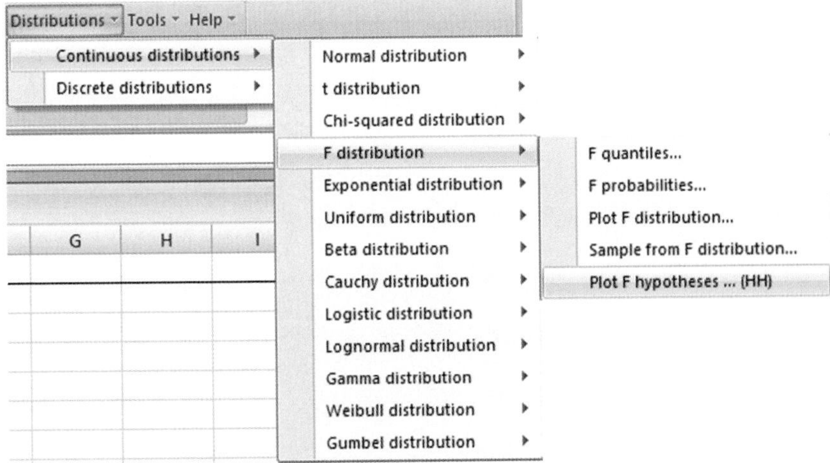

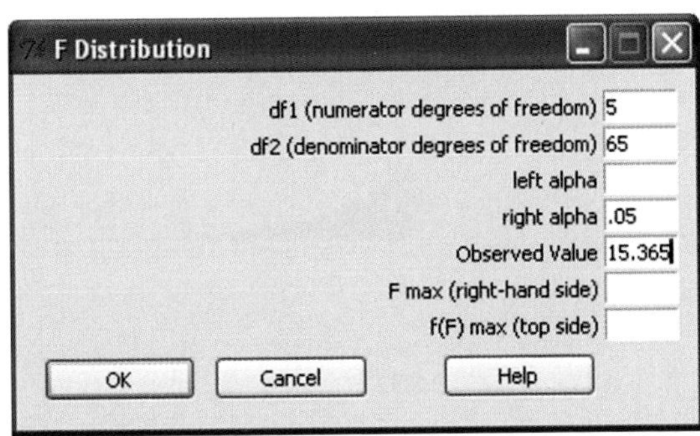

Fig. 7.10 The ANOVA table showed a significant F-value, with $F = 15.365$ with 5 and 65 degrees of freedom and $p5.936 \times 10^{-10}$. We can look up that observed value of F in the F table and locate it on the plot of the F distribution. Use the Distributions ► Continuous distributions ► F distribution ► Plot F hypotheses... menu item and its dialog box. Enter the degrees of freedom and observed F-value from the ANOVA table.

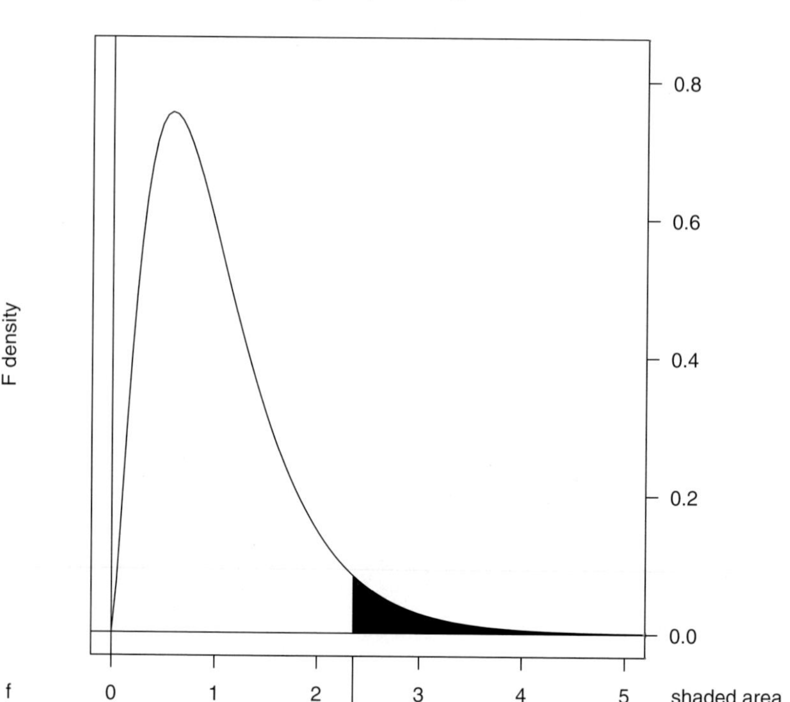

Fig. 7.11 The observed value of 15.365 is so far from the default setting of the scale that we do not see it on the graph. We will need to redraw it with control of the right side.

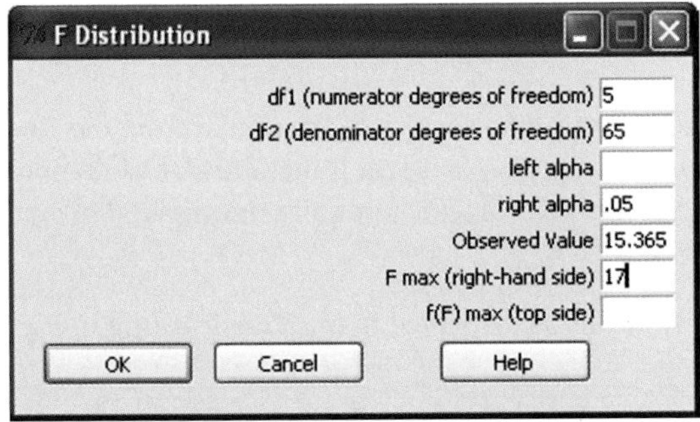

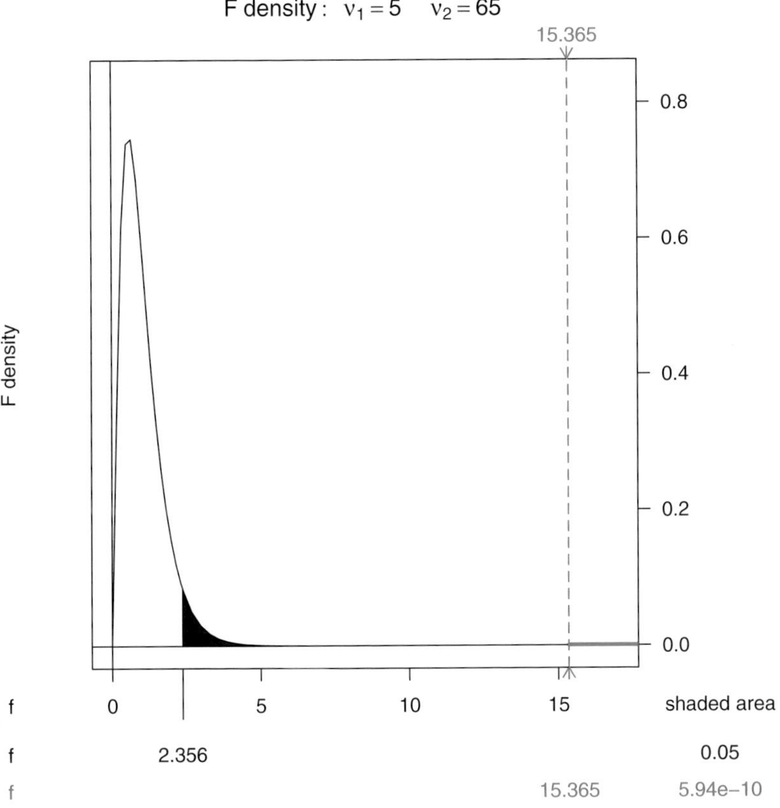

Fig. 7.12 Respecify the plot, this time using the F max (right-hand side) field. The observed value is very far in the tail and clearly in the rejection region for any reasonably sized significance level. The graph shows the density of the $F_{5,65}$ distribution with the $\alpha = 0.05$ critical value of 2.356 printed in blue to go with the blue coloring of the rejection region. The observed F-value of 15.365 is printed in green, and the area associated with the p-value of 5.94×10^{-10} is outlined in green. The observed F-value is in the blue rejection region.

7.5 Table of Means

The table of means is the second section of the output from the One-Way Analysis of Variance dialog box in Fig. 7.9. We repeat it in Table 7.4 as it appears in the Rcmdr Output Window and in Table 7.5 as it is normally reformatted in a table in a report.

Table 7.4 Table of means as displayed in the Rcmdr listing in Fig. 7.1.

```
> numSummary(chickwts$weight,
+    groups=chickwts$feed,
+    statistics=c("mean", "sd"))
              mean       sd  n
casein    323.5833 64.43384 12
horsebean 160.2000 38.62584 10
linseed   218.7500 52.23570 12
meatmeal  276.9091 64.90062 11
soybean   246.4286 54.12907 14
sunflower 328.9167 48.83638 12
```

Table 7.5 Table of means from the Rcmdr listing in Fig. 7.1 reformatted as it is normally displayed in a printed report.

Feed	Mean	Standard deviation	Sample size
casein	323.6	64.4	12
horsebean	160.2	38.6	10
linseed	218.8	52.2	12
meatmeal	276.9	64.9	11
soybean	246.4	54.1	14
sunflower	328.9	48.8	12

7.6 Multiple Comparisons

Assuming inferences are independent, the probability of simultaneously making three correct inferences, when each of the three individually has

$$P(\text{correct inference}) = 1 - \alpha = 0.95$$

is only $(1-\alpha)^3 = 0.95^3 = 0.857$. Alternatively, the probability of making at least one incorrect inference is $1 - 0.857 = 0.143 \approx 3\alpha$. In general, the more simultaneous inferences we make at one time, the smaller the probability that all are correct; equivalently, the higher the probability that at least one is incorrect. The goal of multiple comparisons is to control the probability of making at least one incorrect inference.

We consider all inferences in a related *family* of inferences. The family we consider here is the set of all $\binom{k}{2}$ pairwise comparisons $\bar{x}_i - \bar{x}_j$ for $1 \le i, j \le k$.

The way we control the probability of making at least one incorrect inference is to use a larger critical value for each test than we would use for the tests in isolation. Here we will use the Tukey Studentized Range Test for determining the critical value. For $k = 6$ means and $\nu = 66$ degrees of freedom, we will use the critical value $q_{\text{Tukey}}(0.95, 6, 66)/\sqrt{2} = 2.935$ instead of the $t_{.025,66} = 1.997$ value that would have been used without the adjustment for multiple comparisons. The critical values for the Studentized Range Test are calculated with the `qtukey` function in R. The tables for q are based on the distribution of $(\bar{x}_1 - \bar{x}_k)$. The number $q/\sqrt{(2)}$ that we use is scaled for confidence intervals on individual $\bar{x}_i$. All the hard work is done by the `ghlt` function that is specified either by checking the Pairwise comparison of means box on the One-way ANOVA... or by using the MMC Plot... (HH) menu.

Table 7.6 Table of confidence intervals for pairwise differences of means of the treatments. This table was produced by the dialog box in Fig. 7.9 and is included in the output displayed in Fig. 7.1. The critical value for the table, 2.935 in this example, is from the Studentized Range distribution and is calculated with

```
> qtukey(.95, 6, 66)
[1] 4.150851
> qtukey(.95, 6, 66)/sqrt(2)
[1] 2.935095
```

The critical value adjusts for simultaneous tests and is therefore larger than the $t_{.025,66} = 1.997$ value that would have been used without the adjustment. The hypotheses are ordered alphabetically by the level names. This is usually not a useful ordering. We replace the alphabetical ordering by a data-dependent ordering in Section 7.7.

```
           Simultaneous Confidence Intervals

Multiple Comparisons of Means: Tukey Contrasts


Fit: aov(formula = count ~ spray, data = InsectSprays)

Estimated Quantile = 2.9347
95% family-wise confidence level


Linear Hypotheses:
           Estimate lwr      upr
B - A == 0   0.8333  -3.8654   5.5321
C - A == 0 -12.4167 -17.1154  -7.7179
D - A == 0  -9.5833 -14.2821  -4.8846
E - A == 0 -11.0000 -15.6988  -6.3012
F - A == 0   2.1667  -2.5321   6.8654
C - B == 0 -13.2500 -17.9488  -8.5512
D - B == 0 -10.4167 -15.1154  -5.7179
E - B == 0 -11.8333 -16.5321  -7.1346
F - B == 0   1.3333  -3.3654   6.0321
D - C == 0   2.8333  -1.8654   7.5321
E - C == 0   1.4167  -3.2821   6.1154
F - C == 0  14.5833   9.8846  19.2821
E - D == 0  -1.4167  -6.1154   3.2821
F - D == 0  11.7500   7.0512  16.4488
F - E == 0  13.1667   8.4679  17.8654
```

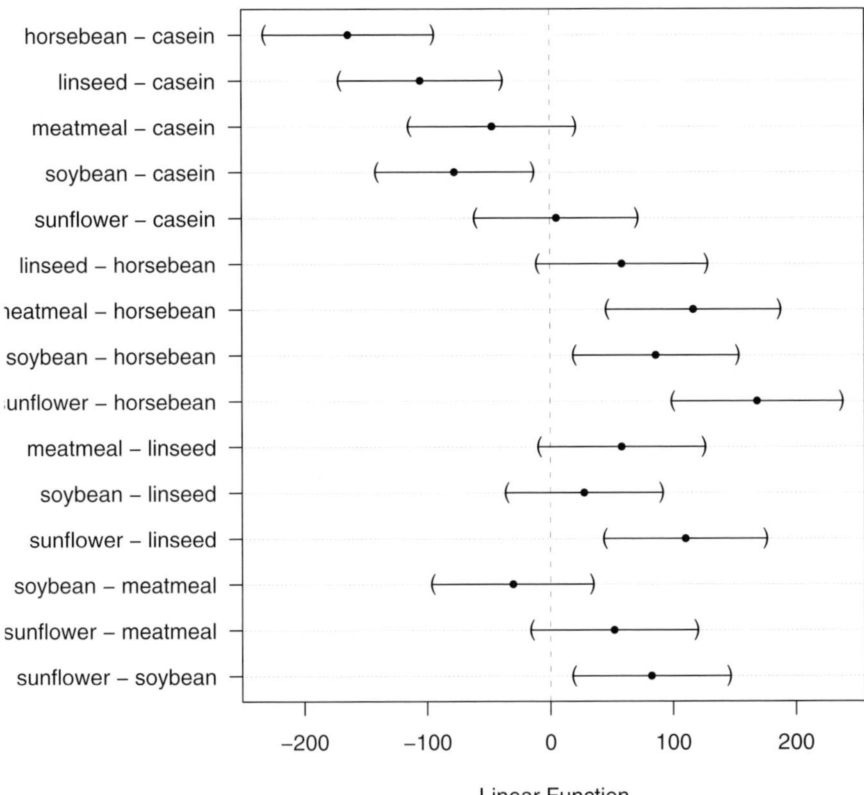

Fig. 7.13 Plot of confidence intervals for pairwise differences of means of the treatments. This figure was produced by the dialog box in Fig. 7.9. It shows the same intervals as in Table 7.6. We will replace the alphabetical order of the contrasts in this figure with a data-dependent ordering in Figs. 7.16 and 7.17.

7.7 Mean–Mean Multiple Comparisons Plot

The Mean–Mean Multiple Comparisons Plot (MMC plot) [Heiberger and Holland, 2006] is a single plot that displays all of

1. the sample means themselves, with correct relative distances.
2. the point and interval estimates of the $\binom{k}{2}$ pairwise differences.
3. the point and interval estimates for arbitrary contrasts of the level means.
4. declarations of significance.
5. confidence interval widths that are correct for unequal sample sizes.

The MMC plot in Fig. 7.16 and the corresponding table in Table 7.7 are specified with the dialog box in Fig. 7.15. In this example, the averages of many of the contrasting means are similar. We therefore also print the tiebreaker plot in Fig. 7.17. Since we frequently need both plots at the same time, it is important to turn on graphics history as indicated in Fig. 7.14.

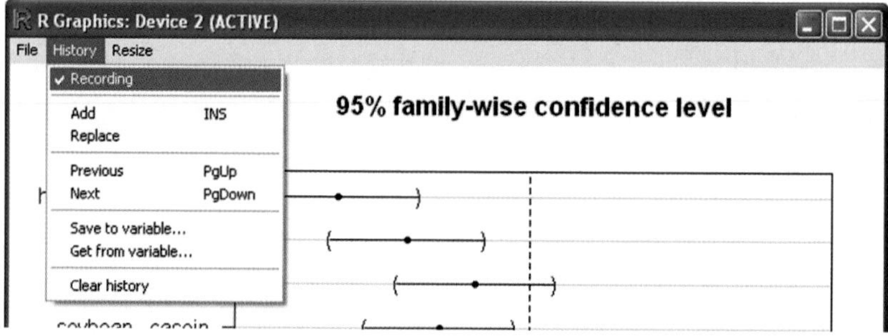

Fig. 7.14
Verify at this time that the Graphics Device history is on. From the Graphics Device menu, click History ► Recording to put the checkmark in place.

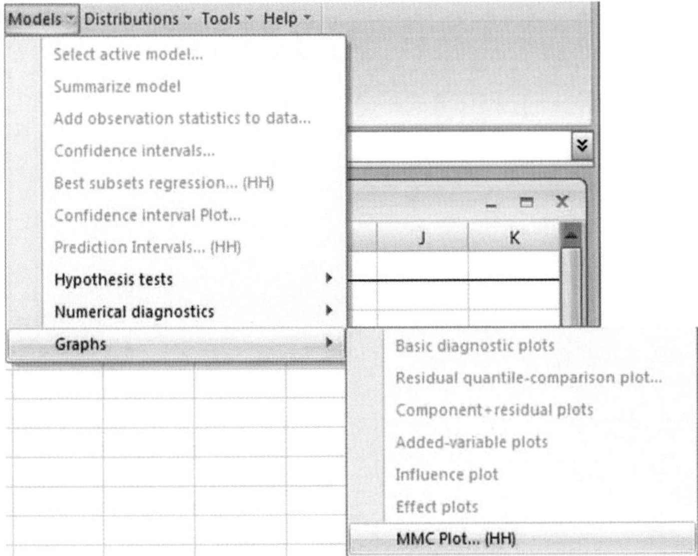

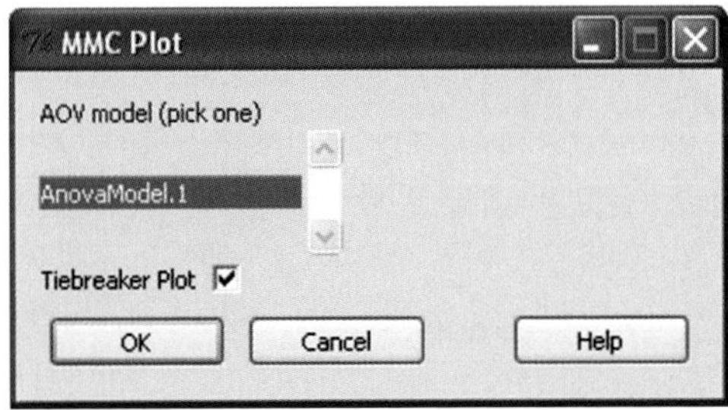

Fig. 7.15 Specify the MMC plot with the Models ► Graphs ► MMC Plot... (HH) menu and its dialog box. Check the Tiebreaker Plot checkbox. This dialog box specifies Figs. 7.16 and 7.17 and Table 7.7.

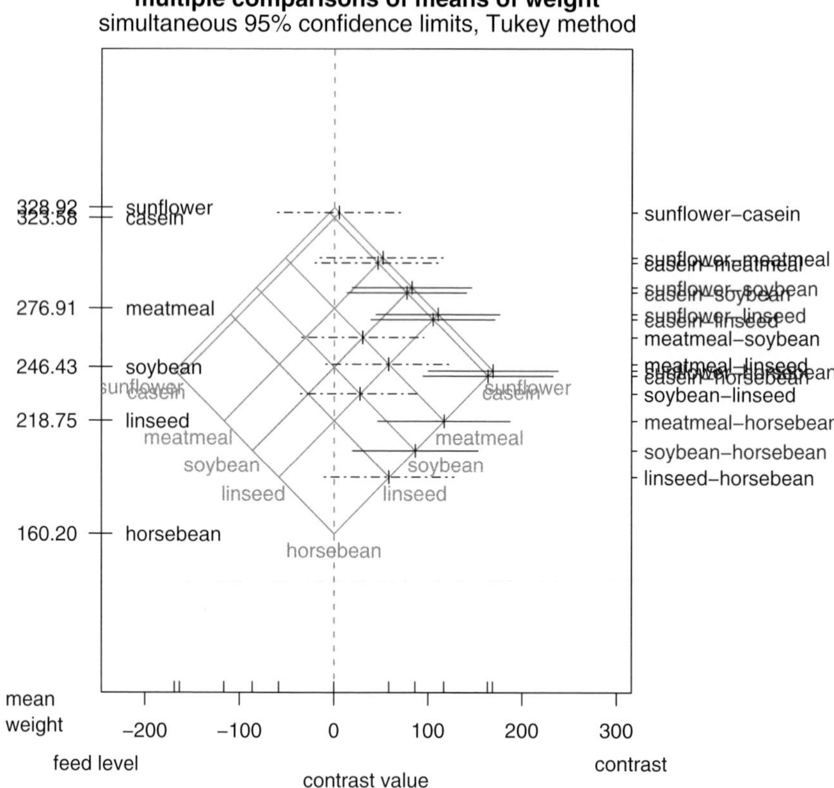

Fig. 7.16 MMC plot of confidence intervals for pairwise differences of means of the treatments. This plot and its tiebreaker plot in Fig. 7.17 were specified in the dialog box in Fig. 7.15. The tiebreaker, specified by checking the Tiebreaker Plot checkbox, is needed to separate the contrast labels in the right margin. Each confidence interval is plotted at a height equal to the average of the means of the two treatments compared in that contrast. The labels in this MMC plot are overprinted because the averages of many pairs of treatment means are similar.

The left axis of the MMC plot is labeled with the means for the treatments. The bottom axis is labeled in contrast units, differences between the treatment means. Each horizontal line representing a confidence interval is at a height that is the average of the two treatment means it compares. Solid red lines do not cross the vertical $x = 0$ line and therefore represent a significant contrast at the specified confidence level, in this example 95% after the Tukey adjustment for simultaneous tests. Dashed black lines represent nonsignificant contrasts.

We discuss the content of the MMC plot in Fig. 7.17.

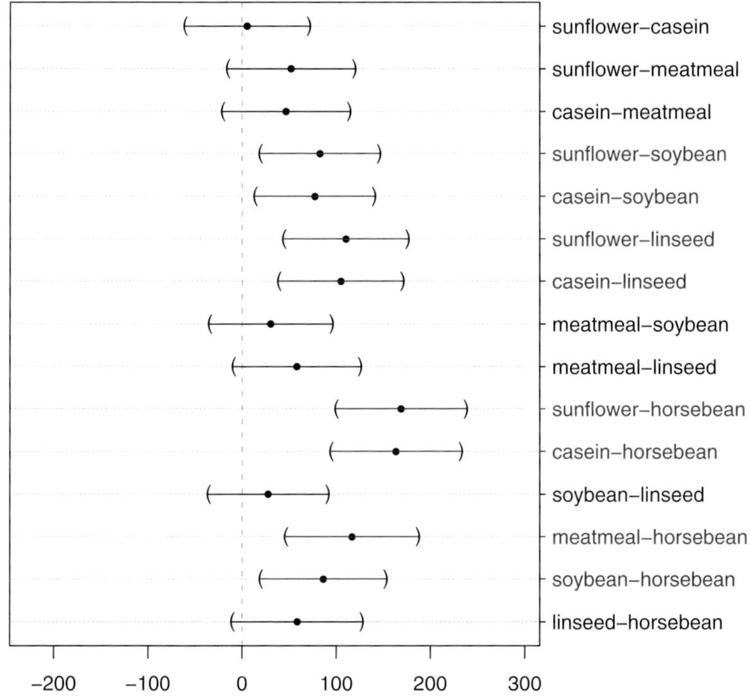

Fig. 7.17 The tiebreaker plot shows the same set of contrasts on the same left-to-right scale and in the same bottom-to-top order as the MMC plot in Fig. 7.16. The tiebreaker plot spaces the contrasts equidistantly in the bottom-to-top direction.

In this example, the significant contrasts on the upper right edge of the isomeans grid in Fig. 7.16 indicate that the sunflower and casein means are different from most of the other treatment means. The significant contrasts on the lower right edge of the isomeans grid indicates that the horsebean mean is different from most of the others. The sunflower–casein contrast crosses the vertical 0-line, indicating that the means of sunflower and casein are indistinguishable from each other. The three contrasts in the center of the MMC plot (meatmeal–soybean, meatmeal–linseed, and soybean–linseed) show that the three treatments meatmeal, soybean, and linseed are similar to each other.

Taken together, these contrasts suggest that there are three clusters of treatments (sunflower, casein), (meatmeal, soybean, and linseed), and (horsebean). We will investigate this suggestion in Section 7.8.

Table 7.7 Tabular output from the MMC dialog box. The `$mca` contrasts are the values from which Fig. 7.16 was constructed. The numerical values are identical to those in Table 7.6. The items in the `$mca` section are ordered by the `height` (the average of the two treatment means each compares) column. The items in the `none` section (meaning no contrasts, but rather the estimates of the means for each treatment level) are ordered by the observed means (in the `estimate` column). The `ry` and `x.offset` arguments to the `plot` command and the `omd` argument to the `par` command together control the placement of the plot in the plotting window. See ?MMC for details.

```
> old.omd <- par(omd=c(0, 0.8, 0,1))

> AnovaModel.1.mmc <- glht.mmc(AnovaModel.1)

> AnovaModel.1.mmc
Tukey contrasts
Fit: aov(formula = weight ~ feed, data = chickwts)
Estimated Quantile = 2.935338
95% family-wise confidence level
$mca
                     estimate  stderr     lower    upper  height
sunflower-casein      5.33333 22.3925 -60.39472  71.0614 326.250
sunflower-meatmeal   52.00758 22.8958 -15.19770 119.2129 302.913
casein-meatmeal      46.67424 22.8958 -20.53103 113.8795 300.246
sunflower-soybean    82.48810 21.5780  19.15095 145.8252 287.673
casein-soybean       77.15476 21.5780  13.81762 140.4919 285.006
sunflower-linseed   110.16667 22.3925  44.43861 175.8947 273.833
casein-linseed      104.83333 22.3925  39.10528 170.5614 271.167
meatmeal-soybean     30.48052 22.0998 -34.38831  95.3493 261.669
meatmeal-linseed     58.15909 22.8958  -9.04619 125.3644 247.830
sunflower-horsebean 168.71667 23.4855  99.78050 237.6528 244.558
casein-horsebean    163.38333 23.4855  94.44717 232.3195 241.892
soybean-linseed      27.67857 21.5780 -35.65857  91.0157 232.589
meatmeal-horsebean  116.70909 23.9658  46.36304 187.0551 218.555
soybean-horsebean    86.22857 22.7102  19.56816 152.8890 203.314
linseed-horsebean    58.55000 23.4855 -10.38617 127.4862 189.475
$none
          estimate   stderr    lower    upper   height
sunflower 328.9167 15.83391 282.4388 375.3946 328.9167
casein    323.5833 15.83391 277.1054 370.0612 323.5833
meatmeal  276.9091 16.53798 228.3645 325.4537 276.9091
soybean   246.4286 14.65936 203.3984 289.4587 246.4286
linseed   218.7500 15.83391 172.2721 265.2279 218.7500
horsebean 160.2000 17.34518 109.2860 211.1140 160.2000

> plot(AnovaModel.1.mmc, x.offset=34.468926055317,
+   ry=c(114.392542547306, 374.724124119361))

> plot.matchMMC(AnovaModel.1.mmc$mca, xlabel.print=FALSE)

> par(old.omd)
```

7.8 Linear Contrasts

This section illustrates a more advanced concept, user-specified linear contrasts among the levels of the factor. It uses techniques that are not available on the menu system and must therefore be written directly in the R language.

There are 5 degrees of freedom in the ANOVA in Table 7.2, yet 15 contrasts in Figs. 7.16 and 7.17. We can summarize Figs. 7.16 and 7.17 to show just 5 contrasts. We noted in Fig. 7.17 that the feeds seem to cluster into three groups, (sunflower and casein), (meatmeal, soybean, and linseed), and (horsebean). We formalize that impression by defining a set of orthogonal contrasts in Table 7.8 and using them in the ANOVA table in Table 7.10 and in the MMC plot in Table 7.11 and Figure 7.18. The first two contrasts distinguish between the three groups. The last three contrasts will be used to verify that there is no significant difference within the groups.

Table 7.8 Specification of a contrast matrix. We specify a set of contrasts in the treatment levels. The first contrast compares the average of the casein and sunflower treatments to the average of the other four treatements. The second contrast compares the average of the cluster of (meatmeal, soybean, and linseed) treatments to the average of the horsebean treatment. The remaining contrasts are an orthogonal completion of the contrast matrix. The constructed matrix `chickwts.focus.lmat` is an orthogonal matrix. The data for this example does not have an equal number of observations in each group. When the contrast matrix is used to specify the dummy variables in an example with unequal sample sizes, the orthogonality is lost. We discuss how we handle the unequal sample size situation in Table 7.9.

```
> chickwts.focus.lmat <-
+ ##                        ca  ho  li  me  so  su
+   cbind("su.ca-rest"=c(  2, -1, -1, -1, -1,  2),
+              "msl-h"=c(  0, -3,  1,  1,  1,  0),
+              "su-ca"=c( -1,  0,  0,  0,  0,  1),
+              "me-sl"=c(  0,  0, -1,  2, -1,  0),
+              "so-li"=c(  0,  0, -1,  0,  1,  0))

> dimnames(chickwts.focus.lmat)[[1]] <-
+          levels(chickwts$feed)

> chickwts.focus.lmat
          su.ca-rest msl-h su-ca me-sl so-li
casein             2     0    -1     0     0
horsebean         -1    -3     0     0     0
linseed           -1     1     0    -1    -1
meatmeal          -1     1     0     2     0
soybean           -1     1     0    -1     1
sunflower          2     0     1     0     0
```

Table 7.9 In this example, the number of observations for each feed level are not the same. The numbers are close. Therefore, the orthogonality in the contrast matrix (`crossprod(chickwts.focus.lmat)`) is diagonal) implies only near-orthogonality in the matrix of dummy variables (the matrix `crossprod(chickwts.aov$x)` is close to diagonal).

```
> with(chickwts, tapply(weight, feed, length))
   casein horsebean   linseed  meatmeal   soybean sunflower
       12        10        12        11        14        12
> crossprod(chickwts.focus.lmat)
           su.ca-rest msl-h su-ca me-sl so-li
su.ca-rest         12     0     0     0     0
msl-h               0    12     0     0     0
su-ca               0     0     2     0     0
me-sl               0     0     0     6     0
so-li               0     0     0     0     2
> chickwts.aov <- update(chickwts.aov, x=TRUE)

> crossprod(chickwts.aov$x)
               (Intercept) feedsu.ca-rest feedmsl-h feedsu-ca feedme-sl feedso-li
(Intercept)             71              1         7         0        -4         2
feedsu.ca-rest           1            143        -7         0         4        -2
feedmsl-h                7             -7       127         0        -4         2
feedsu-ca                0              0         0        24         0         0
feedme-sl               -4              4        -4         0        70        -2
feedso-li                2             -2         2         0        -2        26
```

Table 7.10 We recalculated the ANOVA table, this time using the contrasts defined in Table 7.8. We then partitioned the ANOVA table to show that the two degrees of freedom distinguishing the clusters are highly significant and the remaining three degrees of freedom are not significant. See ?summary.aov for details. The details of the arithmetic for sequential sums of squares assure us that the partitioning of the sums of squares is correct even though the matrix of dummy variables is not orthogonal.

```
> contrasts(chickwts$feed) <- chickwts.focus.lmat
> chickwts.aov <- aov(weight ~ feed, data=chickwts)
> summary(chickwts.aov)
            Df Sum Sq Mean Sq F value    Pr(>F)
feed         5 231129   46226  15.365 5.936e-10 ***
Residuals   65 195556    3009
---
Signif. codes:  0 '***' 0.001 '**' 0.01 '*' 0.05 '.' 0.1 ' ' 1
> summary(chickwts.aov,
+         split=list(feed=list(
+         'su.ca-msl-h'=1:2,
+         'rest'=3:5)))
                    Df Sum Sq Mean Sq F value    Pr(>F)
feed                 5 231129   46226 15.3648 5.936e-10 ***
  feed: su.ca-msl-h  2 211546  105773 35.1574 4.477e-11 ***
  feed: rest         3  19583    6528  2.1697    0.1000
Residuals           65 195556    3009
---
Signif. codes:  0 '***' 0.001 '**' 0.01 '*' 0.05 '.' 0.1 ' ' 1
```

Table 7.11 We recalculate the multiple comparisons, this time using the contrasts defined in Table 7.8 in addition to the pairwise contrasts. The printed output of the recalculated chickwts.mmc contains all of Table 7.7 plus the $lmat section listed here. The plot showing the contrasts specified here is displayed in Figure 7.18. The contrasts here are not totally independent as a consequence of the unbalance in the sample sizes for the feeds. The magnitudes of the sums of squares are such that the conclusions are still valid.

```
> chickwts.mmc <-
+      glht.mmc(AnovaModel.1,
+               focus.lmat=chickwts.focus.lmat)

> chickwts.mmc$lmat
              estimate  stderr     lower     upper  height
su-ca          5.33333 22.3925 -60.3947   71.0614 326.250
su.ca-rest 100.67808 13.7969  60.1805 141.1757 275.911
me-sl         44.31981 19.7461 -13.6402 102.2798 254.749
so-li         27.67857 21.5780 -35.6586   91.0157 232.589
msl-h         87.16255 19.5699  29.7198 144.6053 203.781

> old.omd <- par(omd=c(0, 0.8, 0,1))
> plot(chickwts.mmc, x.offset=34.4705974297444,
+      ry=c(114.391957566256, 374.724709100411))
> par(mfrow=c(2,1))
> plot.matchMMC(chickwts.mmc$lmat, col.signif='blue')
> par(mfrow=c(1,1))
> par(old.omd)
```

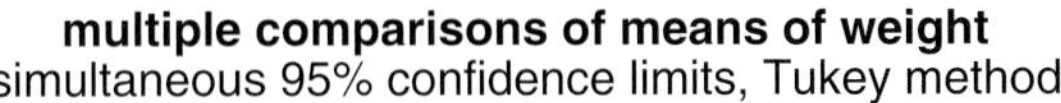

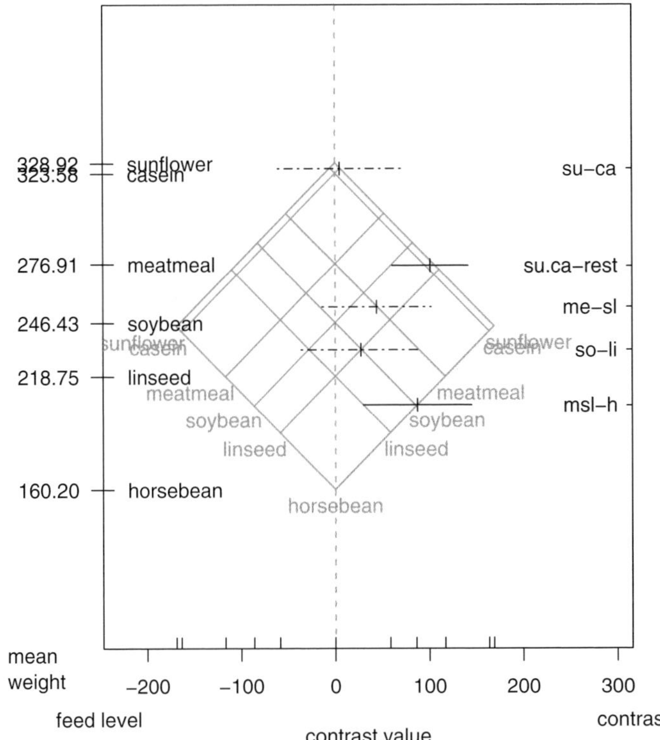

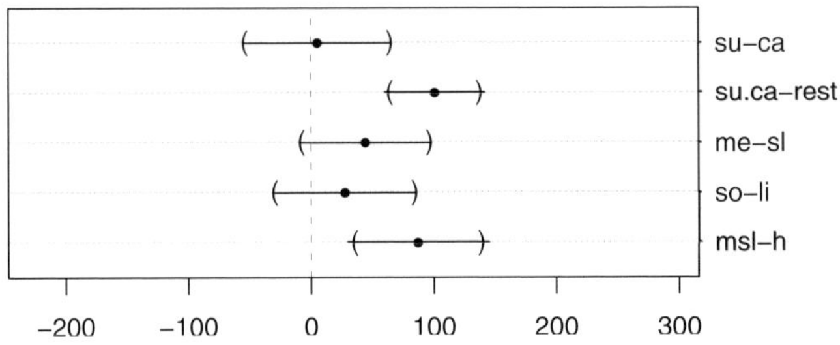

Fig. 7.18 This figure is specified by the R statements in Table 7.11. There are five contrasts, corresponding to the five degrees of freedom in the ANOVA table for the six feeds. The two contrasts distinguishing the three clusters are all significant and do not cross the vertical 0-line. The three contrasts within the clusters are not significant and do cross the 0-line. We show the tiebreaker plot even though it is not absolutely needed here.

Chapter 8
Simple Linear Regression

Abstract Linear regression by the least-squares method is a way of fitting a straight-line model to observed data.

Linear regression is one of the fundamental techniques in the statistical analysis of data. We assume a straight-line model for a response variable y as a function of one or more predictor (or explanatory) variables x. In this chapter, we look at exactly one predictor variable. Beginning with Chapter 10, we will look at two or more predictor variables.

The key model assumption is that the mean value of ys for a given x depends linearly on the value of x. In addition, the model assumes that the observed y values are distributed according to a normal distribution whose mean is linear in x and whose standard deviation is independent of the value of x. That is, the variability of the y data around the mean is independent of x. For one x-variable, the model is

$$\begin{aligned} y_i &= \beta_0 + \beta_1 x_i + \varepsilon_i \\ \varepsilon_i &\sim N(0, \sigma^2) \end{aligned}$$

for data consisting of a response variable y and a single predictor variable x. We fit the model with the least-squares estimates

$$\begin{aligned} \hat{\beta}_1 &= \frac{\Sigma(x_i - \bar{x})(y_i - \bar{y})}{\Sigma(x_i - \bar{x})^2} \\ \hat{\beta}_0 &= \bar{y} - \hat{\beta}_1 \bar{x} \\ \hat{y}_i &= \hat{\beta}_0 + \hat{\beta}_1 x_i \\ s^2 &= \frac{\Sigma(y_i - \hat{y})^2}{n-2} \end{aligned}$$

The estimates are usually calculated by a computer program. We will usually first graph the data and then use the Rcmdr Statistics ► Fit Models ► Linear regression ... menu item to access the R `lm` function.

R.M. Heiberger, E. Neuwirth, *R Through Excel*, Use R,
DOI 10.1007/978-1-4419-0052-4_8,

8.1 Least-Squares Regression with RExcel/Rcmdr

Our initial illustration of regression uses the artificial data in Table 8.1. We will enter the data into a new Excel workbook in Fig. 8.1.

Table 8.1 Artificial data for initial regression example.

x	y
1	−0.16
2	−0.80
3	0.00
4	0.60
5	1.36
6	1.28
7	1.40
8	0.72
9	1.04
10	1.36

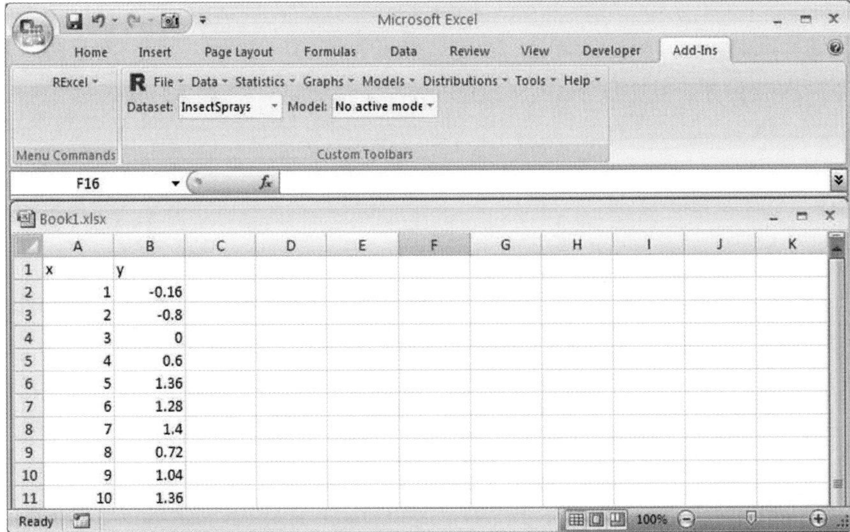

Fig. 8.1 When the numbers are first entered, Excel by default formats them without aligning decimal points. Unaligned decimal points are very difficult to read; therefore, in Fig. 8.2, we will align them as we did in Fig. 6.2.

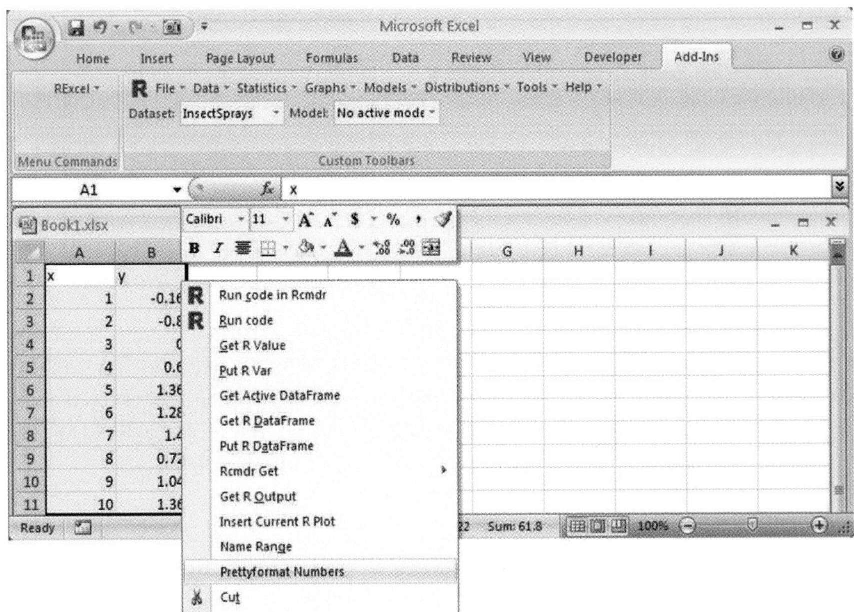

Fig. 8.2 Highlight the region (including the column labels in row 1) containing the poorly formatted numbers, and then right-click Prettyformat Numbers to get Fig. 8.3.

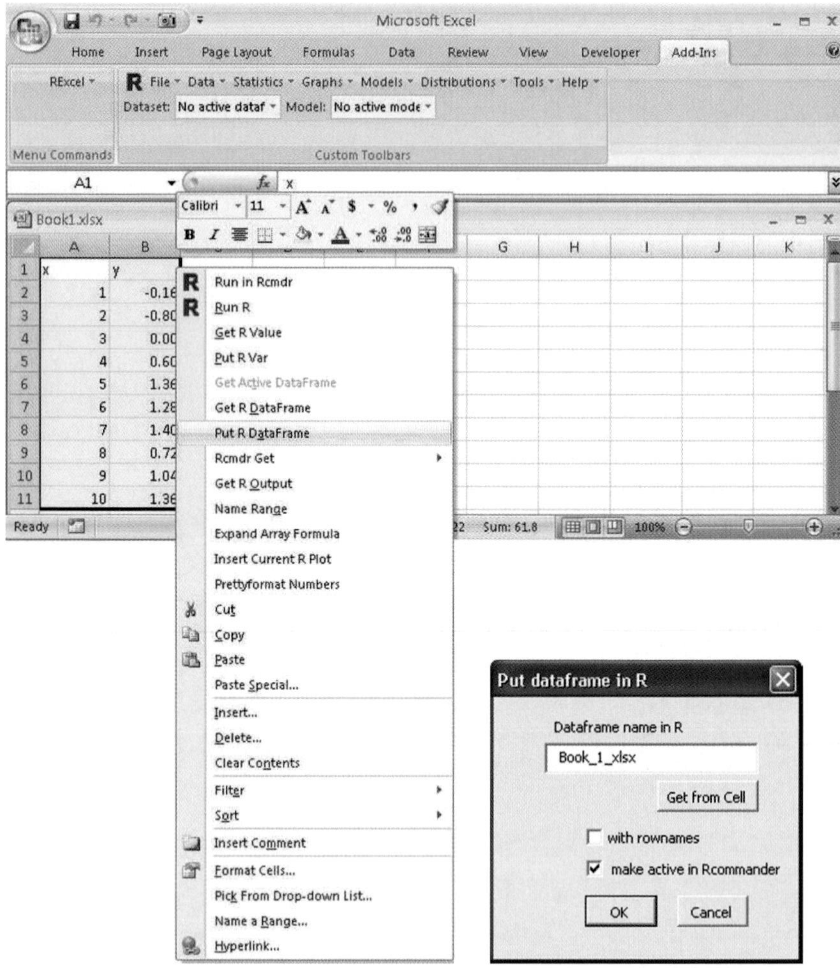

Fig. 8.3 The numbers are now aligned. Since they are still highlighted from Fig. 8.2, we can send them to R by right-clicking Put R DataFrame. RExcel gives a dialog box with a suggested name for the R dataframe that has been constructed from the name of the Excel workbook. Excel and R have different restrictions on the formation of valid names. The suggested name satisfies both restrictions.

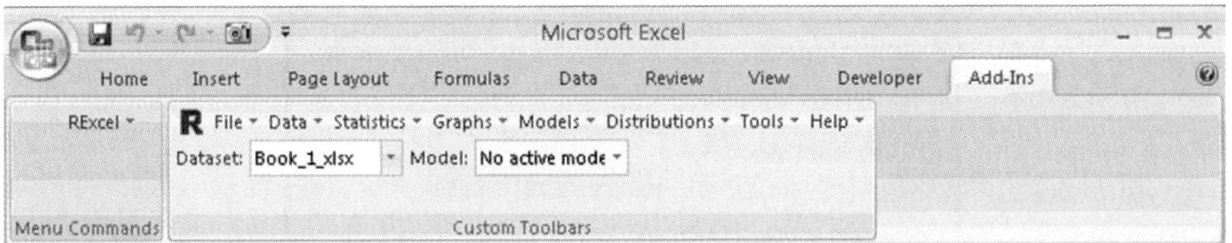

Fig. 8.4 Once the dataframe has been put into R, the Dataset field in the Rcmdr menu shows the name of the now active dataframe. All menu items on the Rcmdr menu refer to variables that are columns in the active dataframe.

8.2 Scatterplot

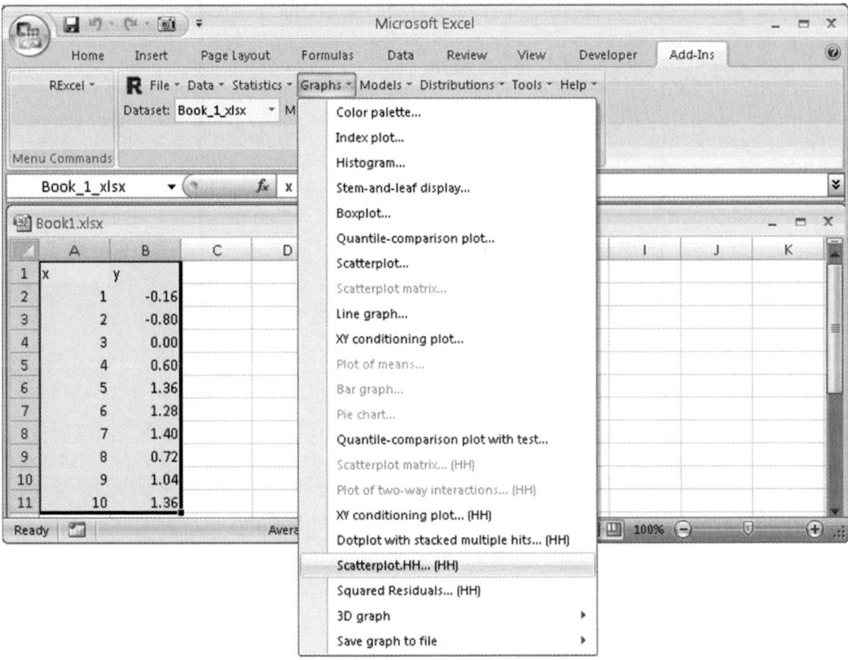

Fig. 8.5 Now that the data is in R, we are ready to begin the analysis. Almost always an analysis begins with a plot of the data. Here we show the Graphs ► Scatterplot.HH... (HH) menu item, which opens the dialog box in Fig. 8.6.

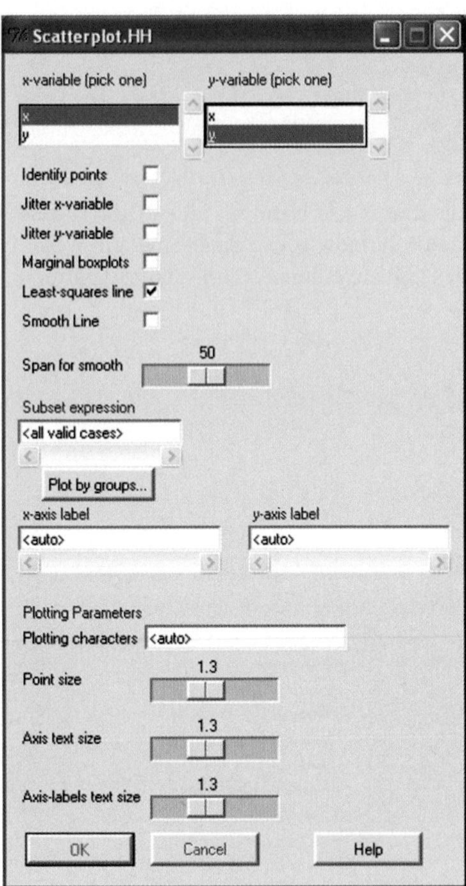

Fig. 8.6 Scatterplot.HH dialog box specifying the scatterplot in Fig. 8.7. We highlighted the x-variable on the left and the y-variable on the right. This figure shows our default settings for the various options in the dialog box. They are different from the defaults for the Scatterplot... menu item. We have checked only the Least-squares line box and unchecked all others. Our default Plotting characters is 16 (to specify solid dots), and we increased the size of Point size, Axis text size, and Axis-labels text size.

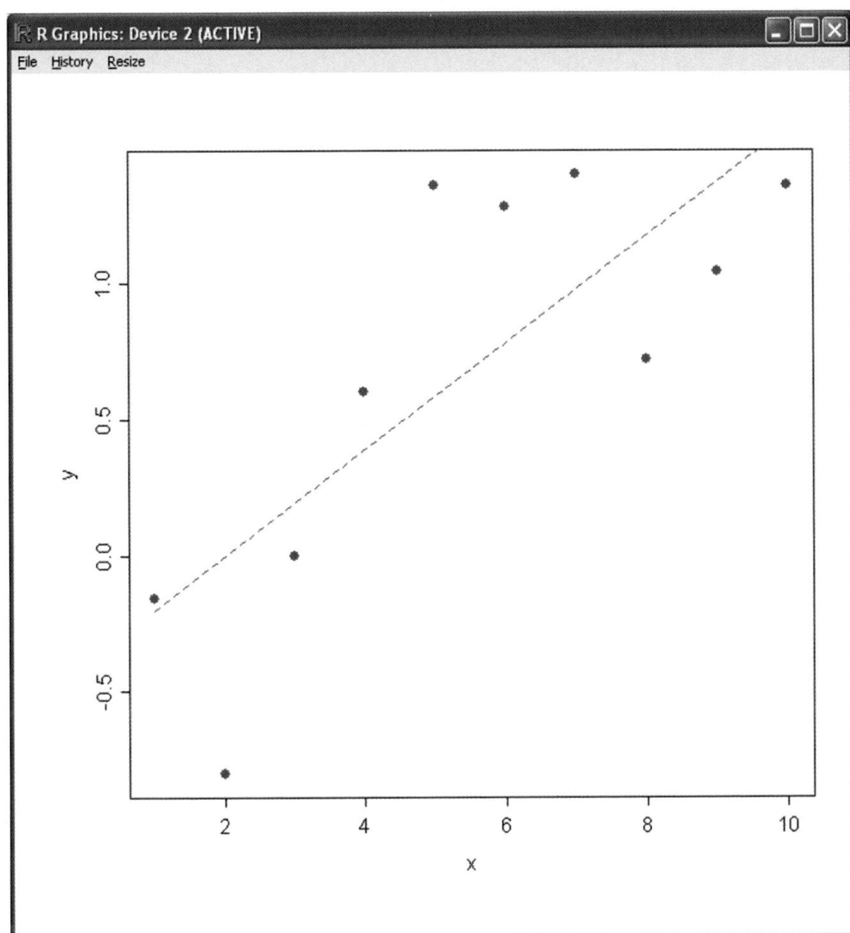

Fig. 8.7 Scatterplot specified in Fig. 8.6. The straight line is the least-squares line. We calculate its coefficients in the next few figures.

8.3 Linear Regression Analysis

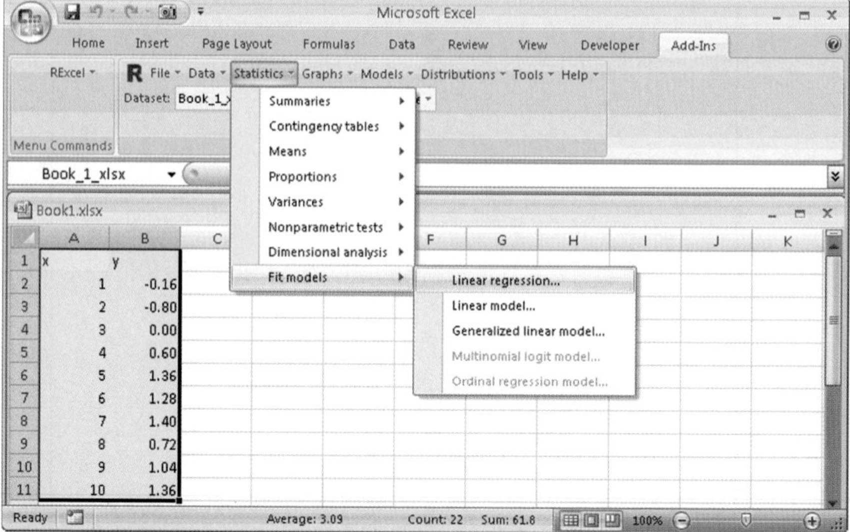

Fig. 8.8 Statistics ► Fit Models ► Linear regression... requests the linear regression dialog box in Fig. 8.9.

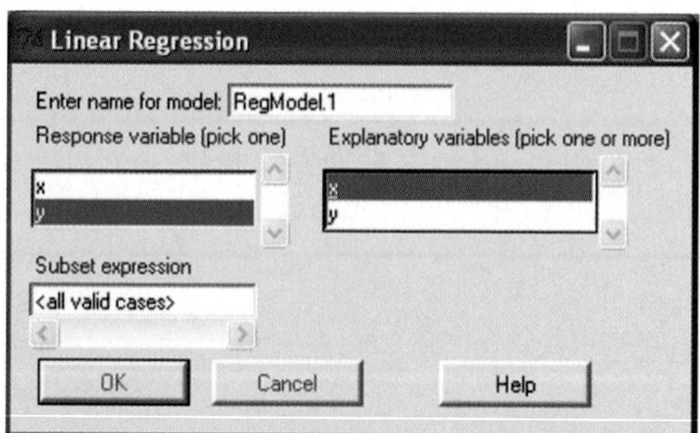

Fig. 8.9 Regression dialog box. We specify the response variable y and the explanatory (predictor) variable x.

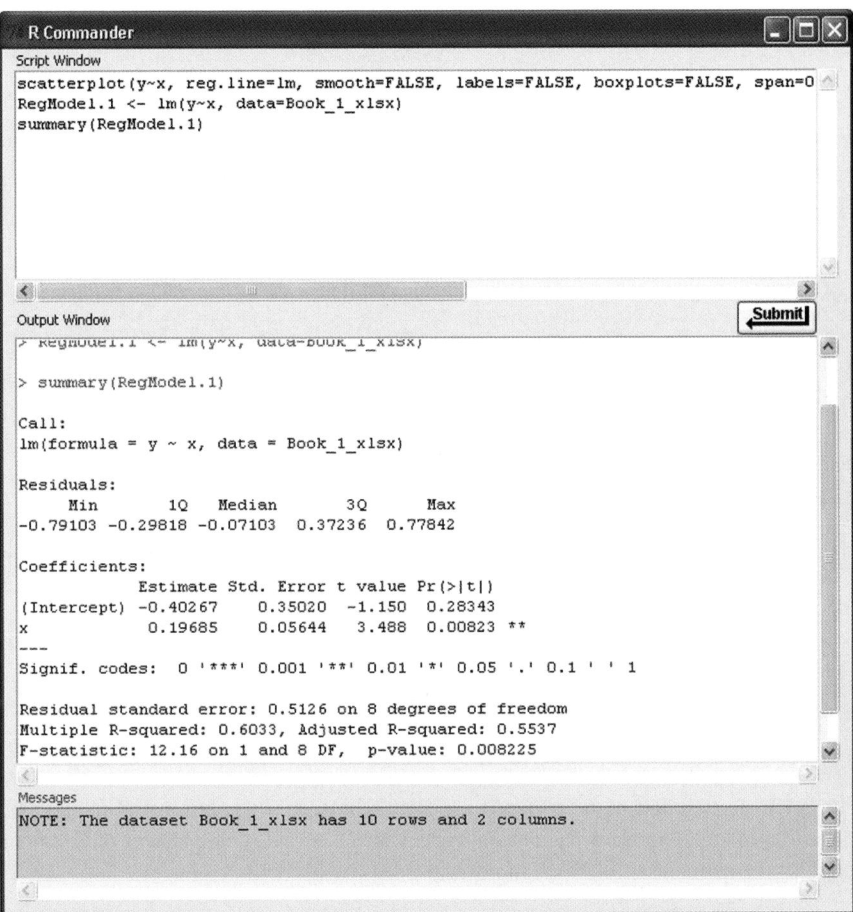

Fig. 8.10 The regression model has been calculated and stored in the model object `RegModel.1`. The model `RegModel.1` is now the active model in Rcmdr. The regression coefficients, the intercept and slope of the straight-line fit, are displayed. Also included in the standard display are the test statistics for the coefficients. In this example, the slope $\beta_1 = 0.19685$ is significant at $p = 0.00823$. The double "$\star\star$" is a reminder that the p-value is between 0.001 and 0.01.

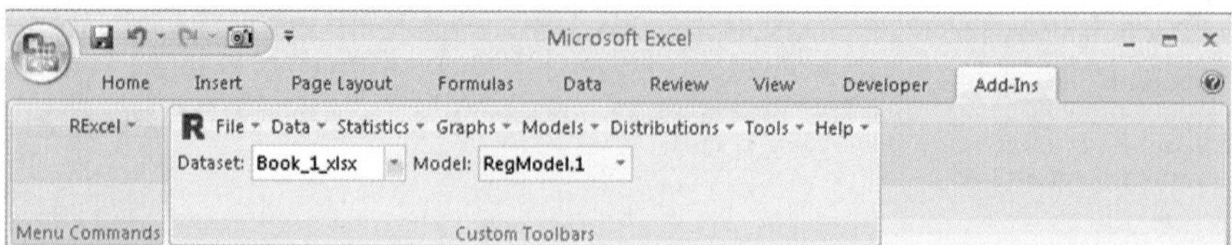

Fig. 8.11 The name of the active model now appears in the Model field on the Rcmdr menu.

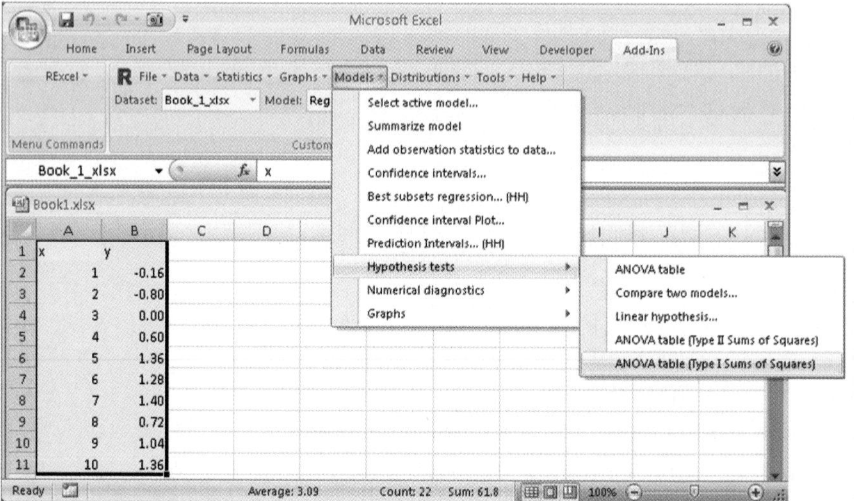

Fig. 8.12 The Models menu is used to specify additional calculations or displays of the active model. Models ► Hypothesis Tests ► ANOVA Table (Type I Sums of Squares) requests the sequential ANOVA table displayed in Fig. 8.13.

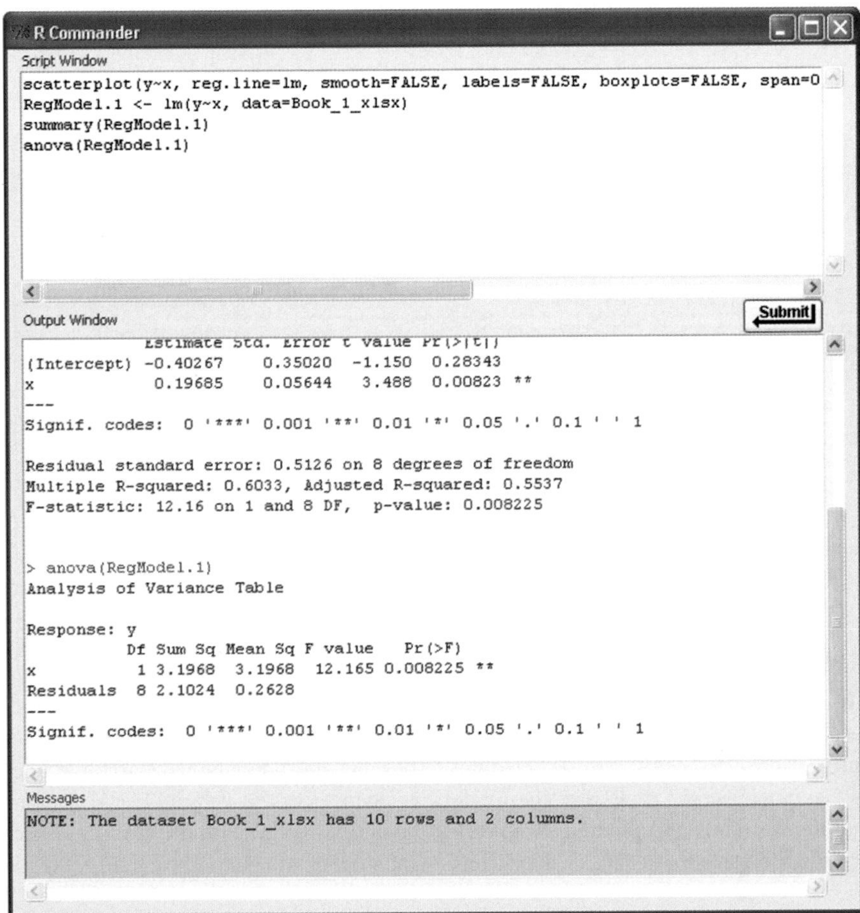

Fig. 8.13 ANOVA table for regression analysis in Fig. 8.10. The *p*-value for *x* in the ANOVA table is identical to the *p*-value for *x* in the table of coefficients in Fig. 8.10. The mean square (Mean Sq) on the Residuals line of the ANOVA table is the square of the Residual standard error.

8.4 Residuals Analysis

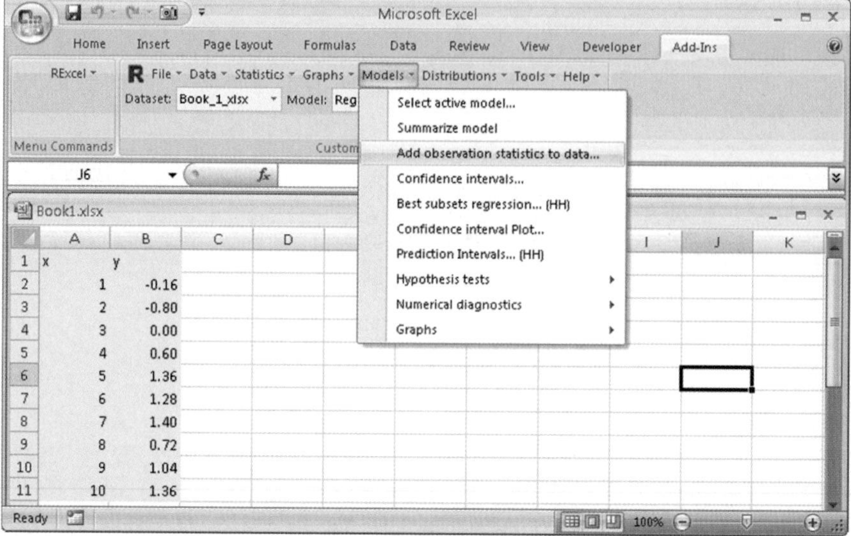

Fig. 8.14 We normally look at the residuals after fitting a model. Recall that the residual standard error is given by $s^2 = (\sum(y_i - \hat{y})^2)/(n-2)$. The terms inside the summation $e_i = y_i - \hat{y}$ are the residuals. They are the unexplained part of y, the *leftover* or *residual* part, after the model has been fit to the x-variable. We calculate the residuals and predicted values for the active model with the Models ▶ Add observation statistics to data... menu item, which opens the dialog box in Fig. 8.15.

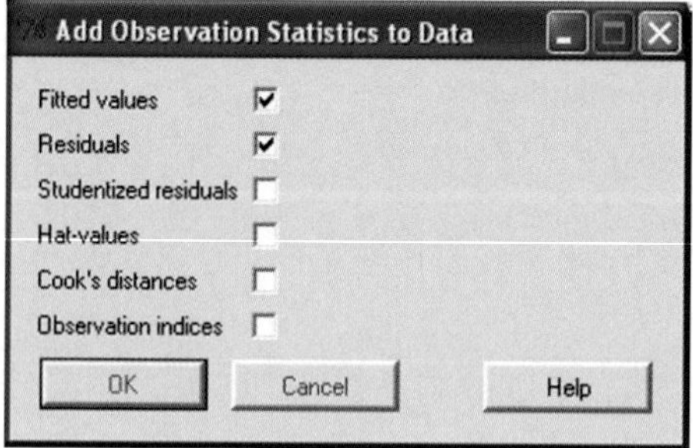

Fig. 8.15 At this time we check just the fitted values and residuals. These will be added as variables to the active dataset in R.

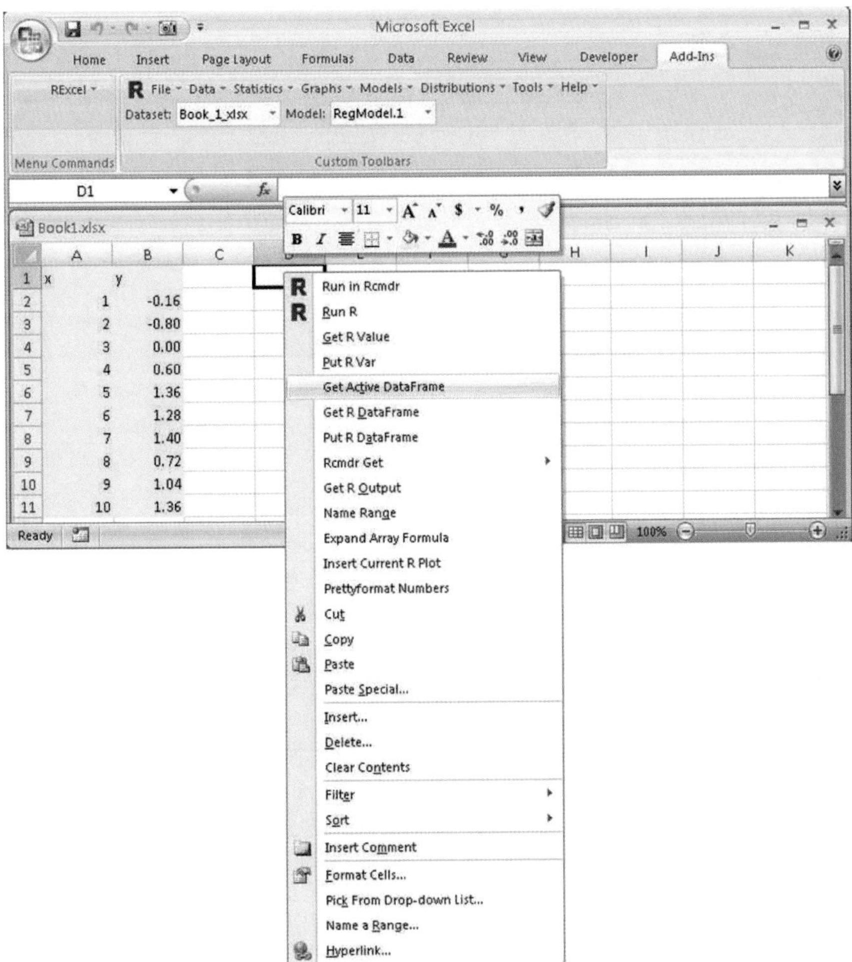

Fig. 8.16 We can see the dataframe as revised with the additional columns by placing the cursor on an empty cell to the right of the existing cells and then right-clicking Get Active DataFrame.

a. Default formatting with unaligned decimal points.

Book1.xlsx

	A	B	C	D	E	F	G	H	I	J	K
1	x	y			x	y	fitted.Reg	residuals.RegModel.1			
2	1	-0.16		1	1	-0.16	-0.20582	0.045818			
3	2	-0.80		2	2	-0.8	-0.00897	-0.79103			
4	3	0.00		3	3	0	0.187879	-0.18788			
5	4	0.60		4	4	0.6	0.384727	0.215273			
6	5	1.36		5	5	1.36	0.581576	0.778424			
7	6	1.28		6	6	1.28	0.778424	0.501576			
8	7	1.40		7	7	1.4	0.975273	0.424727			
9	8	0.72		8	8	0.72	1.172121	-0.45212			
10	9	1.04		9	9	1.04	1.36897	-0.32897			
11	10	1.36		10	10	1.36	1.565818	-0.20582			

b. Aligned decimal points after right-clicking Prettyformat Numbers.

Book1.xlsx

	A	B	C	D	E	F	G	H	I	J	K
1	x	y			x	y	fitted.Reg	residuals.RegModel.1			
2	1	-0.16		1	1	-0.16	-0.20582	0.0458182			
3	2	-0.80		2	2	-0.80	-0.00897	-0.7910303			
4	3	0.00		3	3	0.00	0.18788	-0.1878788			
5	4	0.60		4	4	0.60	0.38473	0.2152727			
6	5	1.36		5	5	1.36	0.58158	0.7784242			
7	6	1.28		6	6	1.28	0.77842	0.5015758			
8	7	1.40		7	7	1.40	0.97527	0.4247273			
9	8	0.72		8	8	0.72	1.17212	-0.4521212			
10	9	1.04		9	9	1.04	1.36897	-0.3289697			
11	10	1.36		10	10	1.36	1.56582	-0.2058182			

Fig. 8.17 The dataset with the additional columns is displayed. Initially, it has unaligned decimal points; therefore, we align them by right-clicking Prettyformat Numbers. See Fig. 8.2 for a display of the right-click menu showing Prettyformat Numbers.

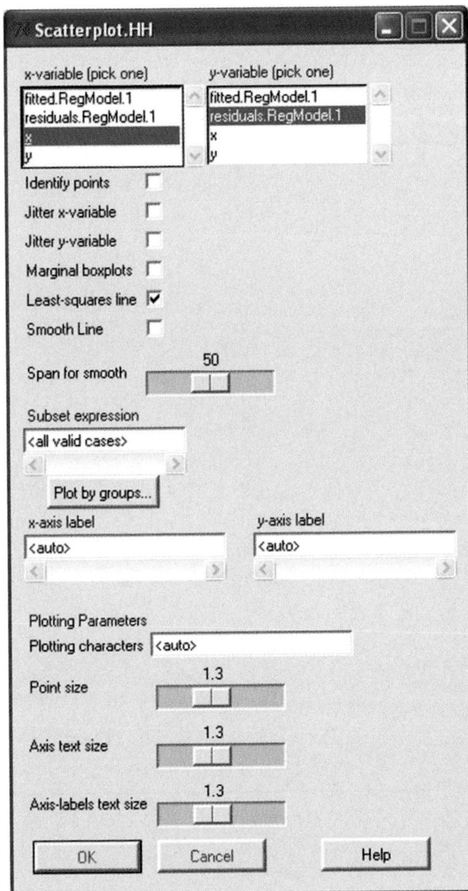

Fig. 8.18 We specify a scatterplot of the residuals variable residuals.RegModel.1 against the predictor x-variable.

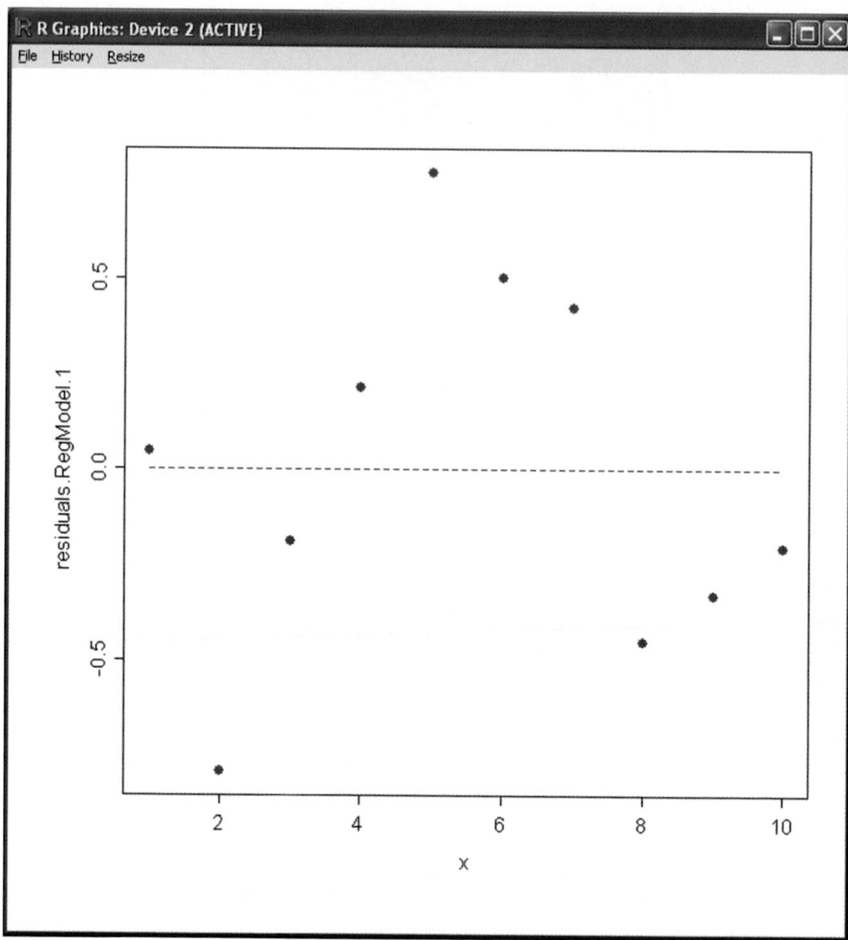

Fig. 8.19 This plot of the residuals against the x-variable shows no structure. If any structure were visible, we would attempt to fit it with a more complex model. We show such examples in the next few chapters.

8.5 Confidence Bands and Prediction Bands

Once we have estimated a linear model, we need to use it.

We need to make statements about the location of the fitted line. These statements take the form of confidence bands around the fitted line. The confidence bands provide an estimate of the expected mean value of ys for a given value of x and a given confidence level.

We need to make predictions, based on the fitted straight line, of the y-values of new observations for which we know the x-values. The prediction bands gives an estimate of an interval which will contain observed values (not means) for a given value of x and a given confidence level.

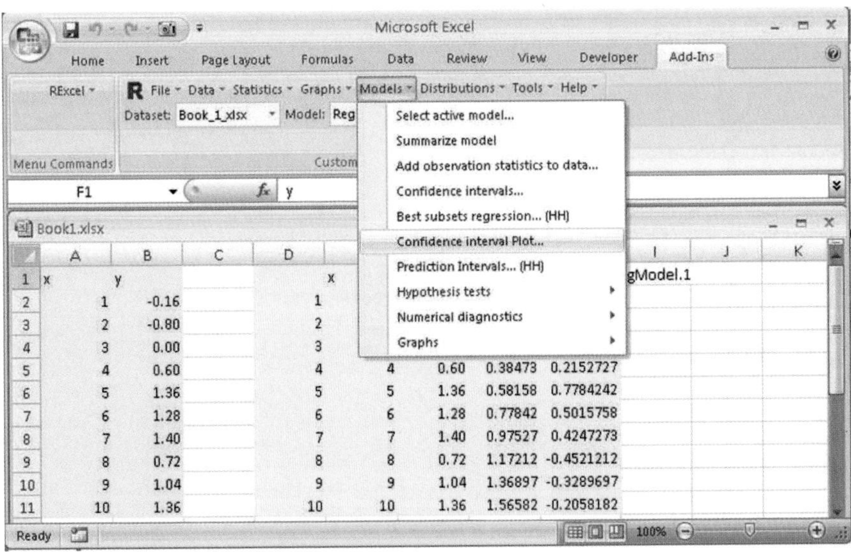

Fig. 8.20 Use the Models ▸ Confidence interval Plot... menu item to request the dialog box in Fig. 8.21 and the display in Fig. 8.22 of the data and least-squares regression line from the model of Figs. 8.10 and 8.13. Fig. 8.22 also shows the confidence bands for estimating the regression line's y-value for a specified x:

$$\mu_{y|x} = E(y|x) = \beta_0 + \beta_1 x$$

and the prediction bands for predicting the y-values of new observations at specified x:

$$y|x = \mu_{y|x} + \varepsilon = \beta_0 + \beta_1 x + \varepsilon.$$

The prediction bands are wider than the confidence bands because they include the uncertainty ε of the new observation.

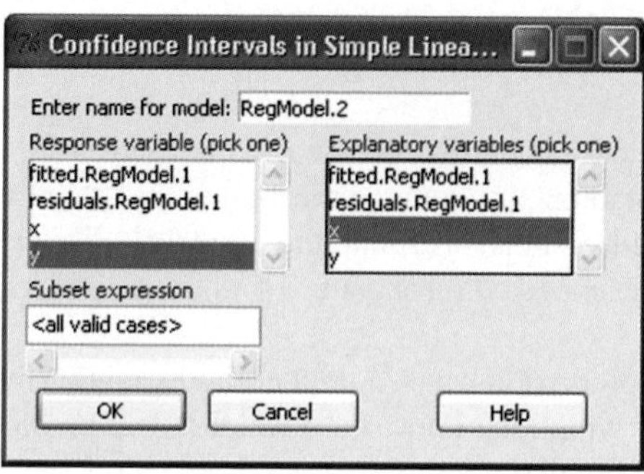

Fig. 8.21 Dialog box for confidence intervals. In addition to drawing Fig. 8.22, this dialog box recalculates the regression analysis and places it in model object `RegModel.2`.

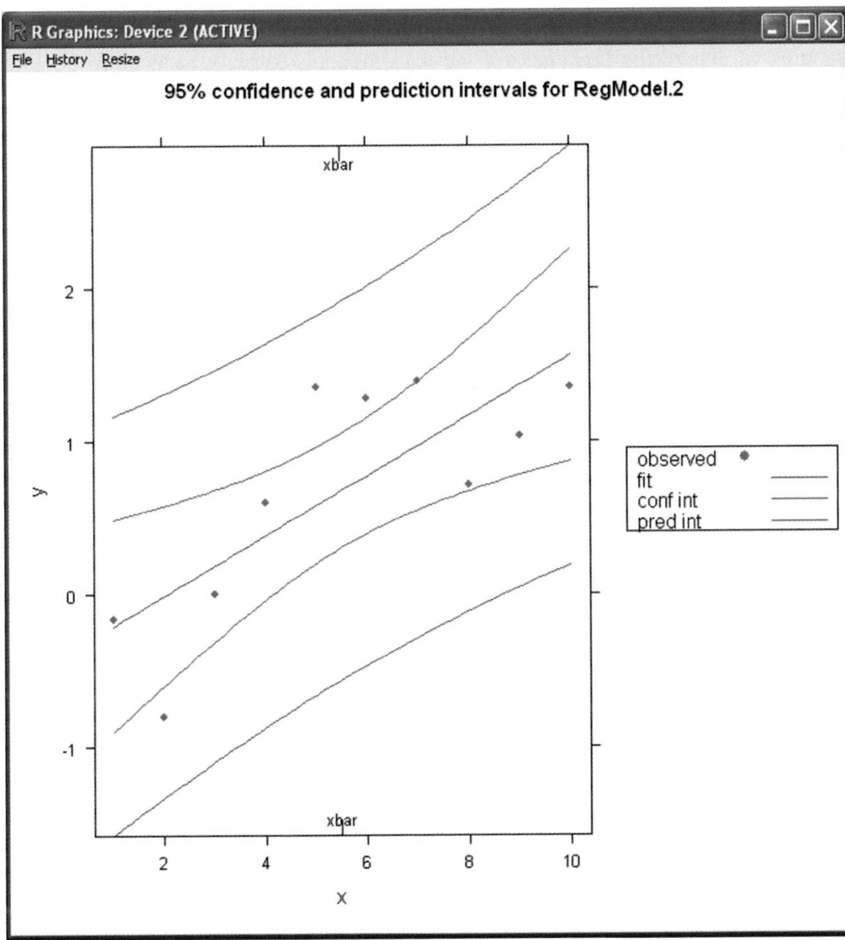

Fig. 8.22 Data points (in blue) and least-squares regression line (in magenta) along with the confidence bands (in green) for estimating the regression line's y-value for a specified x (this corresponds to predicting the mean of many observations with this value of the independent variable):

$$\mu_{y|x} = E(y|x) = \beta_0 + \beta_1 x$$

and the prediction bands (in red) for predicting the y-values of new observations at x:

$$y|x = \mu_{y|x} + \varepsilon$$

The prediction bands are wider than the confidence bands because they include the uncertainty ε of the new observation.

The prediction and confidence intervals displayed in Fig. 8.22 are calculated with formulas similar to the formulas for the hat diagonals to be introduced in Section 9.3.

Define

$$h_0 = \frac{1}{n} + \frac{(x_0 - \bar{x})^2}{\sum_{j=1}^{n}(x_j - \bar{x})^2} \tag{8.1}$$

where x_0 is not necessarily one of the original x-values.

The confidence bands (in green) in Fig. 8.22 for estimating the regression line's y-value for a specified x_0

$$\mu_{y|x_0} = E(y|x_0) = \beta_0 + \beta_1 x_0$$

are given by

$$\begin{aligned}\hat{\mu}_{y|x_0} \pm t_{\frac{\alpha}{2},n-2}\, s\, \sqrt{h_0} &= E(y|x_0) \pm t_{\frac{\alpha}{2},n-2}\, s\, \sqrt{h_0} \\ &= \hat{\beta}_0 + \hat{\beta}_1 x_0 \pm t_{\frac{\alpha}{2},n-2}\, s\, \sqrt{h_0} \end{aligned} \tag{8.2}$$

The prediction bands (in red) in Fig. 8.22 for predicting the y-values of new observations at x_0:

$$y|x_0 = \mu_{y|x_0} + \varepsilon$$

are given by

$$\hat{y}|x_0 \pm t_{\frac{\alpha}{2},n-2}\, s\, \sqrt{1+h_0} = \hat{\beta}_0 + \hat{\beta}_1 x_0 \pm t_{\frac{\alpha}{2},n-2}\, s\, \sqrt{1+h_0} \tag{8.3}$$

Note in Fig. 8.22 that both sets of bands are farther from the regression line for x_0 points farther away from $\bar{x}$ than for points closer to $\bar{x}$.

Chapter 9
What Is Least Squares?

Abstract The linreg workbook distributed with this book allows us to explore linear regression dynamically. We discuss the meaning of least squares, hat diagonals, leverage, and residuals.

9.1 Minimizing the Sum of Squares

The linreg workbook [Heiberger and Neuwirth, 2008] (either `linreg.xlsx` in Excel 2007 or `linreg.xls` in Excel 2003) allows us to explore linear regression dynamically.

This workbook uses the automatic recalculation mode of Excel to update the R graph as numerical values or control tools are changed in the workbook. The workbook directly accesses the same R function that the dialog box in Fig. 11.14 uses.

Fig. 9.2 shows artificial data (the same data we used in Fig. 8.2), the table of coefficients, and the ANOVA table from a linear regression of that data. Fig. 9.3 shows the graph of the data along with the least-squares line, the predicted values, and the residuals.

The arithmetic for calculation of the regression coefficients is displayed in region E1:I12. The residuals e_i in column H are squared to e_i^2 and displayed in column I. Their sum $\sum e_i^2$ is displayed in cell I12. This is the same number as is displayed in the ANOVA table as the "Sum of Squares for Residuals" in cell N9.

R.M. Heiberger, E. Neuwirth, *R Through Excel*, Use R,
DOI 10.1007/978-1-4419-0052-4_9,

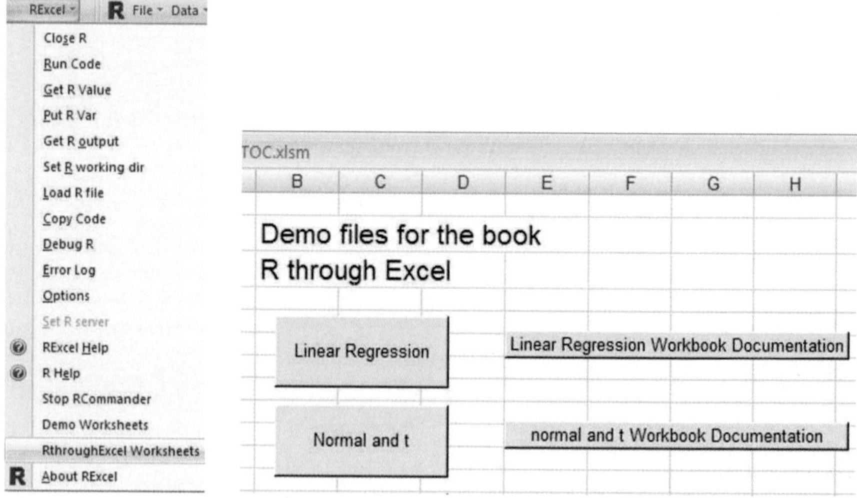

Fig. 9.1 Open the normal.and.t.dist workbook by clicking on RExcel ► RthroughExcel Worksheets. This opens an Excel workbook BookFilesTOC with the names of the workbooks for this book. Click on linreg to open the linreg workbook displaying cells A1:Q25 as in Fig. 9.2 and an R graph reproducing Fig. 9.3. The full BookFilesTOC is shown in Fig. 3.2. (If the RthroughExcel Worksheets menu item is missing, see step 4 of Section A.3.3.) (If the values in the workbook don't match the ones in the figures, then click cell on A17 and choose the scenario R through Excel. Double-click it to reset the workbook to the default values. See the illustration and discussion in Section 9.4.)

linreg.xlsm

	A	C	E	F	G	H	I	J
1	color	sliders for y	x	y	y.hat	resid	resid²	hat(x)
2	red		1	-0.16	-0.21	0.05	0.0021	0.3455
3	purple		2	-0.80	-0.01	-0.79	0.6257	0.2485
4	green		3	0.00	0.19	-0.19	0.0353	0.1758
5	gold		4	0.60	0.38	0.22	0.0463	0.1273
6	orange		5	1.36	0.58	0.78	0.6059	0.1030
7	deep pink		6	1.28	0.78	0.50	0.2516	0.1030
8	forest green		7	1.40	0.98	0.42	0.1804	0.1273
9	brown		8	0.72	1.17	-0.45	0.2044	0.1758
10	salmon		9	1.04	1.37	-0.33	0.1082	0.2485
11	blue		10	1.36	1.57	-0.21	0.0424	0.3455
12							2.1024	

Regression Coefficients

	Estimate	Std. Error	t value	Pr(>|t|)
(Intercept)	-0.4027	0.3502	-1.1498	0.2834
x	0.1968	0.0564	3.4878	0.0082

ANOVA table

	Df	Sum Sq	Mean Sq	F value	Pr(>F)
x	1	3.1968	3.1968	12.1646	0.0082
Residuals	8	2.1024	0.2628		
Total	9	5.2992			

	E	F	G	H	I
14	x	y	y.alt	res.alt	res.alt²
15	1	-0.16	-0.25	0.09	0.0090
16	2	-0.80	-0.11	-0.69	0.4807
17	3	0.00	0.04	-0.04	0.0017
18	4	0.60	0.19	0.41	0.1686
19	5	1.36	0.34	1.02	1.0458
20	6	1.28	0.49	0.79	0.6315
21	7	1.40	0.63	0.77	0.5878
22	8	0.72	0.78	-0.06	0.0038
23	9	1.04	0.93	0.11	0.0122
24	10	1.36	1.08	0.28	0.0799
25					3.0211

use alternate
reset Alt to LS
-0.4027
0.1480
Graph on Top
Residual display: none, line, square
ColorRestore
Sheet1

Fig. 9.2 Artificial data with x_i and y_i in columns E and F and a color name in column A. The y_i-values in column F are controlled by the sliders in column C. The table of regression coefficients is in region L1:P4 and the ANOVA table for the regression is in region L6:Q10. The data is plotted in Fig. 9.3. The predicted values $\hat{y}_i$ are in column G and the residuals $e_i = (y_i - \hat{y}_i)$ are in column H.

The term "least squares" means that the regression coefficients $\hat{\beta}_0$ in cell M3 and $\hat{\beta}_1$ in cell M4 are the values that minimize the sum of squared differences between the observed and predicted y-values. That is,

$$\Sigma_{i=1}^{n} e_i^2 = \Sigma_{i=1}^{n} (y_i - \hat{y}_i)^2 = \Sigma_{i=1}^{n} (y_i - (\beta_0 + \beta_1 x_i))^2$$

is at its minimum value when $\beta_0 = \hat{\beta}_0$ and $\beta_1 = \hat{\beta}_1$. The differences, labeled *residuals*, are in column H, and the squared differences are in column I. The sum of squared differences is in cell I12 and in the ANOVA table in cell N9.

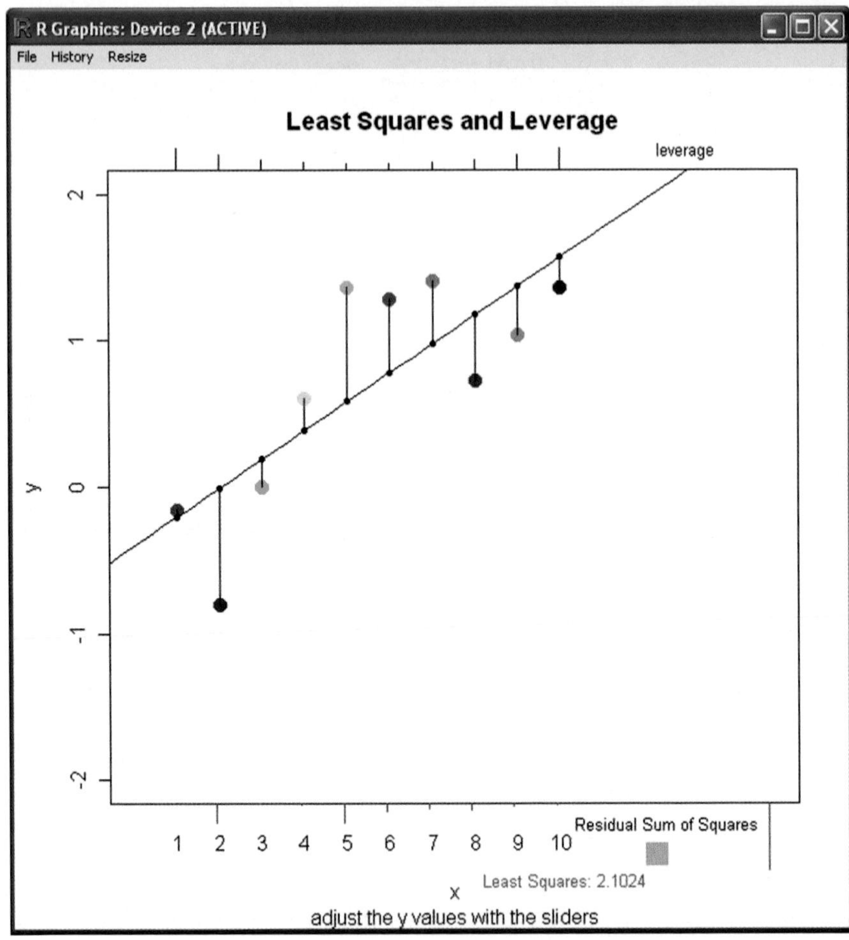

Fig. 9.3 Plot of artificial data in the spreadsheet of Fig. 9.2. Each observed point (x_i, y_i) from columns E and F is plotted in the color specified in column A. The least-squares line for this data is in black. Each predicted value $\hat{y}_i$ is marked with a small black dot on the least-squares line. Residuals are indicated with the vertical lines $e_i = (y_i - \hat{y}_i)$ at each value of x_i.

Additional features on the graph are

1. Subtitle adjust the y values with the sliders. Reminder that this graph is directly connected to the workbook in Fig. 9.2.
2. Bottom rug. The lengths at the tick marks are proportional to the squared residuals and their sum (cells I2:I11, I12).
3. The numerical value of the sum of squared residuals (cell I12) is displayed.
4. Gray box. The area is proportional (with a different factor) to the sum of squared residuals (cell I12).
5. Top rug: leverage. The lengths are proportional (yet another proportionality factor) to the hat(x) values in cells J2:J11.

linregErichRmh3.xlsm

color	sliders for y	x	y	y.hat	resid	resid²	hat(x)
red		1	-0.16	-0.21	0.05	0.0021	0.3455
purple		2	-0.80	-0.01	-0.79	0.6257	0.2485
green		3	0.00	0.19	-0.19	0.0353	0.1758
gold		4	0.60	0.38	0.22	0.0463	0.1273
orange		5	1.36	0.58	0.78	0.6059	0.1030
deep pink		6	1.28	0.78	0.50	0.2516	0.1030
forest green		7	1.40	0.98	0.42	0.1804	0.1273
brown		8	0.72	1.17	-0.45	0.2044	0.1758
salmon		9	1.04	1.37	-0.33	0.1082	0.2485
blue		10	1.36	1.57	-0.21	0.0424	0.3455
						2.1024	

Regression Coefficients

	Estimate	Std. Error	t value	Pr(>|t|)
(Intercept)	-0.4027	0.3502	-1.1498	0.2834
x	0.1968	0.0564	3.4878	0.0082

ANOVA table

	Df	Sum Sq	Mean Sq	F value	Pr(>F)
x	1	3.1968	3.1968	12.1646	0.0082
Residuals	8	2.1024	0.2628		
Total	9	5.2992			

use alternate

reset Alt to LS

-0.4027

0.1480

x	y	y.alt	res.alt	res.alt²
1	-0.16	-0.25	0.09	0.0090
2	-0.80	-0.11	-0.69	0.4807
3	0.00	0.04	-0.04	0.0017
4	0.60	0.19	0.41	0.1686
5	1.36	0.34	1.02	1.0458
6	1.28	0.49	0.79	0.6315
7	1.40	0.63	0.77	0.5878
8	0.72	0.78	-0.06	0.0038
9	1.04	0.93	0.11	0.0122
10	1.36	1.08	0.28	0.0799
				3.0211

Residual display

none

line

square

ColorRestore

Graph on Top

Sheet1

Fig. 9.4 We can see that the least-squares line minimizes the sum of squared residuals by looking at the individual squares in the sum. Click cell L19 to display the squares of each residual. This click yields Fig. 9.5.

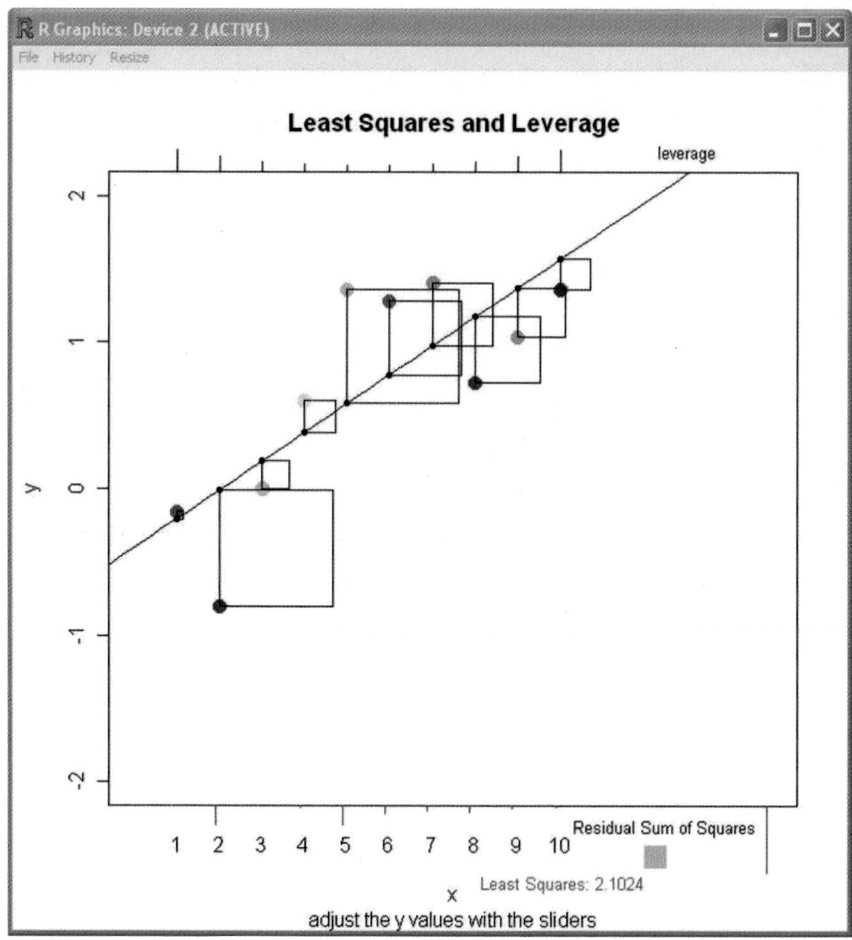

Fig. 9.5 We click cell L19 to produce this figure, which is a repeat of Fig. 9.3 with the residuals indicated by squares, each of whose side is the length of the residual $e_i = (y_i - \hat{y}_i)$. The squares are visual squares; the number of inches used on the page or screen for the horizontal side is the same as the number of inches used by the vertical side $e_i = (y_i - \hat{y}_i)$.

You may construct a similar plot for your own data using the menu shown in Figs. 11.14 and 11.15.

linreg.xlsm

	color	sliders for y	x	y	y.hat	resid	resid²	hat(x)
2	red	< >	1	-0.16	-0.21	0.05	0.0021	0.3455
3	purple	< >	2	-0.80	-0.01	-0.79	0.6257	0.2485
4	green	< >	3	0.00	0.19	-0.19	0.0353	0.1758
5	gold	< >	4	0.60	0.38	0.22	0.0463	0.1273
6	orange	< >	5	1.36	0.58	0.78	0.6059	0.1030
7	deep pink	< >	6	1.28	0.78	0.50	0.2516	0.1030
8	forest green	< >	7	1.40	0.98	0.42	0.1804	0.1273
9	brown	< >	8	0.72	1.17	-0.45	0.2044	0.1758
10	salmon	< >	9	1.04	1.37	-0.33	0.1082	0.2485
11	blue	< >	10	1.36	1.57	-0.21	0.0424	0.3455
12							2.1024	

Regression Coefficients

	Estimate	Std. Error	t value	Pr(>|t|)
(Intercept)	-0.4027	0.3502	-1.1498	0.2834
x	0.1968	0.0564	3.4878	0.0082

ANOVA table

	Df	Sum Sq	Mean Sq	F value	Pr(>F)
x	1	3.1968	3.1968	12.1646	0.0082
Residuals	8	2.1024	0.2628		
Total	9	5.2992			

	x	y	y.alt	res.alt	res.alt²
15	1	-0.16	-0.25	0.09	0.0090
16	2	-0.80	-0.11	-0.69	0.4807
17	3	0.00	0.04	-0.04	0.0017
18	4	0.60	0.19	0.41	0.1686
19	5	1.36	0.34	1.02	1.0458
20	6	1.28	0.49	0.79	0.6315
21	7	1.40	0.63	0.77	0.5878
22	8	0.72	0.78	-0.06	0.0038
23	9	1.04	0.93	0.11	0.0122
24	10	1.36	1.08	0.28	0.0799
25					3.0211

☑ use alternate
reset Alt to LS
< > -0.4027
< > 0.1480

☑ Graph on Top

Residual display
○ none
○ line
◉ square
ColorRestore

Sheet1

Fig. 9.6 We click use alternate in cell C16 to produce Fig. 9.7. The least-squares line in Fig. 9.5, based on the least-squares coefficients in cells M3:M4, is still visible as a dashed gray line. The residuals and squared residuals shown here are distances from the arbitrary line specified by the coefficients in cells C18:C19. The alternate line goes through the alternate points y.alt in cells G15:G24. The alternate residuals in cells H15:H24 are squared in I15:I24. The sum of squares of the alternate residuals are shown in cell I25. The alternate sum of squares in cell I25 is always greater than or equal to the residual sum of squares in cell I12.

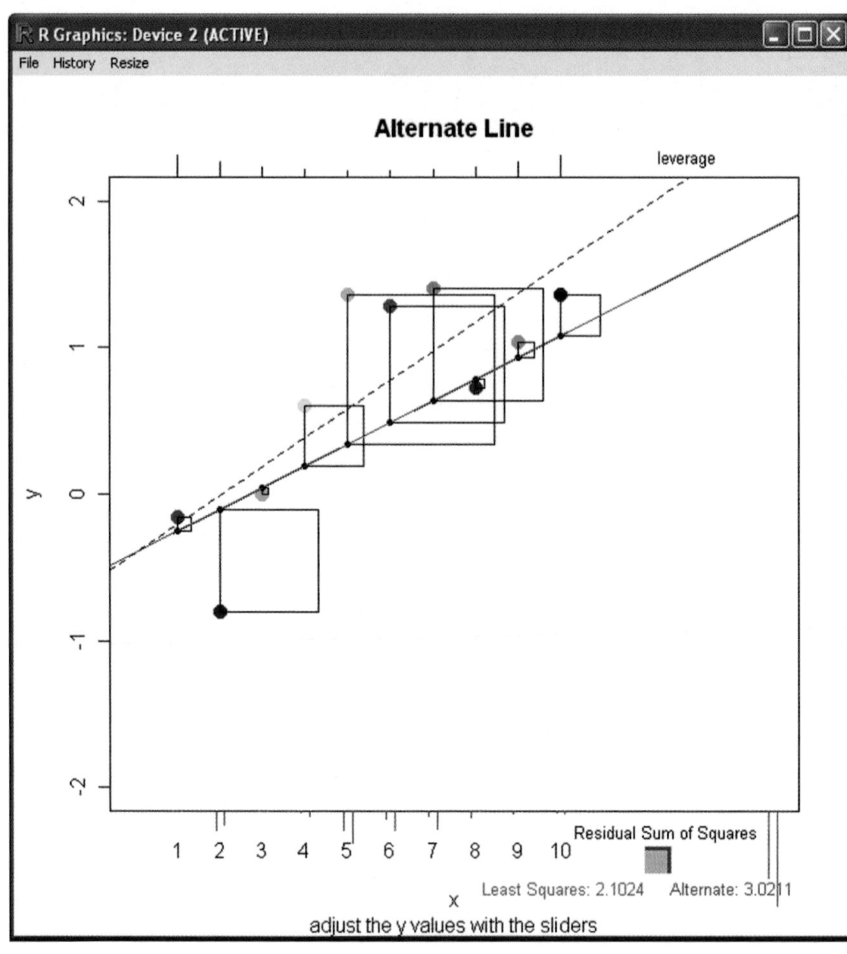

Fig. 9.7 The observed points, identical to those in Fig. 9.5, are plotted along with the alternate line specified by the coefficients in cells C18:C19. The squares of the alternate residuals are visibly bigger than the squares of the least-squares residuals in Fig. 9.4. In this example, the alternate line has much larger squared residuals at the larger values of x, and slightly smaller squared residuals at the smaller values of x. This pair of plots works very well on a live screen, where it is possible to toggle between them.

linregErichRmh3.xlsm

color	sliders for y	x	y	y.hat	resid	resid²	hat(x)
red		1	-0.16	-0.21	0.05	0.0021	0.3455
purple		2	-0.80	-0.01	-0.79	0.6257	0.2485
green		3	0.00	0.19	-0.19	0.0353	0.1758
gold		4	0.60	0.38	0.22	0.0463	0.1273
orange		5	1.36	0.58	0.78	0.6059	0.1030
deep pink		6	1.28	0.78	0.50	0.2516	0.1030
forest green		7	1.40	0.98	0.42	0.1804	0.1273
brown		8	0.72	1.17	-0.45	0.2044	0.1758
salmon		9	1.04	1.37	-0.33	0.1082	0.2485
blue		10	1.36	1.57	-0.21	0.0424	0.3455
						2.1024	

Regression Coefficients

	Estimate	Std. Error	t value	Pr(>|t|)
(Intercept)	-0.4027	0.3502	-1.1498	0.2834
x	0.1968	0.0564	3.4878	0.0082

ANOVA table

	Df	Sum Sq	Mean Sq	F value	Pr(>F)
x	1	3.1968	3.1968	12.1646	0.0082
Residuals	8	2.1024	0.2628		
Total	9	5.2992			

x	y	y.alt	res.alt	res.alt²
1	-0.16	-0.25	0.09	0.0090
2	-0.80	-0.11	-0.69	0.4807
3	0.00	0.04	-0.04	0.0017
4	0.60	0.19	0.41	0.1686
5	1.36	0.34	1.02	1.0458
6	1.28	0.49	0.79	0.6315
7	1.40	0.63	0.77	0.5878
8	0.72	0.78	-0.06	0.0038
9	1.04	0.93	0.11	0.0122
10	1.36	1.08	0.28	0.0799
				3.0211

use alternate

reset Alt to LS

-0.4027

0.1480

Residual display: none / line / square

ColorRestore

Graph on Top

Sheet1

Fig. 9.8 We can make a direct graphical comparison of the squares associated with the two lines. Double-click the resid² value of the point at $x = 7$ in both the least-squares and the alternate displays (cells I8 and I21). The cell values are now colored the associated color in cell A8. The squared residuals from both lines are also now colored the associated color in Fig. 9.9.

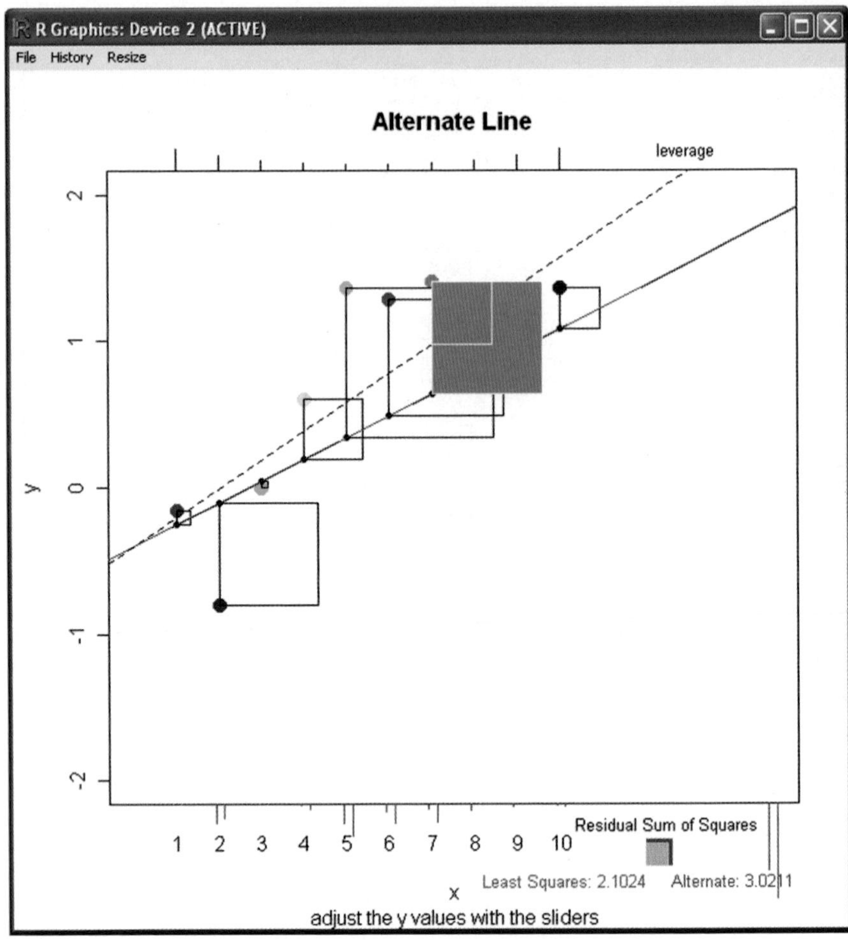

Fig. 9.9 The squared residuals from both lines are now colored the associated color in cell A8 in Fig. 9.8. In this example, we immediately see that the alternate squared residual is larger than the least-squares squared residual for this point at $x = 7$. The bottom red rugs are proportional to the squared alternate residuals in cells H15:24. The alternate sum of squared residuals in cell I25 is shown on the graph both numerically and as a red square that is always larger than the gray square for the residual sum of squares calculated by least squares.

9.2 Hat Diagonals and Leverage

We can adjust the sliders and see the least-squares line shift a lot for values of x_i on the extremes of the range of the x-values and shift not very much for intermediate values of x_i. In this example, in Fig. 9.2, both points 5 at (5, 1.36) and 10 at (10, 1.36) have the same y-value of 1.36. In Fig. 9.10, we first clicked reset Alt to LS in cell C17 to set the alternate coefficients to match the least-squares coefficients.

Then, in Figs. 9.10 and 9.11, we change the y-value for point 5 to 0.36 and note that the regression line has not moved very much. In Figs. 9.12 and 9.13, we change the y-value for point 10 to 0.36 and note that the regression line has moved a lot to follow the changed point.

We collect Figs. 9.5, 9.11, and 9.13 into Fig. 9.14 to make it easier to compare them.

The amount of shift in $\hat{y}_i$ for a unit shift in y_i is called *leverage* and is given by the *hat* value h_i in cells J2:J11. For simple linear regression (one x-variable as in this example), the leverage values are given by

$$h_i = \frac{1}{n} + \frac{(x_i - \bar{x})^2}{\sum_{j=1}^{n}(x_j - \bar{x})^2} \tag{9.1}$$

The term "leverage" is used by analogy with physical levers. The farther away we are from the center of the x-values, the more we can move the regression line with the same change to the y-values.

We can approximate the calculation of the leverage from the observed changes. The difference by which we make a small shift in y_i is called Δy_i. The amount by which $\hat{y}_i$ changes in response is called $\Delta\hat{y}_i$.

In this example, Fig. 9.11 shows

$$\frac{\Delta\hat{y}_i}{\Delta y_i} = \frac{0.54 - 0.58}{0.36 - 1.36} = 0.10$$

and Fig. 9.13 shows

$$\frac{\Delta\hat{y}_i}{\Delta y_i} = \frac{1.43 - 1.57}{0.36 - 1.36} = 0.35$$

Compare these observed ratios to the hat values in column J (0.1030 and 0.3455).

The hat values are precise for infinitesimal shifts, as the amount of change Δy_i goes to 0. It is possible to show

$$\lim_{\Delta y_i \to 0} \frac{\Delta\hat{y}_i}{\Delta y_i} = \frac{\partial\hat{y}_i}{\partial y_i} = h_i$$

linreg.xlsm

	A	B	C	D	E	F	G	H	I	J	K	L	M	N	O	P	Q
1	color		sliders for y		x	y	y.hat	resid	resid^2	hat(x)		Regression Coefficients					
2	red				1	-0.16	-0.33	0.17	0.0300	0.3455			Estimate	Std. Error	t value	Pr(>|t|)	
3	purple				2	-0.80	-0.13	-0.67	0.4487	0.2485		(Intercept)	-0.5360	0.2901	-1.8478	0.1018	
4	green				3	0.00	0.07	-0.07	0.0053	0.1758		x	0.2029	0.0468	4.3403	0.0025	
5	gold				4	0.60	0.28	0.32	0.1052	0.1273							
6	orange				5	0.36	0.48	-0.12	0.0141	0.1030		ANOVA table					
7	deep pink				6	1.28	0.68	0.60	0.3583	0.1030			Df	Sum Sq	Mean Sq	F value	Pr(>F)
8	forest green				7	1.40	0.88	0.52	0.2659	0.1273		x	1	3.3967	3.3967	18.8378	0.0025
9	brown				8	0.72	1.09	-0.37	0.1349	0.1758		Residuals	8	1.4425	0.1803		
10	salmon				9	1.04	1.29	-0.25	0.0626	0.2485		Total	9	4.8392			
11	blue				10	1.36	1.49	-0.13	0.0177	0.3455							
12									1.4425								
13																	
14					x	y	y.alt	res.alt	res.alt^2								
15					1	-0.16	-0.21	0.05	0.0021			Residual					
16			☑ use alternate		2	-0.80	-0.01	-0.79	0.6257			display					
17			reset Alt to LS		3	0.00	0.19	-0.19	0.0353			○ none					
18			-0.4027		4	0.60	0.38	0.22	0.0463			◉ line					
19			0.1968		5	0.36	0.58	-0.22	0.0491			○ square					
20					6	1.28	0.78	0.50	0.2516			ColorRestore					
21					7	1.40	0.98	0.42	0.1804								
22	☑ Graph on Top				8	0.72	1.17	-0.45	0.2044								
23					9	1.04	1.37	-0.33	0.1082								
24					10	1.36	1.57	-0.21	0.0424								
25									1.5455								

Sheet1

Fig. 9.10 Use the slider to change the *y*-value of point 5. The regression coefficients in cells M3:M4 have shifted not very much from the values in Fig. 9.5 (and retained here as the alternate values in cells C18:C19).

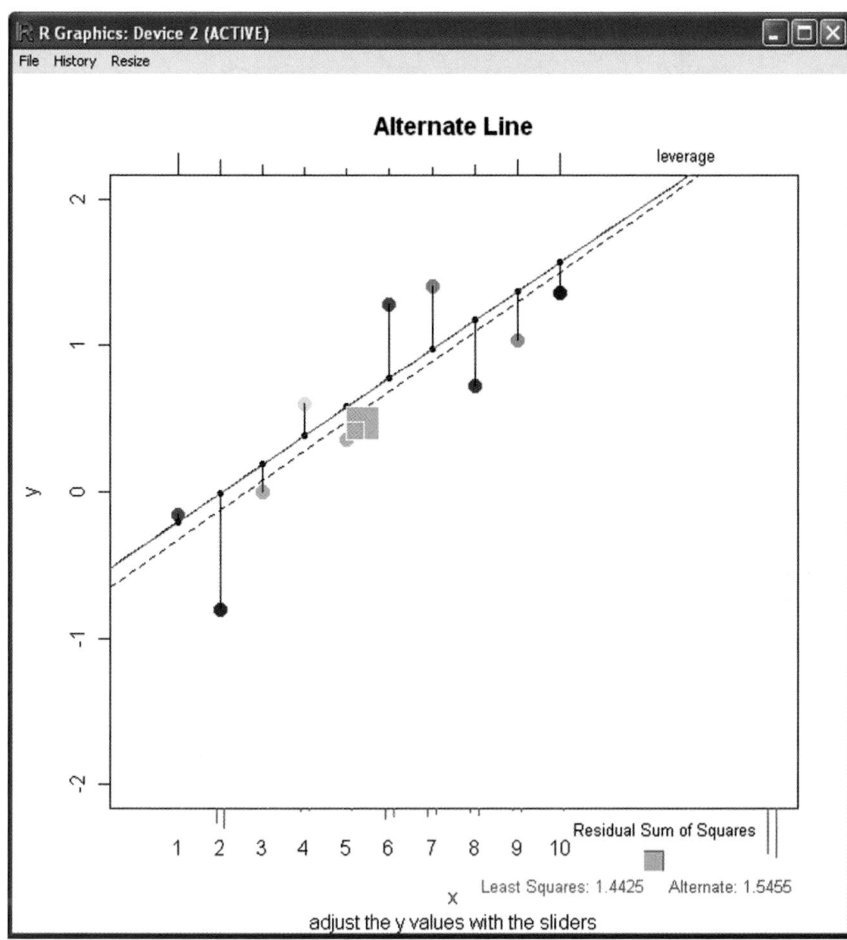

Fig. 9.11 Moving the y-value of a point with an intermediate x, in this case $x = 5$, does not change the regression line very much. The residual for the new location of the point at $x = 5,\ y = 0.36$ to the original line (red) is larger than that from the new location to the new line (dashed gray). Neither residual is the same as in Fig. 9.5. This figure is repeated in Fig. 9.14 for ease of comparison.

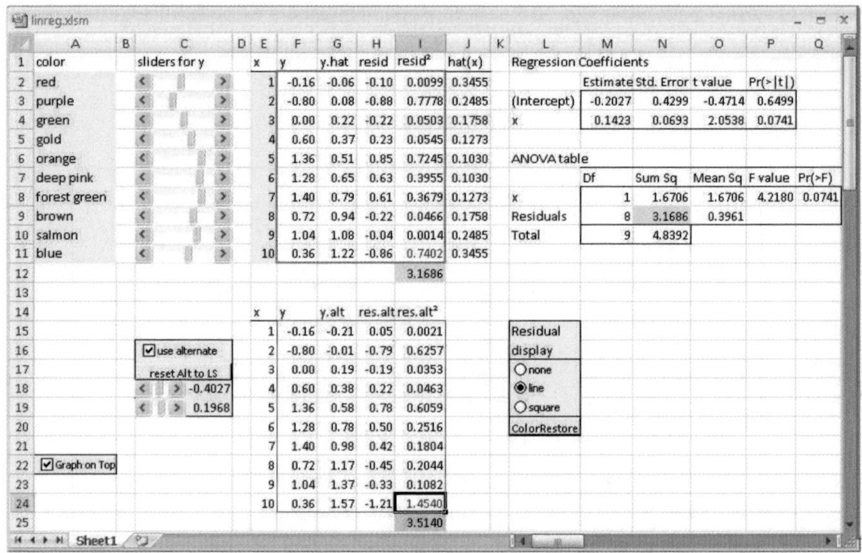
linreg.xlsm

color	x	y	y.hat	resid	resid²	hat(x)
red	1	-0.16	-0.06	-0.10	0.0099	0.3455
purple	2	-0.80	0.08	-0.88	0.7778	0.2485
green	3	0.00	0.22	-0.22	0.0503	0.1758
gold	4	0.60	0.37	0.23	0.0545	0.1273
orange	5	1.36	0.51	0.85	0.7245	0.1030
deep pink	6	1.28	0.65	0.63	0.3955	0.1030
forest green	7	1.40	0.79	0.61	0.3679	0.1273
brown	8	0.72	0.94	-0.22	0.0466	0.1758
salmon	9	1.04	1.08	-0.04	0.0014	0.2485
blue	10	0.36	1.22	-0.86	0.7402	0.3455
					3.1686	

Regression Coefficients

	Estimate	Std. Error	t value	Pr(>|t|)
(Intercept)	-0.2027	0.4299	-0.4714	0.6499
x	0.1423	0.0693	2.0538	0.0741

ANOVA table

	Df	Sum Sq	Mean Sq	F value	Pr(>F)
x	1	1.6706	1.6706	4.2180	0.0741
Residuals	8	3.1686	0.3961		
Total	9	4.8392			

x	y	y.alt	res.alt	res.alt²
1	-0.16	-0.21	0.05	0.0021
2	-0.80	-0.01	-0.79	0.6257
3	0.00	0.19	-0.19	0.0353
4	0.60	0.38	0.22	0.0463
5	1.36	0.58	0.78	0.6059
6	1.28	0.78	0.50	0.2516
7	1.40	0.98	0.42	0.1804
8	0.72	1.17	-0.45	0.2044
9	1.04	1.37	-0.33	0.1082
10	0.36	1.57	-1.21	1.4540
				3.5140

Fig. 9.12 Use the sliders to return y_5 to its original value and to change the y-value of point 10. The regression coefficients in cells M3:M4 have shifted a lot from the values in Fig. 9.5 (and retained here as the alternate values in cells C18:C19).

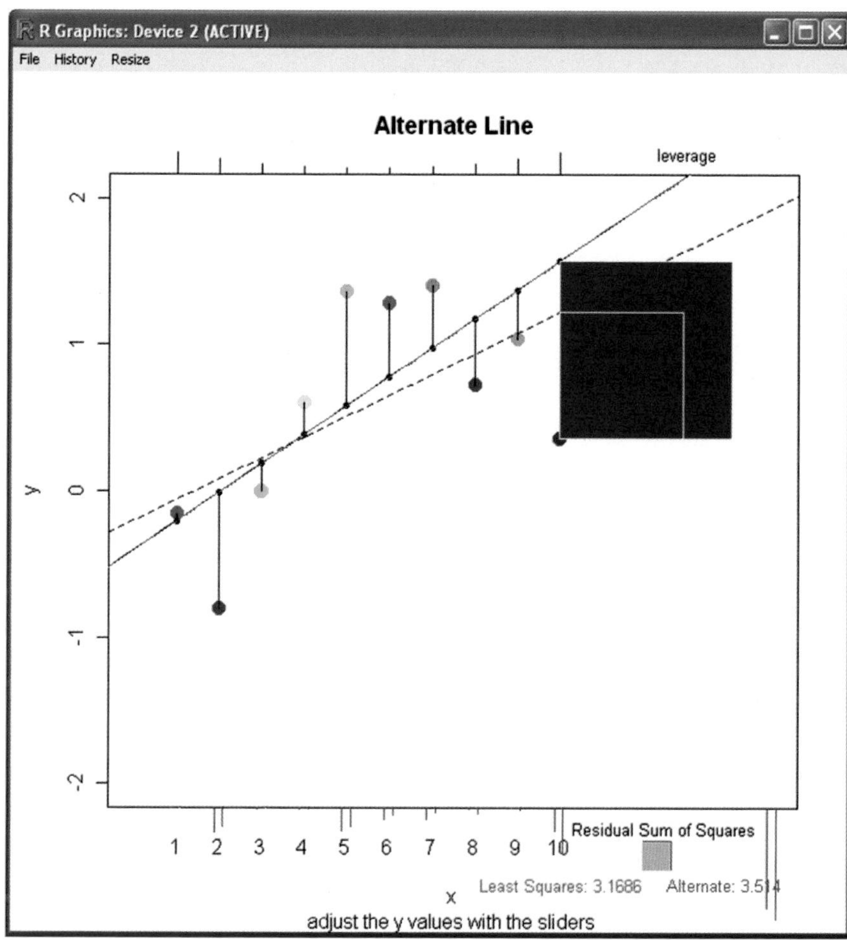

Fig. 9.13 Moving the y-value of a point with an extreme x, in this case $x = 10$, changes the regression line a lot. The residual for the new location of the point at $x = 10$, $y = 0.36$ to the original line (red) is larger than that from the new location to the new line (dashed gray). Neither residual is the same as in Fig. 9.5. This figure is repeated in Fig. 9.14 for ease of comparison.

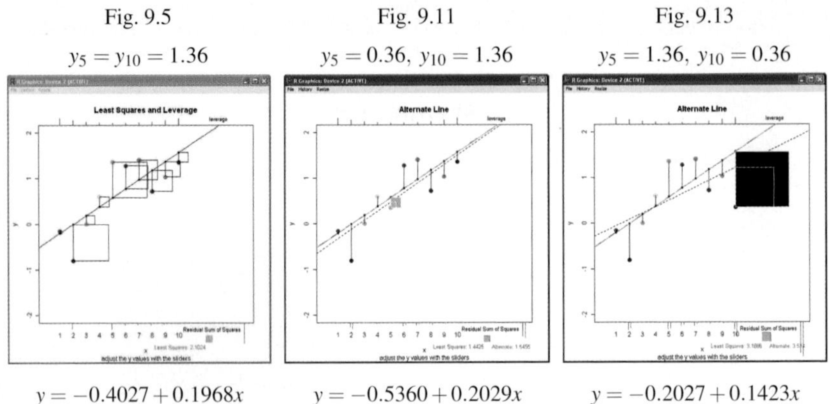

Fig. 9.14 Figs. 9.5, 9.11, and 9.13 repeated, so we can easily compare their regression lines and the sizes of the squared residuals. The regression lines for the first two panels, original data and with point 5 changed, are similar. The line for the third panel, with point 10 changed, is different. In the right two panels, the original line is shown as a solid red line and the the new lines are dashed gray lines. In the second panel, the residuals of the new point from both lines are similar. Point $x = 5$ is in the center of the range of x-values. Therefore, changing its y-value does not have a large effect on the line. In the third panel, the residual of the new point from the original line is larger than from the new line. This is to be expected because the new line follows the change in the y-value of point $x = 10$, which is on the extreme of the x-values.

9.3 Residuals and Leverage

R provides Basic diagnostic plots, a set of plots that help us interpret the results of the regression analysis.

Close the linreg workbook and reopen a fresh copy of the linreg workbook. This will restore the values in the cells to the values used in the figures here.

The workbook operates by automatically sending a dataframe xy.aov.total to R every time the user changes a value with a slider, or changes a checkbox or button. R then calculates, and stores in model xy.lm, the regression analysis on that revised dataframe. In Fig. 9.15, the dataset xy.aov.total and the model xy.lm are shown as the active dataset and active model. If they are not shown as the active dataset and model, then use the dropdown boxes to set those values.

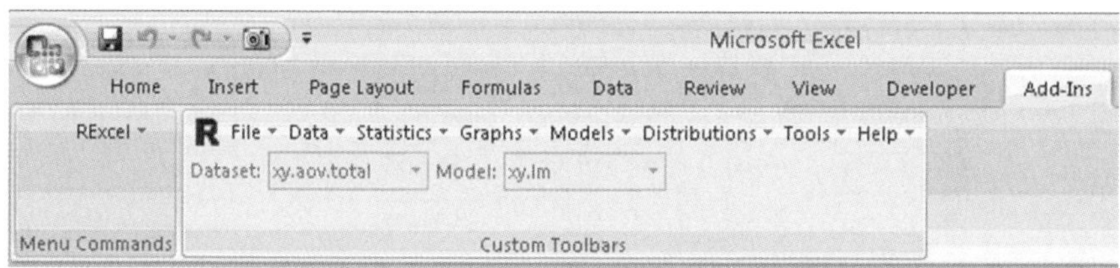

Fig. 9.15 The active dataset is xy.aov.total and the active model is xy.lm.

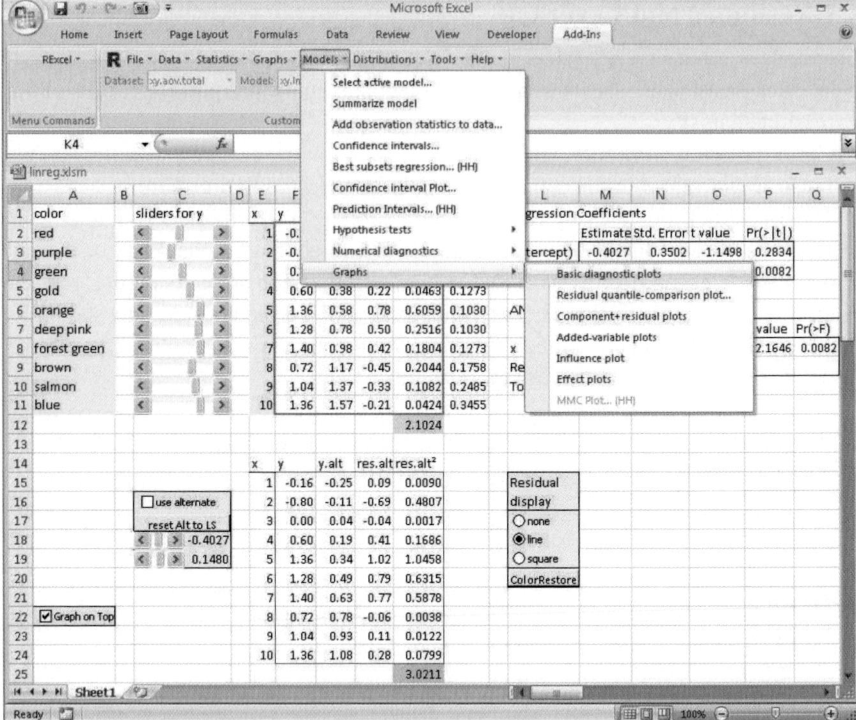

Fig. 9.16 Request the Basic diagnostic plots, a set of plots that help us interpret the results of the regression analysis. The plots are displayed in Fig. 9.17. The plots are more heavily used in multiple regression (more than one x-variable) than they are in simple regression (one x-variable).

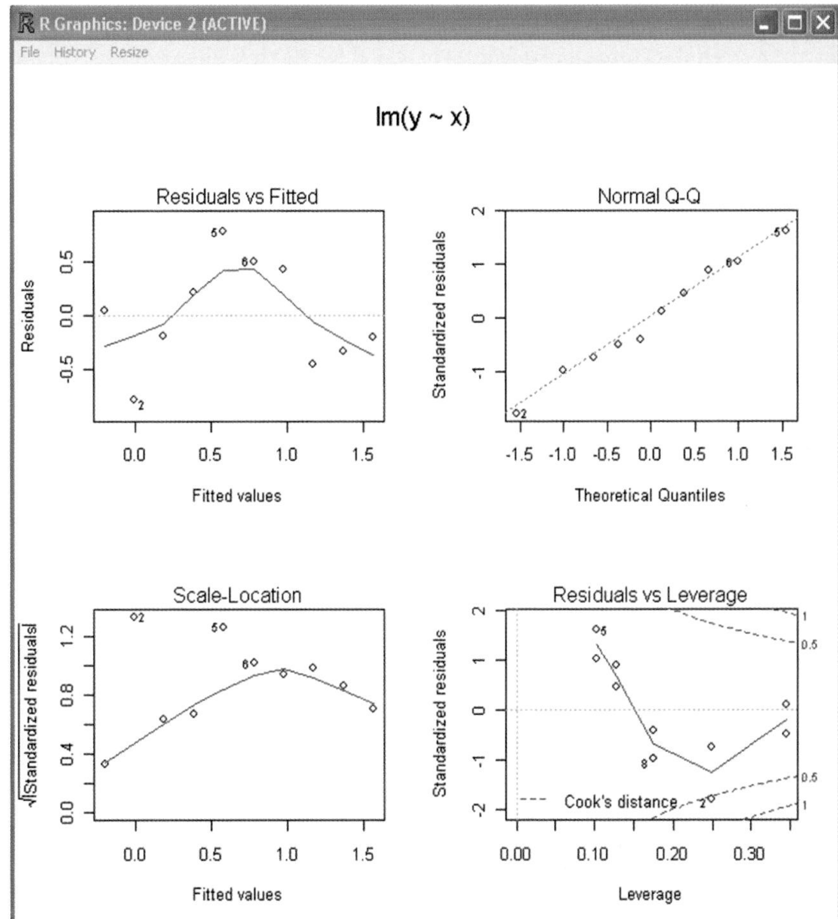

Fig. 9.17 Basic diagnostic plots for the regression analysis in Figs. 8.10 and 8.13. These plots give visual feedback on the effectiveness of the model `y ~ x` in capturing the information in the data. The upper left plot Residuals vs Fitted plots cells H2:H11 (`resid` $= e$) against cells G2:G11 (`y.hat` $= \hat{y}$). A well-fitting model will give a Residuals vs Fitted plot with no apparent pattern. The remaining three plots in this figure are discussed in the body of this section. Three of the plots show a smoothed curve for the points. See `?panel.smooth` and `?lowess` for details.

Three of the four plots in Fig. 9.17 need further discussion. The Scale–Location plot, the Normal Q–Q (quantile–quantile) plot, and the Residuals vs Leverage plot use the standardized residuals, which have identical variance under the null hypothesis. The standardized residuals are given as

$$e_i^* = \frac{e_i}{s\sqrt{1-h_i}} \tag{9.2}$$

where the leverages h_i are the hat values displayed in cells J2:J11 and calculated for simple linear regression models by

$$h_i = \frac{1}{n} + \frac{(x_i - \bar{x})^2}{\sum_{j=1}^{n}(x_j - \bar{x})^2} \tag{9.3}$$

For multiple regression (more than one x-variable), the hat values are calculated as the diagonal entries of the hat matrix `influence()$hat`; see `?hat` and `?influence`.

The Scale–Location plot, also called the Spread–Location or S–L plot, in the lower left panel of Fig. 9.17 takes the square root of the absolute residuals in order to diminish skewness; ($\sqrt{|e^*|}$ is much less skewed than $|e^*|$ for Gaussian zero-mean e).

The Q–Q plot shows the sorted standardized residuals e^* against the theoretical quantiles q_i, calculated as a set of values equidistant in probability under the assumption of a standard normal distribution. See `?qqnorm` and `?ppoints` for further details.

The Residuals vs Leverage plot, in the lower right panel of Fig. 9.17, shows the standardized residuals e^* against the leverage h_i along with contours of Cook's distance. Cook's distance, a combined measure of the "unusualness" of a case's predictors and response, is defined as

$$D_i = \frac{e_i^2}{ps^2} \frac{h_i}{(1-h_i)^2} \tag{9.4}$$

The contours of constant Cook's distance c are calculated as $\sqrt{c\,p\,(1-h_i)/h_i}$, where p is the number of estimated regression coefficients ($p = 2$ for simple linear regression). By default, contours are plotted for the two c-values 0.5 and 1. Note on the graph that the contour lines are closer to the 0-residual horizontal line for higher leverage values (corresponding to points farther away from $\bar{x}$) than for lower leverage values.

9.4 Reset the Workbook to the Values in the Text

We added two new features to the `linreg` workbook after the screenshots for this chapter were completed. We now have a Reset: cell that restores the workbook values to one of

1. the values illustrated in this chapter.
2. an example with uneven x-spacing.
3. an example with negative slope.

As a consequence, we changed the format of the x-values in column E to show one digit after the decimal point. Fig. 9.4 shows the details.

linregErichRmh8.xlsm

	A	C	E	F	G	H	I	J
1	color	sliders for y	x	y	y.hat	resid	resid²	hat(x)
2	red		1.0	-0.16	-0.21	0.05	0.0021	0.3455
3	purple		2.0	-0.80	-0.01	-0.79	0.6257	0.2485
4	green		3.0	0.00	0.19	-0.19	0.0353	0.1758
5	gold		4.0	0.60	0.38	0.22	0.0463	0.1273
6	orange		5.0	1.36	0.58	0.78	0.6059	0.1030
7	deep pink		6.0	1.28	0.78	0.50	0.2516	0.1030
8	forest green		7.0	1.40	0.98	0.42	0.1804	0.1273
9	brown		8.0	0.72	1.17	-0.45	0.2044	0.1758
10	salmon		9.0	1.04	1.37	-0.33	0.1082	0.2485
11	blue		10.0	1.36	1.57	-0.21	0.0424	0.3455
12							2.1024	
13								
14			x	y	y.alt	res.alt	res.alt²	
15			1.0	-0.16	-0.25	0.09	0.0090	
16	Reset:	use alternate	2.0	-0.80	-0.11	-0.69	0.4807	
17	R through Excel	reset Alt to LS	3.0	0.00	0.04	-0.04	0.0017	
18	R through Excel	scenario	4.0	0.60	0.19	0.41	0.1686	
19	uneven x spacing negative slope	le click	5.0	1.36	0.34	1.02	1.0458	
20			6.0	1.28	0.49	0.79	0.6315	
21			7.0	1.40	0.63	0.77	0.5878	
22	Graph on Top		8.0	0.72	0.78	-0.06	0.0038	
23			9.0	1.04	0.93	0.11	0.0122	
24			10.0	1.36	1.08	0.28	0.0799	
25							3.0211	

Regression Coefficients

	Estimate	Std. Error	t value	Pr(>|t|)
(Intercept)	-0.4027	0.3502	-1.1498	0.2834
x	0.1968	0.0564	3.4878	0.0082

ANOVA table

	Df	Sum Sq	Mean Sq	F value	Pr(>F)
x	1	3.1968	3.1968	12.1646	0.0082
Residuals	8	2.1024	0.2628		
Total	9	5.2992			

Residual display: none / line (selected) / square

ColorRestore

Sheet1

Fig. 9.18 The Reset: cell A17 has a dropdown list that restores the workbook values to one of three scenarios. The default scenario even spacing is the one used in the examples in this chapter. We also show an example with uneven x-spacing and an example with negative slope.

Chapter 10
Multiple Regression—Two X-Variables

Abstract Multiple regression by least squares is the natural generalization of simple linear regression to data with more than one explanatory variable.

10.1 The Multiple Regression Model

Multiple regression is similar to simple linear regression, but with more than one explanatory variable. In this chapter, we look at exactly two x-variables. In Chapter 12 we will look at more than two x-variables.

The model assumptions are the natural generalization of the assumptions for simple linear regression. We assume that the mean value of ys for a given set of variables, $x_1, \ldots, x_k$ ($k = 2$ in this chapter) depends linearly on the values of $x_1, \ldots, x_k$. When $k = 1$ (Chapter 8), that was interpreted as a straight line in a graph of y vs x. In this chapter, with $k = 2$, that is interpreted as a plane in a three-dimensional graph of y in the vertical direction vs x_1 and x_2 defining a base plane. We show a picture of this situation in Fig. 10.7. In Chapter 12, with $k \geq 3$, we interpret it as a hyperplane in $k+1$ dimensions and can't draw a simple graph. Instead, we use a scatterplot matrix (introduced in Fig. 2.23) to show the relation of all possible pairs of variables and many diagnostic plots.

The multiple regression model also assumes, as does the simple linear regression model, that the standard deviation of the y-values at each $x_1, \ldots, x_k$ is independent of the value of the x_i variables. That is, the variability of the y data around the mean hyperplane is independent of the x_i.

In simple linear regression in Chapter 8, we assumed a straight-line model

$$
\begin{aligned}
y_i &= \beta_0 + \beta_1 x_i + \varepsilon_i \\
\varepsilon_i &\sim N(0, \sigma^2)
\end{aligned}
$$

for data consisting of a response variable y and a single predictor variable x. We fit the model with the least-squares estimates

R.M. Heiberger, E. Neuwirth, *R Through Excel*, Use R,
DOI 10.1007/978-1-4419-0052-4_10,

$$\hat{\beta}_1 = \frac{\Sigma(x_i - \bar{x})(y_i - \bar{y})}{\Sigma(x_i - \bar{x})^2}$$
$$\hat{\beta}_0 = \bar{y} - \hat{\beta}_1 \bar{x}$$
$$\hat{y}_i = \hat{\beta}_0 + \hat{\beta}_1 x_i$$
$$s^2 = \frac{\Sigma(y_i - \hat{y})^2}{n-2}$$

In this chapter, with two x-variables, we fit a plane model

$$y_i = \beta_0 + \beta_1 x_{i1} + \beta_2 x_{i2} + \varepsilon_i$$
$$\varepsilon_i \sim N(0, \sigma^2)$$

to observed data with one response variable y and two explanatory variables x_1 and x_2. We fit the model with the least squares-estimates

$$\begin{pmatrix} \hat{\beta}_0 \\ \hat{\beta}_1 \\ \hat{\beta}_2 \end{pmatrix} = \text{solve linear equations with your computer program}$$
$$\hat{y}_i = \hat{\beta}_0 + \hat{\beta}_1 x_{i1} + \hat{\beta}_2 x_{i2}$$
$$s^2 = \frac{\Sigma(y_i - \hat{y})^2}{n-(2+1)}$$

We will usually first graph the data and then use the Rcmdr

Statistics ▶ Fit Models ▶ Linear regression ...

menu item to access the R `lm` function.

10.2 Example

[Davies and Goldsmith, 1972], reprinted in [Hand et al., 1994], investigated the relationship between the `abrasion` loss of samples of rubber (in grams per hour) as a function of `hardness` and tensile `strength` (kg/cm^2). Higher values of `hardness` indicate harder rubber. The dataset appears in the file

```
hh("datasets/abrasion.dat").
```

1. Produce a scatterplot matrix of this dataset. Based on this plot, does it appear that `strength` would be helpful in explaining `abrasion`?
2. Produce a three-dimensional plot of the data.
3. Calculate the fitted regression equation.
4. Find a 95% prediction interval for the abrasion for a new rubber sample having hardness 60 and strength 200.

Fig. 10.1 Read the abrasion data by entering the line

```
abrasion <- read.table(hh("datasets/abrasion.dat"),
                      header=TRUE)
```

into the Rcmdr Script Window and clicking Submit,

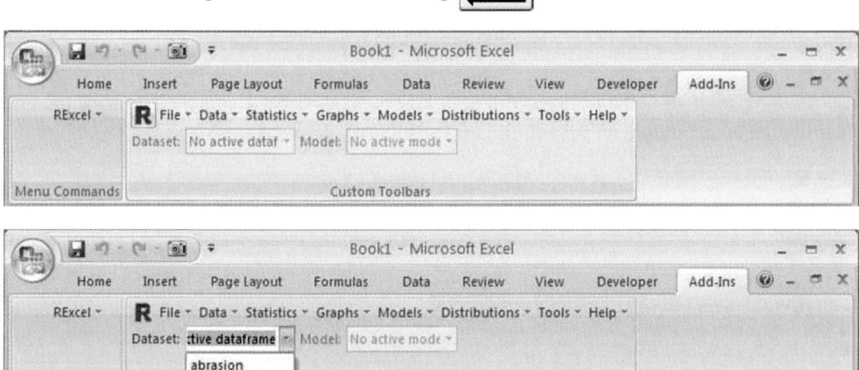

Fig. 10.2 Make abrasion the Rcmdr active dataset with two steps. Click the blue **R** on the RExcel Rcmdr menu to let the menu know that we have added a dataframe to R by means other than using the menu. Then click on the Dataset dropdown menu and make abrasion the active dataset. Making abrasion the active dataset places its variable names into all the Rcmdr dialog boxes.

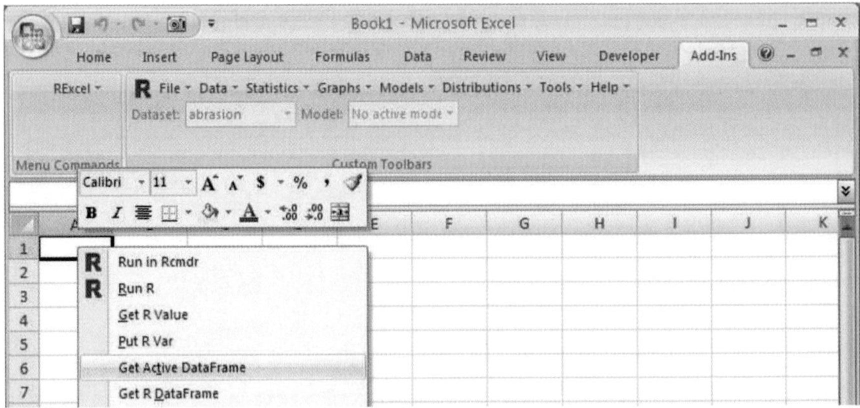

Fig. 10.3 Bring `abrasion` into a new Excel worksheet from the context menu. Place the cursor on cell A1 and then right-click Get Active DataFrame.

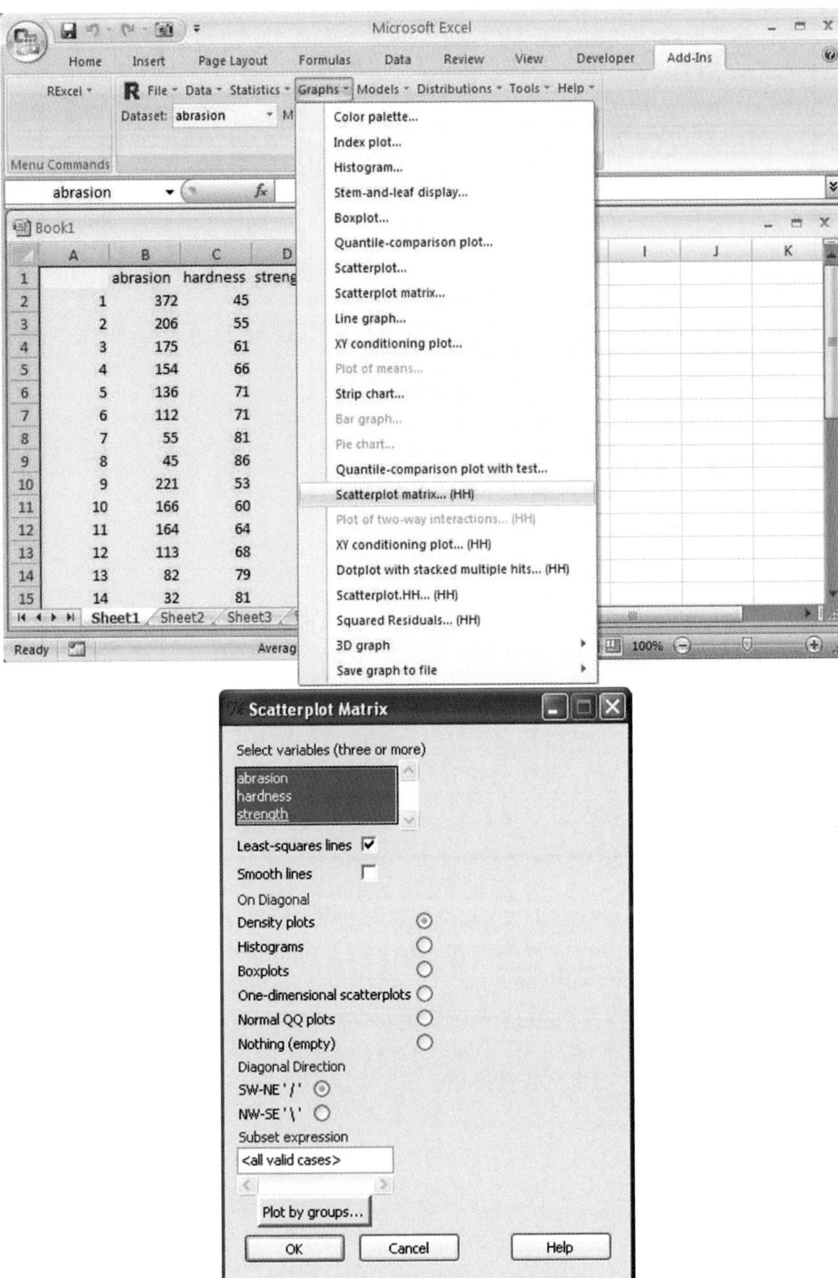

Fig. 10.4 Plot the data with the Graphs ► Scatterplot. . . (HH) menu item. The menu brings up the dialog box. Highlight all three variable names and click OK.

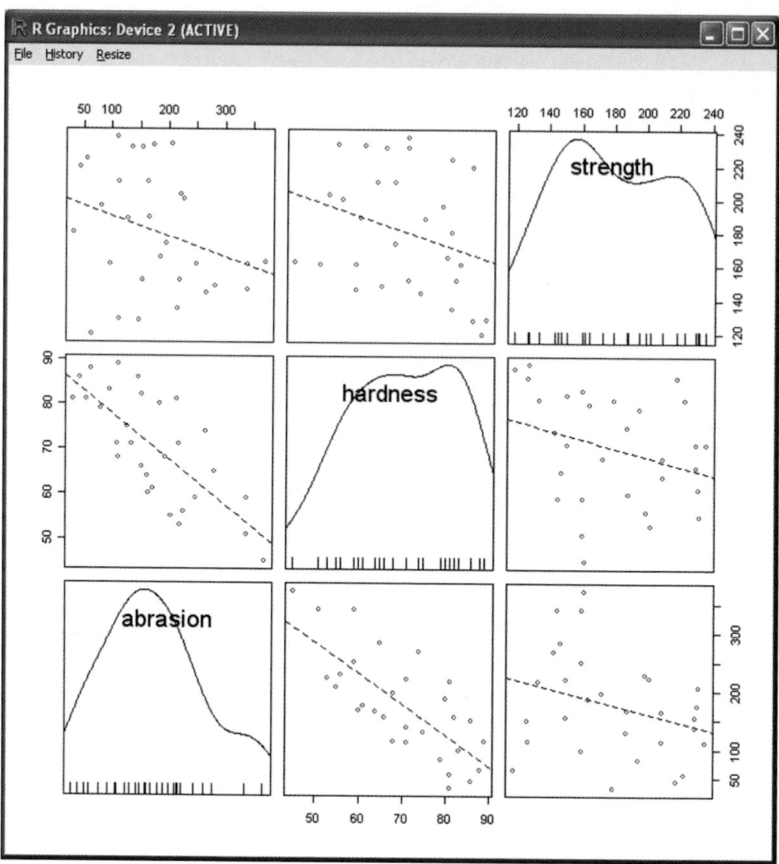

Fig. 10.5 This figure shows all the two-variable plots of these three variables in the off-diagonal panels of the scatterplot matrix plus a marginal density plot for each single variable along the main diagonal. The response variable `abrasion` is in the bottom row. We can see a tight downhill trend in the `abrasion ~ hardness` panel, and a weaker downhill trend in the `abrasion ~ strength` panel. We also need to look at the three-variable plot in Fig. 10.7.

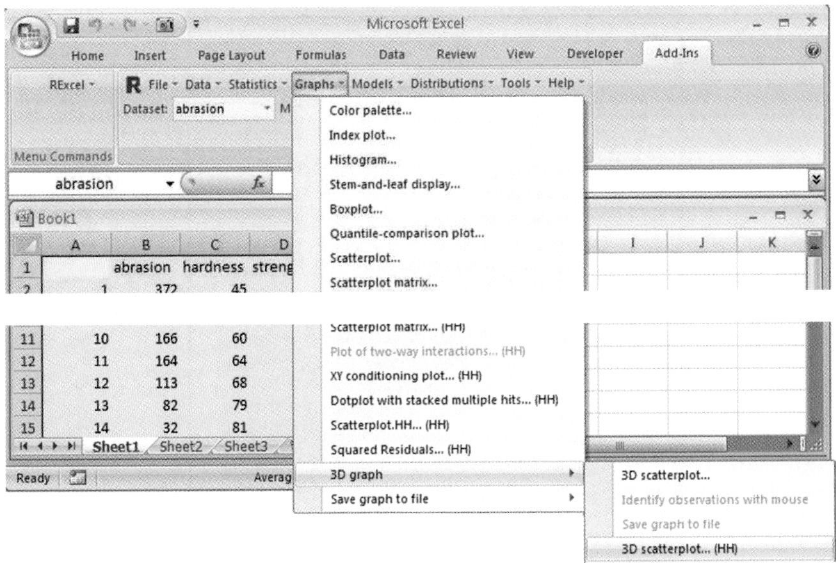

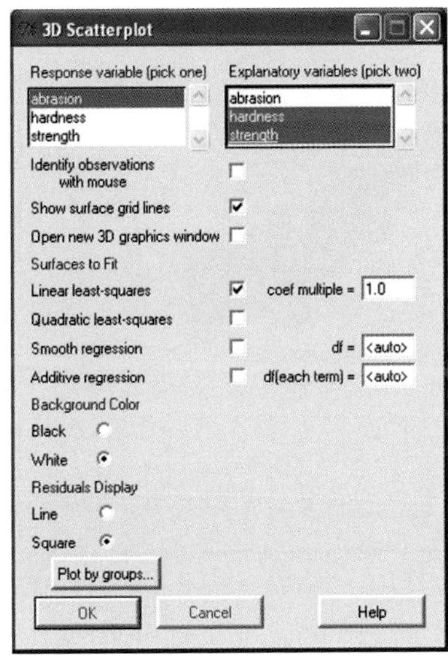

Fig. 10.6 The Graphs ► 3D Graph ► 3D scatterplot...(HH) menu item brings up the dialog box.

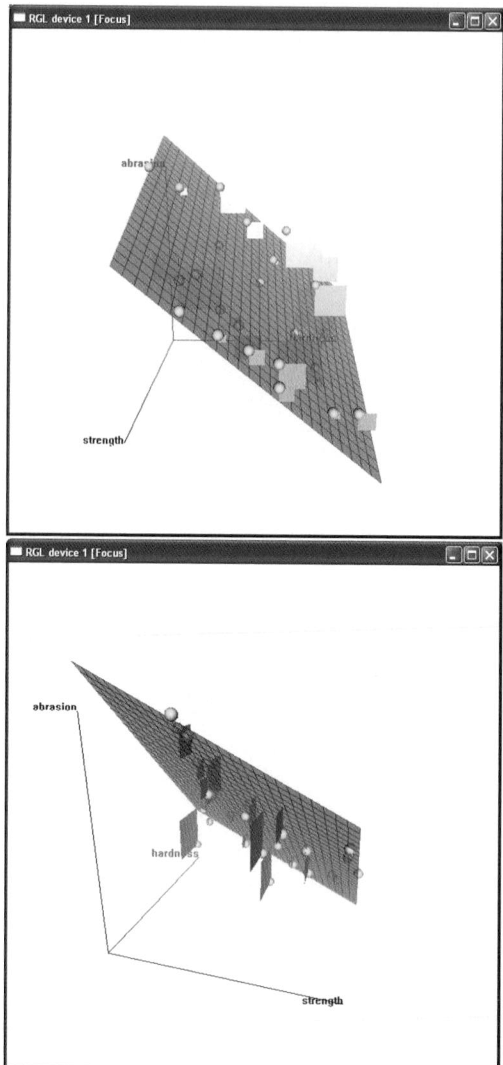

Fig. 10.7 Dynamic 3D plot specified in Fig. 10.6. The top panel is the opening position. The bottom panel is after rotation by the mouse. The user can rotate the figure in any direction. The estimated plane through the points is the natural extension of a straight line in two dimensions to the analogous geometry in three dimensions. The vertical lines connecting the points to the plane are the residuals. The squares of each residual are shown. The least-squares fit produces the plane that has the smallest sum of squares of the residuals of any plane. See Section 9.1 for the illustration of this concept in two dimensions.

10.3 Specify and Fit Several Linear Models

When there is more than one potential predictor variable for the response variable, we don't know which, if any, will give the best fit to the data. In this section, we fit several different models and compare them. The abrasion dataset has two potential predictor variables: hardness and strength. We will look at three models, with each of the variables alone and with both variables.

In Section 10.4, we show graphical comparisons of the three models. In Section 10.5, we show tabular comparisons of the three models.

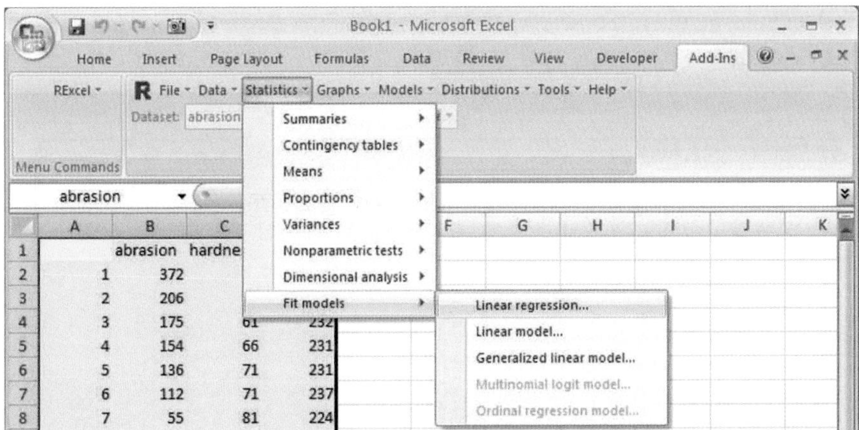

Fig. 10.8 Specification of linear regression. All three models we will look at— the two one-x models in Figs. 10.12 and 10.10 and the two-x model in Fig. 10.14—begin with the Statistics ► Fit models ► Linear regression... menu.

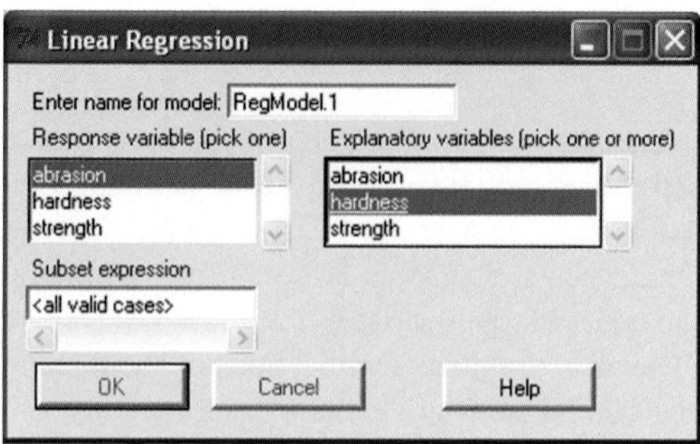

Fig. 10.9 Dialog box for the model `abrasion ~ hardness`. In this figure, we have highlighted the response variable abrasion and the single explanatory variable hardness. Clicking OK generates Fig. 10.10.

R Commander

Script Window

```
abrasion <- read.table(hh("datasets/abrasion.dat"), header=TRUE)
scatterplot.matrix(~abrasion+hardness+strength, reg.line=lm, smooth=FALSE, span=
RegModel.1 <- lm(abrasion~hardness, data=abrasion)
summary(RegModel.1)
```

Output Window Submit

```
> summary(RegModel.1)

Call:
lm(formula = abrasion ~ hardness, data = abrasion)

Residuals:
   Min     1Q Median     3Q    Max
-86.15 -46.77 -19.49  54.27 111.49

Coefficients:
            Estimate Std. Error t value Pr(>|t|)
(Intercept) 550.4151    65.7867   8.367 4.22e-09 ***
hardness     -5.3366     0.9229  -5.782 3.29e-06 ***
---
Signif. codes:  0 '***' 0.001 '**' 0.01 '*' 0.05 '.' 0.1 ' ' 1

Residual standard error: 60.52 on 28 degrees of freedom
Multiple R-Squared: 0.5442,     Adjusted R-squared: 0.5279
F-statistic: 33.43 on 1 and 28 DF,  p-value: 3.294e-06
```

Messages

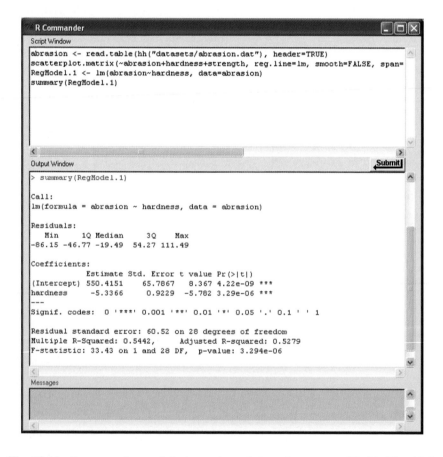

Fig. 10.10 Summary for model `abrasion ~ hardness` specified in Fig. 10.9. The residual standard error is 60 and the R^2 is 0.544.

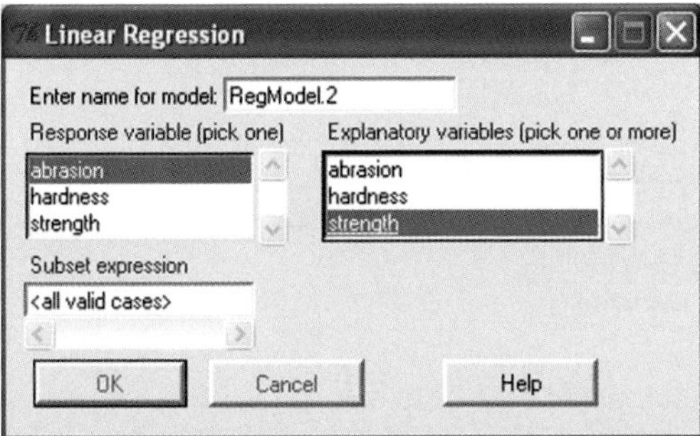

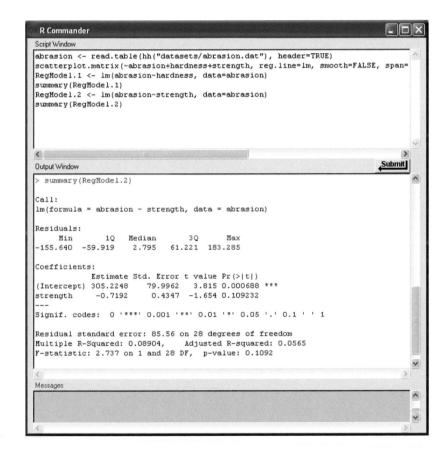

Fig. 10.11 A second use of the menu in Fig. 10.8 gives us the dialog box. This time we fill it out for the model `abrasion ~ strength`.

R Commander

Script Window

```
abrasion <- read.table(hh("datasets/abrasion.dat"), header=TRUE)
scatterplot.matrix(~abrasion+hardness+strength, reg.line=lm, smooth=FALSE, span=
RegModel.1 <- lm(abrasion~hardness, data=abrasion)
summary(RegModel.1)
RegModel.2 <- lm(abrasion~strength, data=abrasion)
summary(RegModel.2)
```

Output Window

```
> summary(RegModel.2)

Call:
lm(formula = abrasion ~ strength, data = abrasion)

Residuals:
     Min       1Q   Median       3Q      Max
-155.640  -59.919    2.795   61.221  183.285

Coefficients:
            Estimate Std. Error t value Pr(>|t|)
(Intercept) 305.2248    79.9962   3.815 0.000688 ***
strength     -0.7192     0.4347  -1.654 0.109232
---
Signif. codes:  0 '***' 0.001 '**' 0.01 '*' 0.05 '.' 0.1 ' ' 1

Residual standard error: 85.56 on 28 degrees of freedom
Multiple R-Squared: 0.08904,    Adjusted R-squared: 0.0565
F-statistic: 2.737 on 1 and 28 DF,  p-value: 0.1092
```

Messages

Fig. 10.12 Summary for model `abrasion ~ strength`. The residual standard error is 85 and the R^2 is 0.089. The single variable `hardness` in Fig. 10.10 is a much better predictor of `abrasion` than the single variable `strength`.

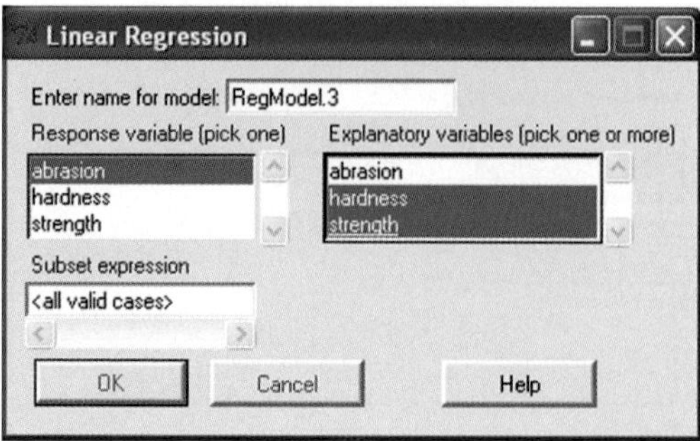

Fig. 10.13 A third use of the menu in Fig. 10.8 gives us the dialog box. This time we fill it out for the model `abrasion ~ hardness + strength`.

R Commander

Script Window

```
abrasion <- read.table(hh("datasets/abrasion.dat"), header=TRUE)
scatterplot.matrix(~abrasion+hardness+strength, reg.line=lm, smooth=FALSE, span=
RegModel.1 <- lm(abrasion~hardness, data=abrasion)
summary(RegModel.1)
RegModel.2 <- lm(abrasion~strength, data=abrasion)
summary(RegModel.2)
RegModel.3 <- lm(abrasion~hardness+strength, data=abrasion)
summary(RegModel.3)
```

Output Window Submit

```
> summary(RegModel.3)

Call:
lm(formula = abrasion ~ hardness + strength, data = abrasion)

Residuals:
    Min      1Q  Median      3Q     Max
-79.385 -14.608   3.816  19.755  65.981

Coefficients:
            Estimate Std. Error t value Pr(>|t|)
(Intercept) 885.1611    61.7516  14.334 3.84e-14 ***
hardness     -6.5708     0.5832 -11.267 1.03e-11 ***
strength     -1.3743     0.1943  -7.073 1.32e-07 ***
---
Signif. codes:  0 '***' 0.001 '**' 0.01 '*' 0.05 '.' 0.1 ' ' 1

Residual standard error: 36.49 on 27 degrees of freedom
Multiple R-Squared: 0.8402,     Adjusted R-squared: 0.8284
F-statistic:    71 on 2 and 27 DF,  p-value: 1.767e-11
```

Messages

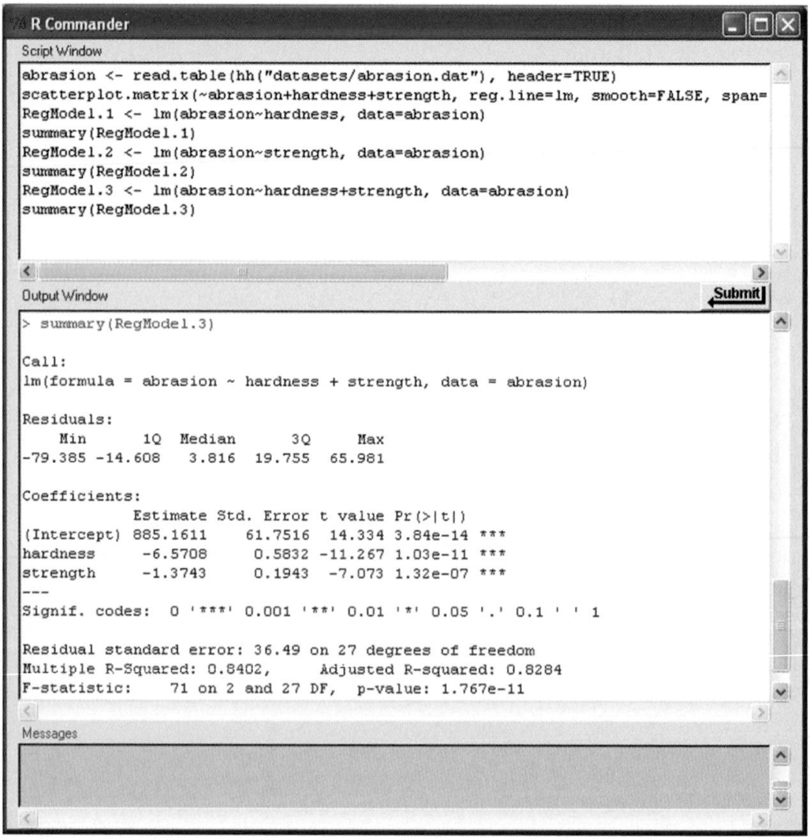

Fig. 10.14 Summary for model `abrasion ~ hardness + strength`. The residual standard error is lowered to 36 and the R^2 is increased to 0.840. The variables `hardness` and `strength` together are a much better predictor of `abrasion` than either variable alone.

10.4 Graphical Comparison of Models

In this section, we study the residuals and fitted values for the three regression models we have looked at for the abrasion data. We calculate and plot the residuals and fitted values for each model here. In Section 10.5, we compare the models numerically with the analysis of variance table.

a. Specify model.

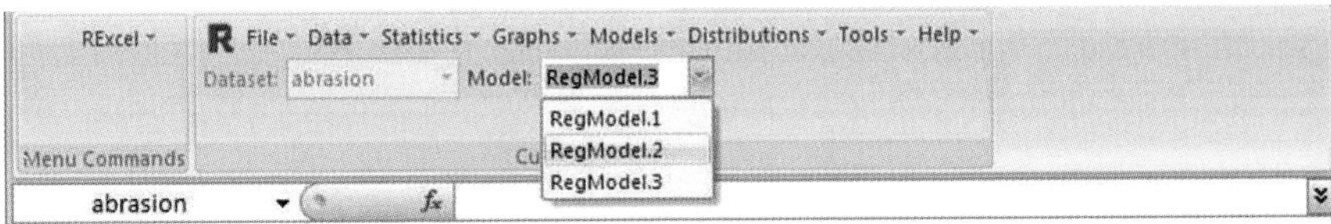

b. Models ▶ Add observation statistics to data...

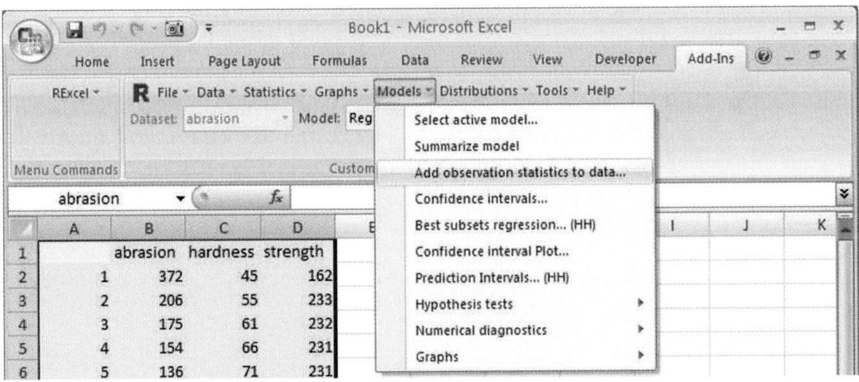

c. Specify fitted values and residuals.

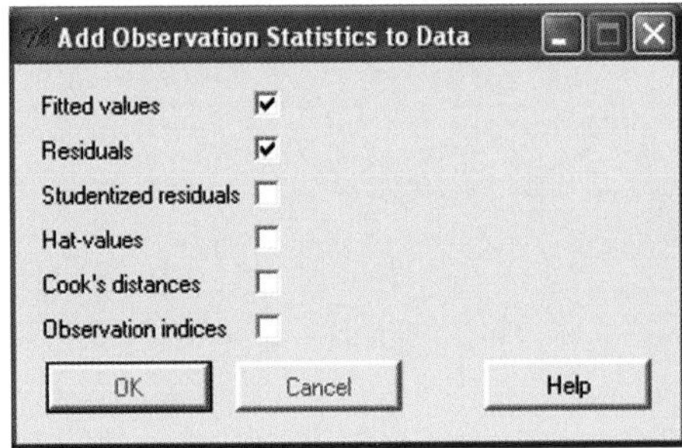

Fig. 10.15 We need to plot the fitted values and residuals from each of the models we have looked at. We do these steps three times, once for each model.

a. Specify the active model for Rcmdr. The dropdown box for Model in the Rcmdr menu bar shows all models defined in this session.

b. As in Fig. 8.14, we calculate the fitted values and residuals for the active model with the Models ▶ Add observation statistics to data... menu item.

c. Check the Fitted Values and Residuals boxes, and leave the other boxes unchecked.

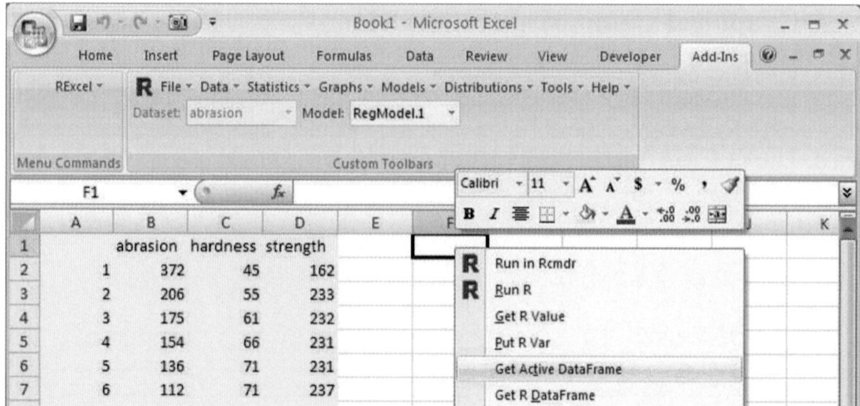

Fig. 10.16 In Fig. 10.15, we added the fitted values and residuals for the three models to the dataframe in R. Now we bring the revised dataframe back to Excel. Place the cursor on row 1, one column beyond the end of the existing data (in this example, the data is in columns A:D, so we place the cursor in column F). Get the revised active dataset, now containing the sets of predicted values and residuals, one set for each of the three models we have looked at, into the Excel worksheet with the right-click Get Active DataFrame menu. This produces Fig. 10.17.

	G	H	I	J	K	L	M	N
1	abrasion	hardness	strength	fitted.Reg	residuals.	fitted.Reg	residuals.	fitted.I
2	372	45	162	366.8353	5.164742	188.7145	183.2855	310.2702 61.72976
3	206	55	233	203.5508	2.449176	137.6514	68.34858	256.9
4	175	61	232	165.5002	9.499844	138.3706	36.62938	224.88
5	154	66	231	134.0203	19.97968	139.0898	14.91018	198.2
6	136	71	231	101.1662	34.83383	139.0898	-3.08982	171.51
7	112	71	237	92.9203	19.0797	134.7746	-22.7746	171.51
8	55	81	224	45.07805	9.921946	144.1242	-89.1242	118.15
9	45	86	219	19.09546	25.90454	147.7202	-102.72	91.471
10	221	53	203	257.9218	-36.9218	159.2274	61.77262	267.57
11	166	60	189	231.1664	-65.1664	169.2962	-3.29617	230.22
12	164	64	210	176.0225	-12.0225	154.193	9.807008	208.87
13	113	68	210	149.7392	-36.7392	154.193	-41.193	187.52
14	82	79	196	96.70044	-14.7004	164.2618	-82.2618	128.82
15	32	81	180	105.5478	-73.5478	175.769	-143.769	118.15
16	228	56	200	242.3323	-14.3323	161.385	66.61502	251.56

Calibri 11

Run in Rcmdr
Run R
Get R Value
Put R Var
Get Active DataFrame
Get R DataFrame
Put R DataFrame
Rcmdr Get
Get R Output
Name Range
Insert Current R Plot
Prettyformat Numbers
Cut

Fig. 10.17 The revised abrasion dataset, now containing fitted values and residuals for all three models, is shown here. The columns of residuals and fitted values are not well formatted—the decimal points are not aligned. We highlight all the new columns and format them with the right-click Prettyformat Numbers... menu to get Fig. 10.18.

	G	H	I	J	K	L	M	N	O	P	Q
1	abrasion	hardness	strength	fitted.Reg	residuals.	fitted.Reg	residuals.	fitted.Reg	residuals.RegModel.1		
2	372	45	162	366.835	5.1647	188.715	183.285	310.270	61.730		
3	206	55	233	203.551	2.4492	137.651	68.349	256.905	-50.905		
4	175	61	232	165.500	9.4998	138.371	36.629	224.885	-49.885		
5	154	66	231	134.020	19.9797	139.090	14.910	198.203	-44.203		
6	136	71	231	101.166	34.8338	139.090	-3.090	171.520	-35.520		
7	112	71	237	92.920	19.0797	134.775	-22.775	171.520	-59.520		

Fig. 10.18 Now the columns are aligned, hence legible. The default names for the columns of fitted values and residuals are truncated in the cells in the display of row 1 of the worksheet. The full names are visible in the formula bar.

10.4.1 *Plot* Residuals ~ Fitted

We will plot the residuals against the fitted values for each of the three models we have viewed in Figs. 10.10, 10.12, and 10.14.

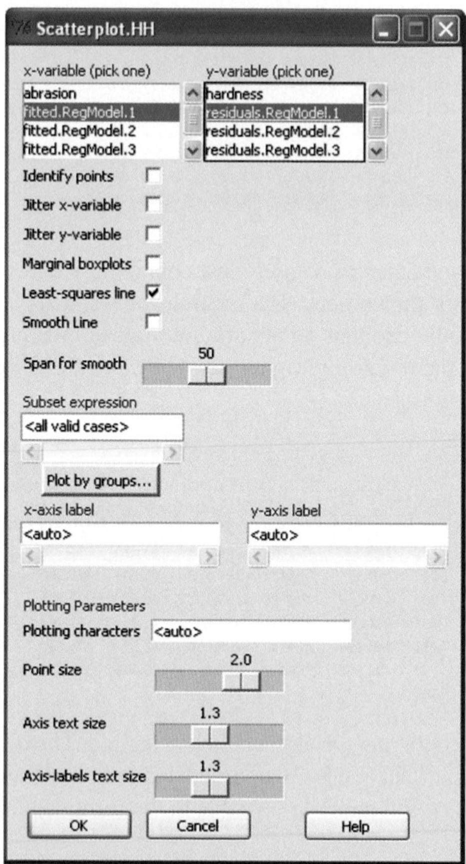

Fig. 10.19 The scatterplot dialog box is specified on the Graphs ► Scatterplot.HH...(HH) menu. We will plot the residuals against the fitted values for each of the three models we have viewed in Figs. 10.10, 10.12, and 10.14. In this illustration, we have highlighted the x-variable fitted.RegModel.1 and the y-variable residuals.RegModel.1. All three individual graphs are displayed in Fig. 10.20. The graphs are shown very small; therefore, we made the dots much larger than normal by adjusting the slider to increase the Point size to 2.0.

abrasion ~ hardness, $s = 60, R^2 = 0.544$

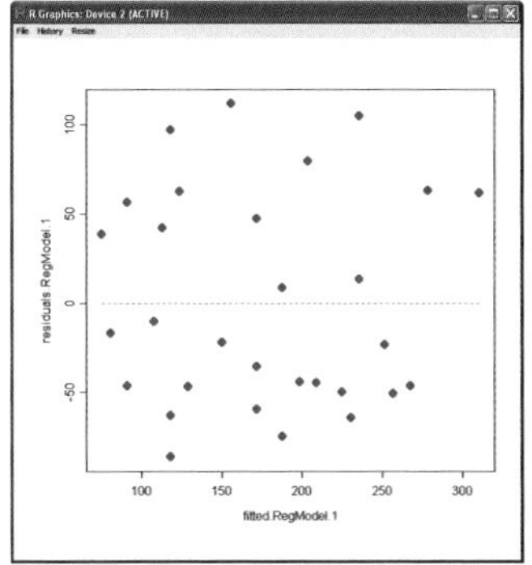

abrasion ~ strength, $s = 85, R^2 = 0.089$

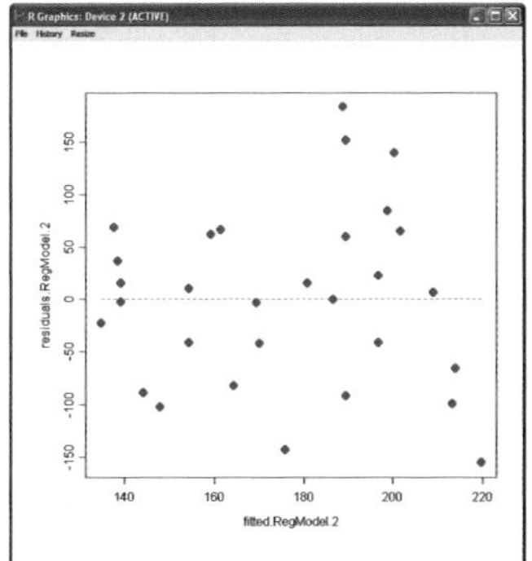

abrasion ~ hardness + strength, $s = 36, R^2 = 0.840$

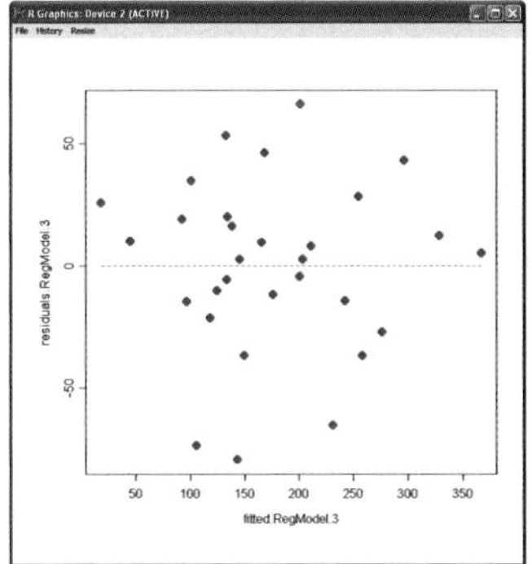

Fig. 10.20 Plots of the residuals against the fitted values for each of the three models in Figs. 10.10, 10.12, and 10.14. The graphs of the models are hard to compare, as each has a different set of x- and y-limits. We therefore repeat these plots with a common scaling in Figs. 10.21 and 10.31.

10.4.2 Rescale Plots for Ease of Comparison

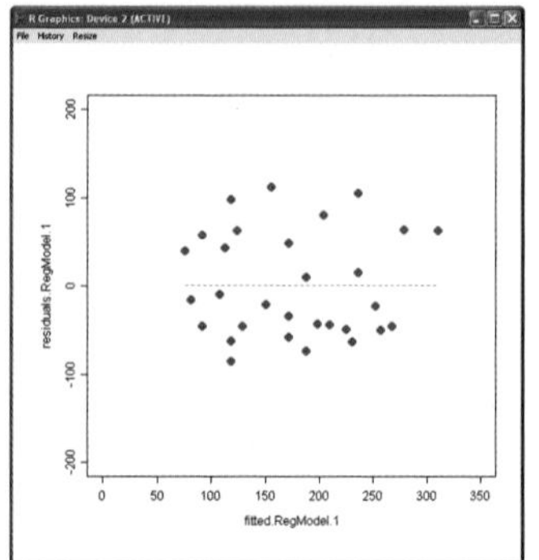

abrasion ~ strength, $s = 85, R^2 = 0.089$

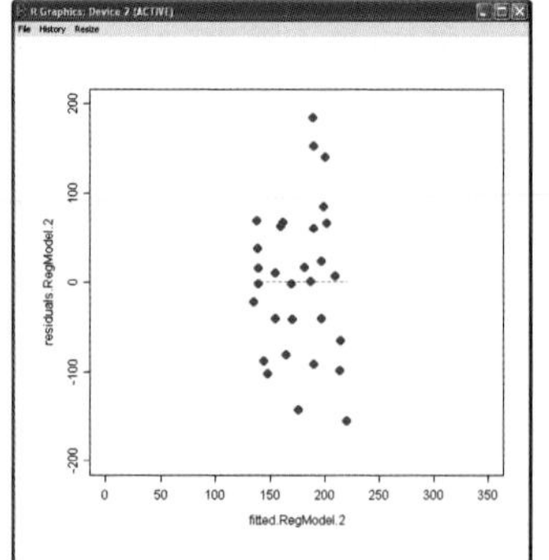

abrasion ~ hardness + strength, $s = 36, R^2 = 0.840$

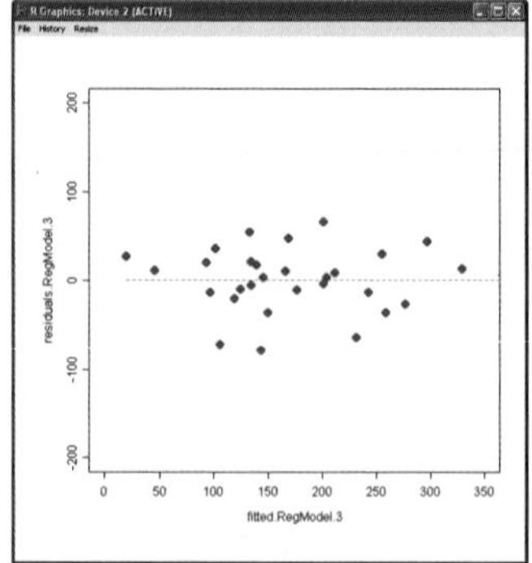

Fig. 10.21 Repeats, with common scaling, of the plots of the residuals against the fitted values for each of the three models in Figs. 10.12, 10.10, and 10.14. As s decreases, we see that the residuals have a smaller and smaller vertical range. As R^2 increases, we see that the fitted values have a wider and wider horizontal range as they do a better job of approximating the observed response values. The commands we used to control the scaling are illustrated in Fig. 10.22.

```
scatterplot(residuals.RegModel.3~fitted.RegModel.3, reg.line=lm,
  smooth=FALSE, labels=FALSE, boxplots=FALSE, span=0.5, cex=1.3,
   cex.axis=1.3,
   cex.lab=1.3, pch=16, data=abrasion)

scatterplot(residuals.RegModel.3~fitted.RegModel.3, reg.line=lm,
  smooth=FALSE, labels=FALSE, boxplots=FALSE, span=0.5, cex=1.3,
   cex.axis=1.3,
   cex.lab=1.3, pch=16, data=abrasion,
   xlim=c(0,350), ylim=c(-200,200))
```

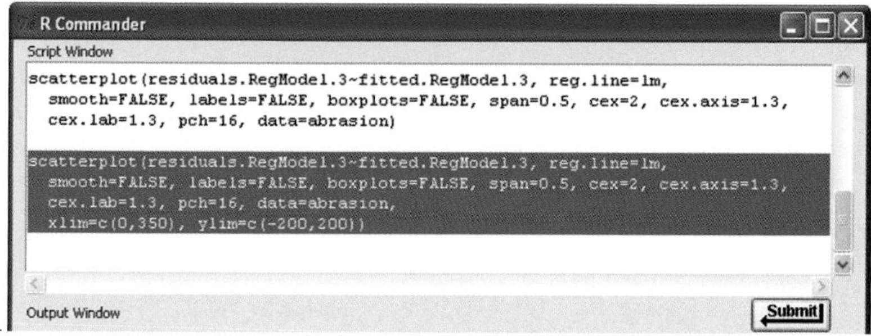

Fig. 10.22 The three plots in Fig. 10.20 were plotted with commands similar to the first command shown here for model RegModel.3. These commands were generated directly by Rcmdr from repeated use of the dialog box in Fig. 10.19. The three plots in Fig. 10.21 were plotted by editing those commands and submitting them. We show the editing for RegModel.3. We copied the command generated by Rcmdr and edited it by adding the last line specifying wider x- and y-limits for the plot. The values here were chosen by looking at the three graphs in Fig. 10.20 and selecting new limits that covered the range of all three graphs. We manually specified the `xlim` and `ylim` arguments to force all three on the same scale. The common scaling is specified by adding the two arguments

```
xlim=c(0,350), ylim=c(-200,200)
```

to the generated commands. The top panel shows the original and edited commands. In the bottom panel, we highlighted the entire four-line edited command and submitted it to Rcmdr by clicking the Submit button.

10.4.3 Lattice Plots with Coordinated Scales

There is another way to get all three plots scaled alike by using the Graphs ► XY conditioning Plot... (HH) menu item and dialog box. This menu and dialog box use R's Lattice package to coordinate the scaling of all panels with a single call. This dialog box requires stacking the fitted and residuals columns from all models and distinguishing the three models with a new factor named model. The stacked data is shown in Fig. 10.23.

In Section 10.4.4, we construct the stacked columns in Fig. 10.23 with the RExcel right-click Paste as Stacked menu item. Column T contains the group labels. The column labels in Fig. 10.18, generated by the Models ► Add observation statistics to data... menu item in Fig. 10.15, include the model name RegModel.n. Here, we have stacked all three fitted.RegModel.n columns into a single column fitted and all three residuals.RegModel.n columns into a single column residuals. The numerical names n (selected from 1, 2, 3 here) are arbitrary. It is much more informative to use the model formula as the label, and we have done so in column T.

Book1.xlsx

	S	T	U	V	W
1		model	fitted	residuals	
2		abrasion ~ hardness	310.27	61.73	
3		abrasion ~ hardness	256.905	-50.905	
4		abrasion ~ hardness	224.885	-49.885	
30		abrasion ~ hardness	118.154	96.846	
31		abrasion ~ hardness	91.472	56.528	
32		abrasion ~ strength	188.715	183.285	
33		abrasion ~ strength	137.651	68.349	
60		abrasion ~ strength	208.852	6.148	
61		abrasion ~ strength	213.887	-65.887	
62		abrasion ~ hardness + strength	366.835	5.1647	
63		abrasion ~ hardness + strength	203.551	2.4492	
90		abrasion ~ hardness + strength	168.766	46.2339	
91		abrasion ~ hardness + strength	145.532	2.4679	
92					

Sheet1 Sheet2 Sheet3

Fig. 10.23 Here we show the entire stacked dataset containing the fitted values and residuals from the three models shown in Fig. 10.18. In this figure, we show the first few and last few observations for each model. The remaining rows were hidden by highlighting the Excel row numbers and using the right-click hide menu item.

10.4.4 Stacking with the Right-Click Menu

Here we show how to use the RExcel right-click Paste as Stacked menu item to create the columns illustrated in Fig. 10.23 from the three sets of residuals and fitted values in Fig. 10.18.

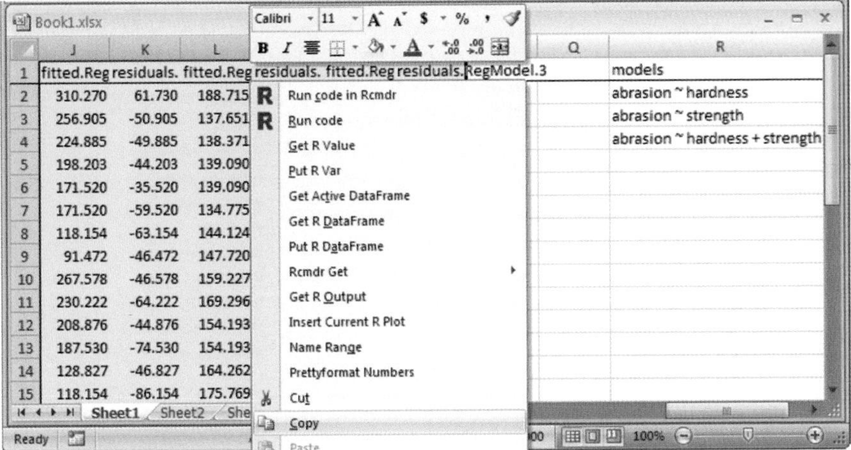

Fig. 10.24 We show two steps here. In cells R1:R4, we write the three model formulas for later use in Fig. 10.26. We begin with Fig. 10.18 and highlight the six columns in cells J1:O31 and right-click Copy.

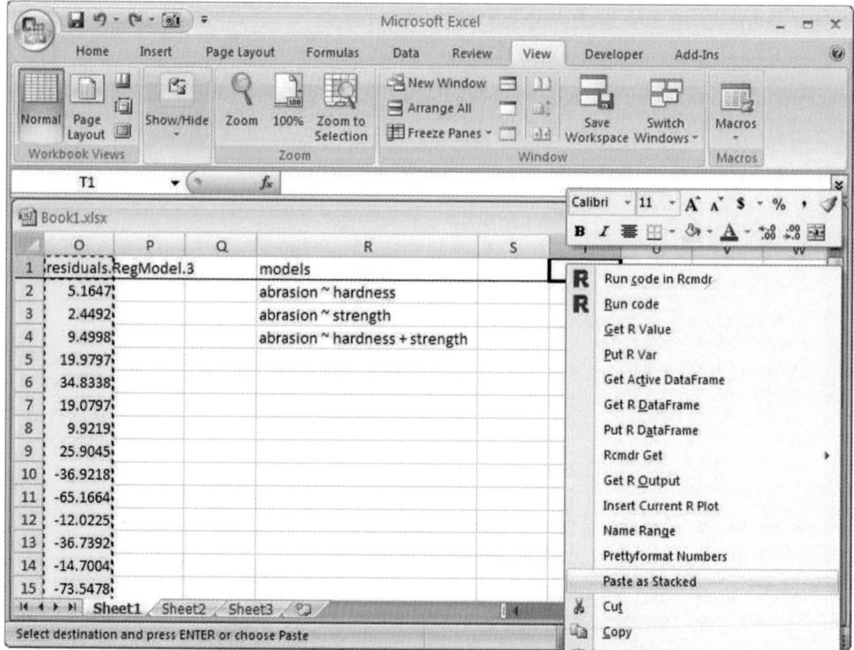

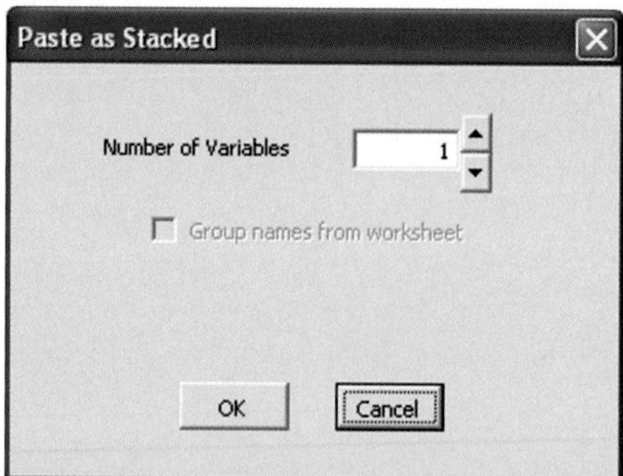

Fig. 10.25 We move the cursor to cell T1 and right-click Paste as Stacked to get the dialog box shown here. The dialog box opens with Number of Variables at 1 and Group names from worksheet grayed out. In this example, there are two columns in each of the groups, so we move to Fig. 10.26 to make that change in the dialog box.

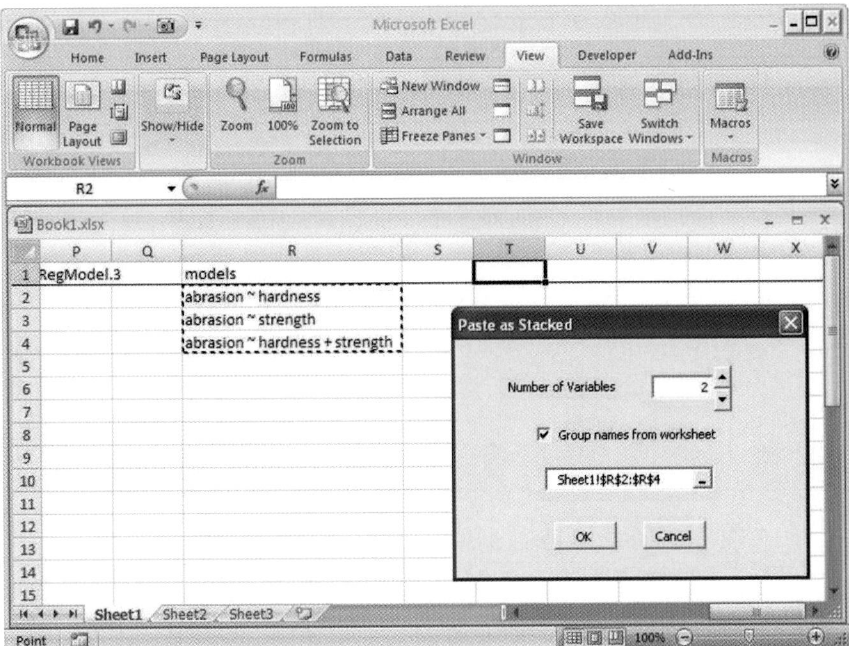

Fig. 10.26 We click the up arrow in the spinner to change the number of variables to 2 and to ungray the Group names from worksheet checkbox. Check the checkbox, and the entry box for the group names appears. With the mouse, select the model names that we previously placed in cells R2:R4 and click OK to get Fig. 10.27.

a. Default column names from Paste as Stacked.

Book1.xlsx

	P	Q	R	S	T	U	V	W	X
1	RegModel.3		models		group	fitted.Reg	residuals.RegModel.1		
2			abrasion ~ hardness		abrasion ~	310.27	61.73		
3			abrasion ~ strength		abrasion ~	256.905	-50.905		
4			abrasion ~ hardness + strength		abrasion ~	224.885	-49.885		
5					abrasion ~	198.203	-44.203		
6					abrasion ~	171.52	-35.52		
7					abrasion ~	171.52	-59.52		
8					abrasion ~	118.154	-63.154		
9					abrasion ~	91.472	-46.472		
10					abrasion ~	267.578	-46.578		
11					abrasion ~	230.222	-64.222		
12					abrasion ~	208.876	-44.876		
13					abrasion ~	187.53	-74.53		
14					abrasion ~	128.827	-46.827		
15					abrasion ~	118.154	-86.154		

Sheet1 Sheet2 Sheet3

Ready 100%

b. More appropriate column names and column widths.

Book1.xlsx

	R	S	T	U	V	W	X
1	models		model	fitted	residuals		
56			abrasion ~ strength	189.434	151.566		
57			abrasion ~ strength	200.222	139.778		
58			abrasion ~ strength	198.783	84.217		
59			abrasion ~ strength	201.66	65.34		
60			abrasion ~ strength	208.852	6.148		
61			abrasion ~ strength	213.887	-65.887		
62			abrasion ~ hardness + strength	366.835	5.1647		
63			abrasion ~ hardness + strength	203.551	2.4492		
64			abrasion ~ hardness + strength	165.5	9.4998		
65			abrasion ~ hardness + strength	134.02	19.9797		
66			abrasion ~ hardness + strength	101.166	34.8338		
67			abrasion ~ hardness + strength	92.92	19.0797		
68			abrasion ~ hardness + strength	45.078	9.9219		
69			abrasion ~ hardness + strength	19.095	25.9045		

Sheet1 Sheet2 Sheet3

Edit

Fig. 10.27 The three columns created in Panel a have default names and default widths. To get to Panel b, we type more appropriate names in cells T1:V1 and change the width of column T by placing the cursor in the row names between T and U and double-clicking.

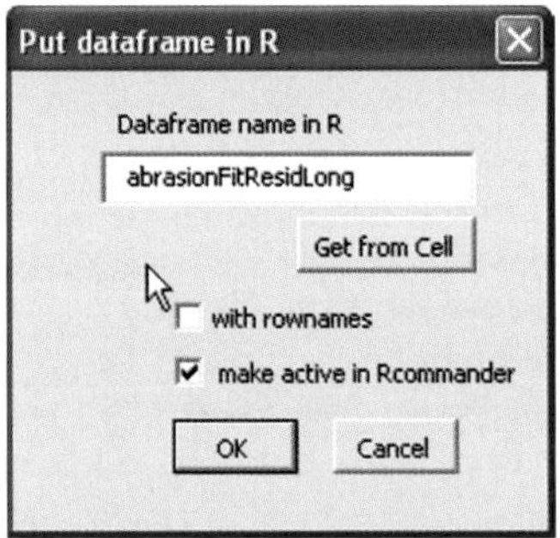

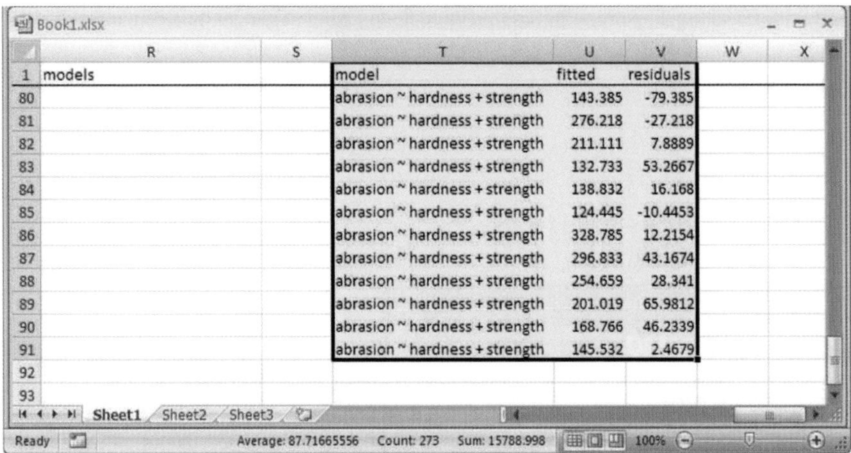

	R	S	T	U	V	W	X
1	models		model	fitted	residuals		
80			abrasion ~ hardness + strength	143.385	-79.385		
81			abrasion ~ hardness + strength	276.218	-27.218		
82			abrasion ~ hardness + strength	211.111	7.8889		
83			abrasion ~ hardness + strength	132.733	53.2667		
84			abrasion ~ hardness + strength	138.832	16.168		
85			abrasion ~ hardness + strength	124.445	-10.4453		
86			abrasion ~ hardness + strength	328.785	12.2154		
87			abrasion ~ hardness + strength	296.833	43.1674		
88			abrasion ~ hardness + strength	254.659	28.341		
89			abrasion ~ hardness + strength	201.019	65.9812		
90			abrasion ~ hardness + strength	168.766	46.2339		
91			abrasion ~ hardness + strength	145.532	2.4679		
92							
93							

Fig. 10.28 We are now ready to put the stacked data into R. Highlight cells T1:V891 and right-click Put R DataFrame (not shown here) to get the dialog box. Choose the name abrasionFitResidLong and click OK. The appearance of the worksheet is the same (except for hiding the rows) as in Fig. 10.23. One more step is needed to make the graph in Fig. 10.31 correct. Factor levels are, by default, ordered alphabetically, which is usually not the right order. In this case, the alphabetical order of the models is

```
abrasion ~ hardness
abrasion ~ hardness + strength
abrasion ~ strength
```

We need to match the ordering:

```
abrasion ~ hardness
abrasion ~ strength
abrasion ~ hardness + strength
```

(top to bottom) of Fig. 10.31.

a. Reorder factor levels menu item.

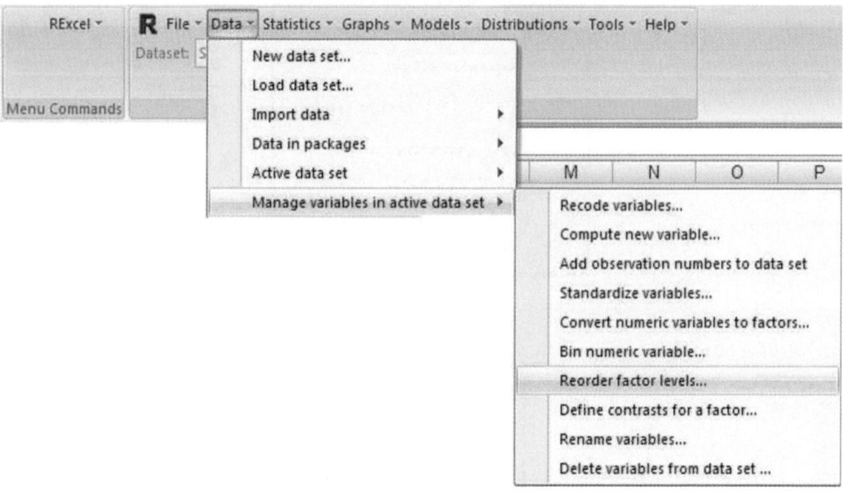

b. Variable selection dialog box. c. Order specification dialog box.

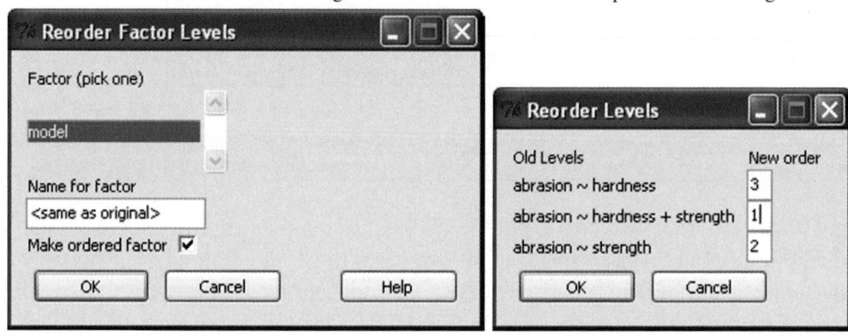

Fig. 10.29 We use the Rcmdr menu item for reordering factor levels. In Panel a, click Data ► Manage variables in active data set ► Reorder factor levels.... This gives the Reorder Factor Levels dialog box in Panel b. When we take the default <same as original>, we get the warning message that we are about to overwrite the variable. In this example, overwriting is OK. Click Yes to accept overwriting. In Panel c, we specify the new order. Lattice panels are ordered from bottom to top, so we specify the bottom level `abrasion ~ hardness + strength` as number 1. We are now ready for the graph specification in Fig. 10.30.

10.4.5 Menu and Dialog Box for Lattice Plot

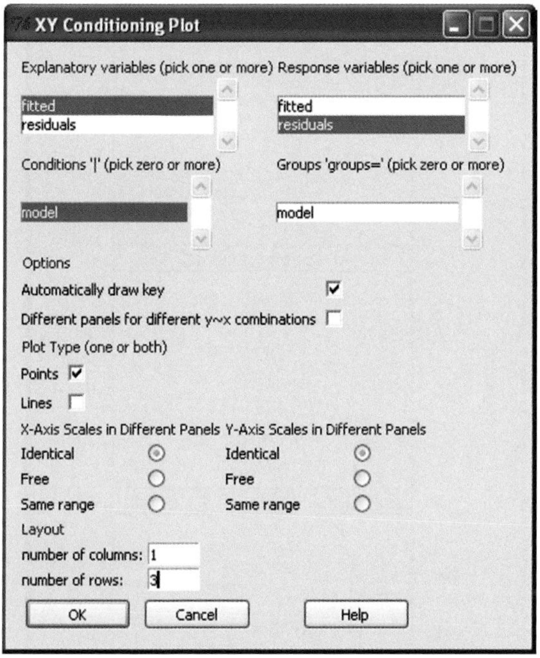

Fig. 10.30 We continue from Fig. 10.29. Specify model as the conditioning factor. Specify one column and three rows for the layout of the figures. The default value, Identical, for the axis scales forces the common scaling.

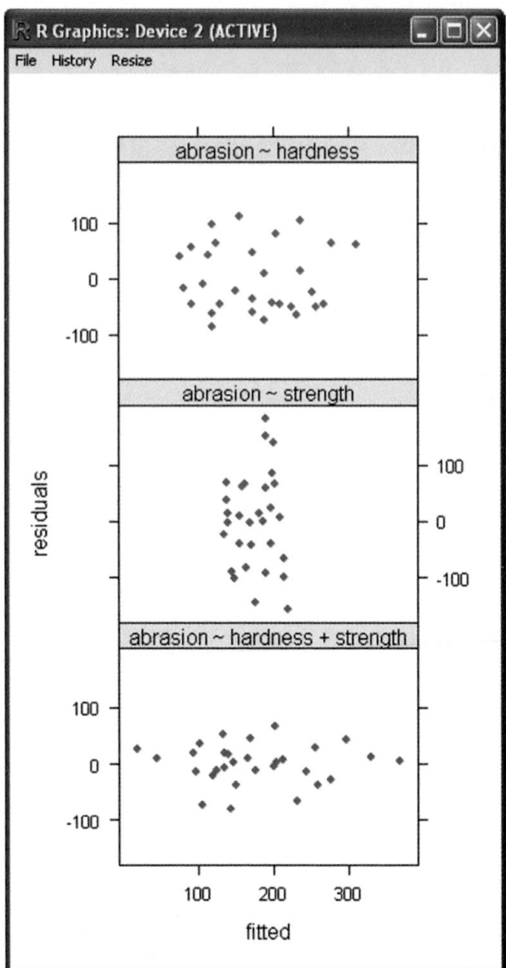

Fig. 10.31 We narrowed the Graphics window by grabbing its left side and pulling it toward the right to improve the aspect ratio. The *strip label* identifies the model in each panel. The strip labels are automatically generated from the levels of the conditioning factor.

Compare the three panels in this figure, specified with a single dialog box in Fig. 10.29, to the similar content and scaling in the three panels in Fig. 10.21 that were individually specified as described in Fig. 10.22.

10.5 ANOVA Table

The display of a regression analysis usually includes an ANOVA (analysis of variance) table. The sequential ANOVA table (each line includes the additional sum of squares from its term, after accounting for all preceding terms) is specified by the ANOVA table (Type I Sums of Squares) menu.

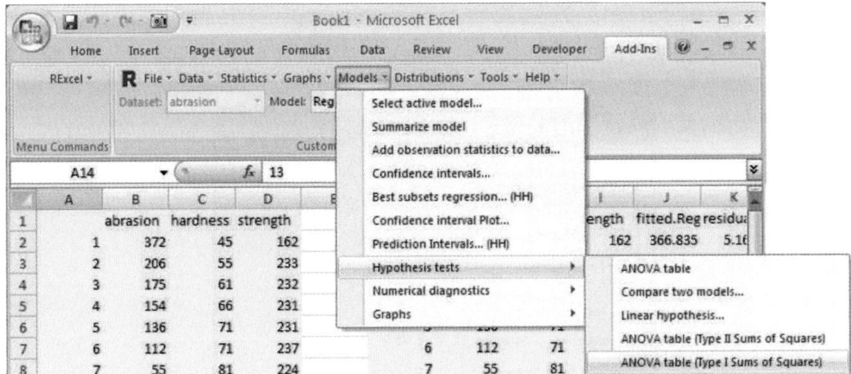

Fig. 10.32 Specify the sequential ANOVA table from the menu.

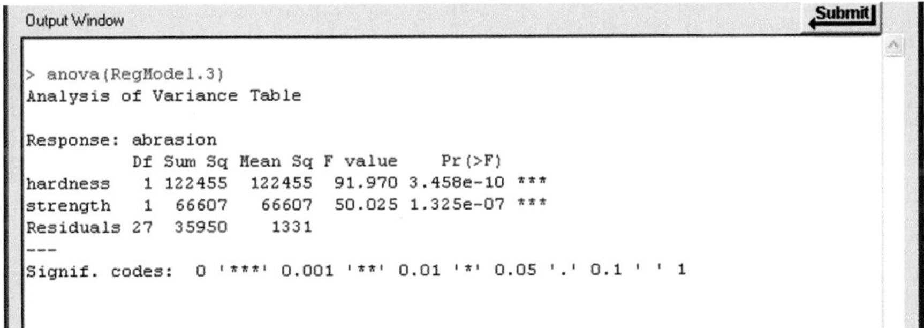


```
> anova(RegModel.3)
Analysis of Variance Table

Response: abrasion
          Df Sum Sq Mean Sq F value    Pr(>F)
hardness   1 122455  122455  91.970 3.458e-10 ***
strength   1  66607   66607  50.025 1.325e-07 ***
Residuals 27  35950    1331
---
Signif. codes:  0 '***' 0.001 '**' 0.01 '*' 0.05 '.' 0.1 ' ' 1
```

Fig. 10.33 The total sum of squares is partitioned into three components. The `hardness` term accounts for 122,455, the `strength` term explains an additional 66,607, and the `Residuals` the remainder (residual) 35,950. The total sum of squares is not displayed in this figure. We calculate the total sum of squares in Fig. 10.34.

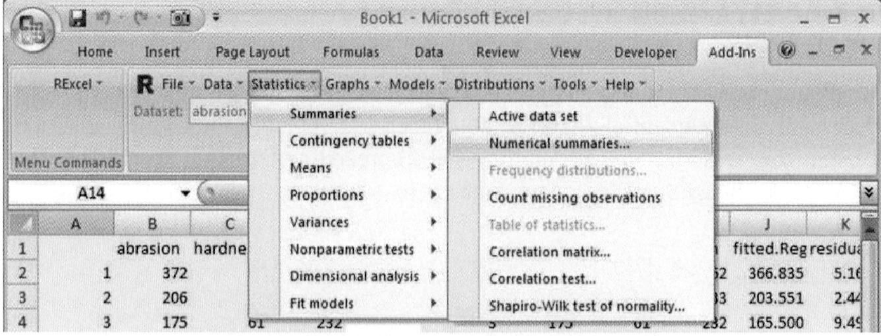

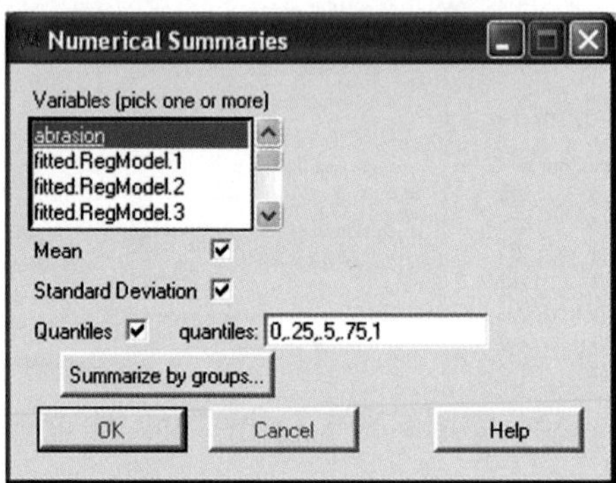


```
> numSummary(abrasion[,"abrasion"], statistics=c("mean", "sd", "quantiles"))
     mean       sd 0%    25% 50%   75% 100%  n
 175.4333 88.08526 32 113.25 165 220.5  372 30

> 29*88.08526^2
[1] 225011.4

> 122455 + 66607 + 35950
[1] 225012
```

Fig. 10.34 The total sum of squares is identical to the sum of the squared mean-centered differences $\sum_i (y_i - \bar{y})^2 = (n-1)\, s_y^2$. We use the numerical summaries menu and dialog box to get the summary. The last line shows the summation of the sums of squares in Table 10.33. The last two lines were manually entered into the Rcmdr script window.

```
> 29*88.08526^2
[1] 225011.4
> 122455 + 66607 + 3590
[1] 192652
```

10.6 Confidence Intervals and Prediction Intervals

Fig. 10.7 shows the least-squares regression plane constructed from the observed values of $y =$ `abrasion` fit to the observed predictor variables $x_1 =$ `hardness` and $x_2 =$ `strength`. We are usually interested in estimating the y location on the regression plane for any specified values of the x_1- and x_2-variables. There is a population mean $\mu_{y|x}$ of y

$$\mu_{y|x} = E(y|x) = \beta_0 + \beta_1 x_1 + \beta_2 x_2$$

that we cannot know. We find a point estimate of this value as

$$\hat{y}|x = \hat{\beta}_0 + \hat{\beta}_1 x_1 + \hat{\beta}_2 x_2$$

The blue plane in Fig. 10.7 shows the set of point estimates for all values of x_1 and x_2.

In simple linear regression, we calculated confidence intervals for estimating the population $\mu_{y|x}$ at each value of the x-variables with Equation (8.2). We also calculated prediction intervals for predicting the y-value corresponding to new observations of the x-values with Equation (8.3). We can do the same for multiple regression.

We calculate a confidence interval for the mean abrasion of a very large sample of rubber having a common value of hardness and strength with the formula for estimating the confidence interval of a population mean $\mu_{y|x}$

$$\hat{y}|x \pm t_{\frac{\alpha}{2},n-3}\; s\, \sqrt{h} \tag{10.1}$$

where h is defined in Equation (10.3). Equation (10.1) is the analog of Equation (8.2). The calculation is specified by the first interval in Fig. 10.36 using the Models ► Prediction Intervals...(HH) menu with the confidence interval for mean box checked.

We calculate a prediction interval for the abrasion for one sample of rubber with a specific value of both hardness and strength

$$y|x = \mu_{y|x} + \varepsilon$$

using the formula for the prediction interval for a new observation

$$\hat{y}|x \pm t_{\frac{\alpha}{2},n-3}\; s\, \sqrt{1+h} \tag{10.2}$$

Equation (10.2) is the analog of Equation (8.3). The calculation is specified by the second interval in Fig. 10.36 using the Models ► Prediction Intervals...(HH) menu with the prediction interval for individual box checked. The prediction intervals are wider than the confidence intervals because they include the uncertainty ε of the new observation.

For simple linear regression, we gave the formula for h in Equation (8.1). For multiple regression, the h-value is usually calculated by software using an analogous matrix equation

$$h = x(X'X)^{-1}x' \tag{10.3}$$

where the vector x for the new point is defined by $x = (1\ x_1\ x_2)$ and the matrix $X = (\mathbf{1}\ X_1\ X_2)$ consists of three columns: $\mathbf{1}$ is the column of all ones, X_1 is the column of x_{i1} for the n original observations, and X_2 is the column of x_{i2} for the n original observations.

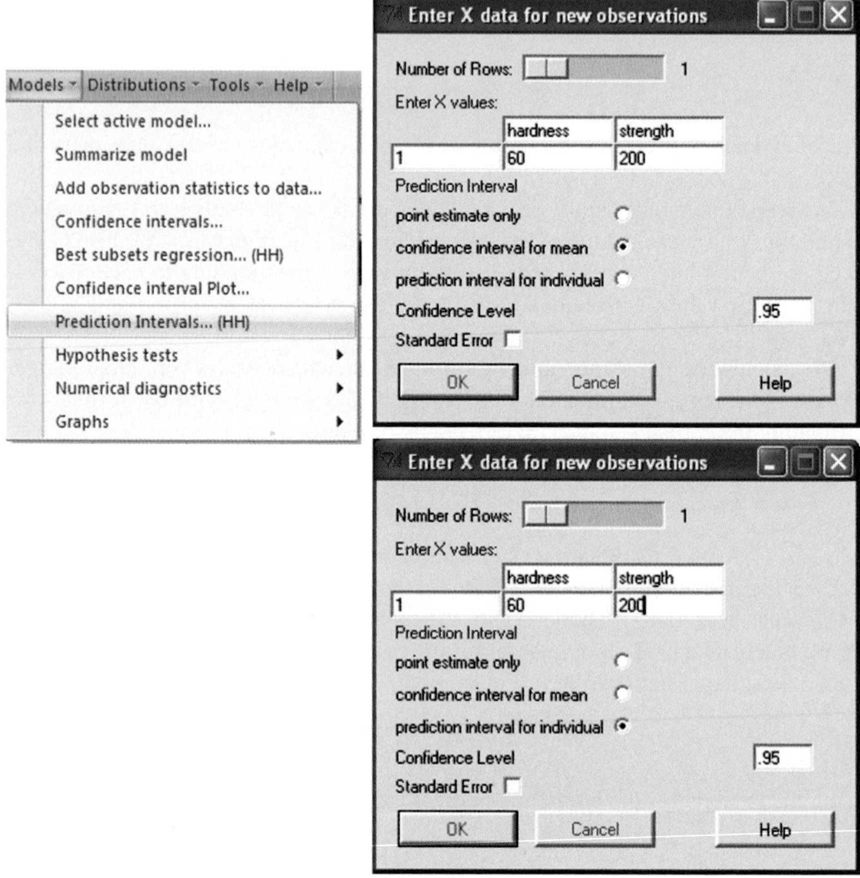

Fig. 10.35 The confidence interval and prediction interval for new observations are calculated by the Models ▶ Prediction Intervals... (HH) menu and its dialog box. Two specifications of the dialog box are shown here. The first shows the confidence interval specification and the second shows the prediction interval specification. The printed output for the two dialog boxes is in Fig. 10.36.

```
> .NewData <- data.frame(hardness=60, strength=200, row.names="1")

> .NewData  # Newdata
  hardness strength
1       60      200

> predict(RegModel.1, newdata=.NewData, interval="confidence",
+   level=.95,  se.fit=FALSE)
       fit      lwr      upr
1 216.0490 197.5783 234.5196

> .NewData <- data.frame(hardness=60, strength=200, row.names="1")

> .NewData  # Newdata
  hardness strength
1       60      200

> predict(RegModel.1, newdata=.NewData, interval="prediction",
+   level=.95,  se.fit=FALSE)
       fit      lwr      upr
1 216.0490 138.9343 293.1636
```

Fig. 10.36 The confidence interval and prediction interval for a new observation as specified by the two dialog boxes in Fig. 10.35. The table here was taken from the Rcmdr Output Window.

Chapter 11
Polynomial Regression

Abstract If the relationship between a response variable Y and an explanatory variable X is believed to be nonlinear, it is sometimes possible to model the relationship by adding an X^2-term to the model in addition to an X-term. For example, if Y is product demand and X is advertising expenditure on the product, an analyst might feel that beyond some value of X, there is "diminishing marginal returns" on this expenditure. Then the analyst would model Y as a function of X and X^2, and possibly other predictor variables, and anticipate a significant negative coefficient for X^2. Occasionally a need is encountered for higher-order polynomial terms.

11.1 Regression on a Quadratic Function of X

Our example illustrates use of the quadratic model

$$y = \beta_0 + \beta_1 x + \beta_2 x^2 + \varepsilon \qquad (11.1)$$

which can be fit with the same procedures as multiple regression.

We use as our example the hardness data (from [Heiberger and Holland, 2004] and from [Hand et al., 1994], original reference [Williams, 1959]). In this section, we investigate the modeling of $Y =$ `hardness` as a quadratic function of $X =$ `density`.

Hardness of wood is more difficult to measure than density. Modeling hardness in terms of density is therefore desirable. This dataset comes from a sample of Australian Janka timbers. In Fig. 11.1, we show the result of fitting both linear and quadratic model to this data.

R.M. Heiberger, E. Neuwirth, *R Through Excel*, Use R,
DOI 10.1007/978-1-4419-0052-4_11,

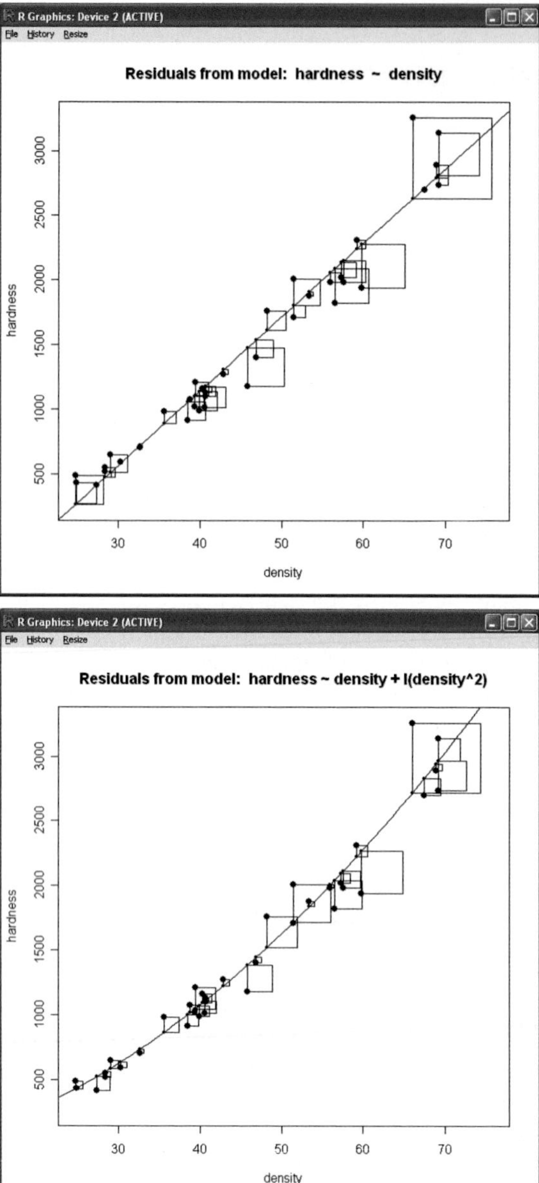

Fig. 11.1 The linear model $y = \hat{\beta}_0 + \hat{\beta}_1 x$ is fit to the hardness data in the top panel. The quadratic model $y = \hat{\beta}_0 + \hat{\beta}_1 x + \hat{\beta}_2 x^2$ is fit to the hardness data in the bottom panel. We can see that the quadratic model fits the points more closely than the linear model. We see it both in terms of closeness of the fitted line to the observed points and in terms of the sizes of the squared residuals. Refer back to Section 9.1 for a discussion of the display of squared residuals. We show the dialog boxes that generate these graphs in Fig. 11.14.

Let us now build up to the display in Fig. 11.1. Read the data by entering

```
hardness <- read.table(hh("datasets/hardness.dat"),
                       header=TRUE)
```

in the Rcmdr Script Window and then click the Submit button. Bring the data into Excel by clicking the blue **R** icon to make Rcmdr aware of the dataframe, and then right-click Get Active DataFrame to get Fig. 11.2. See Fig. 10.2 for a screenshot of the blue **R** icon. Note the `density` column on the left side of Fig. 11.2 does not have aligned decimal points, making it very difficult for a reader to make visual comparisons of numbers in the same column. We need to format the `density` column uniformly with the right-click Prettyformat Numbers menu item, in this case to always show one digit after the decimal point. The properly formatted data is shown on the right side of Fig. 11.2.

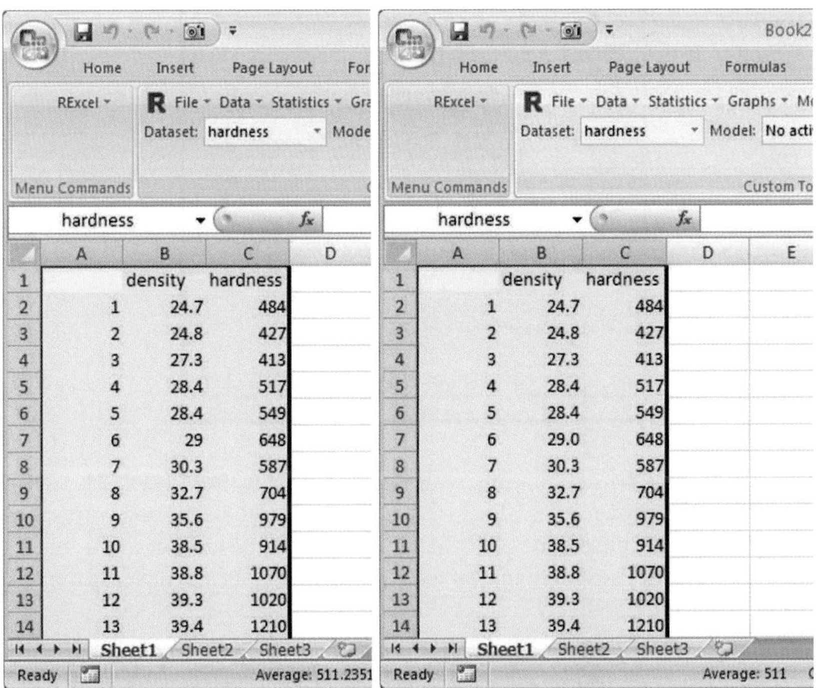

Fig. 11.2 The hardness data is brought into Excel with right-click Get Active DataFrame. Note the `density` column on the left side of the figure does not have aligned decimal points. We formatted the `density` column to one digit after the decimal point by right-clicking Prettyformat Numbers. We show the properly formatted data on the right side of the figure.

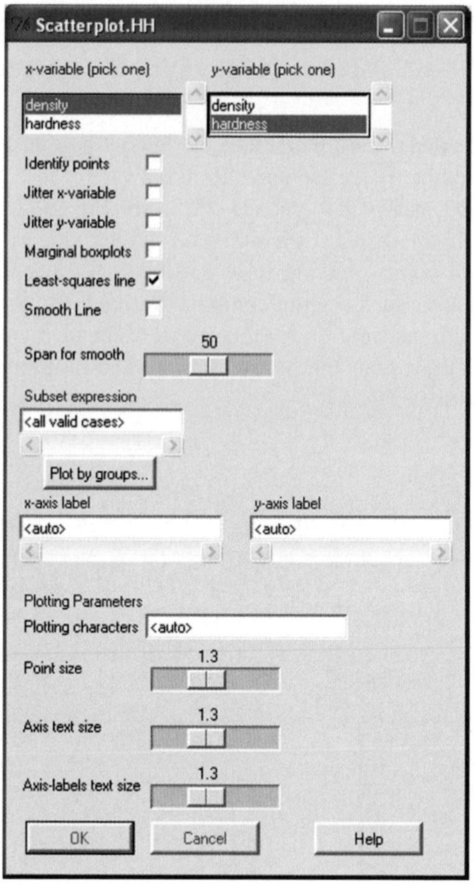

Fig. 11.3 We plot the data starting with Rcmdr Graphs ► Scatterplot.HH... (HH) to get the dialog box shown here, where we specify the x- (predictor) and y- (response) variables. [The Scatterplot.HH... (HH) menu is based on Scatterplot menu, but uses different defaults. It uses plotting character 16 for solid dots and increase the labels to size 1.3. The only option checked by default is the Least-squares line.]

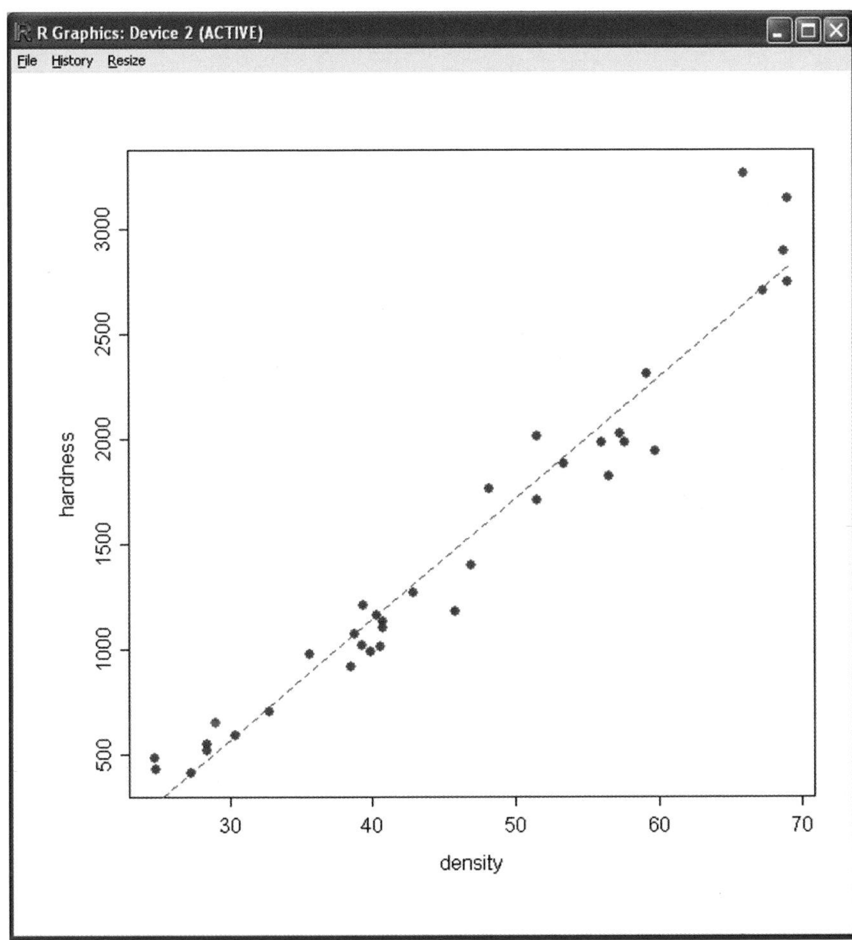

Fig. 11.4 The scatterplot shows most of the points on both ends of the `density` range to be above the least-squares line and a greater proportion of points in the center of the `density` range to be below the least-squares line. This is the first indicator that a straight-line fit will not be sufficient and that a quadratic fit may be needed.

11.2 Linear Fit

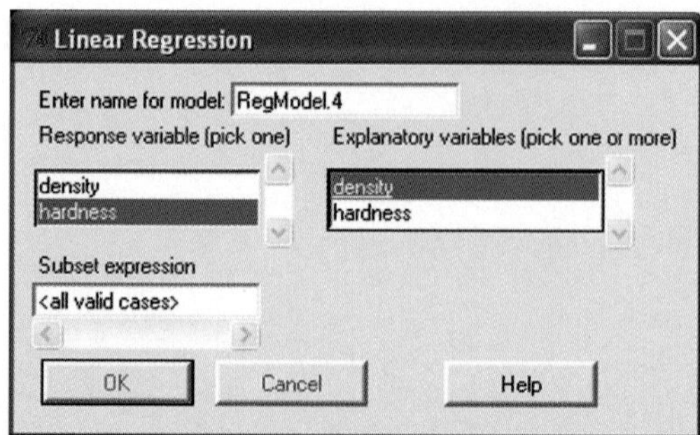

Fig. 11.5 We specified the linear regression with the Rcmdr Statistics ► Fit models ► Linear regression... menu item to get the dialog box shown here. We specify the single-x regression and get the summary table displayed in Fig. 11.6.

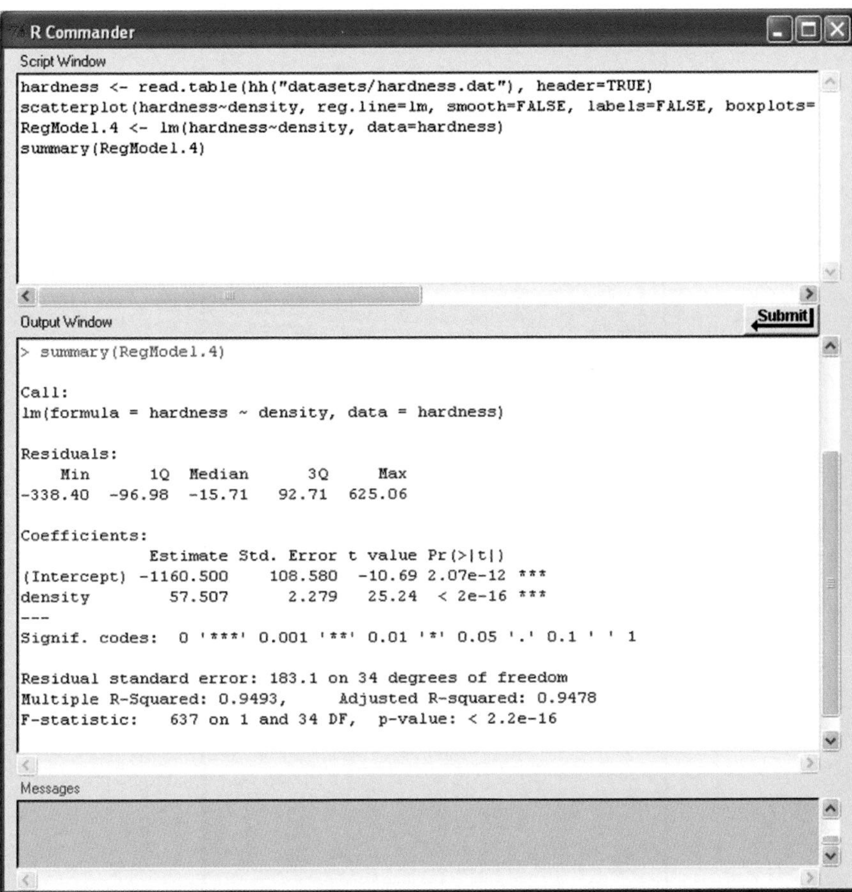

Fig. 11.6 The straight-line model has a p-value of $p = 2 \times 10^{-16}$ and a residual standard error $s = 183.1$.

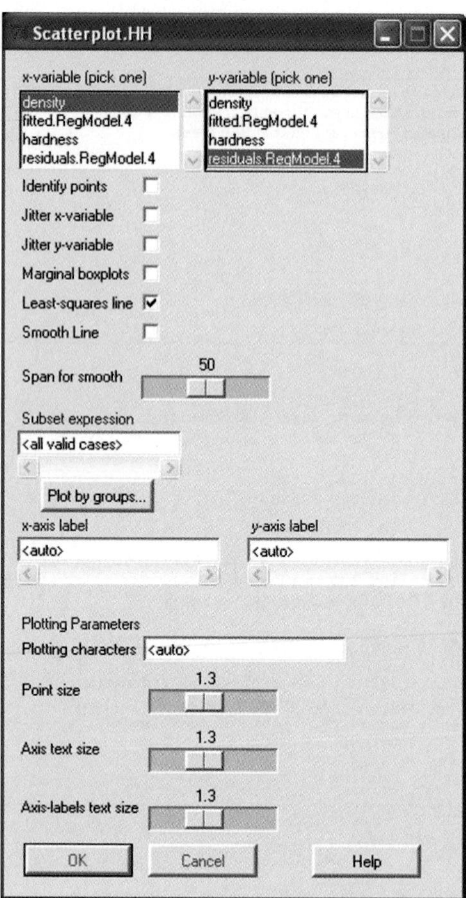

Fig. 11.7 We add the residuals and fitted values of the regression model `RegModel.4` to the dataset `hardness` with the Rcmdr Models ► Add observation statistics to data... menu. We then use the Rcmdr Graphs ► Scatterplot.HH...(HH) menu to get the dialog box shown here. This dialog box specifies the plot of `residuals ~ density` that we show in Fig. 11.8.

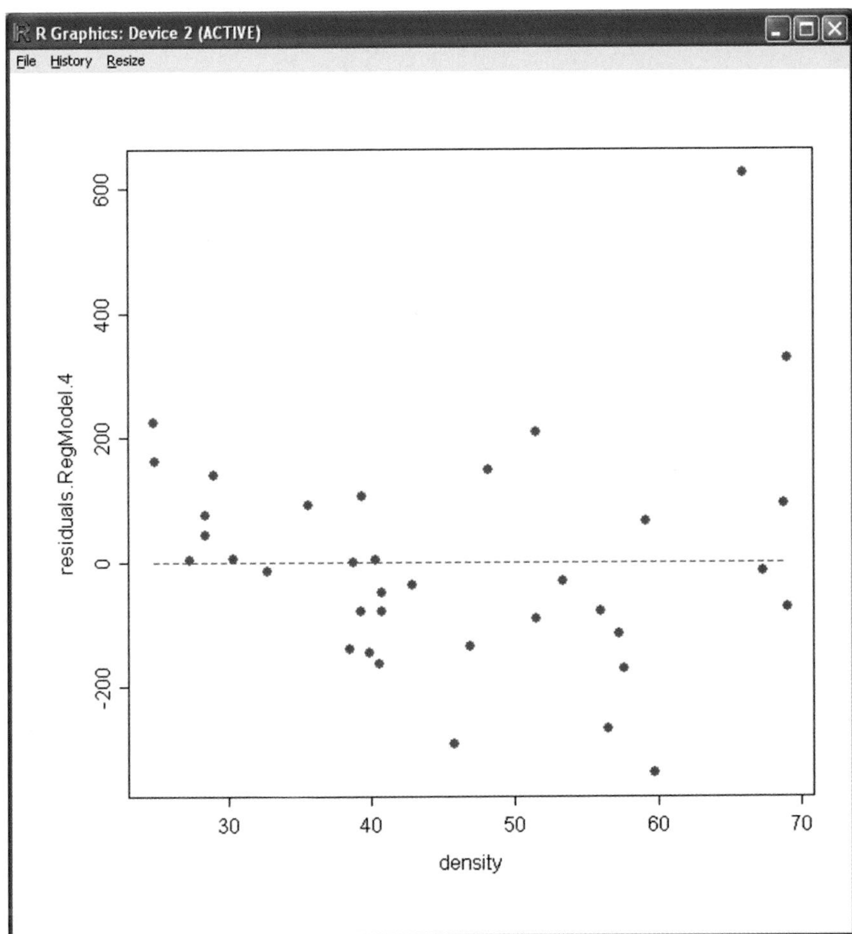

Fig. 11.8 Compare this residual plot to the data plot in Fig. 11.3. We see much more clearly now that there the residuals show quadratic behavior when plotted against the $x =$ `density` variable. Most of the points on the left and right of the plot are above the x-axis. Most of the points in the center of the plot are below the x-axis. We must model the quadratic behavior and test whether it is large enough to keep in the model.

11.3 Quadratic Fit

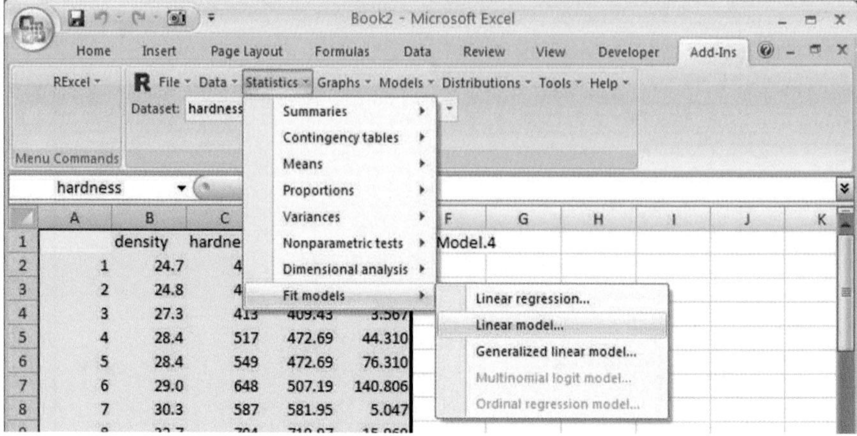

Fig. 11.9 In order to specify the quadratic term, we must use a new menu item. We specify the Linear model... menu item to give the dialog box in Fig. 11.10.

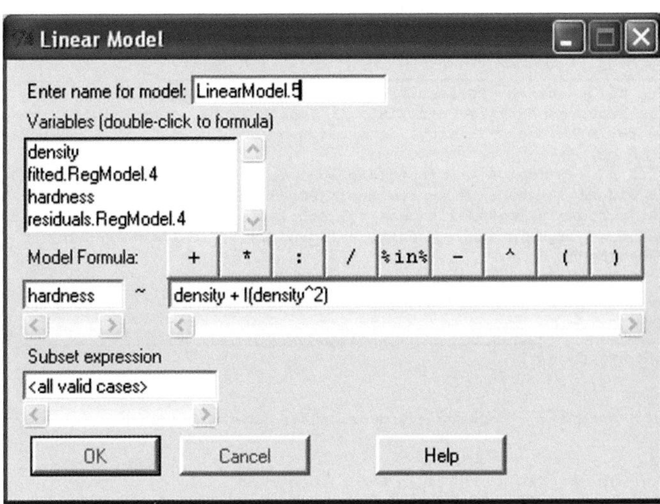

Fig. 11.10 The linear model dialog box allows the right-hand side of the linear model specification to be a complicated function of one or more predictor variables. We are using the quadratic model specification `hardness ~ density + I(density^2)`. (There are several other formulations that would also work.) We find it easier to enter the model by typing rather than by clicking the variables' names and function buttons.

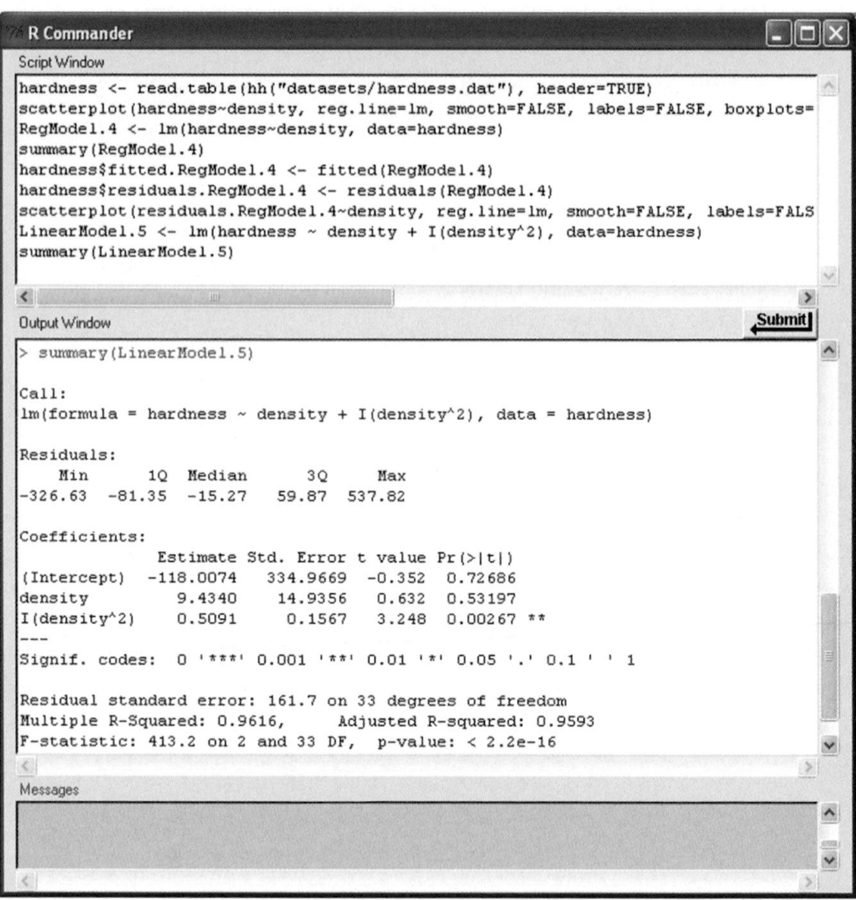

Fig. 11.11 The quadratic model has a smaller standard error $s = 161.7$, compared to the value $s = 183.1$ for the linear model in Fig. 11.6. The p-value for the additional term $x^2 =$ `I(density^2)` is significant at $p = 0.00267$. We also note that the marginal test for the coefficient for $x =$ `density` is not significant. The marginal test means the additional effect of the linear coefficient after the quadratic coefficient is included. A better test is the sequential test shown in the sequential ANOVA table in Figs. 11.12 and 11.13. In the sequential test of the quadratic term, we assume the linear term and test whether the inclusion of an additional quadratic term improves the fit. We will almost always retain the linear term in the model whenever the quadratic term is significant, even when the marginal test of the linear effect is not significant. The geometry of quadratic functions also argues for keeping the linear term. A quadratic function without a linear term $y = a + cx^2$ is symmetric around the origin. Such symmetry is unlikely in most data situations.

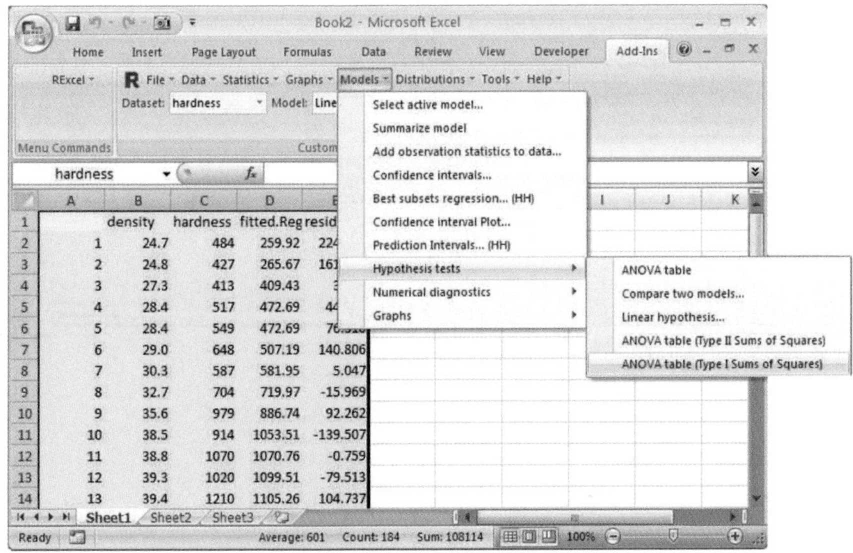

Fig. 11.12 We specify the sequential analysis of variance (ANOVA) table with the Models ► Hypothesis tests ► ANOVA table (Type I Sums of Squares) menu item.

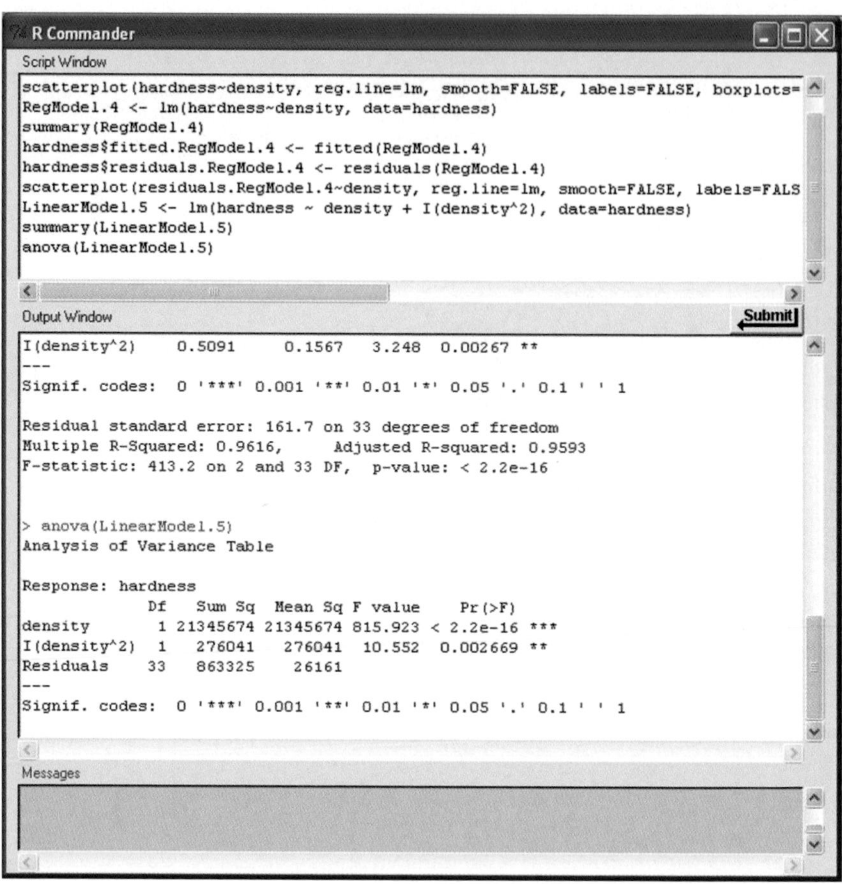

Fig. 11.13 In the sequential ANOVA table, we see that $x =$ `density` is significant. In addition, the increment to the sum of squares explained by the model from the quadratic term $x^2 =$ `I(density^2)` is also significant. We must therefore keep both terms.

11.4 Plot of Squared Residuals

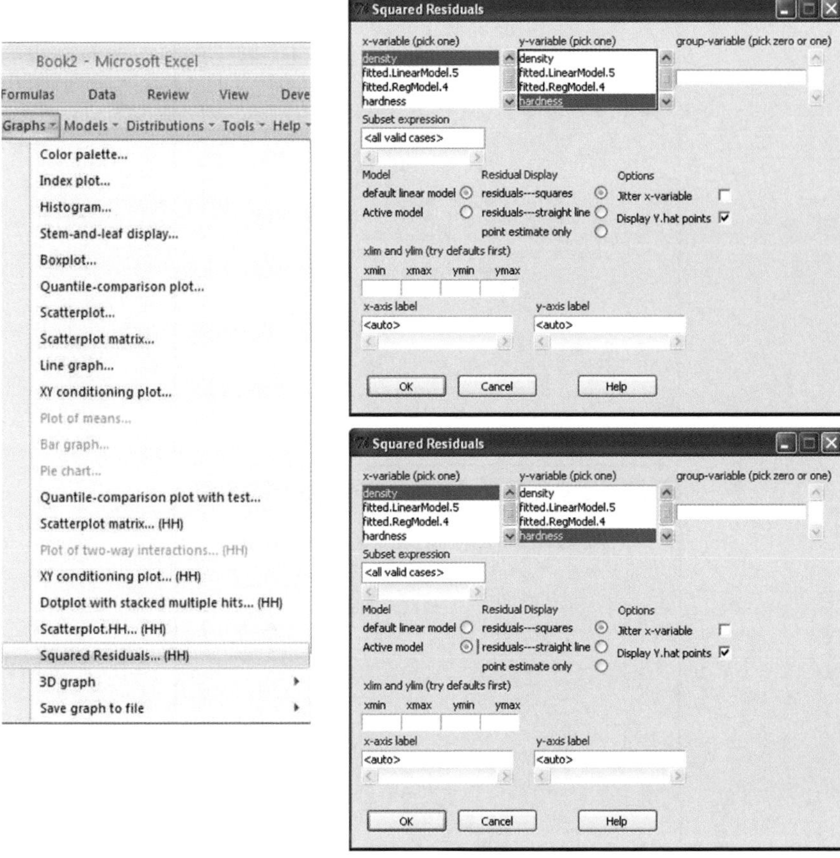

Fig. 11.14 We specify the display of squared residuals with the Graphs ► Squared Residuals...(HH) menu item and its dialog box. Two dialog boxes are shown here. On the top, we accept the default simple linear regression seen on the top in Fig. 11.15. On the bottom, we specify the active model, in this case `LinearModel.5`, which holds the quadratic fit, seen on the bottom in Fig. 11.15.

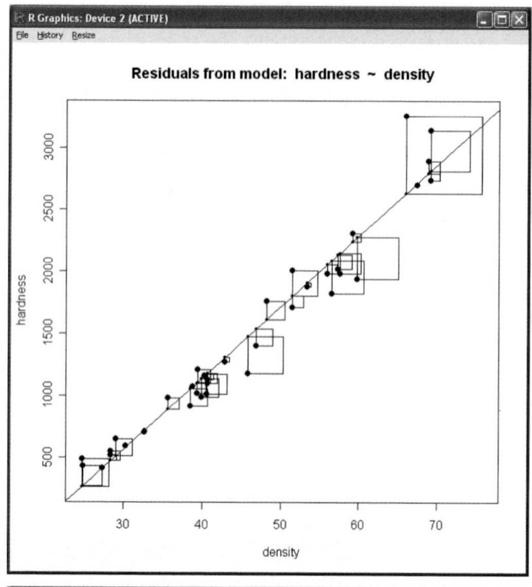

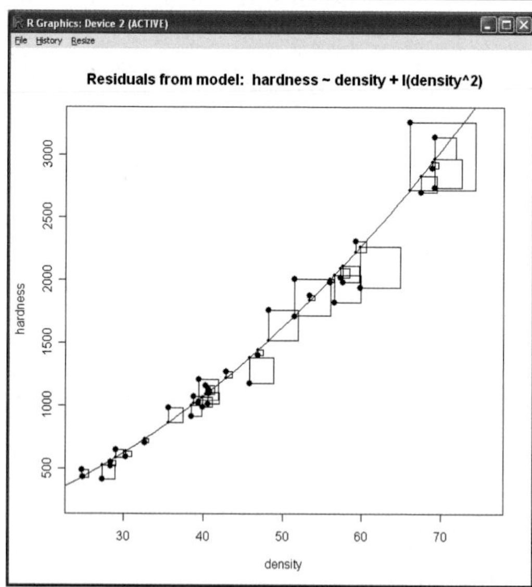

Fig. 11.15 This is a repeat, in context, of the display in Fig. 11.1. On the top, we show the squared residuals from the linear model in Fig. 11.6. On the bottom, we show the squared residuals from the quadratic model in Fig. 11.11. The quadratic model fits the points more closely than the linear model. We see it both in terms of closeness of the fitted line to the observed points and in terms of the sizes of the squared residuals. An additional virtue of the quadratic model is that its intercept term differs insignificantly from zero ($p = 0.726$ from Fig. 11.11); this is not true of the straight-line model for these data ($p = 2 \times 10^{-12}$ for the intercept in Fig. 11.6). (If wood has zero hardness, it certainly has zero density.)

Chapter 12
Multiple Regression—Three or More X-Variables

Abstract Multiple regression is often the method of choice for analysis of datasets that have many potential predictor variables. In this chapter, we illustrate the basic techniques of fitting a model with three or more x-variables and some of the techniques for testing the quality of the fit and for viewing the data and the fit.

Multiple regression with more than one x-variable fits the model

$$\begin{aligned} y_i &= \beta_0 + \beta_1 x_{i1} + \beta_2 x_{i2} + \ldots + \beta_p x_{ip} + \varepsilon_i \\ \varepsilon_i &\sim N(0, \sigma^2) \end{aligned}$$

to observed data consisting of one response variable y and p explanatory variables $x_1, x_1, x_2, \ldots, x_p$. We fit the model with the least-squares estimates

$$\begin{pmatrix} \hat\beta_0 \\ \hat\beta_1 \\ \hat\beta_2 \\ \vdots \\ \hat\beta_p \end{pmatrix} = \text{solve linear equations with your computer program}$$

$$\begin{aligned} \hat y_i &= \hat\beta_0 + \hat\beta_1 x_{i1} + \hat\beta_2 x_{i2} + \ldots + \hat\beta_p x_{ip} \\ s^2 &= \frac{\Sigma(y_i - \hat y)^2}{n - (p+1)} \end{aligned}$$

As in Chapter 10, we will usually first graph the data and then use the Rcmdr Statistics ► Fit Models ► Linear regression ... menu item to access the R `lm` function.

R.M. Heiberger, E. Neuwirth, *R Through Excel*, Use R,
DOI 10.1007/978-1-4419-0052-4_12,

12.1 Shoe Sizes of Austrian Students

The dataset `StudentData` [Neuwirth, 2008] consists of measurements on 1,126 Austrian undergraduates over the past 10 years. We will look at several variables that will help us investigate shoe sizes: `Sizes` are heights in cm. `Size` is the student's height, while `SizeFather` and `SizeMother` are the heights of the student's father and mother. `Weight` is in kg. `Shoesize` is European sizes. `Gender` has the values `male` and `female`.

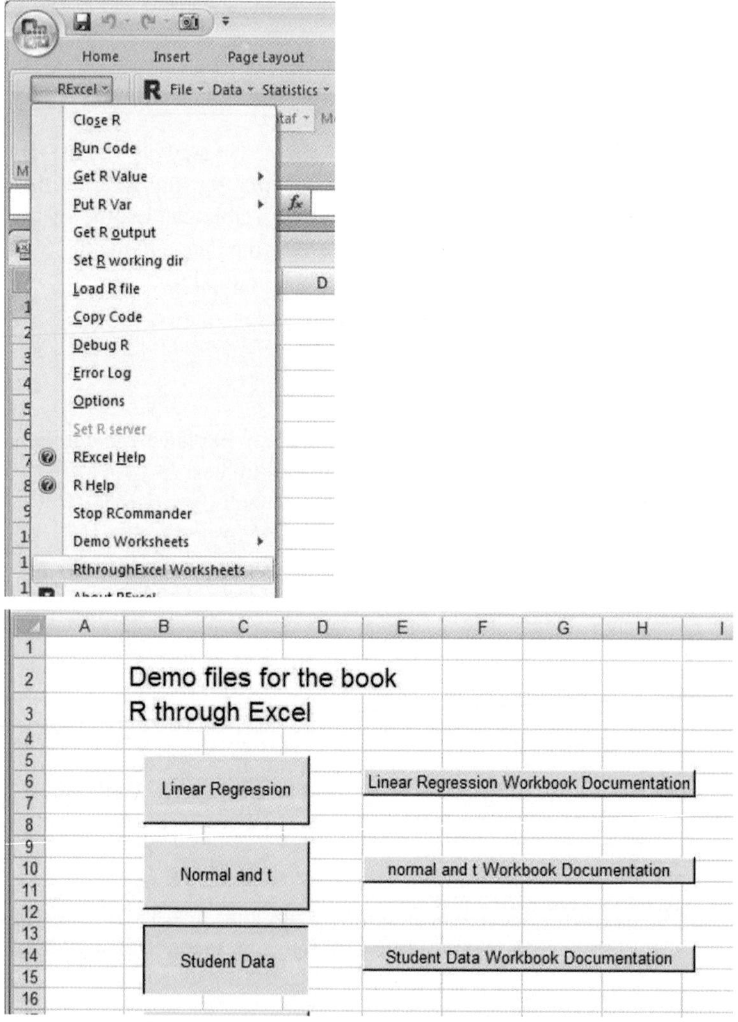

Fig. 12.1 The data is included as one of the Excel workbooks on the RExcel ▶ RthroughExcel Worksheets menu. Click the Student Data button to get Fig. 12.2. Click the Student Data Workbook Documentation button to see the description of the variables in this dataset.

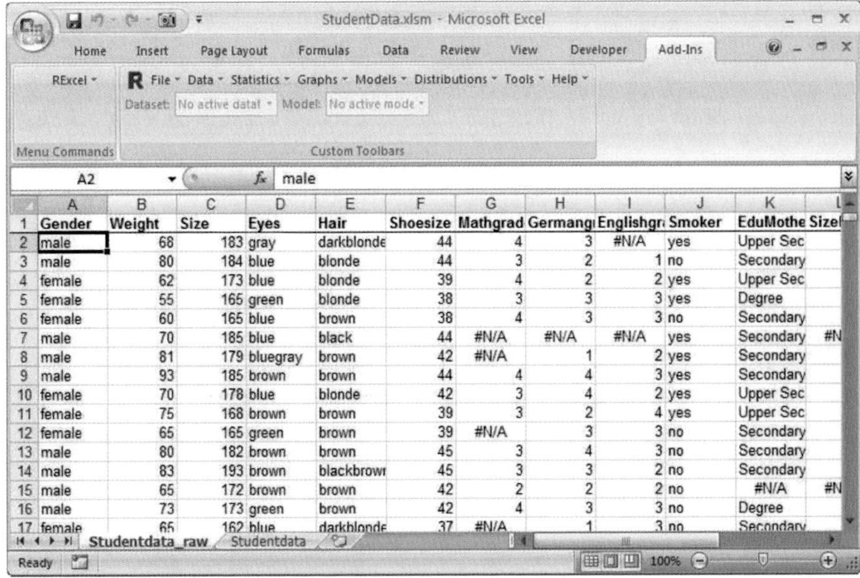

	A	B	C	D	E	F	G	H	I	J	K	L
1	Gender	Weight	Size	Eyes	Hair	Shoesize	Mathgrad	Germang	Englishgr	Smoker	EduMothe	Size
2	male	68	183	gray	darkblonde	44	4	3	#N/A	yes	Upper Sec	
3	male	80	184	blue	blonde	44	3	2	1	no	Secondary	
4	female	62	173	blue	blonde	39	4	2	2	yes	Upper Sec	
5	female	55	165	green	blonde	38	3	3	3	yes	Degree	
6	female	60	165	blue	brown	38	4	3	3	no	Secondary	
7	male	70	185	blue	black	44	#N/A	#N/A	#N/A	yes	Secondary	#N
8	male	81	179	bluegray	brown	42	#N/A	1	2	yes	Secondary	
9	male	93	185	brown	brown	44	4	4	3	yes	Secondary	
10	female	70	178	blue	blonde	42	3	4	2	yes	Upper Sec	
11	female	75	168	brown	brown	39	3	2	4	yes	Upper Sec	
12	female	65	165	green	brown	39	#N/A	3	3	no	Secondary	
13	male	80	182	brown	brown	45	3	4	3	no	Secondary	
14	male	83	193	brown	blackbrowi	45	3	3	2	no	Secondary	
15	male	65	172	brown	brown	42	2	2	2	no	#N/A	#N
16	male	73	173	green	brown	42	4	3	3	no	Degree	
17	female	65	162	blue	darkblonde	37	#N/A	1	3	no	Secondary	

Fig. 12.2 Note that we froze the first line containing the variable names. This way the variable names are always visible as we scroll through the file.

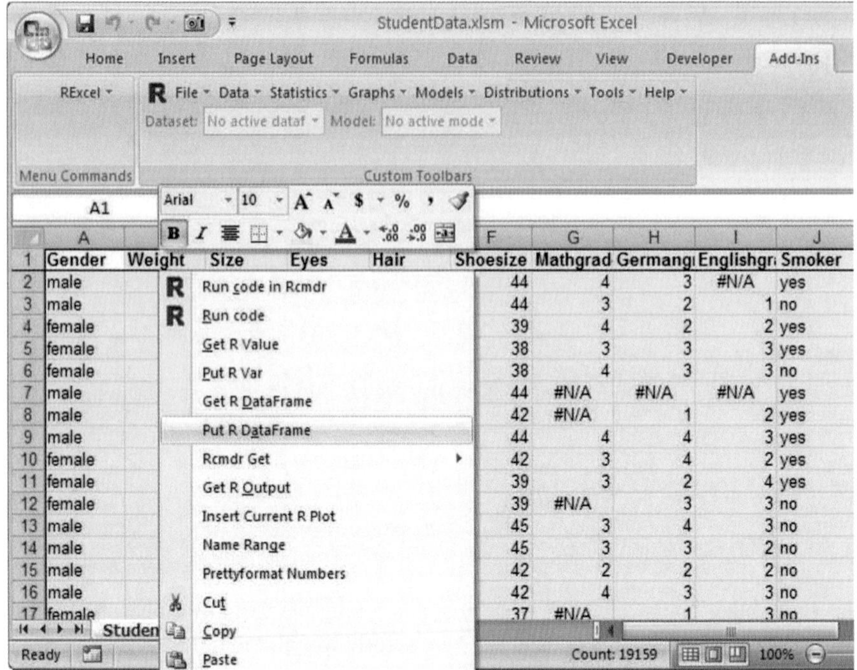

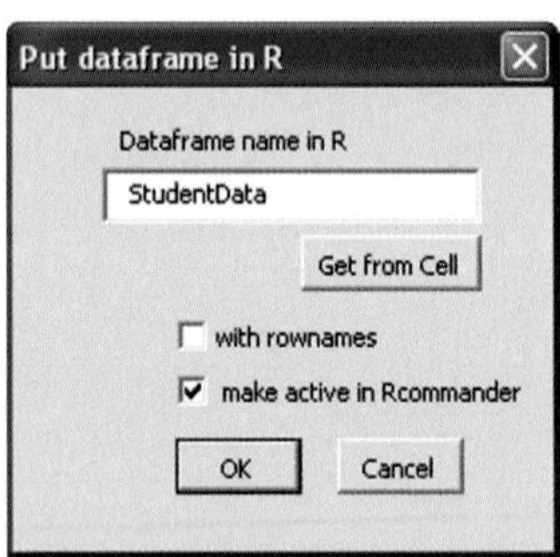

Fig. 12.3 Put the StudentData into R by highlighting the entire worksheet with Ctrl-Shift * and then right-clicking the Put R DataFrame menu item and dialog box. RExcel proposes the dataframe name StudentData, which we kept. All menu items on the Rcmdr menu refer to variables that are columns in the active dataframe.

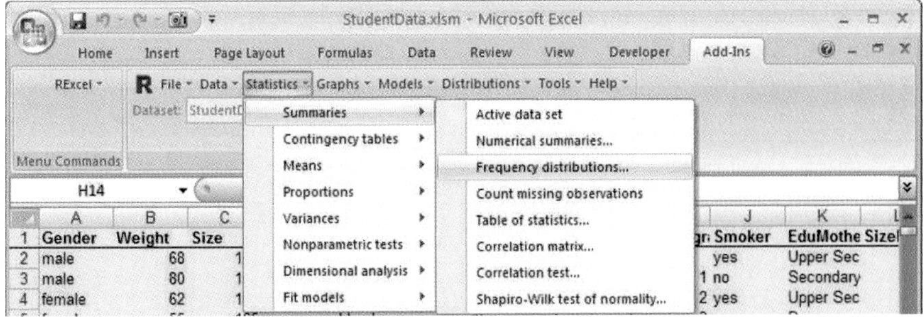

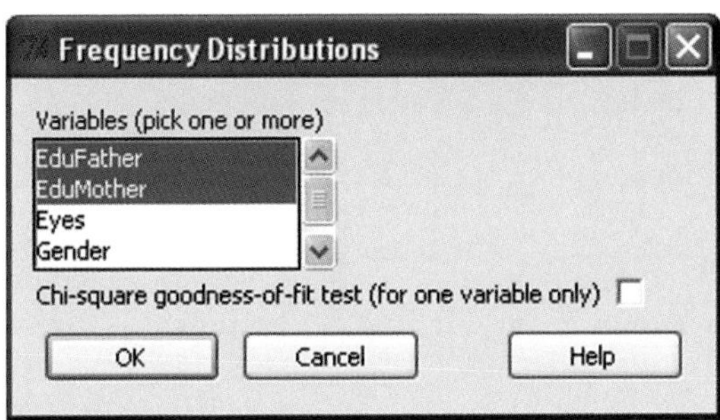

Fig. 12.4 The student data for the Austrian students has additional variables. We look at three here. EduMother and EduFather are the educational levels of the student's mother and father. The correct order of the levels is `Secondary`, `Upper Secondary`, `Degree`. ZodiacSign should be ordered by the positions of the constellations in the sky. We need to verify the ordering of these three ordered factors. We do so with the Statistics ► Summaries ► Frequency distributions... menu item and its dialog box. We select the three variables with Ctrl-left-click (only two are visible in the scroll window) and click OK.

We see in Table 12.1 that the education variables are ordered alphabetically: `Degree`, `Secondary`, `Upper Secondary`. Similarly, we see that the signs of the zodiac are initially ordered alphabetically. We correct both orderings in Fig. 12.5.

Table 12.1 Levels of the three factors are ordered alphabetically by default. This table is a subset of the output printed in the Rcmdr Output Window that was specified by the Frequency Distributions dialog box in Fig. 12.4.

```
> .Table  # counts for EduFather

      Degree        Secondary Upper Secondary
         377              465             255

> .Table  # counts for EduMother

      Degree        Secondary Upper Secondary
         225              505             377

> .Table  # counts for ZodiacSign

       Aquarius        Aries      Cancer   Capricorn
             82           97          84          67
         Gemini          Leo       Libra      Pisces
             94          118          80          96
    Sagittarius      Scorpio      Taurus       Virgo
             87           70          99          86
```

Table 12.2 Levels of the three factors sorted as specified in the Reorder Factor Levels dialog boxes in Figs. 12.5 and 12.6. This table is a subset of the output printed in the Rcmdr Output Window that was specified by a repeat of the Frequency Distributions dialog in Fig. 12.4.

```
> .Table  # counts for EduFather

    Secondary Upper Secondary          Degree
          465             255             377

> .Table  # counts for EduMother

    Secondary Upper Secondary          Degree
          505             377             225

> .Table  # counts for ZodiacSign

          Aries       Taurus      Gemini      Cancer
             97           99          94          84
            Leo        Virgo       Libra     Scorpio
            118           86          80          70
    Sagittarius    Capricorn    Aquarius      Pisces
             87           67          82          96
```

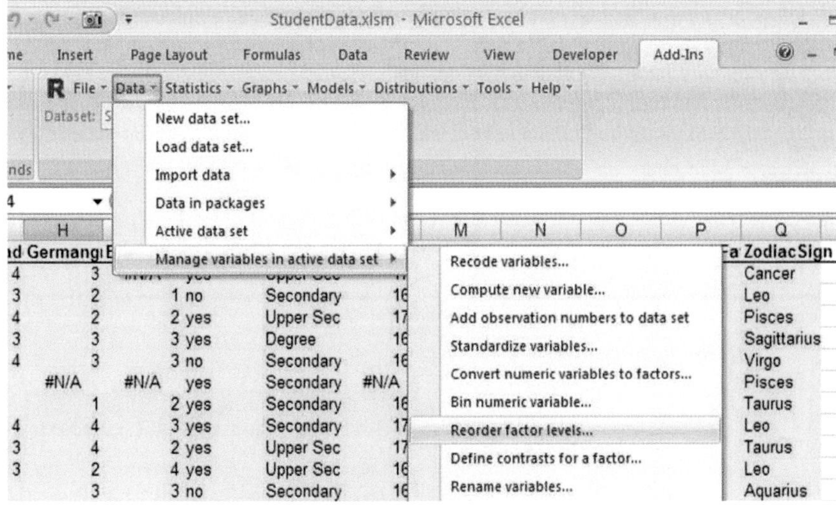

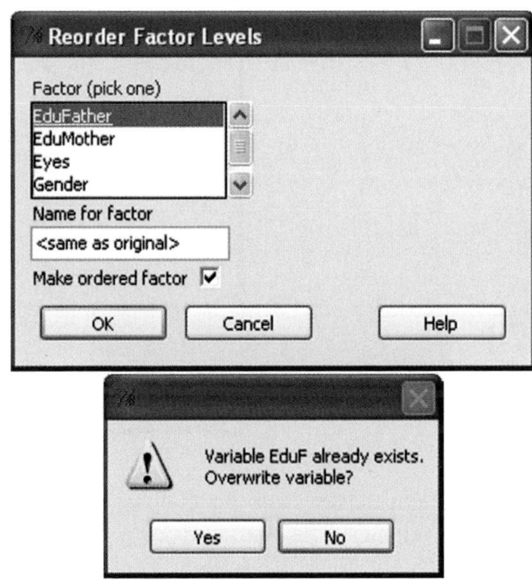

Fig. 12.5 Rcmdr has a menu item for reordering factor levels. We will use this menu item and its dialog box three times, once for each variable to be reordered. Click Data ▶ Manage variables in active data set ▶ Reorder factor levels.... This gives the Reorder Factor Levels dialog box. We show the EduFather variable highlighted. Repeat for the other two variables. When we take the default <same as original>, we get the warning message that we are about to overwrite the variable. In this example, overwriting is OK. Click Yes to get the dialog boxes in Fig. 12.6. The Make ordered factor checkbox is used to determine the type of contrasts used for the factor. The default is *treatment* contrasts. When checked, the contrasts are *orthogonal polynomial* contrasts. See `?contrasts` for more information. We do not use the contrasts in this book.

EduFather and EduMother Before

EduFather and EduMother After

ZodiacSign After

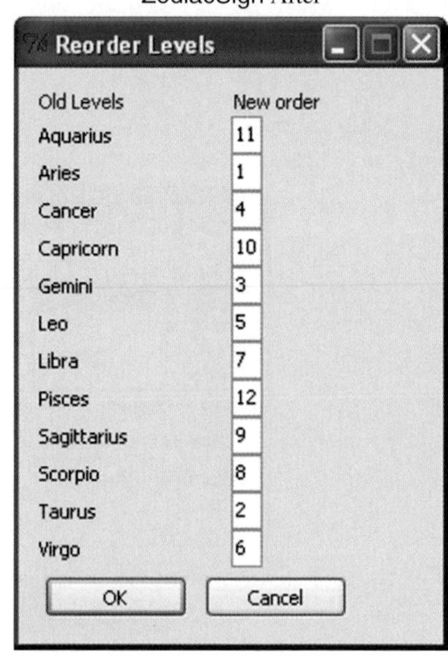

Fig. 12.6 The top two dialog boxes show the Before and After settings for the EduMother and EduFather variables. The bottom dialog box shows the After setting for the ZodiacSign variable.

12.2 Plots

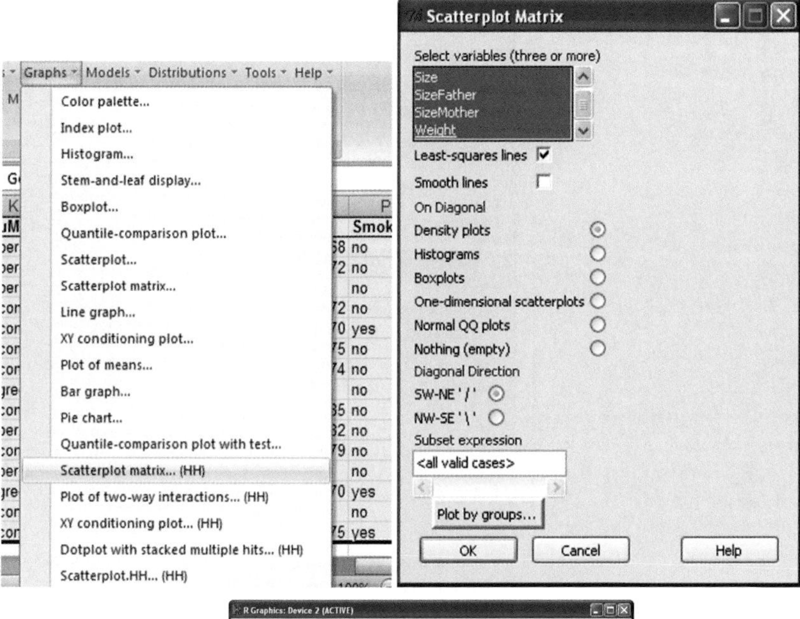

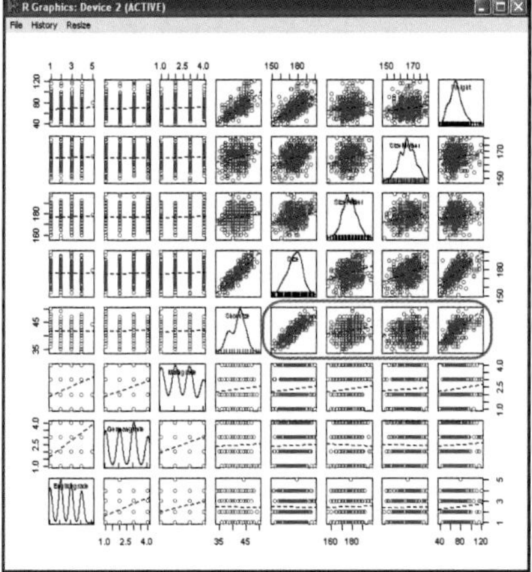

Fig. 12.7 As always, we begin with a plot. We first show the scatterplot matrix from the menu. Only the eight continuous variables show up in the list, and we select all eight. The five variables at the top right are the size and weight variables. They look reasonably normal, although there is some bimodality that might need investigating in Shoesize. We will be using Shoesize as the response variable in the regression analysis; therefore, we are most interested in the four outlined panels in the Shoesize row and the Size and Weight columns of the scatterplot matrix. We will expand these four panels in Figs. 12.8 and 12.9. The three variables in the lower left are grades on a discrete scale of (1, 2, 3, 4). The scatterplots are a lattice, and the univariate densities on the diagonal reflect the discreteness of the variables.

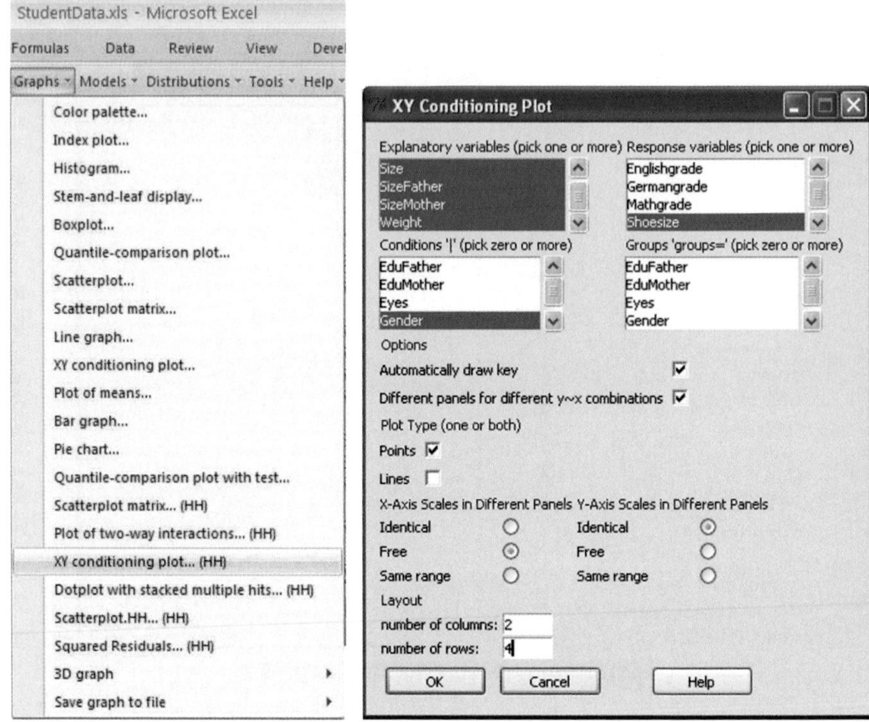

Fig. 12.8 The XY Conditioning Plot. . . (HH) menu gives access to the R lattice plot, a coordinated set of plots. In this example, we expand the outlined panels from Fig. 12.7. We construct four panels, each showing the same response variable Shoesize in the right-side Response variable dropdown menu and the four highlighted variables in the left-side Explanatory variables menu. We highlight Gender in the second row right-side Groups menu to differentially color the points for males and females. Automatically draw key is checked, so the legend telling which is which will be placed on the graph. Each of the four graphs is to appear in its own panel, so we check Different panels for different y~x combinations. Free scaling for the X-Axes means each will be allowed to maximally fill its plot area. Identical scaling would mean that both heights in cm and weights in kg would be scaled from 40 to 200. Most of the area in all four panels would be empty. We specified a 2×2 arrangement of the panels. The graph specified by this dialog box is in Fig. 12.9.

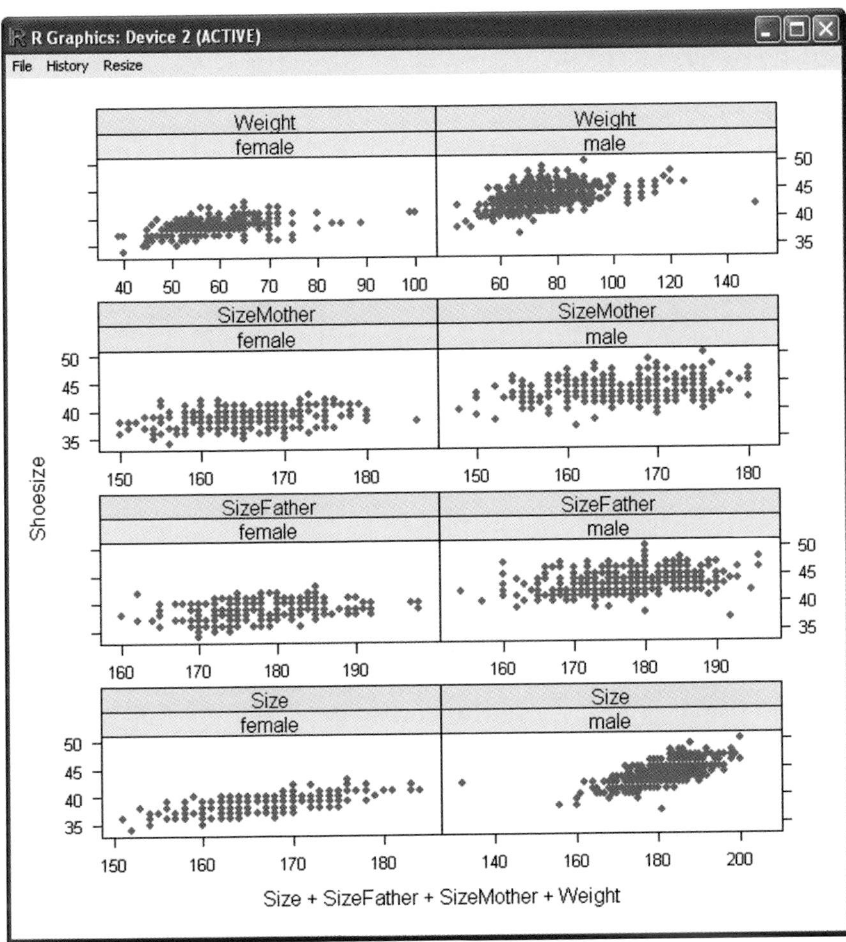

Fig. 12.9 This is the figure specified by the dialog box in Fig. 12.8. We will improve the specification in Fig. 12.11 and redraw the plot in Fig. 12.12. There are three height variables in this set of four panels: `Size`, `SizeFather`, and `SizeMother`. Each has a different set of x-limits, chosen to maximally fill the left-to-right space in its panel. Therefore, our attention is not drawn to one of the most important features of this plot: female students and all mothers have the same height range, and male students and all fathers have the same height range. We must take control of the scaling to make this important finding immediately obvious to the reader of the graph. We do so in Figs. 12.11 and 12.12.

```
xyplot(Shoesize ~
          Size + SizeFather + SizeMother + Weight
           | Gender,
       outer=TRUE, layout=c(2, 4), type="p", pch=16,
       auto.key=list(border=TRUE),
       par.settings=simpleTheme(pch=16),
       scales=list(
         x=list(relation='free'),
         y=list(relation='same')),
       data=StudentData)
```

Fig. 12.10 The Rcmdr dialog box in Fig. 12.8 generated this statement for Fig. 12.9 in the Script Window. The statement shows free scaling for the x-axis of each of the eight panels from the dialog box in Fig. 12.8. We will modify this statement in Fig. 12.11 by changing the `scales` argument.

```
xyplot(Shoesize ~
          Size + SizeFather + SizeMother + Weight
           | Gender,
       outer=TRUE, layout=c(2, 4), type="p", pch=16,
       auto.key=list(border=TRUE),
       par.settings=simpleTheme(pch=16),
       scales=list(
         x=list(relation='free',
                limits=list(
                  c(132,205),c(132,205),
                  c(132,205),c(132,205),
                  c(132,205),c(132,205),
                  c(0,150),   c(0,150))),
         y=list(relation='same')),
       data=StudentData)
```

Fig. 12.11 We constructed this modified statement, based on the generated statement in Fig. 12.10, to take control of the x-axes. The important feature for programming is to let the dialog box do as much of the thinking as possible. Only at the end do we intervene and make some small changes to the generated code. This modified statement specifies Fig. 12.12. We replaced the `scales` argument by the more elaborate statement here. The x-axes for the six size panels are the same as each other and wide enough to include all observations in all panels. The x-axis for the two weight panels are the same as each other and extended on the left to make the left–right positioning of the weight point cloud approximately the same as the size point cloud.

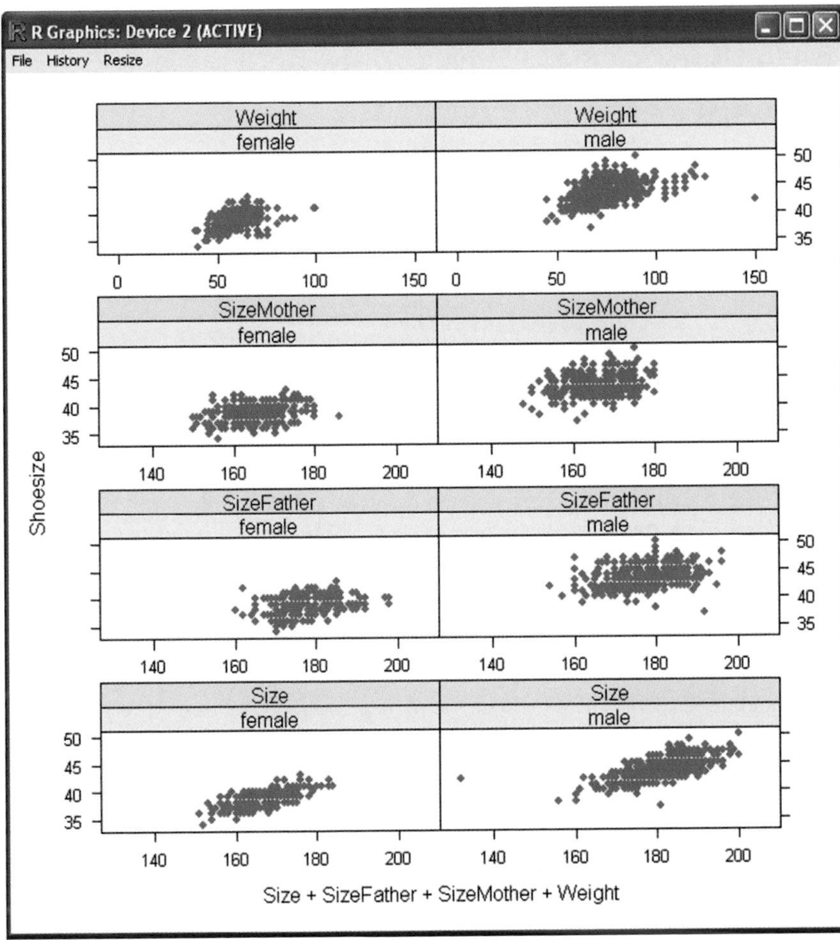

Fig. 12.12 This is the enhanced version of the plot in Fig. 12.9 that was constructed with the command-line statement in Fig. 12.11. Now our attention is drawn to the important feature that female students and all mothers have the same height range. Label the panels $\begin{pmatrix} 7 & 8 \\ 5 & 6 \\ 3 & 4 \\ 1 & 2 \end{pmatrix}$. We see that the dots for female students in the lowerleft panel (Panel 1) have the same x-range as all dots in the SizeMother row (Panels 5 and 6). Similarly, male students (Panel 2) and all fathers (Panels 3 and 4) have the same height range. Because we took control of scaling, this important finding is immediately obvious from the graph. We can do even better, and we do so in Figs. 12.13 and 12.14.

```
xyplot(Shoesize ~ Size + Weight + SizeFather + SizeMother,
       outer=TRUE, layout=c(2, 3),
       skip=c(FALSE,FALSE,FALSE,TRUE,FALSE),
       groups=Gender,
       auto.key=list(border=TRUE, pch=c(17,16)),
       par.settings = simpleTheme(pch=c(17,16)),
       scales=list(relation='free',
         x=list(limits=list(c(132,205), c(39,150),
                            c(132,205),
                            c(132,205))),
         y=list(limits=c(34,50))),
       data=StudentData)
```

Fig. 12.13 In this specification statement, we place all three height variables in the left column. We place the two variables on the students themselves in the bottom row. The `groups=Gender` statement forces separate colors for female and male students. The two `pch=c(17,16)` statements specify solid triangles and solid circles as the plotting characters for the groups. The `pch` statement in the `auto.key` specifies the plotting characters in the legend and the statement in the `par.settings` specifies the characters in the plot itself. Several changes are needed to control the placement of the panels. We changed the layout to two columns and three rows. The panels on the plotting surface are numbered $\begin{pmatrix} 5 & 6 \\ 3 & 4 \\ 1 & 2 \end{pmatrix}$. The default sequence for sending packets to be drawn in the panels is bottom to top, and within each row from left to right. Therefore, we changed the order of the variables in the right side of the specification to match the drawing sequence. We use the `skip` argument to skip the fourth panel. The fourth packet (Shoesize ~ Size) is sent to the fifth panel on the plotting surface. The resulting plot is in Fig. 12.14.

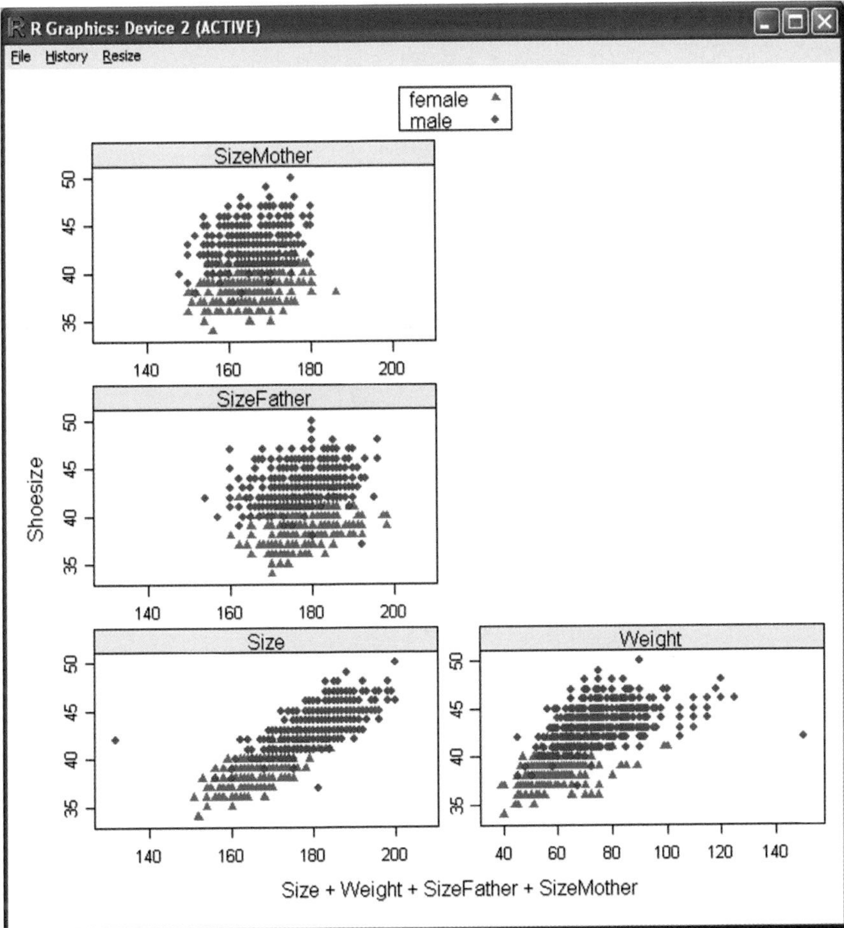

Fig. 12.14 We have two columns and three rows of panels. The left column shows all three height variables. It is now even easier to see that female students (blue triangles in the bottom row) and all mothers (the top panel) have the same height range and that male students (red circles in the bottom row) and all fathers (the panel in the second row) have the same height range. The bottom row shows both height and weight for the students themselves. We now see two potential outliers, observations that need careful investigation in the source data. The accuracy of the data for the male student with Size = 132 cm and Weight = 150 kg needs further investigation. (The second sheet in the StudentData worksheet removes the data for this student.) Similarly, we might wish to check the accuracy of the data for the male with Shoesize = 37.

12.3 Regression Analysis

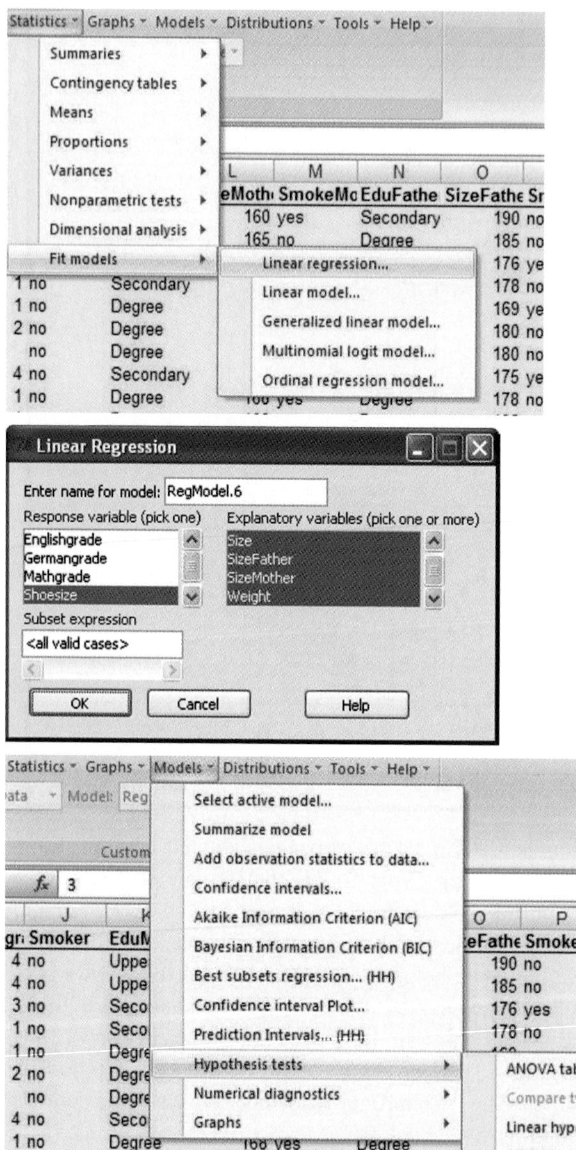

Fig. 12.15 We specify the initial linear model with the Statistics ► Fit models ► Linear regression... menu item and dialog box. This dialog box shows only the continuous variables and places them in alphabetical order. That is an acceptable first step. The dialog box calculates the regression model and displays the summary in Table 12.3. The Models ► Hypothesis tests ► ANOVA table (Type I Sums of Squares) menu item displays the sequential ANOVA table, also shown in Table 12.3.

Table 12.3 All four continuous explanatory variables are shown as significant, although the heights of the parents have p-values of *only* 10^{-3}. Gender, which we see from the graphs is very important, is not in this model. In Fig. 12.16 and Table 12.4, we will construct an improved model based on our insight from this model.

```
> RegModel.6 <- lm(Shoesize~Size+SizeFather+SizeMother+Weight,
+    data=StudentData)

> summary(RegModel.6)

Call:
lm(formula = Shoesize ~ Size + SizeFather + SizeMother + Weight,
    data = StudentData)

Residuals:
     Min        1Q    Median        3Q       Max
-5.50358 -0.90325  0.04158  0.80143  5.48781

Coefficients:
             Estimate Std. Error t value Pr(>|t|)
(Intercept)  9.051955   1.593298   5.681 1.80e-08 ***
Size         0.215778   0.006700  32.204  < 2e-16 ***
SizeFather  -0.024033   0.006877  -3.495 0.000498 ***
SizeMother  -0.029116   0.007964  -3.656 0.000271 ***
Weight       0.055190   0.004218  13.083  < 2e-16 ***
---
Signif. codes:  0 '***' 0.001 '**' 0.01 '*' 0.05 '.' 0.1 ' ' 1

Residual standard error: 1.328 on 905 degrees of freedom
  (216 observations deleted due to missingness)
Multiple R-squared: 0.759,Adjusted R-squared: 0.7579
F-statistic: 712.5 on 4 and 905 DF,  p-value: < 2.2e-16


> anova(RegModel.6)
Analysis of Variance Table

Response: Shoesize
            Df Sum Sq Mean Sq  F value    Pr(>F)
Size         1 4644.0  4644.0 2634.053 < 2.2e-16 ***
SizeFather   1   44.7    44.7   25.381 5.680e-07 ***
SizeMother   1   34.0    34.0   19.297 1.251e-05 ***
Weight       1  301.8   301.8  171.170 < 2.2e-16 ***
Residuals  905 1595.6     1.8
---
Signif. codes:  0 '***' 0.001 '**' 0.01 '*' 0.05 '.' 0.1 ' ' 1
```

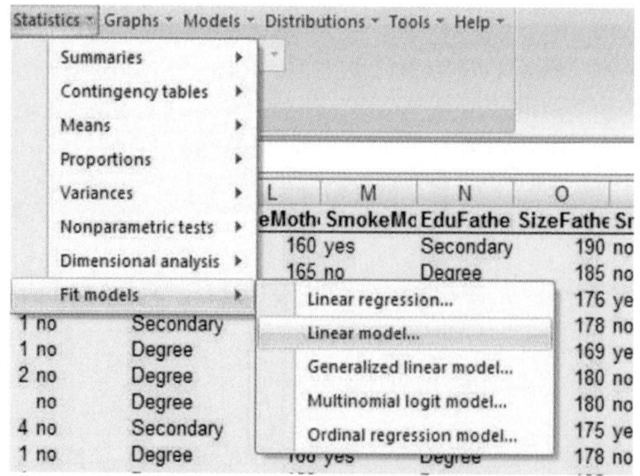

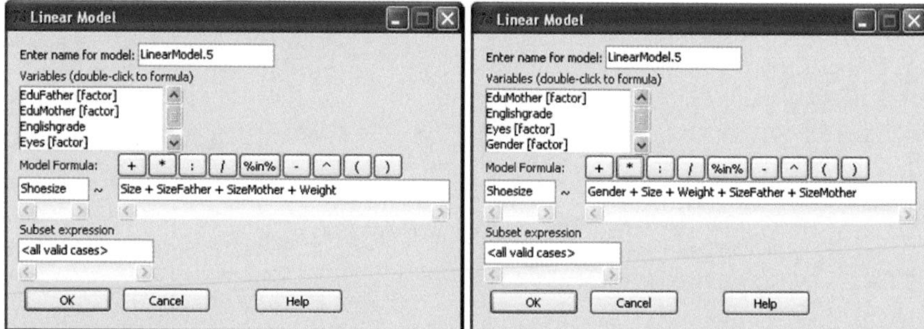

Fig. 12.16 We specify the revised linear model with the Statistics ► Fit models ► Linear model... menu item and dialog box. This dialog box shows factors as well as continuous explanatory variables, allows user control of the order of terms in the model, and gives facilities for specifying interaction and other relationships among the explanatory variables. The dialog box opens (left side of the figure) with the Model Formula Shoesize ~ Size + SizeFather + SizeMother + Weight, the formula for the previous linear regression, in the box. We need to edit it to a better model (right side of the figure). We placed Gender sequentially first and moved SizeFather and SizeMother sequentially last. The new model formula is Shoesize ~ Gender + Size + Weight + SizeFather + SizeMother. Clicking OK calculates the regression model and displays the summary in Table 12.4. The Models ► Hypothesis tests ► ANOVA table (Type I Sums of Squares) menu item (not shown here) displays the sequential ANOVA table, also shown in Table 12.4.

Table 12.4 Linear model with predictor variables ordered by size of the p-value. We see that the gender, height, and weight of the student are sufficient to explain shoe size. The information on parents does not provide significant additional explanatory power. We see the p-value $p_{\text{SizeMother}} = 0.9435$ in both the summary and the ANOVA. Why are they the same numerical value? Had `SizeMother` been sequentially earlier, as in `RegModel.6`, it would have been significant. Why is `SizeMother` not significant here in `RegModel.7`?

```
> LinearModel.7 <- lm(Shoesize ~ Gender + Size + Weight +
+     SizeFather + SizeMother, data=StudentData)

> summary(LinearModel.7)

Call:
lm(formula = Shoesize ~ Gender + Size + Weight + SizeFather +
    SizeMother, data = StudentData)

Residuals:
     Min        1Q    Median        3Q       Max
-6.20646 -0.73868 -0.03658  0.68864  4.59488

Coefficients:
                 Estimate Std. Error t value Pr(>|t|)
(Intercept)    11.8442645  1.3789228   8.590   <2e-16 ***
Gender[T.male]  2.2106553  0.1232408  17.938   <2e-16 ***
Size            0.1393854  0.0071593  19.469   <2e-16 ***
Weight          0.0391494  0.0037406  10.466   <2e-16 ***
SizeFather      0.0071875  0.0061936   1.160    0.246
SizeMother     -0.0004983  0.0070291  -0.071    0.944
---
Signif. codes:  0 '***' 0.001 '**' 0.01 '*' 0.05 '.' 0.1 ' ' 1

Residual standard error: 1.141 on 901 degrees of freedom
  (219 observations deleted due to missingness)
Multiple R-squared: 0.8218,Adjusted R-squared: 0.8208
F-statistic: 831.2 on 5 and 901 DF,  p-value: < 2.2e-16


> anova(LinearModel.7)
Analysis of Variance Table

Response: Shoesize
            Df   Sum Sq  Mean Sq   F value Pr(>F)
Gender       1   4190.7   4190.7 3219.4945 <2e-16 ***
Size         1   1074.6   1074.6  825.5175 <2e-16 ***
Weight       1    142.8    142.8  109.7384 <2e-16 ***
SizeFather   1      1.7      1.7    1.3417 0.2470
SizeMother   1 0.006542 0.006542    0.0050 0.9435
Residuals  901   1172.8      1.3
---
Signif. codes:  0 '***' 0.001 '**' 0.01 '*' 0.05 '.' 0.1 ' ' 1
```

12.4 Basic Diagnostic Plots

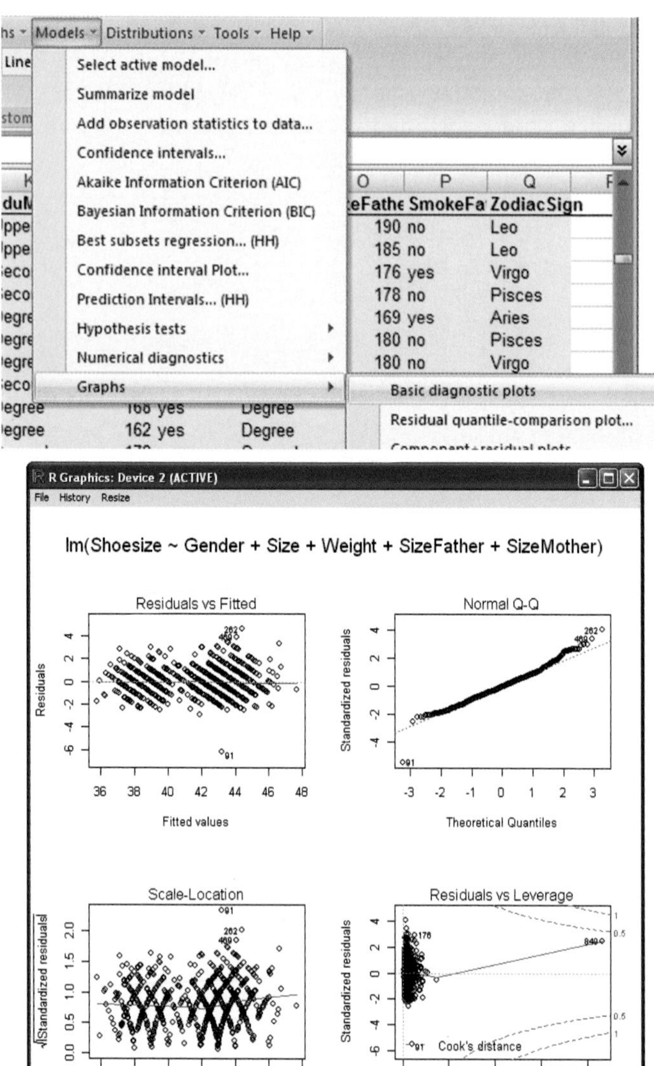

Fig. 12.17 The basic diagnostic plots are displayed with the Models ▶ Graphs ▶ Basic diagnostic plots menu item and dialog box. See Section 9.3 for a general discussion of these plots. In this example, much of the granular structure of the plots can be attributed to the use of a two-level factor Gender. Observation 849, the point with the extremely high leverage on the right in the Residuals vs Leverage plot, is the individual we spotted in Fig. 12.14 with Size = 132 cm and Weight = 150 kg.

12.5 Confidence Intervals

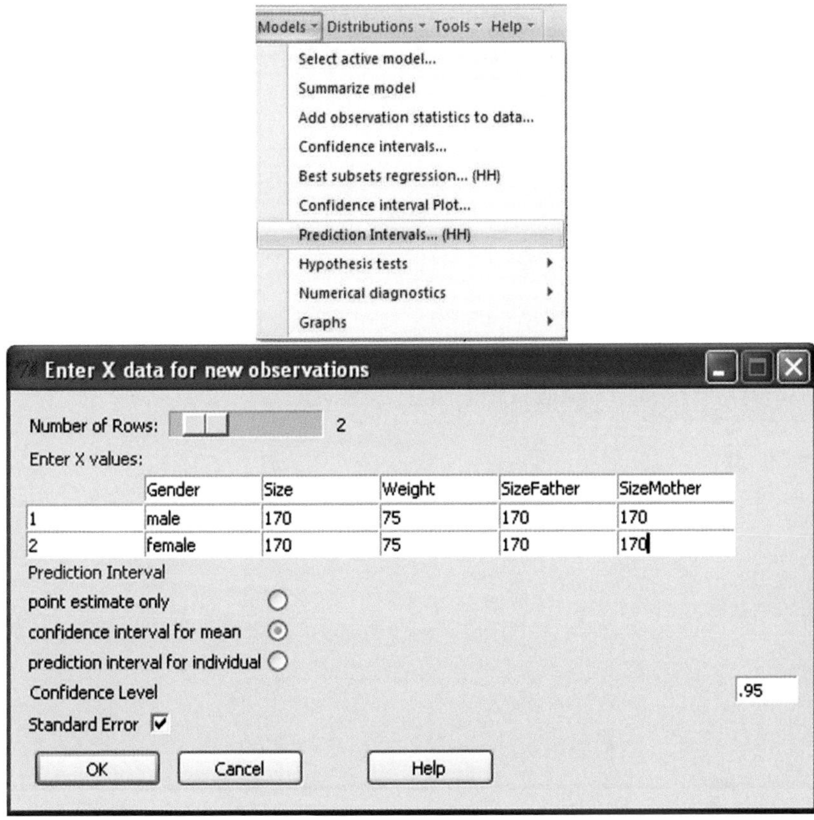

Fig. 12.18 Let's construct confidence intervals for the estimate of the mean Shoesize for a group of males and a group of females, each of whom has a height and parent's height of 170 cm and a weight of 75 kg. We use the Models ► Prediction Intervals... (HH) menu item and dialog box. We wish to construct confidence intervals on the means for two different groups. We use the slider at the top of the dialog box to set the box to accept two rows of data. Then we enter the data. We select the confidence interval for mean option and select Standard Error. Clicking OK generates the statements in the Script Window of Fig. 12.19 and the confidence intervals in the Output Window of Fig. 12.19.

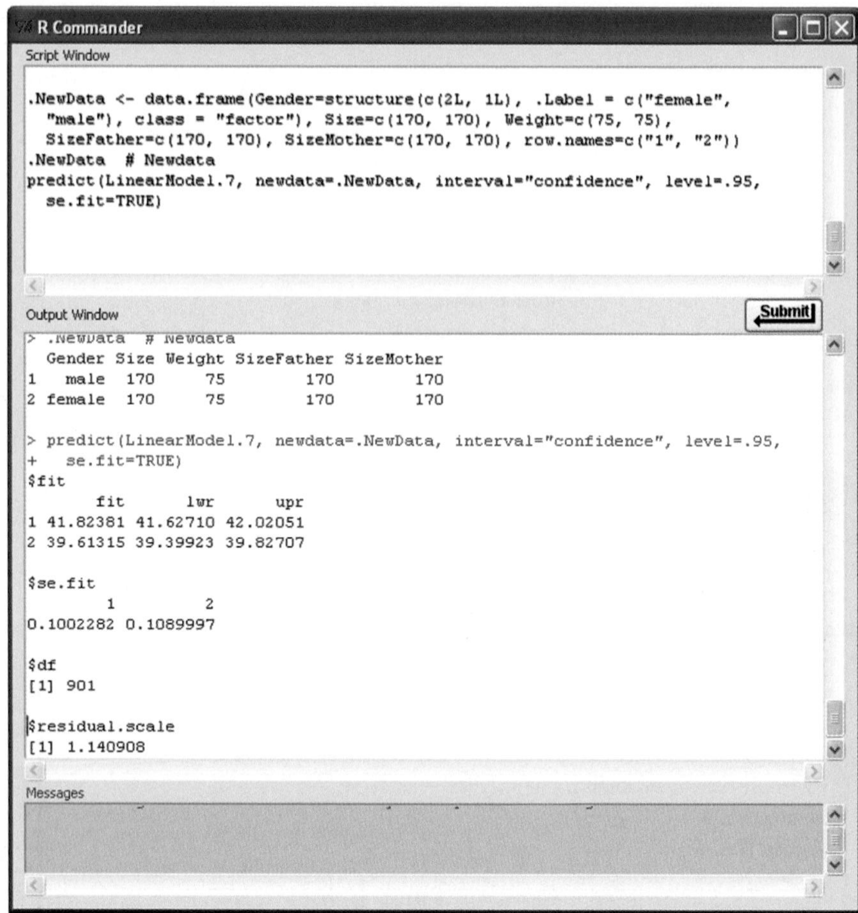

Fig. 12.19 The statements in the Script Window were generated by the dialog box in Fig. 12.18. The Output Window shows the observations that were specified (read them carefully to be sure there were no interpretation errors) and the confidence intervals. Reading from the bottom up, the `df` and `residual.scale` are the degrees of freedom ν and residual standard error s (square root of the `Residuals Mean Sq`) from Table 12.4. The `se.fit` is the standard error of the fit from the formula $s\sqrt{h}$ in Equation (10.1) where h is defined in Equation (10.3). For new observation 1, $\sqrt{h} = 0.0878495$ and for new observation 2, $\sqrt{h} = 0.0955377$. For illustration, we duplicate the calculations for the `fit` and the confidence intervals in Table 12.5. Normally, this arithmetic is done only by the dialog box.

Table 12.5 Selections from the Output Window, where we manually entered commands to duplicate the calculation of the confidence intervals on the means. Normally, this arithmetic is done only by the dialog box.

Case	Fit: $\hat{y}\|x$

New case 1 (male)	`> 11.8442645 +`
	`+ 2.2106553 * 1 +`
	`+ 0.1393854 * 170 +`
	`+ 0.0391494 * 75 +`
	`+ 0.0071875 * 170 +`
	`+ -0.0004983 * 170`
	`[1] 41.82381`

New case 2 (female)	`> 11.8442645 +`
	`+ 2.2106553 * 0 +`
	`+ 0.1393854 * 170 +`
	`+ 0.0391494 * 75 +`
	`+ 0.0071875 * 170 +`
	`+ -0.0004983 * 170`
	`[1] 39.61315`

Case	Lower confidence limit: $\hat{y}\|x - t_{.025,\nu}\ (s\sqrt{h})$
New case 1 (male)	`> 41.82381 - 1.962600 * 0.1002282` `[1] 41.6271`
New case 2 (female)	`> 39.61315 - 1.962600 * 0.1089997` `[1] 39.39923`

Case	Upper confidence limit: $\hat{y}\|x + t_{.025,\nu}\ (s\sqrt{h})$
New case 1 (male)	`> 41.82381 + 1.962600 * 0.1002282` `[1] 42.02052`
New case 2 (female)	`> 39.61315 + 1.962600 * 0.1089997` `[1] 39.82707`

Chapter 13
Contingency Tables and the Chi-Square Test

Abstract Contingency tables are designed to study relationships between two categorical variables or factors. A contingency table has rows and columns labeled with the levels of two factors. The (row i–column j) cell in the table gives the number of observations in the dataset whose value on the first factor is level i and whose value on the second factor is level j. For example, if we have a group of people of both genders, with some smokers and some nonsmokers, we can ask the question, is the percentage of smokers essentially the same for both genders or, equivalently, does the data indicate that there is a significant difference in percentage of smokers?

We will investigate relationships between gender and smoking behavior using the StudentData dataset accompanying this book. We will also investigate relationships between student grades in different subjects and gender.

The variables in the StudentData dataset are described in Chapter 12.

Load the StudentData workbook as illustrated in Fig. 12.1, and click on the second, Studentdata, worksheet. In Chapter 12, we used the first, Studentdata_raw, worksheet. Select a cell in the data range, press Ctrl-Shift *, and then right-click Put R Dataframe to transfer the data to R as a dataframe.

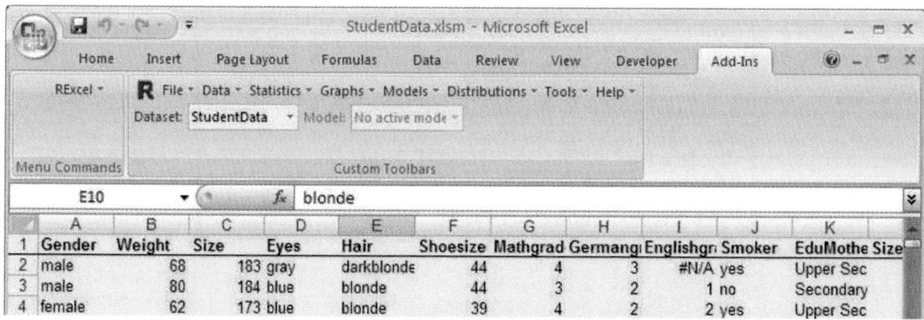

Fig. 13.1 Excel window after transferring the data. The active dataset is indicated as StudentData. The transferred region was colored during the transfer.

R.M. Heiberger, E. Neuwirth, *R Through Excel*, Use R,
DOI 10.1007/978-1-4419-0052-4_13,

13.1 Gender and Smoking

13.1.1 Two-Way Table Chi-Square Test

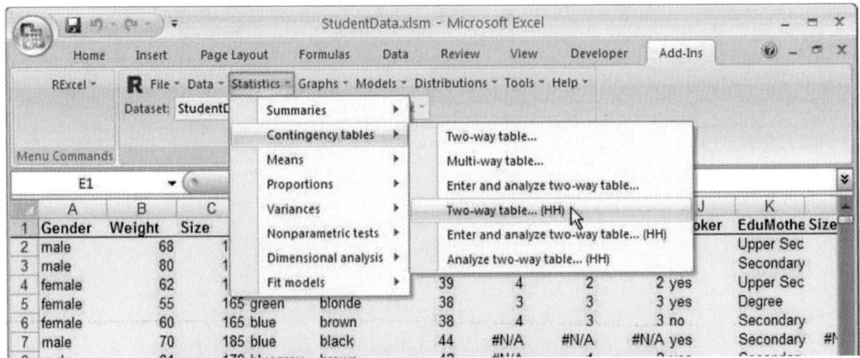

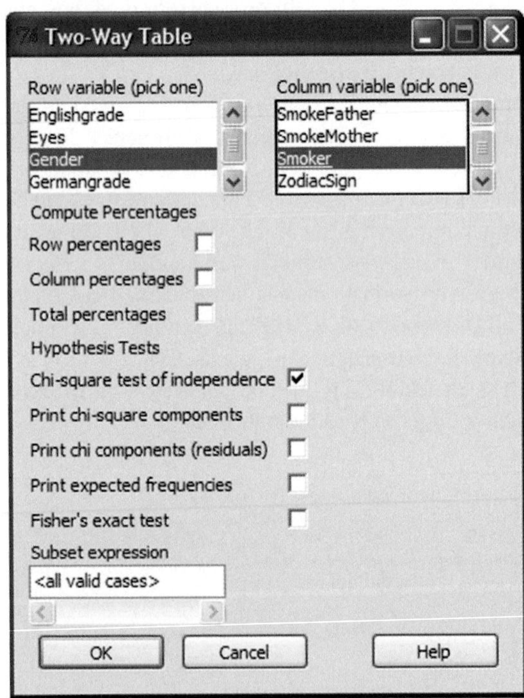

Fig. 13.2 Click the Statistics ▶ Contingency tables ▶ Two-way table...(HH) menu item to get the Two-Way Table dialog box. From the StudentData, we select Gender as the row variable and Smoker as the column variable. From the options, we choose only Chi-square test of independence. This produces test results in the Rcmdr Output Window as shown in Table 13.1.

Table 13.1 The table shown here is from the Rcmdr Output Window. This table shows the analysis specified in Fig. 13.2. There are 229 female and 514 male non-smokers and 107 female and 261 male smokers in our student sample. The proportion of nonsmoker females within all females is $229/(229+107) = 0.682$ and the proportion of nonsmoker males within all males is $514/(514+261) = 0.663$. The p-value for the test for independence of the variables is $p = 0.5512$, so the interpretation of the test result is that there is no significant difference in the nonsmoking percentage between men and women in our sample.

```
> .Table <- xtabs(~Gender+Smoker, data=StudentData)

> .Table
        Smoker
Gender     no yes
  female 229 107
  male   514 261

> .Test <- chisq.test(.Table, correct=FALSE)

> .Test

Pearson's Chi-squared test

data:  .Table
X-squared = 0.3552, df = 1, p-value = 0.5512
```

13.1.2 Two-Sample Proportions Test

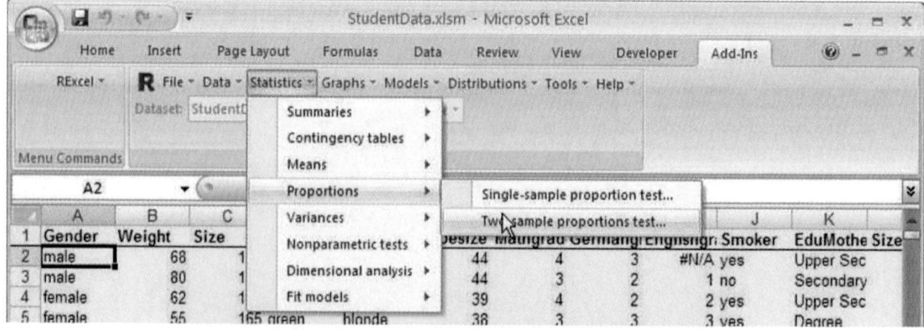

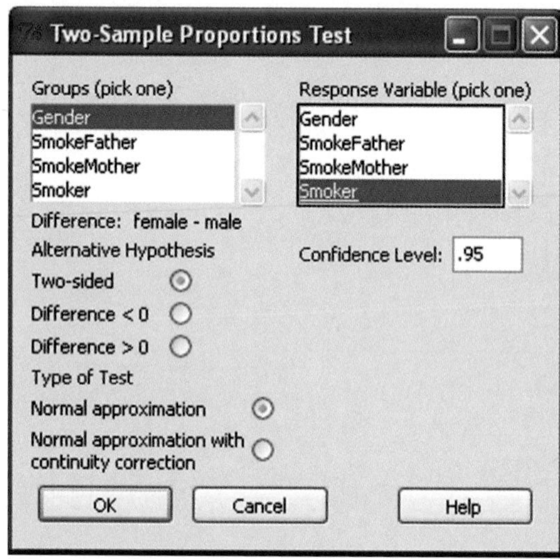

Fig. 13.3 An equivalent test can be performed by choosing Statistics ► Proportions ► Two-sample proportions test.... In the dialog box, we set Gender as the group variable and Smoker as the response variable. As we will see in Table 13.2, the group and response variables are interpreted differently, so specifying them correctly is important.

Computing the test with the Proportions menu is possible only when we have exactly two groups and the percentage is taken for a dichotomous response variable, i.e. a variable with only two possible values. The Rcmdr Two-sample proportions test dialog box displays variables of only this type in the selection boxes. This menu and dialog box give the results shown in Table 13.2.

Table 13.2 This table was specified by the menu and dialog box in Fig. 13.3. By default, the percentages within the groups are displayed. The p-value for the test for independence of the variables is $p = 0.5512$, because statistically this is the same test as the one in Table 13.1.

```
> .Table <- xtabs(~Gender+Smoker, data=StudentData)

> rowPercents(.Table)
        Smoker
Gender     no  yes Total Count
  female 68.2 31.8   100   336
  male   66.3 33.7   100   775

> prop.test(.Table, alternative='two.sided', conf.level=.95,
+   correct=FALSE)

2-sample test for equality of proportions without continuity
correction

data:  .Table
X-squared = 0.3552, df = 1, p-value = 0.5512
alternative hypothesis: two.sided
95 percent confidence interval:
 -0.04158248  0.07822611
sample estimates:
   prop 1    prop 2
0.6815476 0.6632258
```

Sometimes, the two-sample proportions test is performed not by using the chi-square statistic as done by these menus, but with the z-statistic. The hypotheses for the test are

$$H_0\colon\ p_1 - p_2 = 0$$
$$H_1\colon\ p_1 - p_2 \neq 0$$

The formulas for the test statistic are in Table 13.3. The numerical values are in Table 13.4. The arithmetic, substituting the numerical values into the formulas, is shown calculated in R in Table 13.5.

Table 13.3 The test statistic has the form $z = (w - \mu_w)/\sigma_w$, where $w = (\widehat{p}_1 - \widehat{p}_2)$.

Test statistic	$z = \dfrac{(\widehat{p}_1 - \widehat{p}_2) - 0}{\sigma_{(\hat{p}_1 - \hat{p}_2)}}$
Standard deviation	$\sigma_{(\hat{p}_1 - \hat{p}_2)} = \sqrt{\widehat{p}\,(1 - \widehat{p})\left(\frac{1}{n_1} + \frac{1}{n_2}\right)}$

Table 13.4 If $\widehat{p}_1$ and $\widehat{p}_2$ are the sample proportions of the subgroups under consideration (smokers within males and smokers within females in our case), $\hat{p}$ is the percentage of smokers in the whole group (females and males), and if n_1 and n_2 are the group sizes (in this example, the number of females and males), then using the above formula and data, we have $z = -0.5960$.

Computing the p-value of the two-sided z-test with $z = -0.5960$ results in the same $p = 0.5512$ as the p-value Rcmdr computed for the chi-square test. This is no coincidence. For a 2×2 contingency table, the value of the chi-square test is always the square of the value of the z-test. Therefore, the p-value for the chi-square test is the same as the p-value for the two-sided z-test. We show the arithmetic for the z-test in Tables 13.5 and 13.6.

The z-test can also be used for one-sided hypotheses. The chi-square test can be used only with two-sided tests. The chi-square test can be generalized for larger contingency tables, for example, the 4×4 table in Section 13.2, whereas the z-test is applicable only for 2×2 tables.

	Smoker		Row	Row proportion	
Gender	no	yes	Count	no	yes
Female	$x_1 = 229$	107	$n_1 = 229 + 107 = 336$	$\widehat{p}_1 = \frac{229}{336} = 0.682$	$\frac{107}{336} = 0.318$
Male	$x_2 = 514$	261	$n_2 = 514 + 261 = 775$	$\widehat{p}_2 = \frac{514}{775} = 0.663$	$\frac{261}{775} = 0.337$
Both	743	368	$n = 743 + 368 = 1111$	$\widehat{p} = \frac{743}{1111} = 0.669$	$\frac{368}{1111} = 0.331$

Table 13.5 Arithmetic for the z-test in Table 13.3 for the comparison of the proportion of female nonsmokers and male nonsmokers using the data in Table 13.4. Enter the code into the Script Window and click the Submit button. This will place the calculations shown in Table 13.6 into the Output Window.

Rcmdr Script Window

```
x.1       <- 229
n.1       <- 336
p.hat.1   <- x.1/n.1
p.hat.1

x.2       <- 514
n.2       <- 775
p.hat.2   <- x.2/n.2
p.hat.2

n         <- n.1 + n.2
p.hat     <- (x.1 + x.2) / (n.1 + n.2)
p.hat

sigma.sq <- (p.hat*(1-p.hat)) * (1/n.1 + 1/n.2)
sigma.sq

z <- (p.hat.1 - p.hat.2) / sqrt( sigma.sq )
z

p.value <- 2*pnorm(z, lower=FALSE)
p.value
```

Table 13.6 Clicking the Submit button in Fig. 13.5 places the calculations shown here into the Output Window. These computational statements are a direct translation of the formulas in Table 13.3 into the R notation.

Rcmdr Output Window

```
> x.1       <- 229
> n.1       <- 336
> p.hat.1   <- x.1/n.1
> p.hat.1
[1] 0.6815476
>
> x.2       <- 514
> n.2       <- 775
> p.hat.2   <- x.2/n.2
> p.hat.2
[1] 0.6632258
>
> n         <- n.1 + n.2
> p.hat     <- (x.1 + x.2) / (n.1 + n.2)
> p.hat
[1] 0.6687669
>
> sigma.sq <- (p.hat*(1-p.hat)) * (1/n.1 + 1/n.2)
> sigma.sq
[1] 0.0009451083
>
> z <- (p.hat.1 - p.hat.2) / sqrt( sigma.sq )
> z
[1] 0.5959744
>
> p.value <- 2*pnorm(z, lower=FALSE)
> p.value
[1] 0.5511923
>
```

13.2 German and Math Grades

We now study the relationship between German-language grades and math grades for the Austrian students. Grades in Austria vary from 1 (best grade) to 5 (not passed). Since all the students in the sample have passed the final exam of high school, grade 5 is impossible.

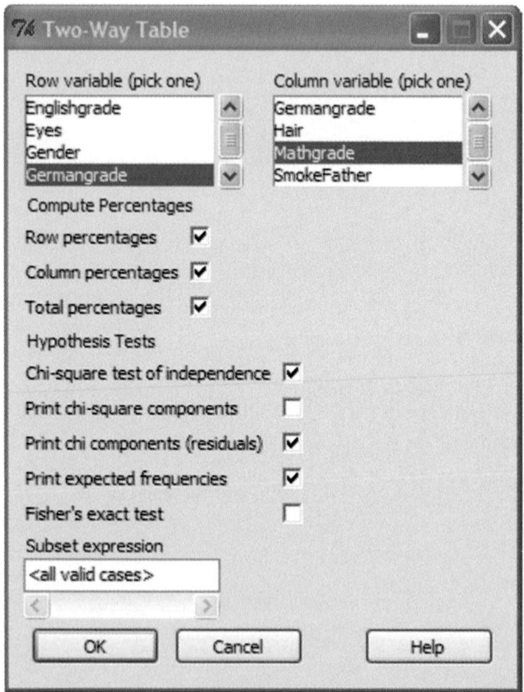

Fig. 13.4 We perform a test for independence (or dependence) between grades in math and grades in German. We select Statistics ► Contingency tables ► Two-way table... (HH) as in the top of Fig. 13.2. We select Germangrade as the row variable and Mathgrade as the column variable. From the options, we choose Chi-square test of independence, Print chi components (residuals), and Print expected frequencies. This dialog box specifies the output, which we have displayed in Tables 13.7–13.10.

Table 13.7 The tables here are the beginning of the output specified by the dialog box in Fig. 13.4. In this part, we display the cross-tabulated frequency table, the row percentages (including counts for each row), the column percentages (including counts for each column) from the Rcmdr Output Window, and the total percentages (including marginal percentages for the rows and columns). The first table has the counts of all possible grade combinations for the 862 students who had valid recorded grades in both subjects. We see that there are 111 students with grade 1 in both subjects. The second table has the row percentages. We see that 53.9% of the students with grade 1 in German also have grade 1 in math. Similarly, the third table with the column percentages shows that 48.9% of the students with grade 1 in math also have grade 1 in German. The fourth table gives the overall (or total) percentages and shows that 12.9% of all students have grade 1 in both German and math.

```
> .Table <- xtabs(~Germangrade+Mathgrade, data=StudentData)

> .Table
           Mathgrade
Germangrade   1   2   3   4
          1 111  49  32  14
          2  46  71  72  38
          3  51  79  78  60
          4  19  40  55  47

> rowPercents(.Table) # Row Percentages
           Mathgrade
Germangrade    1    2    3    4 Total Count
          1 53.9 23.8 15.5  6.8   100   206
          2 20.3 31.3 31.7 16.7   100   227
          3 19.0 29.5 29.1 22.4   100   268
          4 11.8 24.8 34.2 29.2   100   161

> colPercents(.Table) # Column Percentages
           Mathgrade
Germangrade     1     2     3     4
      1      48.9  20.5  13.5   8.8
      2      20.3  29.7  30.4  23.9
      3      22.5  33.1  32.9  37.7
      4       8.4  16.7  23.2  29.6
      Total 100.1 100.0 100.0 100.0
      Count 227.0 239.0 237.0 159.0

> totPercents(.Table) # Total Percentages
         1    2    3    4 Total
1     12.9  5.7  3.7  1.6  23.9
2      5.3  8.2  8.4  4.4  26.3
3      5.9  9.2  9.0  7.0  31.1
4      2.2  4.6  6.4  5.5  18.7
Total 26.3 27.7 27.5 18.4 100.0
```

Table 13.8 The next section of the Rcmdr Output Window contains the chi-square test result. We see that value of the statistic, the degrees of freedom, and the p-value. We have $p < 2.2 \times 10^{-16}$. Therefore, the null hypothesis of independence is rejected. Our data indicate that there is a relationship between the grade in German and that in math. To further investigate the nature of the relationship, we study the expected frequencies in Table 13.9 and then the residuals in Table 13.10.

```
> .Test <- chisq.test(.Table, correct=FALSE)

> .Test

Pearson's Chi-squared test

data:  .Table
X-squared = 126.7532, df = 9, p-value < 2.2e-16
```

Table 13.9 The next section of the Rcmdr Output Window contains the residuals, and the last section contains the expected frequencies. Since we need the expected frequencies to compute the residuals, we will look at the expected frequencies first.

The expected frequencies are the hypothetical frequencies one would anticipate if the German grades were independent of the math grades. Independence means that the percentage of students getting grade 1 in math would be the same for students with grade 1 in German, for students with grade 2 in German, grade 3 in German, and grade 4 in German. In other words, independence assumes that the percentage distribution according to the math grades is the same for each of the four groups defined by the German grades. Assuming independence, we can compute the hypothetical number of students with any grade combination from the overall percentages for the math grades and the German grades.

There are 862 students with valid values for both German grade and math grade. The total percentages table in Table 13.7 shows 23.9% of these students have grade 1 in German, and 26.3% of them have grade 1 in math. Therefore, if the percentage of grade 1 math students among the German grade 1 students were equal to the percentage of grade 1 math students among all students, the percentage of students with grade 1 in math and in German would be 23.9% $\times$ 26.3% = 6.3%; 6.3% of the 862 students is 54.25, which is the value displayed in the table for the expected values. Using this method, we can compute expected counts for all combinations of grades.

```
> round(.Test$expected, 2) # Expected Counts
           Mathgrade
Germangrade     1     2     3     4
          1 54.25 57.12 56.64 38.00
          2 59.78 62.94 62.41 41.87
          3 70.58 74.31 73.68 49.43
          4 42.40 44.64 44.27 29.70
```

Table 13.10 The Rcmdr Output Window displays the residuals table just above the expected frequency table. We discuss the residuals last.

Residuals measure the difference between the observed frequency and the expected frequency. Looking at the students with grade 1 in both subjects, we see that the observed frequency is 111 (see Table 13.7) and the expected frequency is 54.25 (see Table 13.9). The ordinary difference of these two numbers is not the residual. To standardize this residual to a standard normal distribution, we need to divide the difference by the square root of the expected frequency. The result of this computation is $(111-54.25)/\sqrt{54.25}=7.71$. This table shows the residuals computed this way for all grade combinations.

If the distribution of the grades for the two subjects were independent, all the residuals would follow a standard normal distribution. The values in our residual table definitely do not follow a standard normal distribution. Too many of these values lie outside the range between -2 and 2, which would contain about 95% of the values if they were normal. The residual value for the combination {Germangrade = 1 and Mathgrade = 1} is 7.71. This indicates that the observed value is noticeably higher than the expected value. Further inspection of the residuals table shows that all the values on the main diagonal (equal grades in German and math) are high and that all the values where the difference between the grades is 2 or more are low. This indicates that there is a tendency that high marks in one subject more often than expected by pure chance occur simultaneously with high marks in the other subject. Similarly, low grades also tend to occur simultaneously.

```
> round(.Test$residuals, 2) # Chi Components (residuals)
           Mathgrade
Germangrade     1     2     3     4
          1  7.71 -1.07 -3.27 -3.89
          2 -1.78  1.02  1.21 -0.60
          3 -2.33  0.54  0.50  1.50
          4 -3.59 -0.69  1.61  3.18
```

Appendix A
Installation of RExcel

Abstract

- Excel is the most prevalent software used for data storage, analysis, and interpretation. Elementary and medium-quality mathematical and statistical functions are included with Excel. Good statistical analysis in Excel with more advanced methods than just frequency counts, however, requires an add-in package.
- R is one of the best and most powerful statistics programs currently available.
- RExcel integrates a menu system, based on the R Commander package, that puts complete access to the full power of R onto the Excel menu bar. Results from the analyses in R can be returned to the spreadsheet. Ordinary formulas in spreadsheet cells can use functions written in R.

A.1 Basic Installation Procedures

The easiest way to install R, RExcel, and the additionally needed software modules and tools is to download the current version of RAndFriendsSetup from http://rcom.univie.ac.at. Running this program will install everything needed for a working configuration on your machine. A detailed description of the installation is in Section A.3. You will need a working internet connection during the installation process because one module, `statconnDCOM`, is not under the GPL license that covers most of R. `statconnDCOM` must be downloaded separately during the installation. More information on the license is in Section A.8.

If you already have a working version of R (version 2.8.1 or later) on your machine, you can simply install the R packages RExcelInstaller and RthroughExcelWorkbooksInstaller (and the packages they require) from CRAN. Section A.4 gives more details about this process.

R.M. Heiberger, E. Neuwirth, *R Through Excel*, Use R,
DOI 10.1007/978-1-4419-0052-4,

A.2 Supported Excel Versions

The RExcel add-in is supported for the following versions of MS Windows Excel:

- Excel 2002 (=Excel XP)
- Excel 2003
- Excel 2007

If Excel 2007 is found on your machine, the Excel add-in will be installed for Excel 2007. If Excel 2002 or 2003 are found on your machine, the add-in will be installed for the latest of these Excel versions. If you have Excel 2007 and an earlier version of Excel on your machine, then the installer will install both versions of the RExcel add-in.

If you do not have Excel, or if Excel is installed in an unusual location, then the installer will still install R and Rcmdr. It will give information on how to install RExcel at a later time when Excel becomes available. See step 3 in Section A.3.3 for installing RExcel later. See Section A.6 for information on working without Excel.

The RExcel interface works only with MS Windows Excel. The material in this book that uses the R Commander menu system (from the Rcmdr package available on all platforms where R is available) will work on any R installation. For Macintosh and Linux systems, see Section A.6. For the Open Office spreadsheet, see Section A.7.

A.3 Download and Installation of R and RExcel for MS Windows

The home website for RAndFriends [Neuwirth, 2009] is http://rcom.univie.ac.at/. Click on the Download tab on the website. You will find a download link to the latest version of the RAndFriends installer. RAndFriends includes the current release of R [R Development Core Team, 2008] and the

- rcom [Baier, 2007],
- RExcelInstaller [Neuwirth et al., 2008]
- HH [Heiberger, 2008a],
- RthroughExcelWorkbooksInstaller [Heiberger and Neuwirth, 2008],
- Rcmdr[Fox et al., 2007],
- RcmdrPlugin.HH [Heiberger, 2008b],

packages, and other packages. This is a large file (approximately 150MB), so this is best done with a fast internet connection.

Download the RAndFriendsSetup*.exe file to a temporary location.

A.3.1 Preparation

The installation requires Administrator access to your PC because the RExcel add-in uses the Windows Registry to configure communication between Excel and R through the. On Vista, the installation requires a user with Administrator privileges to start `RAndFriendsSetup*.exe` by right-clicking the RAndFriendsSetup icon and explicitly clicking the run-as-Administrator item. Once the program is installed, Administrator privileges are no longer needed.

A.3.2 An Ancient Previous Version of RExcel Must Be Uninstalled

If you have an ancient installation of RExcel [from an earlier version of the RAndFriends installer, the (D)COM package, or the RExcelInstaller package], you will need to uninstall the Excel add-in and the (D)COM package before installing the newer version. *Ancient* means an RExcel version older than 3.0.0. To find out: Open Excel and click on the RExcel ► About RExcel menu item. If the version is 3.0.0 or higher, then you do not have to do the uninstall step.

If you determine that you must uninstall the ancient version, you have to do it in the following way:

1. For Excel 2003 and earlier (with the add-in installed), start Excel and go to

   Tools ► Add-Ins

   and uncheck the checkbox next to the entry RExcel. Close Excel.
2. For Excel 2007 (with the add-in installed), start Excel and go to

   Office Button ► Excel Options ► Add-Ins ► Go...

   and uncheck the checkbox next to the entry RExcel2007. Close Excel.
3. Remove old programs using Control Panel.

   a. Open the Windows XP Add or Remove Programs window with
   Start ► Control Panel ► Add or Remove Programs.

   b. Open the Windows Vista Programs and Features window with
   Start ► Control Panel ► Programs and Features ► Installed Programs.

   Remove any of the following:

   - RDACCSD
   - R (D)COM Server
   - R/Scilab...

This completes the uninstall. After this, you can install the current version of RAndFriends.

If any version conflicts remain, particularly for a user other than the Administrator, see the Wiki at http://rcom.univie.ac.at/ for suggestions.

A.3.3 Installation

1. Close Excel and any previous version of R.
2. Execute installer. In Windows Explorer, double-click the downloaded file

   ```
   RAndFriendsSetup*.exe
   ```

   The installer may take up to 15 minutes. It will install R with RExcel and R Commander and will give you the option to install

   - 'R through Excel' book demo files. You MUST check 'R through Excel' book demo files, which contains the *R through Excel* book's workbook files.
   - Rggobi. Rggobi is a very powerful 3D graphing program. It is not discussed in this book. You are invited to explore it yourself. Clicking Rggobi also installs Glade and GTK+.
   - Notepad++ and NppToR. Notepad++ is a text editing program; NppToR enhances Notepad++ by adding an R mode. These programs are not used in this book. If you choose to install them, we strongly recommend that you uncheck checkmarks for all file types (particularly `.txt` and `.text` files) for which you are happy with the editor you are using. If you use Emacs with ESS for your R programs, or any other editor with a special mode for R code, you probably don't need to install Notepad++ and NppToR.

   The RAndFriendsSetup installer will install R and place an R icon on the desktop of the user performing the installation. RAndFriendsSetup will install the RExcel add-in to your installed version(s) of Excel if it finds Excel (if not, see step 3 of Section A.3.3). It will install a digital certificate for RExcel (see Section A.9). If it finds Excel 2007, it will pop up a message saying that RExcel is installed for Excel 2007. If it finds an earlier version of Excel, it will pop up a message saying that RExcel is installed for Excel 2003 or Excel 2002. The installer will put an RExcel with RCommander icon on the desktop of the installing user for whichever versions of Excel it finds. It also will put one or two items on the Start ▶ All Programs ▶ R ▶ RExcel Windows menu. These items "Activate RExcel Add-in" and/or "Activate RExcel 2007 Add-in" allow other users to make the RExcel add-in(s) available for themselves.

   After RExcel is installed, the RAndFriends installer will start additional installers for the checked items and it will need to download statconnDCOM from the internet. The 'R through Excel' workbooks installer (which you must check) will install a digital certificate for RthroughExcel (see Section A.9).

   The other two installers (if you select them) pop up many boxes. Take the defaults.
3. If Excel is present and the installer can't find Excel...

   This sometimes happens when an earlier version of RExcel is already on the machine or when Excel 2007 has recently been installed and Excel 2003 removed. In this case, start R from the R icon. On XP, just click the icon. On Vista, right-click the icon and click run-as-Administrator to run as Administrator. At the R prompt, enter

```
library(RExcelInstaller)
installRExcel()
```

Pop-up messages will ask for administrative privileges. RExcel needs administrative privileges because it uses the Windows Registry for setting up communication between R and Excel. Follow the pop-up instructions precisely. The installer needs a working internet connection.

4. Verify the installation of the RthroughExcel worksheets.
   Click the RExcel with RCommander icon. When it finishes loading, the cursor will be in Excel. In Excel 2007, click the Add-Ins tab (Fig. 1.2) to get the RExcel menu (Fig. 2.1). In Excel 2003, the RExcel menu is on the main Excel menubar (Fig. 2.2). Click the RExcel menu and verify that the RthroughExcel Worksheets item is there (Fig. 2.4). This is the menu for the worksheets in the *R through Excel* book.
   If the RthroughExcel Worksheets item is missing, then there is one more step. On the Windows taskbar, click the **R** R Console item. Type the following two lines exactly into the R Console window. Punctuation and capitalization must be correct.

```
library(RthroughExcelWorkbooksInstaller)
installRthroughExcel()
```

   The installer needs a working internet connection. Then close R and Excel.
5. The installation is now complete. Congratulations!
   You now have a copy of one of the world's best statistical software systems fully integrated into your MS Excel.
   The installer file `RAndFriendsSetup*.exe` is no longer needed.
6. Using RExcel. Please see Chapters 1 and 2 for detailed information, including screenshots, on how to use RExcel and Rcmdr.

A.4 Installing RExcel for MS Windows When R Is Already Installed

RExcel is easily added to an already installed R. We recommend that you first update your R installation to the most recent. See Section A.5.

Start R from the R icon. On XP, just click the icon. On Vista, right-click the icon and click run-as-Administrator to run as Administrator.

You will need to install the RExcelInstaller, RthroughExcelWorkbooksInstaller, Rcmdr, HH, and RcmdrPlugin.HH packages and additional packages they require.

From the R command prompt, enter

```
install.packages(c("RExcelInstaller",
                   "RthroughExcelWorkbooksInstaller",
                   "RcmdrPlugin.HH"),
                 dependencies=TRUE")
```

At the R prompt, enter

```
library(RExcelInstaller)
installRExcel()
library(RthroughExcelWorkbooksInstaller)
installRthroughExcel()
```

Pop-up messages might ask for administrative privileges. RExcel needs administrative privileges because it uses the Windows Registry to setup communication between R and Excel. Follow the pop-up instructions precisely. The installation needs a working internet connection.

After the installation is complete, type

```
library(RcmdrPlugin.HH)
```

The Rcmdr window will open. Additional packages might be downloaded and installed.

Close R and reopen R from the RExcel with RCommander icon.

A.5 Upgrade an Existing R Installation

The best way to upgrade an existing R installation and add a new package is to follow the recommendations of R-Core. Do not blindly copy packages from one release of R to the next. See the "R for Windows FAQ" on this topic:

http://www.r-project.org/

Then click in the left panel:

FAQs ► R Windows FAQ ► "2.8 What's the best way to upgrade?"

There is a Wiki page at the RExcel website expanding on the R-Core recommended way to maintain the package selections in the next release.

http://rcom.univie.ac.at/

then click at the top

WIKI ► "How to upgrade R with our packages installed".

A.6 R and Rcmdr Without Excel—Windows, Macintosh, Linux

The material in this book that uses the R Commander menu system (from the Rcmdr package available on all platforms where R is available) will work on any R installation on Windows, Macintosh, or Linux systems.

On Windows, Excel is not free. On Macintosh, although Excel is available, it uses a different protocol to communicate with the rest of the computer: hence, RExcel doesn't work.

See Section A.7 for information on R for Open Office.

Other spreadsheet programs may be available for data handling. They don't communicate directly with R, but they usually permit you to save files in several formats, most likely including the Excel `.xls` format, and then you can read them into Rcmdr as described in Section A.6.3.

A.6.1 Install the Rcmdr, HH, and RcmdrPlugin.HH packages

You will need to install the Rcmdr [Fox et al., 2007], HH [Heiberger, 2008a], and RcmdrPlugin.HH [Heiberger, 2008b] packages and additional packages they require. From the R command prompt, enter

```
install.packages(c("Rcmdr","HH","RcmdrPlugin.HH"),
                 dependencies=TRUE)
```

After the installation is complete, type

```
library(RcmdrPlugin.HH)
```

The Rcmdr window will open. Additional packages might be downloaded and installed. The installation needs a working internet connection.

Close R and reopen R.

A.6.2 Use the R Commander Directly

Start R. At the R prompt, enter

```
library(RcmdrPlugin.HH)
```

You now have R and Rcmdr running and access to many examples in this book.

A.6.3 Data Input

There are several options to get data in:

1. Use the Rcmdr Data ► Import data ► from Excel, Access, or dBASE data set... menu item.
2. Use the `read.xls()` function from the Rcmdr Script Window. Either

```
library(xlsReadWrite)
?read.xls ## see the help file
```

   or

```
library(gdata)
?read.xls ## see the help file
```

   The xlsReadWrite and/or gdata packages must be downloaded from CRAN and installed.
3. Enter data manually with the Rcmdr Data ► New data set... menu. This gives a spreadsheet data entry screen. Close the data entry screen when ready, and the dataframe will be saved and will be made the active dataset.

A.7 R and Open Office

A working prerelease of ROOo, R for Open Office, is currently available at

http://rcom.univie.ac.at/

in the Download section. The web site and the WIKI on the site discuss this add-in in more detail. When fully released, ROOo will behave nearly identically on Windows, Macintosh, and Linux.

A.8 License for statconnDCOM

Not all of the components installed by the RExcelInstaller package are licensed under the GPL or LGPL, the licenses used by R and many of the packages on CRAN. The critical module statconnDCOM, the module which interfaces with the MS COM interprocess communication system, is not under GPL. Instead, it has a license that permits free and unlimited use, but does not permit redistribution. Full details are in the license distributed with the package. Other software developers who wish to use the statconnDCOM software infrastructure should visit http://www.statconn.com for information on negotiating a commercial license.

A.9 Digital Certificate

The RExcelInstaller and RthoughExcelWorkbooksInstaller packages each ask for permission to install a digital certificate. You do not need to install either certificate. Without the RExcel certificate, Excel, depending on your macro security settings, might open pop-up message boxes asking for permission to run macros every time an Excel session running RExcel is started. Similarly, without the RthroughExcelWorkbooksInstaller certificate, Excel might open pop-up message boxes asking for permission to run macros every time one of the workbooks on the RExcel ► RthroughExcel Worksheets is started.

Appendix B
Nuisances—Installation, Startup, or Execution

Abstract This appendix collects various nuisance problems, with installation, startup, or execution, that may appear.

B.1 Installation

1. Everything looks right, but it doesn't work. This can happen if an older version of the R(D)COM library is still on your machine. Uninstall the older version from the Start ► All Programs ► R ► (D)Com Server menu. You might also need to uncheck RExcel from the Excel Add-Ins menu. See Section A.3.2 for details.
2. Excel is not found. One or both of the following messages may appear.

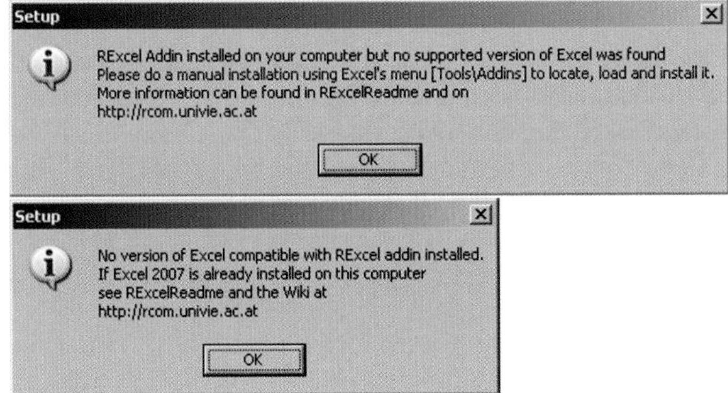

   If either appears, see step 3 in Section A.3.3.
3. Excel messages about conflicts with installation of previous versions of RExcel. These are usually a complaint that it can't find a file whose pathname begins with something like c:/Program Files/R/(D)COM.... See Section A.3.2 for this situation.

B.2 Startup

1. We recommend starting with one of the RExcel with RCommander icons illustrated in Fig. 1.1. Things run more smoothly. Other options for starting—clicking the Excel icon or double-clicking an `xls` file—are more likely to have transient problems.
2. Missing RExcel with RCommander icon. The icon is initially placed on Desktop of the user who ran the RExcelInstaller. If the icon is not visible for another user, it can easily be made accessible. From the Start button, click All Programs ► R ► RExcel ► Activate RExcel Add-in.
3. "R Server not available" message. See Fig. B.1.

Fig. B.1 This is usually a spurious message. It usually means that Excel is looking for R before R is ready. The program automatically tries again and succeeds. Just click OK.

4. The RExcel menu item is either missing entirely or present and non-functional on a machine that previously had RExcel working. In multi-user settings, for example, a classroom computer used by several instructors, another instructor may have unchecked the RExcel Add-In. You need to check it again. The details depend on the version of Excel.

   Excel 2007 Open Excel. Click the Office Button ► Excel Options (at the bottom of the window) ► Add-Ins (in the left pane) ► Go... (bottom) ► RExcel2007 (make sure it is checked). Then click OK all the way back.

   Excel 2003 Open Excel. Click the Tools (main menu) ► Add-Ins... ► RExcel (make sure it is checked) Then click OK all the way back.

B.3 Execution

1. When Excel gets scrambled, you can often (not always) fix it with
   Ctrl-Shift-Alt-F9.
2. If the Rcmdr menu is scrambled or items are grayed out, then click the blue **R** on the Rcmdr menu.
3. There are built-in inconsistencies in the Rcmdr menus. Read them closely.
   The Rcmdr scatterplot menu has x on the left, y on the right.
   The Rcmdr linear regression menu has y on the left, x on the right.

4. OLE actions. See Fig. B.2.

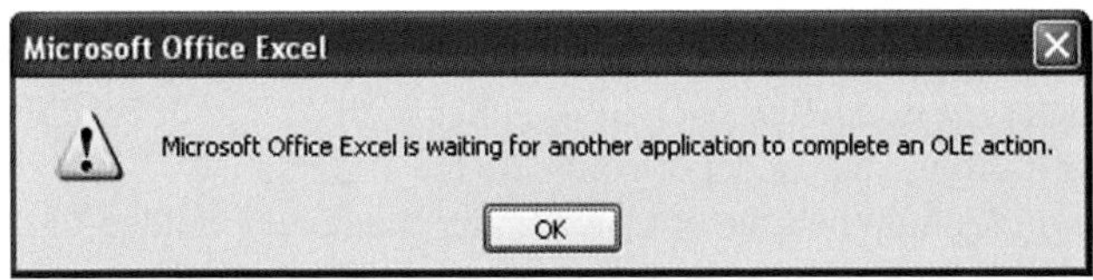

Fig. B.2 This means you are taking longer to fill in a dialog box than Excel is comfortable with. Click OK and take your time filling out the dialog correctly.

5. The variable names are X followed by numbers in the range of the data values. See Fig. B.3. This probably means that the dataset was transferred to R without column names and that the first row of the data has been incorrectly interpreted as column names. See Section 3.3.

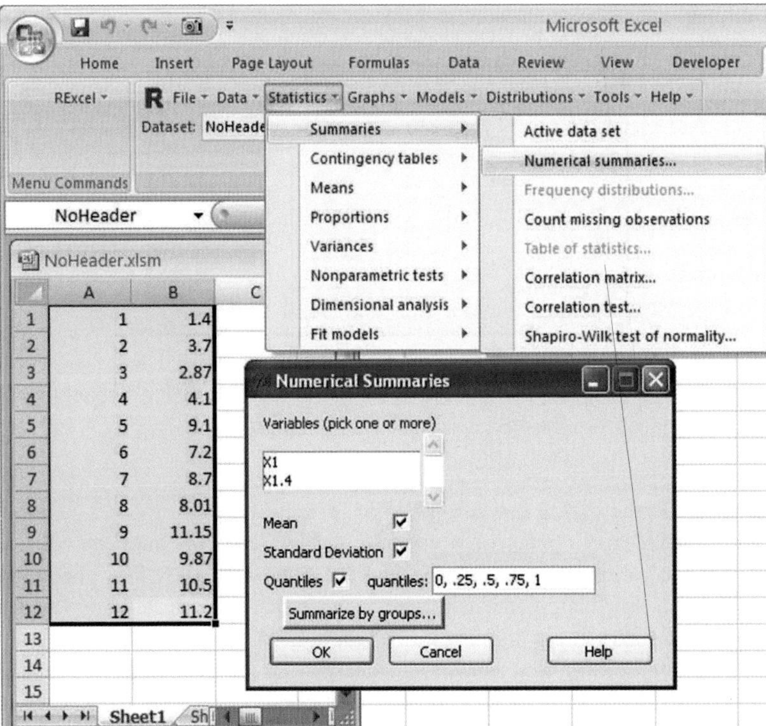

Fig. B.3 This usually means that the dataset was transferred to R without column names. See Chapter 3, specifically Section 3.3, for a discussion of how to make the transfer correctly.

6. Similar menu names: Excel 2003 has File, Data, Tools, and Help menu items. So does the Rmcdr menu. Excel 2007 has a Data menu item on the main menu. So does the Rmcdr menu.
7. Excel, RExcel, and R are all frozen. This usually means you have an open Rcmdr dialog box. Switch back to it, either with Alt-Tab or by clicking on the Windows taskbar, and cancel or complete the dialog box.
8. Hidden windows. When the R Commander window is hidden, it does not automatically come to the top when the Rcmdr menu in Excel writes to it. Similarly, when a new graph is drawn, the Graphics window does not automatically come to the top. Should a window be hidden, it is easily found with the Windows taskbar or use of the Alt-Tab key. There is an option on RExcel ► Options to change the behavior. Check RCommander gets focus with output, and then RExcel will bring either the Commander window or the Graphics window, as appropriate, to the top.
9. The RExcel and Rcmdr menus have vanished in Excel 2007. That can happen when you click another tab to get access to some other menus in the ribbon. Just click on the Add-Ins tab as in Fig. 1.2.
10. `Run-time error '13': Type mismatch`. See Fig. B.4.

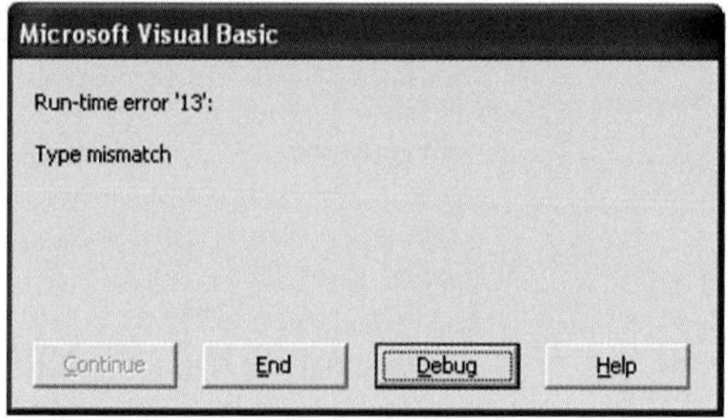

Fig. B.4 This usually means you should close Excel and leave R running. Then start RExcel again from the RExcel with RCommander icon.

11. Variables in the dialog box are not used. The Rcmdr dialog box's variable selection boxes may open with a variable highlighted. This happens when there is only one variable that makes sense and it is needed. They may also open not highlighted, for example, when there is more than one variable that would be appropriate. They may also open not highlighted when they are optional. For example, in the Graphs ► Dotplot with stacked multiple hits... dialog box, the selection boxes for both Factors and | Groups open not highlighted because they are optional.
12. Excel quits and restarts by itself. When it comes back, the Rcmdr window is present without the Rcmdr menu, and the RExcel menu item says R is running but there is no Rcmdr menu on the Excel menu bar. The solution is to stop

Rcmdr from the RExcel menu, then reopen Rcmdr with Excel menus from the RExcel menu.

13. The Rcmdr menu is visible and working in Excel, but the RExcel menu item is missing. Close Excel and reopen Excel.
14. Numbers are interpreted strangely in non-English Windows systems. This could mean that Excel and R have been given different information about the operating system decimal notation and/or time conventions.

    R (and therefore Rcmdr) uses the operating system's information. In German and Austrian Windows, for example, Excel typically uses "," as the decimal point, so numbers entered as "1.5" will be converted to something weird (e.g., the first of May, 2009). See the R help files `?locales` and `?localeconv` for further information.

    Excel uses information on the Windows Start ▶ Control Panel ▶ Regional and Language Options ▶ Regional Options ▶ Customize... dialog boxes and on the Excel Tools ▶ International tab.

    RExcel has a worksheet function RNumber which, when dealing with numbers as strings, always does the right thing in conversion.

References

Adobe Systems Incorporated, 1999. Adobe Systems Incorporated (1999). *PostScript language reference manual*, 3rd edition. http://www.adobe.com/products/postscript/pdfs/PLRM.pdf.

Baier, 2007. Baier, T. (2007). rcom: R COM Client Interface and Internal COM Server. R package version 1.5-2.2, http://www.r-project.org.

Baier et al., 2006. Baier, T., Heiberger, R., Schinagl, K., and Neuwirth, E. (2006). Using R for teaching statistics to nonmajors: Comparing experiences of two different approaches. In *UserR! Conference*. R-Project. http://www.r-project.org/useR-2006/Slides/BaierEtAl.pdf.

Baier and Neuwirth, 2007. Baier, T. and Neuwirth, E. (2007). Excel :: Com :: R. *Computational Statistics*, 22(1):91–108.

Davies and Goldsmith, 1972. Davies, O. L. and Goldsmith, P. L., editors (1972). *Statistical Methods in Research and Production*. Oliver and Boyd, 4th edition.

Fox et al., 2007. Fox, J. et al. (2007). Rcmdr: R Commander. R package version 1.3-11; additional contributors: Michael Ash, Theophilius Boye, Stefano Calza, Andy Chang, Philippe Grosjean, Richard Heiberger, G. Jay Kerns, Renaud Lancelot, Matthieu Lesnoff, Samir Messad, Martin Maechler, Erich Neuwirth, Dan Putler, Miroslav Ristic, Peter Wolf.; http://www.r-project.org, http://socserv.socsci.mcmaster.ca/jfox/Misc/Rcmdr/.

Hand et al., 1994. Hand, D. J., Daly, F., Lunn, A. D., McConway, K. J., and Ostrowski, E. (1994). *A Handbook of Small Data Sets*. Chapman and Hall.

Heiberger, 2008a. Heiberger, R. M. (2008a). HH: Statistical analysis and data display: Heiberger and Holland. R package, http://www.r-project.org; contributions from Burt Holland.

Heiberger, 2008b. Heiberger, R. M. (2008b). RcmdrPlugin.HH: Rcmdr support for the HH package. R package, http://www.r-project.org; contributions from Burt Holland.

Heiberger and Holland, 2004. Heiberger, R. M. and Holland, B. (2004). *Statistical Analysis and Data Display: An Intermediate Course with Examples in S-Plus, R, and SAS*. Springer. http://springeronline.com/0-387-40270-5.

Heiberger and Holland, 2006. Heiberger, R. M. and Holland, B. (2006). Mean–mean multiple comparison displays for families of linear contrasts. *Journal of Computational and Graphical Statistics*, 14(4):937–955.

Heiberger and Neuwirth, 2008. Heiberger, R. M. and Neuwirth, E. (2008). RthroughExcelWorkbooksInstaller: Excel workbooks supporting statistics courses using *R through Excel*. R package, http://www.R-project.org, http://rcom.univie.ac.at.

Lamport, 1986. Lamport, L. (1986). *LaTeX: A Document Preparation System*. Addison-Wesley.

Microsoft, 2008a. Microsoft (2002–2008a). Microsoft Office Excel.

Microsoft, 2008b. Microsoft (2002–2008b). Microsoft Windows.

Neuwirth, 2008. Neuwirth, E. (2008). Student data collected in classes, 1998–2008. Distributed on CRAN as part of the RthroughExcelWorkbooksInstaller package [Heiberger and Neuwirth, 2008].

Neuwirth, 2009. Neuwirth, E. (2009). Randfriendssetup: Installer with r, rexcel, rthroughexcelworkbooks, hh, rcmdr, rcmdrplugin.hh and other packages for ms windows. http://rcom.univie.ac.at.

Neuwirth and Arganbright, 2004. Neuwirth, E. and Arganbright, D. (2004). *The Active Modeler: Mathematical Modeling with Microsoft Excel.* Brooks/Cole.

Neuwirth et al., 2008. Neuwirth, E. et al. (2008). Rexcelinstaller: Integration of r and excel, (use r in excel, read/write xls files). R package, http://www.R-project.org, http://rcom.univie.ac.at; with contributions by Richard Heiberger, Christian Ritter, Jan Karel Pieterse, and Jurgen Volkering.

R Development Core Team, 2008. R Development Core Team (2008). *R: A Language and Environment for Statistical Computing.* R Foundation for Statistical Computing, Vienna, Austria. ISBN 3-900051-07-0.

Williams, 1959. Williams, E. J. (1959). *Regression Analysis.* Wiley.

Index

J

L

M

N

O

P

R

S

T

V

W

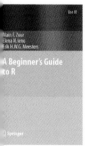

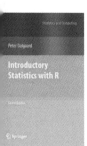

Printed in the United States of America